W9-CDY-603

Afghanistan

Paul Clammer

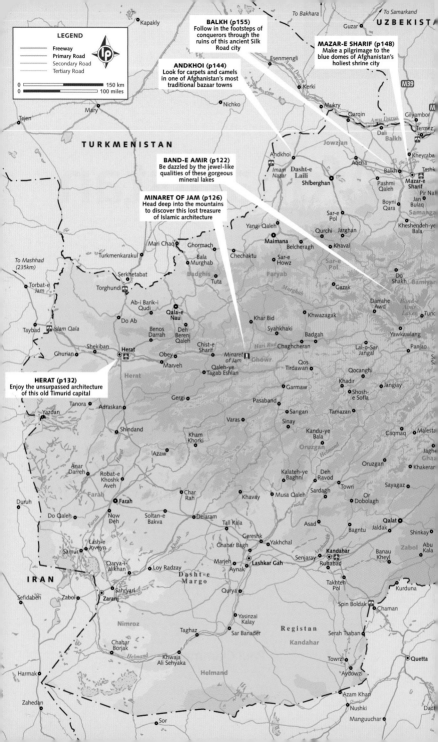

BALKH (p155)
Follow in the footsteps of conquerors through the ruins of this ancient Silk Road city

MAZAR-E SHARIF (p148)
Make a pilgrimage to the blue domes of Afghanistan's holiest shrine city

ANDKHOI (p144)
Look for carpets and camels in one of Afghanistan's most traditional bazaar towns

BAND-E AMIR (p122)
Be dazzled by the jewel-like qualities of these gorgeous mineral lakes

MINARET OF JAM (p126)
Head deep into the mountains to discover this lost treasure of Islamic architecture

HERAT (p132)
Enjoy the unsurpassed architecture of this old Timurid capital

LEGEND

Freeway
Primary Road
Secondary Road
Tertiary Road

0 ——— 150 km
0 ——— 100 miles

UZBEKISTAN

To Bakhara
To Samarkand
Kapakly
Guzar

TURKMENISTAN

Tejen
Mary
Nichko

Esenmengli
Kerki
Mukry
Qarqin
Amu Darya
Gilyambor
Termez
Dali
Balkh
Kheyraba
Tashk
Mazar-e Sharif
Pir Na
Jan

Andkhoi
Dasht-e Laili
Imam Nazar
Shiberghan
Aqcha
Pashmi Qaleh
Balkh
Boyni Qara
Samanga

To Mashhad (235km)
Turkmenkarakul
Mari Chaq
Ghormach
Bala Murghab
Tuta

Yangi Qaleh
Sar-e Pol
Qurchi
Jarghan
Do Shakh
Bamiya

Serkhetabat
Torghundi

Chechaktu
Sar-e Howz
Maimana
Belcheragh
Khaval
Sar-e Pol
Faryab

Darrahe Awd
Band-i Amir Lakes
Tund
Yawkawlang

Ab-i Barik-i Qudi
Qala-e Nau

Khar Bid
Khwazagak
Gazak

Torbat-e Jam
Do Ab

Benos Darrah
Deh Berenj Qaleh
Chist-e Sharif

Syahkhaki
Badgah
Badghis

Lal-o-Sar Jangal
Panjao

Taybad
Islam Qala
Shekiban

Herat
Obey
Marveh

Minaret of Jam
Qaleh-ye Tagab Eshlan
Ghowr

Chaghcheran
Qos
Tirdawan

Qocanghi
Jangiay

Ghurian
Hari Rud
Herat

Gergi

Pasaband
Sangan
Sinay

Khadir
Shosh-e Sofla
Tamazan

Qaqmaq
Malesta
Jaghe
Ghaz

Tanora
Yazdan
Adraskan

Garmaw

Varas
Kandu-ye Bala

Oruzgan
Khakerar

Shindand

Kham Khorki

Kalateh-ye Baghni
Deh Ravod
Towri

Or Dobolagh
Sayagaz

Anar Darreh
Robat-e Khoshk Aveh
Azaw

Char Rah
Khavay
Musa Qaleh
Sardagh
Oruzgan

Duruh
Farah

Now Deh
Soltan-e Bakva
Delaram
Tall Kala
Asad

Bagntu
Jaldak
Qalat
Shinkay
Zabol
Abu Kala

Do Qaleh
Lashe Joveyn

Chahar Bagh
Gereshk
Yakhchal
Senjaray
Kandahar
Ruhabad

Banau Kheyl

Samur
Qarya-i-alikhan
Loy Radzay
Marjeh
Aynak
Lashkar Gah
Qurya

Takhteh Pol
Spin Boldak
Chaman
Kurduna

IRAN
Sahryari
Zaranj
Sefidabeh
Zabol

Dasht-e Margo
Nimroz

Kandahar
Registan
Serah Tsahan

Chahar Borjak
Helmand

Yasinzai Kalay
Sar Banader
Taghaz

Towrzi
Aydowzi
Quetta

Harmak

Khwaja Ali Sehyaka
Helmand

Zahedan

Sor

Azam Khan
Nushki
Manguuchar
Dad

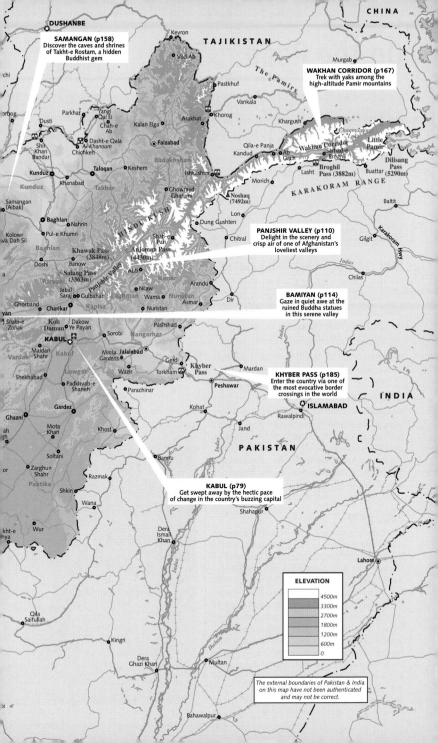

CHINA

DUSHANBE

SAMANGAN (p158)
Discover the caves and shrines of Takht-e Rostam, a hidden Buddhist gem

TAJIKISTAN

Keyron

Vod Ab

Murgab

Pastkhuf

The Pamirs

WAKHAN CORRIDOR (p167)
Trek with yaks among the high-altitude Pamir mountains

Vankala

Parkhar

Yangi
Qal Ei

Chah-e

Kalan Elga

Arakhat

Khorog

Khargush

Chaqmaqtin
Lake

Dusti

Dasht-e Qala

Al
Khanoum

Faizabad

Qila-e Panja

Wakhan Corridor

Ab
Gach

Samad-e

Little
Pamir

Shir
Khan
Bandar

Chichkeh

Kandud

Broghli

Dilisang
Pass
(5290m)

Kunduz

Khanabad

Taloqan

Keshem

Ishkashim

Morich

Lasht

Broghli
Pass (3882m)

Buattar

Kunduz

Badakhshan

KARAKORAM RANGE

Samangan
(Aibak)

Baghlan

Nahrin

Takhar

Ghowrayd
Gharami

Noshaq
(7492m)

Lon

Dung Gushten

Baltit

Kolowr
va Dah Sil

Pul-e Khumri

HINDU KUSH

Shah-e
Pari

Chitral

PANJSHIR VALLEY (p110)
Delight in the scenery and crisp air of one of Afghanistan's loveliest valleys

Gilgit

Karakoram Hwy

Baghlan

Khawak Pass
(3848m)

Anjoman Pass
(4430m)

Doshi

Banow

Auti

Indus

Chilas

Salang Pass
(3363m)

Jabal
Saraj

Gulbahar

Nilaw

Wama

Nuristan

Arandu

Ghorband

Charikar

Kapisa

Asmar

Dir

BAMIYAN (p114)
Gaze in quiet awe at the ruined Buddha statues in this serene valley

Shahr-e
Zohak

Koh
Daman

Dakow
Ye Payan

Sorobi

Nangarhar

Pashshad

Indus

KABUL

Kabul

Nimla
Gardens

Jalalabad

Maidan
Shahr

Logwar

Wazir

Gerdi

Khyber
Pass

Mardan

Vardak

Shekhabad

Padkhvab-e
Shaneh

Parachinar

Torkham

Peshawar

KHYBER PASS (p185)
Enter the country via one of the most evocative border crossings in the world

INDIA

Gardez

Mota
Khan

Kohat

Jand

Rawalpindi

ISLAMABAD

Ghazni

Khost

PAKISTAN

Soltani

Zarghun
Shahr

Khost

Razmak

Bannu

Paktika

Shkin

Wana

KABUL (p79)
Get swept away by the hectic pace of change in the country's buzzing capital

Wur

Dera
Ismail
Khan

Indus

Shahapur

Lahore

Qila
Saifullah

Kingri

Jhelum

ELEVATION

	4500m
	3300m
	2700m
	1800m
	1200m
	600m
	0

Dera
Ghazi Khan

Multan

The external boundaries of Pakistan & India on this map have not been authenticated and may not be correct.

Bahawalpur

On the Road

PAUL CLAMMER Coordinating Author

For me, late summer is the best time to be in Afghanistan, and researching this book was no exception. I missed out on the winter *buzkashi* (Afghan rugby on horseback, with a dead goat) season, but there was ample compensation in the endless fruit – sweet grapes from the Shomali Plain, fat Kandahari pomegranates and melons everywhere. The country might not be the most straightforward to write a travel guide for, dealing with terrible roads and security concerns, but the rewards (like so many things unexpected in Afghanistan) were always the sweetest.

DON'T MISS!

Any trip to Afghanistan should start by entering through the Khyber Pass (p185). I'll stop in Kabul (p79) to catch up with friends before heading out of the city for the vistas of Bamiyan (p114) and the Band-e Amir lakes (p122). If I can brave the bad roads I'd bump my way to the Minaret of Jam (p126), or fly from Kabul to finish in Herat (p132), my favourite Afghan city.

PAUL'S BIO

Paul grew up near Cambridge. After a false start as a molecular biologist he spent several years kicking around the Islamic world from Casablanca to Kashgar, eventually becoming a tour guide in Morocco, Turkey and Pakistan. Having watched *The Man Who Would Be King* at an impressionable age, the Khyber Pass was always in his sights, and in 2001 he finally made it to Afghanistan, only to find himself having dinner with two Taliban ministers a fortnight before the September 11 attacks. When the dust settled he wrote *Kabul Caravan*, one of the first travel websites dedicated to Afghanistan, and is now the first Lonely Planet writer to cover the country since the mid-1970s.
See contributing author bios on p236.

Opposite: The trinket trade still flourishes in Herat (p132)

Highlights

Sights

The blue-tiled Shrine of Khoja Abu Nasr Parsa
(p155) is a classic example of Timurid architecture

The awe-inspiring Large Buddha niche
(p117), Bamiyan

Embrace the local transportation in Bamiyan (p114)

Step back in time at Kabul's Ka Faroshi Bird Market (p90),
which remains untouched by modernisation

The brilliant blue lakes of Band-e Amir (p122) are reputed to have great healing powers

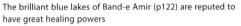

The Minaret of Jam (p126) rises unexpectedly from the rocky landscape

Pilgrims pay their respects at the Shrine of Hazrat Ali (p152) in Mazar-e Sharif

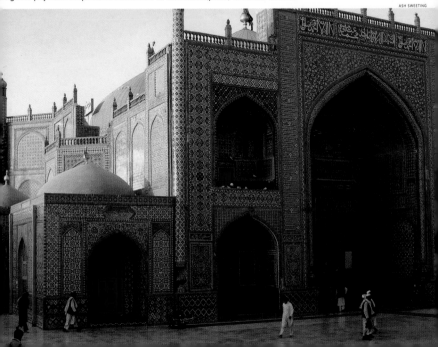

People

Taking time out from the bustle of the central bazaar, Jalalabad (p182)

ASH SWEETING

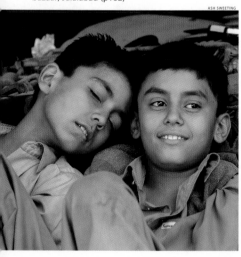

ASH S

Cutting and scraping opium poppy (p73) in Badakhshan

Musicians strike a chord in Panjshir (p110)

ASH S

ASH SWEETING

It's cold work on the Salang Pass (p112): truck drivers light a fire to thaw their vehicle's frozen engine

Follow the leader: a shepherd steers his flock down from the mountains of Nangahar province (p182)

ASH SWEETING

LINA ABIRAFEH

Raising a smile and the next generation in the capital, Kabul (p79)

Landscapes

ASH SWEETING

The old city of Kabul (p94) spreads like a
blanket across the valley

ASH

The white-water Panjshir River (p110)

The ancient city of Faizabad (p164) straddles the gushing Kokcha River

ASH

ASH SWEETING

Mir Samir (p187) was made famous by Eric Newby's *A Short Walk in the Hindu Kush* (p18)

Mineral deposits on the lake shores of Band-e Amir (p122) have built up over time to create bizarre curtain walls

ASH SWEETING

Daily Life

Players tee it up at Kabul Golf Club (p109)

No sport captures the Afghan spirit like *buzkashi* (p57)

Solemn evening prayers in Arghandab (p19

Firefighting Afghan style: Kandahar (p190) locals take the fire to the water in an effort to save their truck

Contents

On the Road	4
Destination Afghanistan	15
Getting Started	16
Itineraries	20
History	25
The Culture	41
Food & Drink	59
Environment	64
Safety in Afghanistan	68
Working in Afghanistan	76

Kabul 79

History	81
Climate	82
Orientation	83
Information	84
Dangers & Annoyances	87
Sights	87
Festivals & Events	95
Sleeping	95
Eating	98
Drinking	101
Entertainment	102
Shopping	102
Getting There & Away	103
Getting Around	104

Around Kabul 106

Istalif	107
Paghman	108
Qargha Lake	108
Bagram	109
Panjshir Valley	110
Salang Pass	112

Bamiyan & Central Afghanistan 113

Climate	114
Getting There & Away	114
BAMIYAN	**114**
History	114
Orientation	116
Information	117
Sights	117
Sleeping	120
Eating	121
Getting There & Away	121
Around Bamiyan	122
THE CENTRAL ROUTE	**124**
Practicalities	124
Bamiyan to Chaghcheran	125
Chaghcheran to Herat	126

Herat & Northwestern Afghanistan 130

Climate	132
Getting There & Away	132
HERAT	**132**
History	134
Orientation	135
Information	135
Dangers & Annoyances	135
Sights	135
Sleeping	140
Eating & Drinking	140
Shopping	141
Getting There & Away	141
Getting Around	142
THE NORTHWEST	**142**
Herat to Maimana	142
Maimana	143
Andkhoi	144
Shiberghan	145

Mazar-e Sharif & Northeastern Afghanistan 147

Climate	148
Getting There & Away	148
MAZAR-E SHARIF	**148**
History	149
Orientation	151
Information	151
Dangers & Annoyances	152

Sights	152
Sleeping	153
Eating & Drinking	153
Shopping	154
Getting There & Away	154
Getting Around	155
AROUND MAZAR-E SHARIF	**155**
Balkh	155
MAZAR-E SHARIF TO BADAKHSHAN	**158**
Tashkurgan	158
Samangan (Aibak)	158
Pul-e Khumri	159
Kunduz	160
Ai khanoum	162
BADAKHSHAN	**163**
Faizabad	164
Lake Shewa	166
South to the Anjoman Pass	166
Ishkashim	167
Wakhan & The Afghan Pamir	167

Life Along the Silk Road 173

Jalalabad & Eastern Afghanistan 181

Climate	182
Getting There & Away	182
JALALABAD	**182**
Orientation	183
Information	183
Sights	183
Sleeping & Eating	184
Getting There & Around	184
Around Jalalabad	184
NURISTAN	**186**
History	186
Culture	187
Travel in Nuristan	187

Kandahar & Southern Afghanistan 188

Climate	190
Getting There & Away	190
KANDAHAR	**190**
History	190
Orientation	191
Information	191
Dangers & Annoyances	193
Sights	193
Sleeping	194
Eating & Drinking	194
Shopping	194
Getting There & Away	195
Getting Around	195
THE SOUTH	**195**
Ghazni	196
Lashkar Gah	197

Directory 198

Transport 212

Health 221

Language 227

Glossary 233

Contributing Authors 236

Behind the Scenes 238

Index 241

Map Legend 244

Regional Map Contents

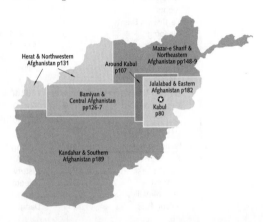

Herat & Northwestern Afghanistan p131

Mazar-e Sharif & Northeastern Afghanistan pp148-9

Around Kabul p107

Jalalabad & Eastern Afghanistan p182

Bamiyan & Central Afghanistan pp126-7

Kabul p80

Kandahar & Southern Afghanistan p189

Destination Afghanistan

When Lonely Planet was hitting the Asia overland trail in the 1970s, Afghanistan was known for its dramatic mountain scenery and the unparalleled hospitality of its people. At the turn of the 21st century the country was more synonymous with war and terrorism, the picture of a failed state. The fall of the Taliban regime in 2001 and the subsequent reconstruction attempts have done much to address this view, but in early 2007 Afghanistan's future remained on a knife-edge.

Having been bled white by 10 years of Soviet occupation, Afghanistan was dropped by the international community almost the minute the last Red Army tank withdrew in 1989, allowing it to slip into the chaos of civil war and the Taliban. Promises not to repeat the same mistake 13 years later proved half-hearted at best. Progress in development of education and the political process (which have seen successful presidential and parliamentary elections) are real enough. Kabul and other cities have boomed with increasing trade and new constructions. Most of the country is at peace, but the state remains perilously weak. The return to power of many of the rejected warlords of the 1990s has cynically proved to Afghans that you can apparently have peace or justice, but not both. The booming economy has failed to touch the countryside where most Afghans live and development programmes have mostly ignored the important agricultural sector, particularly in the Pashtun regions that originally spawned the Taliban.

Afghanistan's rugged landscape and tribal patchwork has never allowed it a strong central government, and attempts by the international community to build one have been patchy. The economy is dependent on aid, and in 2006 domestic revenues raised just US$13 per capita. This pales in comparison with the 6100 tonnes of opium produced in the same period – over half the value of the legal economy. Opium corrodes the fragile state, reaching from bribed provincial cops to the centres of power in Kabul, and out into the developed world. Over 90% of the heroin on the streets of the UK comes from Afghanistan.

Ever the meddling neighbour, Pakistan has continued to play a double game in Afghanistan. Islamabad has been a key partner in public in the War on Terror, but stands accused of giving sanctuary to the Taliban leadership it once helped into power. The Waziristan compact it signed in 2006 to quell a tribal rebellion on its own troubled frontier has provided both a reservoir and safe haven for Taliban fighters operating in southern Afghanistan. Flush with opium money and drawing new inspiration from the Iraqi insurgency, Taliban attacks set swathes of southern Afghanistan ablaze in 2006, drawing NATO forces into heavy combat.

Is the Afghan glass half-empty or half-full? Continued and improved international commitment is crucial for Afghanistan's success. Afghans still welcome foreigners who come to the country to help, knowing full well the cost of neglect. At the time of writing, international sabre-rattling over Iran fuels Afghan fears that the country will again slip off the radar. Progress is slow and painful, but possible. A peaceful, stable Afghanistan is still there to be won – the costs of losing it again are simply too high for everyone.

FAST FACTS

Population: 31 million (2006 estimate)

Population under 14: approximately 14 million

Refugee population outside Afghanistan: approximately 2 million

Adult literacy: 36%

Infant mortality rate: 160 per 1000 live births

Gross Domestic Product per capita: US$800

Main exports: opium, fruits and nuts, handwoven carpets, wool, hides and pelts, gems

Main imports: petroleum products, food, textiles, machinery

Ranking on UN Human Development Index: 173 (out of 178)

Getting Started

By any stretch of the imagination, Afghanistan isn't the simplest country to travel in. For the visitor, it's a world away from backpacking in Thailand or island-hopping in Greece. It's a country recovering from nearly three decades of war, with a host of continuing problems. You'll need to invest time getting the latest safety information, and news from other travellers or colleagues working in the country.

But with the right preparations, and a constant ear to the ground once you're there, travel in Afghanistan is not only a possibility but also incredibly rewarding. The post-Taliban scene has brought investment to the country for the first time in years, and the logistics of getting around and finding somewhere to stay has become increasingly straightforward. Not only that, it's an addictive country to visit. Once in Afghanistan, there's something about the people, the history and even the air that can get in your blood and promise to draw you back again. Do your research, and you'll find Afghanistan a truly rewarding country.

SHOULD YOU GO?

The rebuilding of Afghanistan's shattered infrastructure continues to be painfully slow. Its culture has been pillaged and its people scattered, and discontent in the south and east has reignited into a full-blown Taliban insurgency. While many international workers continue their jobs under often tricky conditions, Afghan embassies are happy enough to give out tourist visas to those who ask. But should you go?

The prime concern is security, and we do not advocate people putting themselves at risk. It's vital to understand that safety and security issues are anything but static in Afghanistan – things can change rapidly and it would be irresponsible of us to give prescriptive safety advice. Be aware that at the time of research, the US, British and Australian governments were all advising against non-essential travel to Afghanistan. For a detailed analysis of security issues in Afghanistan, see the Safety in Afghanistan chapter (p68), but remember that this chapter is only a starting point for your own research. Only you are responsible for your safety, so it's absolutely

Foreign women shouldn't attempt to wear the burqa – for more information on dress codes see p211.

DON'T LEAVE HOME WITHOUT...

- An Afghan visa in your passport (see p210).
- A travel insurance policy that actually covers you for travel to Afghanistan (see p205).
- The latest news from the ground, and safety information (see p68).
- Non-revealing clothes, with arms and legs covered for both sexes. Headscarves for women are strongly recommended. Wearing respectful attire will get you a better reception in Afghanistan.
- Water purification treatment.
- Lip balm, sunscreen, sunglasses and hat for protection against the strong mountain light and desert sun.
- A torch for when the electricity inevitably fails.
- A sleeping bag – essential for winter, and useful for anywhere off the beaten track.
- A taste for tea – no business or social meeting can take place without an endlessly replenished cuppa.

essential that before considering a visit you assess the security situation from reliable, up-to-date sources.

Choosing to travel in an organised tour, where a company has experience on the ground and access to reliable security information can be a preferable alternative to going independently without any support network, and there are now several reliable tour operators working out of Kabul.

If security constraints allow it, we believe that visiting Afghanistan can be a highly positive experience. Tourism is by no means a panacea for Afghanistan's myriad problems, and the tourist vanguard has a special responsibility travelling in a socially conservative country recovering from war. One of the most common laments you'll hear in Afghanistan is how the world forgot them after the Soviet War. Foreigners can help Afghans reconnect with the world, and to allow them to be seen as individuals rather than victims of war, while putting money into the local economy has a more tangible direct benefit.

A visit to Afghanistan, with its amputees and women begging in burqas, can be a shock. If you want to have a more positive impact, you might want to consider donating time or money to aid agencies working in the country. There are dozens to choose from, and some are better than others, so pick carefully. Ask how long they have been working in Afghanistan, what role the local community plays in their projects and how sustainability is monitored.

WHEN TO GO

Assuming that the political climate allows you to make a trip, the most pleasant time to explore Afghanistan is spring or autumn, in particular April to early June and September through October. In spring, north Afghanistan turns from dusty ochre to bright green, as the desert and hills spring into life and are studded with blooms of flowers. Autumn is harvest time and brings the best of the Afghan fruit – melons from the north, grapes from the Shomali Plain and fat pomegranates from Kandahar.

Summers can be blisteringly hot at lower altitudes, with cities like Herat, Mazar-e Sharif, Jalalabad and Kandahar sweltering in temperatures topping 40°C. The mountains mitigate this heatwave, and Kabul, Bamiyan and Faizabad are all more manageable at this time, and their altitude blesses them with deliciously cooler nights. June to September is the best time to head to the higher mountains – much of Badakhshan (including the Wakhan Corridor) is inaccessible for the rest of the year due to snow. The white stuff can also make crossing central Afghanistan to the Minaret of Jam extremely difficult outside these months, as roads and high passes close for the winter. Even the Salang Pass, the main artery between north and south Afghanistan, experiences avalanches and blockages a few times every winter.

See Climate Charts (p201) for more information.

Winter is harsh across the country barring the extreme south, with temperatures sitting below zero and heavy snow in Kabul and elsewhere. The spring melt can bring trouble of its own, with frequent floods washing out poorly maintained roads.

At the end of winter, everyone looks forward to Nauroz on 21 March, the Afghan New Year celebrations. This can be a joyous time to visit the country, and one of the best times to see the national sport, *buzkashi* (p57). Conversely, the month-long fast of Ramazan (Ramadan; p203) can be a trying time to be on the road, as restaurants and teahouses are closed during the day, and frequently shut up shop for the entire month.

COSTS & MONEY

Afghanistan is by turn both an incredibly cheap and very expensive country to travel in. While the daily costs of eating, drinking and travelling by local transport are relatively low, the cost of accommodation can be high, and travelling by private vehicle very expensive. The large influx of foreign workers with large expense accounts and an economy reliant on imported goods has produced a two-tier system, where dual pricing for locals and foreigners is not uncommon. Payment in US dollars is almost as universally accepted as payment in afghanis.

Roughly speaking, if you opt for the simplest hotels, eat only in local restaurants and at street food stands (and avoid imported groceries, which are available in most towns), and travel only using local transport; you can get by on around 1000Afg to 1200Afg per day.

If you've been roughing it and need a night in a comfier bed, or a break from an endless diet of kebabs and rice, a single room at a midrange hotel ranges from 1500Afg to 3000Afg per night. Many places charge a flat rate for the room, so sharing a double can cut costs considerably. Kabul is the most expensive place in the country, and a midrange room can cost up to 4000Afg. Top end hotels – almost all of these are in the capital – cost upwards of this, to around 6000Afg. The recent boom in hotel building in Kabul means that many top end places frequently offer generous discounts, which can bring their rates down to the midrange, so don't be shy about asking. Discounted rates are frequently available for long-term occupancy.

For more details on money issues, see p206.

HOW MUCH?

Internet access (per hour): 50Afg

100km minibus ride: 90Afg

One minute phone call to USA/UK: 20Afg

City taxi ride: 80Afg

2kg melon: 40Afg

TRAVEL LITERATURE

Afghanistan is blessed with incredibly rich travel literature. Any of the following will help prime you for your trip (for other recommendations, see History, p25, and The Culture, p41).

The Sewing Circles of Herat by Christina Lamb wonderfully stitches together accounts of the author's time with the mujaheddin (including a young Hamid Karzai) with a return to post-Taliban Afghanistan to produce a beautifully balanced mix of reportage and travel writing.

The Storyteller's Daughter by Saira Shah is a highly evocative memoir of an Afghan journalist raised in Britain examining her roots through the lens of the war against the Russians and the Taliban chaos. Our favourite book on Afghanistan in the past few years.

The Places In Between by Rory Stewart is the account of an incredible journey walking across central Afghanistan in mid-winter, months after the fall of the Taliban. Pensive and well-observed, it's a great companion for anyone heading for that part of Afghanistan.

Peregrine Hodson's *Under A Sickle Moon* is one of the few 'travels with the mujaheddin' books to stand the test of time, a keen account of one corner of the war that's helped enormously by the author's fluent Dari and eye for character.

Ostensibly a quest for the roots of Islamic architecture, *The Road to Oxiana* by Robert Byron is still the best travel book on Afghanistan (and Persia), more than 70 years after it was written. Few characters in the travel literature genre are as memorable as the show-stealing Afghan ambassador to Tehran.

A Short Walk in the Hindu Kush by Eric Newby is one of the modern classics of travel writing, describing the misadventures of two Englishmen who trekked to the remote Nuristan region in the 1950s. It has one of the best (and funniest) endings of any travel book.

In *An Unexpected Light,* Jason Elliot dazzles the reader with a journey around Afghanistan on the eve of the fall of Kabul to the Taliban. Elliot displays a sympathetic ear and a keen understanding of the richness of Afghan culture and history.

The Light Garden of the Angel King is a scholarly but still colourful account of author Peter Levi's travels in Afghanistan with Bruce Chatwin in the 1970s. Finely written, with suitably distinguished footnotes.

A Bed of Red Flowers by Nelofer Pazira is a lyrical memoir of life growing up in 1970s Kabul, the Soviet occupation and her family's flight to Pakistan and Canada as refugees. The denouement, in Kabul and Moscow, is highly moving.

Kandahar Cockney by James Fergusson takes a different approach to the travel genre, describing the complicated life of an Afghan friend who fled to London as a refugee. A revealing portrait of an under-reported side to recent Afghan history.

Tamim Ansary's *West of Kabul, East of New York* is a revealing memoir of growing up in '50s and '60s Lashkar Gah and Kabul, and a life lived in the USA, straddling the cultures of his Afghan father and American mother.

Magic Bus is Rory Maclean's witty and engaging retracing of the old Hippy Trail from Istanbul to Kabul and Goa. Looking at the changes in the countries en route and the metamorphosis from spaced-out intrepids to modern backpackers, it's highly recommended.

INTERNET RESOURCES

These websites may assist with trip planning, and keep you informed of Afghan news, safety issues, culture and more.

Afghan News Network (www.afghannews.net) Useful news portal covering Afghan current affairs.

Afghan Web (www.afghan-web.com) Generic country portal, with sections on just about all aspects of Afghanistan.

Afghan Wire (www.afghanwire.com) English translations of stories in the Afghan media, with an encyclopaedic 'backgrounder' section on Afghan history, culture and politics.

Institute for War & Peace Reporting (www.iwpr.net) Runs the useful weekly *Afghan Recovery Report,* written by Afghan journalists.

International Crisis Group (www.crisisgroup.org) Heavyweight conflict resolution think-tank, regularly producing excellent reports and analyses of the current Afghan situation.

Juldu.com (www.juldu.com) Comprehensive travel site for trekking in the Wakhan Corridor and the Afghan Pamir.

Kabul Caravan (www.kabulcaravan.com) Countrywide travel information for Afghanistan, run by the main author of this guidebook.

Lonely Planet (www.lonelyplanet.com) The dedicated Central Asia branch of the Thorn Tree forum is one of the best places to get up-to-date travellers' reports on Afghanistan.

Luke Powell (www.lukepowell.com) Beautiful photographs of Afghanistan from before and after the war.

Moby Capital (www.mobycapital.com) Hard to beat daily email service collating news on Afghanistan from the world's media.

Relief Web (www.reliefweb.int) Provides excellent coverage from a humanitarian slant, with news and press releases from the UN and many non government organisations.

Survival Guide to Kabul (www.kabulguide.net) An indispensable resource to the city, aimed primarily at expat workers, and with an excellent bulletin board for up-to-the-minute goings on.

Itineraries
CLASSIC ROUTES

KABUL EXPLORER   One Week

It's easy to get swept up in the hectic atmosphere of **Kabul** (p79), a city struggling through the birth pangs of recovery. There's an enormous amount to check out – the battered but recently reopened Kabul Museum, the wonderfully restored Babur's Gardens and the OMAR Landmine Museum. Take time to experience some of the more traditional corners too, such as the birdsellers of Ka Faroshi and the hustle of Mandayi Market along Kabul River. If you're lucky, you might be in time for a kite-flying festival or a winter game of *buzkashi* – Afghan polo, played with a dead goat. A walk along the old city walls can bring some welcome relief from Kabul's infamous bad air.

For real refreshment, get out of the city. A short drive north across the Shomali Plain will bring you to the traditional mountain village of **Istalif** (p107). The village is famous for its rustic pottery – a great souvenir. Don't forget to stop to buy sweet grapes from roadside sellers on the Shomali Plain. Carrying along the same road, switch northeast as the mountains rise to enter the **Panjshir Valley** (p110). Panjshir was home to the legendary mujaheddin commander Ahmad Shah Massoud, who never allowed it to be captured by the Soviets or the Taliban; his grave lies halfway up the valley.

Closer to home, **Qargha Lake** (p108) is a popular picnic getaway for Kabulis. You can even tee off here for a round at the Kabul Golf Club. The damaged model village of **Paghman** (p108) is nearby – battered but green, and with tremendous views that are worth a detour.

If you're short of time or just based in the capital, this itinerary offers a series of day trips to get you out of the city and give you a quick taste of Afghanistan at large.

HIPPY TRAIL   Two to Three Weeks

Enter Afghanistan by crossing the Iranian border near Mashhad and head to the old Silk Road city of **Herat** (p132). There's an enormous amount to see and do here, from taking in the views from the imposing Citadel to admiring the fabulous mosaic tiling of the Friday Mosque.

After a few days, strike northwest – by air rather than land, as the latter remains a tricky security prospect. At **Mazar-e Sharif** (p148) the blue domes of the Shrine of Hazrat Ali mark Afghanistan's holiest site. The ruins of once-mighty **Balkh** (p155) are a stone's throw away, with crumbling city walls and ancient mosques.

As you leave Mazar-e Sharif, the plains gradually rise into the Hindu Kush mountains. Cross the **Salang Pass** (p112), the main route between north and south Afghanistan. Although the road is good, the traffic is crazy, so you'll be pleased to arrive in the capital, **Kabul** (p79). This is a city with lots to experience, from Mughal gardens to mine museums, as well as Chicken Street – one of the hubs of the Hippy Trail in the 1970s. Kabul's lively restaurant scene will also make a change from the usual diet of kebabs and rice.

From Kabul, allow several days to make a side trip to **Bamiyan** (p114). The Taliban-destroyed Buddha statues have left a yawning hole, but the valley is still one of the most beautiful in Afghanistan. It's a short drive from here to the gorgeous blue lakes of **Band-e Amir** (p122).

Returning to Kabul, you can head for the Pakistan border. Leave Afghanistan through the **Khyber Pass** (p185), an iconic travel experience that has been the gateway to the Indian subcontinent throughout the centuries.

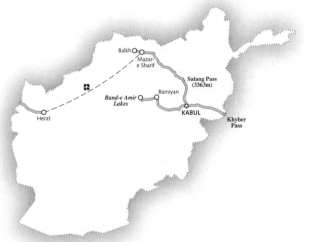

If you have a few weeks to spare, this version of the overland itinerary is the perfect introduction to Afghanistan, taking in the best of its cities, scenery and culture.

ROADS LESS TRAVELLED

ACROSS THE CENTRE   **Three Weeks**

Start your trip in **Kabul** (p79), enjoying its amenities before hitting the rough and ready road ahead.

From Kabul enjoy the good highway across the Shomali Plain, until the road switches west towards **Bamiyan** (p114). The route is bad, but never less than spectacular. If possible, make a stop at the spectacular ruins of **Shahr-e Zohak** (p119) that cling to the red cliffs at the entrance of the Bamiyan valley. Bamiyan is a relaxing place to catch your breath for a few days. Take time to check out the weird geology of nearby **Darya Ajdahar** (p120).

Heading west, the dazzling **Band-e Amir Lakes** (p122), the colour of Afghan lapis lazuli, are an essential stop. From here, the obvious overnight stop is at **Yawkawlang** (p125).

It's a long drive to the regional hub of **Chaghcheran** (p126), over a series of dramatic mountain passes and along narrow valleys. It's the best place to arrange a vehicle to the astounding **Minaret of Jam** (p126), the lonely sentinel left from the Ghorid empire. If you're lucky you'll see camel caravans of nomads along the way.

From Jam, head for **Chist-e Sharif** (p128) with its ruined domed tombs, and the hot springs of **Obey** (p128). Finally, rejoice as the tarmac road reappears, to whisk you along the final stretch to **Herat** (p132), which has all the amenities of a large city.

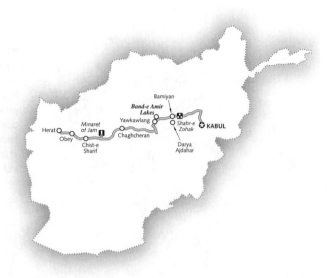

AFGHAN TURKESTAN   Two Weeks

Having enjoyed a few days in **Kabul** (p79), take the road north towards the **Salang Pass** (p112). Once the mountains have been crossed, head northeast towards **Kunduz** (p160), one of the medieval city-states of the north. Crossing the deserts nearby you'll arrive at **Ai Khanoum** (p162), the remains of the easternmost Greek City in the world, looking across the river into Tajikistan.

Backtrack via **Pul-e Khumri** (p140) and continue northwest, break your trip at **Samangan** (p158) to marvel at the Buddhist stupa of Takht-e Rostam. The road continues through the dizzying gorge of **Tangi Tashkurgan** (p158), where roadside sellers offer juicy pomegranates and figs. Having stocked up, take a few days rest at **Mazar-e Sharif** (p148), home to the Shrine of Hazrat Ali and its flocks of pure white doves.

Just outside Mazar-e Sharif is **Balkh** (p155), once the 'Mother of Cities' according to the Arab conquerors. They left Afghanistan's oldest mosque on the outskirts of the town. The road continues west through **Shiberghan** (p145), where the land starts to turn to desert. At the end of the tarmac is the Turkmen and Uzbek town of **Andkhoi** (p144), a centre of carpet production that hosts a fabulous market twice a week.

If you're feeling sturdy, a rough track bumps across the desert to **Maimana** (p143), another old city-state, now a quiet market town with a large Uzbek population.

TAILORED TRIPS

WAKHAN & PAMIR EXPLORER
Three to Four Weeks

This trip into the Wakhan Corridor is highly seasonal and can only be attempted between May and September. Before setting out on this mountain adventure, you'll need to spend some time checking the current requirements for permits (p168), which change regularly. From **Kabul** (p79) drive north to **Faizabad** (p164), the capital of Badakhshan province. It's a two-day drive needing an overnight stay in **Kunduz** (p160), but there are regular flights if you're pushed for time.

In Faizabad, make sure that all your paperwork is in order to allow you to head deep into the mountains, and arrange food and 4WD transport to take you past **Ishkashim** (p167).

From Ishkashim it's a two day drive through stunning mountain scenery to **Sarhad-e Broghil** (p170). You'll overnight at **Khandud** (p169) in the Lower Wakhan, or **Qila-e Panja** (p170), where you can camp near an old royal hunting lodge. It's possible to trek the 90km to Sarhad-e Broghil, which is useful for acclimatisation. The road runs out here at any case.

Sarhad-e Broghil is the trailhead for treks into the **Little Pamir** (p171). It's possible to arrange horses or yaks here for riding or baggage. The Little Pamir is an area of wide alpine grassland 100km long. It's perfect for trekking, and if you're lucky you might spot Marco Polo sheep, or even a snow leopard. The nomadic Kyrgyz herd their flocks amid their yurts here. **Chaqmaqtin Lake** (p172) makes a good trekking destination – a ten-day round trip from the entrance to the Little Pamir.

With sufficient advance preparation, it's possible to trek into Pakistan over the **Dilisang Pass** (p172), a demanding 12-day trek requiring mountaineering experience.

History

As a country, Afghanistan's history is less than 300 years old but it has been playing a key role in the region for over two millennia. The map reveals the reason: Afghanistan sits at the crossroads of Asia, sitting astride the hinterland between Persia, Central Asia and India. These three centrifugal forces have interacted time and again in Afghan history, frequently dividing the country against itself. At other times, Afghanistan has united against invaders and proved a bloody testing ground for foreign empires, as well as occasionally looking beyond its borders to form empires of its own.

FROM THE PERSIANS TO THE GREEKS

The prehistory of Afghanistan has been little studied, but there is evidence of pastoralism and agriculture in the region from around 10,000 years ago. Lapis lazuli from Badakhshan was being traded with Mesopotamia and India for at least 7000 years, and around 1500 BC the country became populated by the Indo-Aryans moving in from the west. Afghanistan doesn't enter written history until around the 6th century BC, when it became part of the Achaemenid Empire of Cyrus the Great. The Persians were the world's superpower of the time, and Afghanistan was divided into satrapies – Ariana (Herat), Arachosia (Kandahar), Bactria (Balkh) and Gandhara (the Kabul Valley). The Bactrians in particular were renowned fighters. At some stage during this period Zoroaster was born in Bactria, giving rise to the Zoroastrian religion that was quickly adopted by the Achaemenids.

Persia's great rival was Greece, and in 334 BC Alexander the Great launched a huge campaign against Darius III. Just 24 years old, Alexander's military genius quickly conquered the Mediterranean coast and the Achaemenid capital at Persepolis in modern Iran. His kingdom in ruins, Darius fled to Afghanistan where he was betrayed by the Bactrian satrap Bessus, who in turn proclaimed himself king. Alexander was outraged and led his army deep into Afghanistan, sweeping through the south before crossing the Hindu Kush and driving Bessus towards the Oxus (Amu Darya). He captured Bactria and Bessus, who was executed for his resistance.

Afghanistan got deep into Alexander's blood. He took his bride Roxanne in Balkh, and founded Bagram as a base for his invasion of India. Moreover he adopted local dress, and tried to set himself up as dictator. Only an eventual troop rebellion quelled his ambition, and he eventually turned for home to die at Babylon in 323 BC, leaving no named heir but having conquered much of the known world.

Alexander left behind ten years of chaos in Bactria, with thousands of Greeks stationed far from home. From the anarchy came Seleucus who began to weld together the foundations of the Graeco-Bactrian kingdom. This Hellenistic state deep in Asia sparked a centuries-long period of profound East-West cultural exchange, disseminating the aesthetics of the Classical world and absorbing the influences of both the central Asian steppe and the Indian subcontinent. Ai Khanoum, the easternmost Greek

Nearly half the infantry and 95% of the cavalry in Alexander the Great's entire empire had to be stationed in Afghanistan to try and pacify the country.

Martin Ewans' highly recommended *Afghanistan – A Short History of its People and Politics* covers the breadth of Afghan history from Alexander the Great to Hamid Karzai with a sure hand and lightness of touch.

330 BC	AD 128
Alexander the Great invades Afghanistan	Kanishka rules Kushan empire from Kapisa (Bagram)

city in the world was a place of gymnasiums and theatres performing the Greek tragedies, temples to the old gods and groves of olive trees.

BUDDHIST AFGHANISTAN

As the Graeco-Bactrian kingdoms flowered in the north, a new power rose in the east. In 302 BC north India became unified under the Mauryans, who quickly took control of southern and eastern Afghanistan. A peace treaty with the north was sealed with gifts of elephants and marriages between the Greeks and Indians. Under the great emperor Ashoka, the Mauryans converted to Buddhism, driven by his guilt at the blood spilled for the formation of his empire. Buddhist monasteries thrived across Afghanistan, together with rock-cut edicts from Ashoka exhorting readers to follow a pious life. One found in modern Kandahar was written in Greek and Aramaic.

Into the Land of Bones – Alexander the Great in Afghanistan by Frank Holt is a lively history of Alexander's Afghan campaign and the Graeco-Bactrian kingdoms that sprung up in its wake.

Buddhism proved irresistible to the Graeco-Bactrians. After Seleucus the kingdom fell into a tumbling succession of warring factions and dynasties, and the Hellenistic traditions were slowly absorbed by local customs. By 150 BC, they were under pressure from other directions – the Parthians from Iran, and then nomad tribes from the north. These were the outermost ripples of a wave of people displaced by the unification of China under the Qin dynasty. Again Afghanistan's direction was influenced by events in distant imperial capitals. Of the nomads that washed up, it was the Yueh-chih in 130 BC that had the greatest impact, when they united under the name of the Kushans.

The Kushans soon settled, and took the best traditions from the Graeco-Bactrians and the Indians to fuse them with the free-spirited

---

THE SILK ROAD

The Silk Road was never a single highway, rather a network of routes stretching over 8000km from Xi'an in modern China across Central Asia to Damascus and Antioch on the Mediterranean. Similarly, no trader ever passed its entire length. Instead, caravans traded along set stages with goods exchanged and becoming ever more expensive at each stop.

The Silk Road really sprang into life in the 1st century BC, when China exchanged embassies with Parthia (modern Iran) and Ferghana in Central Asia. From these were born the Roman craze for silk, supplied by the Parthians. The fabric was so popular – and expensive – that the Roman Senate even tried to ban it, on moral as well as economic grounds. As the Chinese guarded the secret of its production closely, silk was supposed to literally grow on the trees of the far east.

The Parthians and Bactrians were the most avid traders, sending gold, horses, glass and ivory. In return, China sent porcelain, paper, tea, lacquer – and endless bolts of silk. Ideas became an equally important currency. The Kushans sent Buddhist ideas from Afghanistan to China, and Buddhist art to India. Manichaeism and Nestorian Christianity also headed east. Bukhara, Balkh, Yarkand and Dunhuang flourished as great cities of trade and culture.

The Silk Road reached its apogee during the 1st and 2nd centuries AD. The collapse of the Roman and Han Chinese empires caused a collapse in trade, while the rise of Islam further changed the political and economic balance of the region. The Pax Mongolia that briefly followed Genghis Khan allowed Marco Polo to hit the old trade roads to China, but by the time the region had recovered from the depredations of Timur, the powers of Europe were looking elsewhere. The age of sea exploration had arrived, dealing the final death knell for the Silk Road.

6th century	**652**
The Buddhas of Bamiyan carved from cliffside	Arab conquest of Herat brings Islam to Afghanistan

nature of the steppe. In doing so they created a unique culture that ruled Afghanistan for five centuries. The new kingdom was ideally placed to exploit the burgeoning trade along the Silk Road (see boxed text, opposite). From AD 128, the visionary King Kanishka built two capitals at Kapisa (modern Bagram) and Peshawar, forging an empire whose influence travelled as far as the Ganges. Kushan art, also known as Gandharan art, was a vibrant blend of Classical, Indian and Persian styles, and was hugely influential. The kingdom was the first to represent the Buddha in human form, a style it sent to Kashmir, Tibet and China. Monasteries thrived in Balkh, Kandahar, Bamiyan, Samangan, and Hadda near Jalalabad.

Decline eventually came with the demise of the Silk Road, and the Kushans fell before the arrows of their neighbours. In the 3rd century AD the Sassanians arrived from Persia and reduced Kushan power to a rump. A century later the Hephthalites (or White Huns) swept in, and stayed long enough to build the giant Buddha statues at Bamiyan. From the east, the Hindus raised kingdoms in Kabul and Ghazni. Afghanistan was again pushed to the margins of history.

Life Along the Silk Road by Susan Whitfield is a great read for Silk Road enthusiasts, presenting the history of the route through an absorbing set of characters and vignettes.

ISLAMIC EMPIRES

In the 7th century a new power with a new religion was knocking at the door. Having swept the Sassanians aside, the Arab armies arrived in 652, marching under the banner of Islam. Herat and the south were soon subdued, but the north was a harder nut to crack. It took two centuries for Balkh to fall fully under Muslim control, where it was ruled from the Samanid Arab capital at Bukhara, and flourished as a centre of learning and culture. The rest of Afghanistan became a patchwork of squabbling Muslim city-states, far from Bukhara's influence and chafing for independence.

Out of this morass came Alptigin, a Turkish slave-soldier who overthrew his masters and captured the fortress of Ghazni in 961. He quickly died thereafter, but his successors consolidated their power and went onto capture Kabul, Bost, Balkh and Herat, dealing a deathblow to the Arabs. In their place stood the new power of the Ghaznavid dynasty.

Sultan Mahmoud the Great was both an empire builder and patron of the arts. Ghazni was richly endowed with mosques and palaces, becoming one of the greatest cities in Islamic world. He filled his court with poets and artists, his stables with an army of elephants, and whenever the treasury was bare, raided Delhi – introducing Islam to India in the process. Winter was spent in the warmth of Bost and Lashkar Gah, made green with an intricate series of canals. On Mahmoud's death in 1030 his rule stretched almost to Calcutta in the east, and west to the Caspian Sea.

The empire was too swollen to be stable. India and the Afghan north fell almost immediately, and while the Ghaznavid princes fought over the remains they failed to notice new tribes coming down from the mountains with envious eyes. In 1148 the Ghorids, Muslims from central Afghanistan led by Alauddin, 'the World Burner', swept into Ghazni and laid the great city to waste. It took seven days to burn to the ground. From here the Ghorids poured into India and Iran on an orgy of pillage. When they returned they endowed their capitals at Firuzkoh and Herat with fine buildings, leaving the Minaret of Jam and Herat's Friday Mosque as their greatest testaments.

Asia is comparable to a living body composed of soil and water/

The heart that beats inside the body is Afghanistan/

The destruction of Afghans would be the destruction of Asia/

And in their progress and prosperity lies the well-being of Asia

MOHAMMED IQBAL, 1936

11th century	1136
Ghazni flourishes under Mahmoud the Great	Shrine of Hazrat Ali constructed in Mazar-e Sharif

INVADERS FROM THE STEPPES

As the Ghorids settled into what they thought would be a long and prosperous rule, they had no way of knowing that the greatest storm in Afghan history was about to break over them. Thunderheads were gathering in far Mongolia, in the shape of the armies of Genghis Khan. A brilliant tactician and proponent of total war, Genghis Khan swept through central Asia in 1219 after his emmissaries were killed by unwise rulers far to the north of Afghanistan. As one historian put it, Genghis was 'the atom bomb of his day'. Having levelled Samarkand, Bukhara and Merv, the Mongols tore into Afghanistan. Balkh and Herat were dispatched without mercy, leaving little more than barking dogs as witnesses. The south, with its green gardens, orchards and canals was utterly destroyed, a disaster that it arguably has yet to recover from. In Bamiyan, the fate of Shahr-e Gholghola (the 'City of Screams') continues to burn in the folk memory of the locals.

'With one stroke a world which billowed with fertility was laid desolate, and the regions thereof became a desert.'

JUVAINI, THE HISTORY OF CONQUERING THE WORLD, 1259

The Mongols didn't gallop into the sunset, but incorporated the ruins into their empire. Genghis' son Chagatai ruled Afghanistan and most of central Asia. But although the Chagatai dynasty soon converted to Islam, it was never strong. Within decades of Genghis Khan's death the Turkic peoples of the northern steppe began to reassert themselves.

Their vehicle was Timur ('the Lame', or Tamerlane), an Uzbek from near Samarkand. As a tyrant and military leader, Timur was the equal of Genghis (from whom he claimed ancestry), but he was also a man of the arts and loved building cities as much as destroying them and slaughtering their inhabitants. In the 1390s he went on a rampage that landed him an empire from Syria to north India. The great Timurid cities were richly endowed by captured artisans and painters.

Timur died in 1405 and was succeeded by his son Shah Rukh, who moved the empire's capital from Samarkand to Herat, sparking one of Afghanistan's greatest cultural flowerings. Shah Rukh and his formidable wife Gowhar Shad were tremendous patrons of the arts. His court produced poetry that is still widely read in the Persian world, while the painted books from Herat would go on to form the bedrock for both the Persian and Indian style of miniatures. Scientists and philosophers were as highly regarded.

When Timur captured Andkhoi he sought omens from the local saint, who threw a sheep's breastbone at the conqueror – inspiring Timur to conquer Herat and Khorasan, the breastbone of the known world.

The Timurid Renaissance lasted just a century, until a surfeit of wine and poetry turned it flabby and decadent. Warring Uzbek tribes nibbled at its edges until they were strong enough to bite off Samarkand and (in 1507) Herat itself. To the west, the Safavid shahs of Persia were also beginning to covet Afghan territories. At the start of the 16th century, the balance of power was on a knife-edge.

THE AFGHAN KINGDOMS

The man to resurrect Afghanistan was Zahiruddin Babur, a teenage claimant to the Samarkand throne from the Ferghana Valley. Despite repeated attempts to capture and hold his birthright, the Uzbek khan Shaybani kept beating him back until he gave up and looked for a new kingdom to the south. Kabul fit the bill perfectly, and in 1504 its inhabitants welcomed him with open arms for evicting its Kandahari warlord ruler. He visited his Timurid relations in Herat months before it fell to

Ghorid sultan Ghiyassudin erects the Minaret of Jam

Genghis Khan invades and devastates Afghanistan

he hated Uzbeks, and captured Kandahar in a thrice. In that city he left a monument to his achievements – the Forty Steps (Chihil Zina) – directly above the edicts carved by Ashoka 18 centuries before.

On Shaybani's death Babur made one last failed attempt to take Samarkand, before returning to consolidate his Afghan kingdom, laying out palaces and gardens in Kabul, and always writing his memoirs, *The Baburnama*. In 1525 he followed the well-trodden path of the Ghaznavids, Ghorids and Timur and invaded India. He settled in Delhi and Agra, only returning to Kabul in death, but gave birth to the Mughal empire that held sway in India until the arrival of the British.

Kabul was a favourite of Babur's son Humayun, but he held little of his father's gift for politics. Over the next 200 years, the Mughal sphere of Afghanistan was squeezed back until it comprised little more than Kabul and Kandahar. The Safavids pushed far past Herat and into the south, while the Uzbeks continued to hold sway north of the Hindu Kush.

In the early 1700s, the Safavid empire had begun its slow decline, but still managed to capture and hold Kandahar. In 1709 the Ghilzai Pashtun mayor of Kandahar, Mir Wais Khotak sparked a revolt and defeated a Persian army sent to punish him. Not only that, his son Mahmoud marched on the Safavid capital Esfahan and sacked it before the Persians could regain their senses. In retaliation, the Persian leader Nadir Shah tried to play off the Pashtun tribes against each other, supporting the Abdalis against the Ghilzais – a tactic that would be repeated in later centuries, with similar unforseen consequences. Nadir Shah appointed the Abdali Ahmad Khan as commander of his Afghan forces and the royal treasury.

The Abdalis were proven fighters, smashing Ghilzai power in Kandahar, capturing Kabul and pushing far enough into India to thump the Mughals and loot the fabled Peacock Throne and Koh-i Noor Diamond. But just as Ahmad Khan thought the status quo was restored, Nadir Shah was assassinated. Khan quickly realised the opportunity before him. Rich with the Persian treasury, he drew together the Abdalis and made his bid for power. A *jirga* (council) named him Ahmad Shah, *Dur-i Durran* ('Pearl of Pearls') and crowned him with a garland of wheat sheafs. The Abdalis were renamed the Durrani in his honour.

From his new capital at Kandahar, Ahmad Shah Durrani set about laying the borders now recognisable as modern Afghanistan. Herat, Balkh and Badakhshan all fell under his sway in just a few years, and the kingdom extended as far as Srinagar, Delhi and Mashhad. He died of cancer in 1772, and is still remembered as Ahmad Shah 'Baba', the Father of Afghanistan.

> 'Whatever countries I conquer in the world, I would never forget your beautiful gardens. When I remember the summits of your beautiful mountains, I forget the greatness of the Delhi throne.'
>
> AHMAD SHAH DURRANI

SHAH SHUJA, DOST MOHAMMED & THE BRITISH

Inevitably Ahmad Shah Durrani's empire started to contract as soon as he was laid to rest. His son Timur Shah moved the capital to Kabul in 1776, but pretty soon the kingdom descended into fights for succession and tribal revolts. Herat again resurrected itself as an independent city-state and Bukhara resumed its influence over the northern cities. Kabul became a cauldron of rivalries between the Barakzai and Sadozai Durranis, competing for the throne. Of these, history primarily remembers the cruel and

15th century	1504
Timurid empire ruled from Herat	Babur captures Kabul, sowing the first seeds of the Mughal Empire

THE GREAT GAME

Rudyard Kipling immortalised the term 'the Great Game' in his novel *Kim*. It refers to the competition between Britain and Russia over control of Central Asia, in which Afghanistan played a central role. Britain was ever paranoid about approaches to India, the jewel of its empire, while Russia feared any approaches towards the motherland itself.

At the start of the 19th century much of Central Asia was unknown. Russia was rapidly expanding its borders towards the khanates of the old Silk Road cities, while Britain sought to explore and protect the routes through the Himalayas and Hindu Kush that led to the subcontinent. On both sides a motley bunch of explorers, emissaries and officers on 'shooting leave' risked their lives to map the region and try to win the confidence of local rulers. On the home fronts, politicians and pamphleteers kept tensions stoked up to levels of Cold War hysteria. While meddling at the Kabul court always seemed to be at the centre of things, the Great Game span off into Tibet, Chinese Turkestan and northern Pakistan, as Russian and British agents played cat-and-mouse amid the high passes. The Game reached its climax between 1880 and 1890, with war between the powers (over Afghanistan, of course) only narrowly avoided, and the settling of Afghanistan's borders for imperial convenience a few years later.

A century later, the collapse of the Soviet Union and the emergence of the new Central Asian states prompted a revival of the phrase. The 'New Great Game' was all about gas, oil and the rise of radical Islamism – and as if nothing had changed, Afghanistan found itself at the heart of political intrigue yet again.

feckless Shah Shuja, whose main achievement was to lose Peshawar to the expanding Sikh kingdom of Ranjit Singh. He was soon kicked into exile in British India by the rising star of Dost Mohammed Khan, a ruler popular for his learning, piety and sense of justice towards his people.

Dost Mohammed took to the throne at a dangerous time. Both the British and Russian empires were creeping towards his borders in a rivalry that became known as 'the Great Game' (see boxed text, above). In 1836 the British sent Alexander 'Bukhara' Burnes to woo the amir. Dost Mohammed's main preoccupation was regaining his beloved Peshawar, and he sought Burnes' help in this. But Burnes had been sent empty handed, and although sympathetic to the amir's designs, British policy favoured bolstering the Sikhs over all other considerations. While Dost Mohammed clearly saw the danger of being squeezed between imperial rivals (and at the time, Russia was aiding a Persian siege of Herat), he accepted Captain Ivan Vitkevich as an envoy from Moscow, hoping to encourage the British to engage more closely.

The plan backfired in grand scale. The governor-general of India, Lord Auckland, decided that the amir must go, and a friendlier ruler put in his place. Shah Shuja was dusted down from retirement and placed at the head of a British and Indian army to restore him to power.

From the outset the British saw their Army of the Indus as one great victory parade. Invading from the south, resistance at Kandahar was brushed aside, and once the great fortress of Ghazni was taken Dost Mohammed took to the hills. Shah Shuja was crowned amir again in front of a population that was at best indifferent.

The British settled in, the officers sending for their wives while the enlisted men scandalised Kabul by dallying with the Afghan women.

For a brilliant retelling of the 19th century struggle between Britain and Russia in Central Asia, pick up Peter Hopkirk's *The Great Game*, told as the *Boy's Own* adventure it undoubtedly was for many of its protagonists.

1747	1834
Ahmad Shah Durrani crowned, begins creation of modern Afghan state	Peshawar lost to the expanding Sikh kingdom

With horse racing and amateur dramatics, garrison life seemed good. The whole country was 'quiet from Dan to Beersheba,' wrote the British envoy at the close of 1840, wilfully blind to signs that a tribal revolt under Dost Mohammed's son Akbar Khan was brewing in the mountains. Afghan resentments spilled into bloodshed in November 1841 when a mob attacked Burnes' house and hacked him to death. As events spun out of control, the British eventually found themselves hounded from the country, in the disastrous retreat from Kabul (see boxed text, p32).

A year later, the British sent an army of vengeance to level Kabul, but despite the costs in blood and treasure, they realised the folly of interfering in Afghanistan too closely and restored Dost Mohammed to the throne, with a fat subsidy to boot. The amir was never so popular or powerful. He began to build the first national army, and brought Afghan Turkestan back into the nation. In the 1860s Herat was restored too, where Dost Mohammed died, to be buried at the shrine of Gazar Gah.

The British Army invading Afghanistan in 1839 didn't travel lightly – amid the 30,000-strong herd of pack animals were two camels dedicated to carrying regimental cigars, and a pack of hounds for fox-hunting.

SHER ALI & THE IRON AMIR

After the usual confusion following an amir's death, Sher Ali ascended the Kabul throne in 1869. As with Dost Mohammed, he came to power to a background of heightened imperial tensions. Russia had recently annexed Bukhara and Samarkand, steeping Britain in Great Game paranoia. When Sher Ali received an envoy from Moscow in 1878, London insisted that they be allowed to establish a permanent mission in Kabul – and having set themselves an impossibly short time for the amir to reply, sleepwalked into the Second Anglo-Afghan War.

Apparently, no lessons had been learned from the 1840s disaster. No sooner was the British envoy Cavagnari installed by arms in Kabul, he was shot by Afghan soldiers rioting over pay. An army was sent from India to quell the trouble, which they did by imposing a reign of terror on Kabul with mass arrests and summary executions. Soon the whole countryside was ablaze with rebellion. Another British army was trounced, this time at Maiwand near Kandahar. Although the Afghan regular forces were eventually beaten, the British decided that they'd had enough. Amir Abdur Rahman Khan was allowed to take the throne from exile in Bukhara. Foreswearing any contacts with the Russians, he also insisted that no power interfere with internal Afghan affairs, and refused any envoys at his court. The British were only too happy to be shot of Afghanistan, signed a treaty with the amir and marched back to India.

Abdur Rahman unified Afghanistan with ruthless determination, gaining him the moniker of the 'Iron Amir'. He used his British subsidy to build up a strong army, which he then used to pacify the regions and break the old tribal monopolies on power. Over 10,000 Ghilzai families were relocated to the north following an uprising in the east. For the first time, Abdur Rahman claimed divine right to rule. The influence of the mullahs was restrained by bringing them under government control and establishing a unified sharia court system. When the mullahs protested he won them back through campaigns against the Shiite Hazaras and, most spectacularly, capturing and converting the pagan tribes of Kafiristan in 1893 – thence renamed Nuristan, the 'Land of Light'. An effective state administration was created for the first time and taxes were

For an alternative account of the disastrous British campaigns, consult George MacDonald Fraser's essential *Flashman*, memoirs of the Empire's greatest (fictional) cad, coward and hero.

1839–42	1878–80
British occupation of Afghanistan ends in disastrous retreat from Kabul	Second British invasion ends ignominiously; Abdur Rahman Khan takes the throne

---

THE RETREAT FROM KABUL

The First Anglo-Afghan War is remembered for the calamitous retreat of the British army from Kabul, a withdrawal that turned into a frozen death march that has passed into Afghan folk history.

The army was led by the incompetent William Elphinstone, a feeble and perpetually sick general on the verge of retirement, who was bullied by both his subordinates and Macnaghten, the British representative to Shah Shuja. As Kabul rioted after the murder of Burnes, Elphinstone dithered. His camp was far from the city and immediately fell under siege, a position made far worse by the decision to keep the camp supplies outside the perimeter wall.

Attempts to break free were half-hearted and quickly squashed. As more tribes joined the revolt, Afghan sharpshooters with their superior *jezails* (long-barrelled muskets) steadily picked off the British. Macnaghten tried to broker a double-dealing plan with Dost Mohammed's son, Akbar Khan, which only led to his murder at a parley and his body being strung up in the bazaar.

Elphinstone eventually agreed to abandon Kabul, and left the families of the married officers as hostages in return for safe passage to the Indian border. On 5th January 1842, 4500 soldiers and their families and 12,000 camp followers headed into the harsh winter. Almost immediately they were set upon and discipline collapsed. As the Ghilzai tribes snatched at the train of the column, the march turned into a rout. Akbar claimed it was impossible to restrain the wild Ghilzai, and demanded more hostages for protection. Elphinstone acquiesced. The hostages were the lucky ones – in the first five days of the march over 12,000 lives were lost to raids and the freezing winter. As British numbers dwindled, the raids became bolder. The tattered army made its last doomed stand at Gandamack. On January 13, army surgeon Dr William Brydon limped into the garrison at Jalalabad on a half-dead pony, the only officer to carry the British shame and disaster back to the empire.

---

collected. The Iron Amir forged modern Afghanistan through bloo[d] and determination.

There was a price to pay for this state-building. Feeling Afghanistan ha[d] tasted enough foreign interference, Abdur Rahman promoted an isolation ism bordering on xenophobia. Modern developments like the telegrap[h] and railways were firmly rejected, and foreign traders rebuffed. The coun try went from being at the heart of Asia to an inward-looking backwater.

> 'How can a small power like Afghanistan which is like a goat between two lions, or a grain of wheat between two strong millstones of the grinding mill, stand in the midway of the stones without being ground to dust?'
>
> AMIR ABDUR RAHMAN KHAN, 1900

Nonetheless, the amir held to his commitments to the British. When the Russian army advanced to the Afghan border near Herat in 1885 provoking the 'Panjdeh Crisis', he stuck firm to London's line, even t[o] the point of allowing Herat's renowned Musalla Complex to be levelle[d] to give defenders a clear line of fire at any advancing Russians. Whe[n] war was averted, he allowed the British to settle his northern border wit[h] Russia two years later. In 1893 he further allowed the drawing of the Du rand Line, the border between Afghanistan and British India that slice[d] through the Pashtun region – a border so contentious no subsequen[t] Afghan government has yet to formally accept and demarcate it.

EXPERIMENTS IN MODERNISATION

Abdur Rahman was succeeded by his son Habibullah in 1901 – a rar[e] peaceful passing of the crown. Habibullah saw the need to modernis[e] Afghanistan. He set up schools teaching modern curricula and built road[s] and factories. A major influence was Mahmud Beg Tarzi, the founder o[f] the country's first newspaper and a key reformist and nationalist thinker Anti-imperial and pan-Islamist ideologies were beginning to gain mo[re]

Kafiristan forcibly converted to Islam and renamed Nuristan	Durand Line between Afghanistan and British India plotted

mentum in the British empire and seep into Afghanistan. Habibullah rejected the 1907 Anglo-Russian Convention that designated his country as a formal buffer zone between the empires, without even consulting him. After the outbreak of WWI, Habibullah flirted with a German-Turkish delegation aiming to take the war into India, and sought relations with newly Soviet Russia. An assassin's bullet found him in early 1919.

Habibullah's brother Amanullah took the throne, and drove even harder along the modernisation road. Almost his first act after becoming king (the title of amir wasn't suitably 20th century for Amanullah) was to provoke the British into the Third Anglo-Afghan War. It lasted barely the month of May 1919, and brought Afghanistan's first experience of air war, with the bombing of Kabul and Jalalabad by the RAF. But the British were weary from the exertions of WWI and sued for peace. A treaty granted Afghanistan full control over its diplomatic relations. After a century of the Great Game, Amanullah had won Afghanistan back its independence.

> The dispute over their common British-drawn border meant that Afghanistan was the only country to vote against Pakistan's accession to the UN in 1947.

He set about the country with a modernist's zeal, and wowed Europe with an eight-month grand tour. But at home resentments bubbled away with each story of his top hats and motor cars. More scandalous still, Amanullah had allowed Queen Soraya to appear in public unveiled and wearing a sleeveless dress. Rumours abounded that he was allowing the Europeans to import machines that made soap from human corpses. The country rose in revolt, and Amanullah's army had been fatally weakened by the loss of his British subsidy. In early 1929 he fled into exile and the throne was snatched by Bacha Saqao, the first Tajik to rule Afghanistan. Not that he lasted long. General Nadir Khan toppled him in less than a year and made himself him king. He wasn't related to Amanullah, but at least he was a Durrani Pashtun, and he immediately put the brakes on the more overt forms of modernisation.

Nadir Khan barely lasted four years before his murder in 1933, to be succeeded by his teenage son Zahir Shah. Under his rule Afghanistan cautiously made progress with stepwise introduction of education reform, the wearing of the veil made voluntary, and the 1964 constitution that made the country a constitutional democracy. The most imaginative reforms were overseen by prime minister Mohammed Daoud, the king's cousin. Like his forbears, Daoud played the Afghan game of courting several imperial powers, inviting both the USA and USSR to bring trade and aid to the county, as well as rattling sabres at Pakistan over the Durand Line. Briefly dismissed by the king, in 1973 he sidestepped his cousin and declared himself president, backed by a loya jirga and a rewritten constitution.

> American aid to Afghanistan up to the 1970s focussed on the Helmand Valley scheme, aimed in large part at repairing the damage done to south Afghanistan's irrigation system by Genghis Khan and Timur.

THE AFGHAN COMMUNISTS

Although Daoud had close relations with the Soviets, he sought to deepen Afghanistan's neutrality and made approaches to the USA and Iran. The Soviets bit back. They had invested heavily in training the Afghan army, as well as encouraging the embryonic Afghan communists, the People's Democratic Party of Afghanistan. Even at this stage the PDPA had split into two bickering factions, Khalq ('The People') and the mainly Pashtun Parcham ('The Banner'). In April 1978 soldiers stormed the Presidential Palace and killed Daoud and his family. The Khalq leader Mohammed Taraki proclaimed himself president of a revolutionary Marxist regime.

1919	1919–29
Third Anglo-Afghan War results in independence	King Amanullah attempts modernist reform programme, resulting in tribal rebellion

The countryside rose almost immediately against plans for land reform, women's rights and secular education. Zbigniew Brzezinski, President Carter's National Security Advisor pushed for American military support for the rebellion. By the end of 1978 the country was ablaze. An army mutiny in Herat was only quelled by inviting Soviet pilots to carpet bomb the city. The communists had no answers but more force and more radical reform, and fell into infighting and party purges. In September 1979 Moscow replaced Taraki with Hafizullah Amin and drew up plans for military support. But by Christmas Eve their patience finally ran out. KGB troops landed in Kabul and killed Amin. The Parchami Babrak Karmal was installed as president, and the next day the Red Army started to pour across the border, 'invited' in to safeguard the revolution. The Great Game was back on – the Russians were finally in Afghanistan.

Amin Saikal's *Modern Afghanistan – A History of Struggle and Survival* is a key work for understanding the trajectory of Afghanistan in the 20th century.

THE ANTI-SOVIET JIHAD

The Soviets initially expected to be in Afghanistan for just a few months but events soon spiralled out of their control. The invasion not only attracted worldwide condemnation, but as the resistance called a jihad

AFGHANISTAN IN THE HIPPY ERA... AND 35 YEARS LATER   Tony Wheeler

In 1973 Kabul was in danger of becoming a 'fly in, fly out' tourist trap. At least that's what I wrote in the very first Lonely Planet guidebook. I'd passed through Afghanistan the previous year, part of the great Asia Overland exodus, following the 'hippy trail' from London to Kathmandu and on through South-East Asia to Australia.

Looking back it was a magical era and one that still hasn't been adequately recorded, although Rory Maclean's *Magic Bus* and David Tomory's oral history of the trail, *A Season in Heaven,* capture the feel of Afghanistan perfectly. Of course the memories have faded (and if you can remember it clearly, you clearly weren't there) but Sigi's in Kabul felt like the epicentre of the Afghan section of the trail. We lounged on carpets, sipping free mint tea, listening to the music (the rumour was that if Pink Floyd released it in London on Monday the tapes were in Kabul by Friday), occasionally repairing to the courtyard to shift the giant chess pieces around the giant chessboard. Cool.

The Afghans were cool too, 'they were an example to us all, proving that you could be smart, tough, proud, broke, stoned and magnificently dressed, all at once' according to *A Season in Heaven.* Our attempts to look magnificently dressed inevitably failed. I'd no sooner arrived in Herat than I wandered off to a tailor to be fitted out with a Europeanised version of an Afghan suit. A German traveller returning from the tailor at the same time reduced the assembled Afghans hanging around the hotel to gibbering wrecks, laughing so hard they had to lie on the floor.

'No man would wear red,' one of them confided.

It was the travellers' responsibility to entertain as well as be entertained and we did our best. You arrived in Afghanistan slightly spooked; you'd heard so many stories about wild men and craziness and there was no question that crossing borders seemed like something measured on the Richter scale, the number goes up by one but the earthquake factor jumps by 10. Leaving Europe for Turkey was the first big culture shock, then it was x10 when you hit Iran and x100 when you crossed into Afghanistan. And then you relaxed, because it simply wasn't as scary as you'd expected.

Bruce Chatwin may have rejoiced that he visited Afghanistan 'before the Hippies wrecked it', which they did, he claimed, 'by driving educated Afghans into the arms of the Marxists', but Chatwin was a snob and never very happy about anybody who hadn't been to Oxford and didn't do their shopping at Sotheby's.

1920s	1973
Central Asia refugees flood into Afghanistan following the Soviet upheavals	Daoud overthrows King Zahir Shah, declares Afghanistan a republic

against the godless Russians Afghanistan became a beacon for the world-wide Islamist movement. The Americans feared the Cold War expanding towards the warm waters of the Arabian Sea and pledged covert military aid to fight the Soviets 'to the last Afghan'.

The resistance was known as the mujaheddin. Several key leaders were already in exile in Pakistan, having fled Afghanistan in the mid-1970s after Daoud's crackdown on Islamists at Kabul University. These included the Tajiks Burhanuddin Rabbani, founder of Jamiat-e Islami (Society of Islam), and his supporter Ahmad Shah Massoud, and the fundamentalist Ghilzai Pashtun Gulbuddin Hekmatyar, founder of Hezb-e Islami (Party of Islam). Reflecting the disparate nature of Afghan society, the resistance itself was divided. Seven main parties emerged, split between the Islamists, hoping to establish an Islamic state, and the traditionalists, who saw the Jihad as a national liberation struggle.

Funding soon poured in from the USA and Saudi Arabia. Pakistan was the epicentre of resistance, home not only to the mujaheddin parties but also to over three million Afghan refugees. The Pakistani dictator General Zia insisted that all funding and support be funnelled to his secret service,

---

In fact the Afghans look back to the hippy period as a golden age, everything was peaceful and there was lots of money to be made: somebody was buying the carpets even if we weren't. In 2006 I finally returned to Afghanistan and despite the intervening chaos quickly discovered one thing had not changed: the Mustafa Hotel, where Maureen and I stayed in 1972, was still there at the end of Chicken St and still a travellers' favourite. In fact the young trio, 'two guys and a chick' in hippie-era-speak, who tumbled out of the Mustafa as I strolled by, adjusting their backpacks as they emerged, could easily have been time-warped straight from the 1970s.

My recent two-week return trip was a mystifying blend of old and new. In Kabul I couldn't remember Sigi's exact Chicken St location and the shops in the city centre, near the market and river, all seemed to be devoted to mobile phones. The flight across the snow-clad central mountains to Herat – I had zero enthusiasm about risking the road via Kandahar – was spectacularly beautiful and Herat was still a delight. Until very recently the Citadel that dominates the centre of the town had been just as closed as it was on our 1970s visit, but today it's open to visitors (it's a shame there aren't more of them) and the views are dazzling.

From Herat I forayed into central Afghanistan to visit the reclusive Minaret of Jam. I still remember seeing the minaret on a tourist poster on a Herat hotel wall and instantly thinking 'where is that?' followed, of course, by 'I'd like to go there.' It had taken 34 years, but finally I did. From Kabul another central Afghanistan trek to Bamiyan and Band-e Amir followed, where I encountered a couple of intrepid French motorcyclists. A final trip north took me into the Panjshir Valley and up to Mazar-e Sharif.

On my way back south to Kabul I made the short detour to the rock-cut Buddhist stupa at Takht-e Rostam and experienced, once again, that amazing sensation of seeing something that I knew nothing about. I'd read about the millennium-old rock dome in Nancy Hatch Dupree's classic *An Historical Guide to Afghanistan*, but I'd never seen a photograph and had little idea what to expect. Clearly it had similarities to the temples of Ajanta and Ellora in India, also cut out of solid rock, or even the cave temples of Petra in Jordan, but the place it really reminded me of was Lalibela in Ethiopia, where you could also stand at surface level and look down at the marvel at your feet. Here was something too solid for even the Taliban to damage.

April 1978	**December 1978**
Saur Revolution brings Afghan communist Khalq party to power	Soviet army invades Afghanistan and installs new regime

the ISI, and went about moulding the resistance to his own interests. Moderate mujaheddin groups were sidelined in favour of the most radical Islamists like Hekmatyar. Pakistani policy was aimed at installing a pliable Pashtun government in Kabul to quell disputes over the historically unstable Durand Line, and through Hekmatyar the ISI quashed attempts to unify the resistance. Touted by Islamabad and Washington as the most effective mujaheddin leader, Hezb-e Islami spent more time terrorising the refugee camps and killing Afghan rivals than Russians.

Pakistan also encouraged foreign fighters to join the struggle. Around 30,000 radicals from across the Muslim world were trained at arms, with financial support and Islamic guidance from Saudi Arabia. Known as the 'Arab-Afghans' they were deeply xenophobic and saw Afghanistan as a key staging post in a worldwide Islamic revolution. Osama Bin Laden came to Afghanistan at this time, and his co-militants would go on to take their experience to Algeria, Chechnya, Kashmir and beyond.

In the field, the regular mujaheddin fought on heroically. The countryside was ideal for hit-and-run ambushes, and the Red Army gradually found that it had little influence beyond the range of its guns. Scorched earth policies merely drove the resistance on. The Afghan army deserted in droves, and in 1986 the arrival of Stinger missiles from the USA put them further on the back foot, as helicopters and planes were shot from the skies. The new Soviet leader, Mikhail Gorbachev, started looking for a way out. He encouraged reconciliation through Kabul's new headman, Mohammed Najibullah, and when that failed announced a unilateral withdrawal. Gambling on the survival of the PDPA government, troops were pulled out until the last tank crossed the Amu Darya in February 1989. The decade-long war had cost the Soviets over 15,000 men and proved a significant catalyst to the collapse of the USSR. Over 1.5 million Afghans had died, and four times that many had fled the country.

> 'What's most important to the history of the world? The Taliban or the collapse of the Soviet empire? Some stirred-up Muslims or the liberation of Central Europe and the end of the Cold War?'
>
> ZBIGNIEW BRZEZINSKI LOOKS BACK ON US COVERT ASSISTANCE, 1998

CIVIL WAR

The Geneva Accords negotiated between the USSR and USA were meant to end the fighting, but they were barely worth the paper they were written on. The mujaheddin rejected forming an interim coalition government with Najibullah, and all sides continued to arm their proxies.

Kabul was expected to fall the moment the Russians left, but Najibullah held on for three more years. The ISI bribed the mujaheddin into forming an interim government, but it was incapable of capturing and holding territory. A huge assault on Jalalabad in 1989 turned into a bloodbath, and an internal coup against Najibullah was easily quashed. But gradually the mujaheddin gained ground. By early 1992 the mujaheddin were camped outside Kabul, with Hekmatyar to the south and Massoud to the north. At a crucial moment, an army mutiny in the north led by the Uzbek general Rashid Dostum provided the push that was needed to topple the regime. Massoud raced into Kabul to claim the prize, leaving Hekmatyar and his Pakistani handlers spitting with fury.

The birth of the Islamic Republic of Afghanistan merely delivered a slide into fratricidal war. Having liberated the country the mujaheddin set about destroying it. Rabbani ascended to the presidency and Hekmatyar was offered the job of prime minister, a job he accepted while remaining

> *Ghost Wars* by Steve Coll is a gripping and intricately researched history of the CIA's covert funding of the mujaheddin, and the spawning of the Arab-Afghans and Al-Qaeda.

1979–89	1989
Mujaheddin fight jihad against Soviet-backed regime; over 6 million flee country as refugees	Soviet army withdraws from Afghanistan

---

THE SOVIET EXPERIENCE IN AFGHANISTAN

Barring clichés that the mujaheddin effectively toppled the Soviet Union, the effect of Afghanistan on those who fought for the Red Army has been little written about. During the early stages of the invasion, Turkmen and Uzbek Soviet soldiers were in the vanguard, to win hearts and minds of the locals. However, their ranks were swiftly infiltrated by the resistance, so they were withdrawn and replaced by Russian and Ukrainian conscripts.

The soldiers quickly nicknamed the mujaheddin *dukhi* (ghosts), as they were so hard to find and fight. For their part, Afghans called the Red Army the 'Army of Bastards', as it was popularly believed that Soviet soldiers were orphans raised by the military.

The war was hard, with troops frequently confined to base not comprehending why their great socialist mission was being so deeply rejected, and unable to trust the Afghan army they fought with. Stinger missiles made helicopter evacuation of the wounded difficult, causing a further drop in morale. Drug abuse and corruption were rife. Some soldiers even deserted, converting to Islam and joining the mujaheddin.

In *The Hidden War*, the Russian journalist Artyom Borovik wrote: 'We thought that we were civilizing a backwards country by exposing it to TV, to modern bombers, to schools... but we rarely stopped to think how Afghanistan would influence us.' As Moscow lost the political will to continue the fight, disillusioned soldiers questioned the reason for their sacrifices. Forgotten on their return home, many of the veterans, dubbed *Afghantsi*, see themselves today as much victims of the Soviet regime as the Afghans.

---

outside Kabul and shelling the city. Dostum joined Massoud's forces, then switched to Hekmatyar, then went back north to set up his own quasi-state. The newly powerful Hazara militias backed by Iran were in turn fought and favoured. Herat effectively became an independent city-state once more, under Ismail Khan. A council of mujaheddin ruled Jalalabad and the south became an anarchic patchwork of warlord's fiefdoms.

From being the epicentre of the Cold War, Afghanistan simply dropped off the map, awash with arms, manipulated by its neighbours and with no peace in sight. Attempts by the UN to engage in talks repeatedly stalled and the Americans lost all interest the moment Kabul fell, preferring to forget the sacrifices the country had made, and the billions of dollars they'd spent arming the different factions.

It's estimated that over US$42 billion was spent on arms by all sides in Afghanistan between 1978 and 1992.

THE TALIBAN

In July 1994 a group of mullahs led by Mohammed Omar were so outraged by the rape and murder of several women by a warlord near Kandahar that they grouped together students from the local madrassas to enact justice. The warlord was strung up from a tank, and flush with the purity of their cause the students went on to clear the road to the Pakistan border, drawing people to their cause and in no time liberating Kandahar itself. So goes the Taliban creation myth.

The truth is a little more complex. Having invested so heavily in Hekmatyar, Pakistan eventually decided he was a dead letter and looked for another Pashtun horse to back. The Taliban looked like a good prospect to help clear the roadblocks between Kandahar and Quetta, where bribes were cutting into the profits of the Pakistani transport mafia. The

The 2005 report Blood-Stained Hands by Human Rights Watch (www.hrw .org) is a chilling indictment of civil war atrocities perpetrated by the mujaheddin in 1990s Kabul.

April 1992	1994–5
Mujaheddin capture Kabul, triggering the start of civil war	Kandahar and Herat fall under Taliban control

---

AHMAD SHAH MASSOUD – 'LION OF THE PANJSHIR'

Arriving in Kabul for the first time, you could be forgiven for confusing the identity of Afghanistan's president. Pictures of Ahmad Shah Massoud vastly outnumber those of Hamid Karzai.

Hailing from the Panjshir Valley north of Kabul. Massoud was the most formidable mujaheddin leader to fight against the Soviets. Largely ignored by the Pakistanis and Americans, he built a tough guerrilla army that repulsed 10 Russian offensives against the Panjshir, often by evacuating its entire civilian population. His natural charm, fluent French and moderate Islamic beliefs made him a hugely popular figure with Western journalists.

Following the capture of Kabul in 1992, Massoud became the real power behind the throne. While militarily brilliant, Massoud was no politician, and his inability to form alliances with other factions did much to prolong the civil war.

The Taliban reduced Massoud to a rump of power in the northeast. His assassination two days before 11 September 2001 has since cast him permanently in the role of martyr and saviour, his image reproduced everywhere in the style of an Afghan Che Guevara. Politically he has become more influential dead than when he was alive.

Not everyone idolises Massoud. Many Pashtuns resent him as a symbol of Tajik rule, Hazaras for his massacres of their kin, and others for the part he played in reducing Kabul to rubble in the 1990s. While Massoud will surely remain Afghanistan's number one poster boy for the foreseeable future, he's also a reminder that in civil wars few people emerge without any blood on their hands.

Taliban were allowed to capture a major arms dump on the border, and the Pakistani army provided training and logistical support for the nascent militia. Many of the opposing warlords were simply bought off with huge bribes facilitated by the ISI and the Saudis. When Kandahar fell the Taliban were welcomed for returning security to the region.

The mujaheddin government couldn't decide how to handle the situation. Talks sparked on and off, but collapsed when the Taliban raced to capture Herat in 1995, and started looking enviously towards the capital. In a final bid for power Hekmatyar threw his lot in with the hated Massoud, but his troops left the back door open. Rushing in from Jalalabad, the Taliban took Kabul in September 1996. Massoud fled to his Panjshir stronghold.

The fall of Kabul briefly jolted the international community out of their indifference. The Taliban wasted no time setting up the Islamic Emirate of Afghanistan. Najibullah was hauled from his UN-protected compound and publicly lynched. Women were banned from work and education and wearing the burqa was made compulsory. Men had to grow beards, music was banned and shops closed at prayer time.

Over the next two years the Taliban consolidated their control of Afghanistan. Mazar-e Sharif fell, driving Dostum into exile. Uprisings in the Hazarajat were brutally suppressed. Half the population relied on food aid but there was little sign of active Taliban governance, just ever more esoteric Islamic rulings on the minutiae of life. Rabbani clung on the presidency (and Afghanistan's seat at the UN), despite eventually being pinned back to a fiefdom in Badakhshan. In addition, the Taliban became ever more reliant on the Arab-Afghans who had stayed in Afghanistan – most notably Osama Bin Laden, who had reorganised his movement into Al-Qaeda ('The Base') and set up training camps for further jihad. As Bin Laden's

Other things forbidden by the Taliban included nail polish, lipstick, playing cards, chess, neckties, the internet and paper bags (lest they accidentally carry verses of the Quran).

1996	1998
Taliban capture Kabul, and lynch Najibullah	USA fires missiles at training camps in east Afghanistan in retaliation for bombing of US embassies in East Africa

influence grew, the Taliban became ever more radical and unbending. Only Pakistan, Saudi Arabia and the UAE recognised the Taliban as Afghanistan's legitimate government. In the words of the head UN representative, the country was 'a failed state which looks like an infected wound. You don't even know where to start cleaning it.'

WAR, AGAIN

On 9 September 2001, two suicide bombers posing as journalists assassinated Massoud, an act heavily suspected to be the work of Al-Qaeda. Two days later, hijackers flew planes into the Word Trade Centre and the Pentagon, killing over 3000 people. From that moment the Taliban were doomed. Citing the rules of Afghan hospitality, they refused to give up Osama Bin Laden to the USA. Two months later the Americans launched Operation Enduring Freedom to oust the regime. Still mourning their leader, Massoud's Northern Alliance was reconstituted. The CIA returned with suitcases full of money to buy off any waverers, and the American B-52 bombers did the rest from high altitude. Pakistan objected but nevertheless distanced itself from the Taliban, who after a brief fight simply melted away, with Mullah Omar fleeing to the hills. A major offensive against Al-Qaeda at Tora Bora similarly failed to capture Bin Laden. On 13 November 2001 a resurgent Northern Alliance entered Kabul.

A post-war conference in Bonn elected Hamid Karzai as interim leader. An International Assistance Force (ISAF) was mandated to provide security in Kabul, while the Americans continued the hunt on the ground for Al-Qaeda and Taliban remnants. A loya jirga the following summer confirmed Karzai as president and King Zahir Shah returned from a 28-year exile with the new title of 'Father of the Nation'. As floods of refugees and exiles followed, optimism was in the air.

THE ROAD TO RECONSTRUCTION

Although huge gains have been made since the Taliban's ouster, peace was only barely less rocky than the fighting that preceded it. Afghanistan in 2002 was effectively at 'Year Zero', its people traumatised and the infrastructure of the state destroyed. Huge attention was paid to getting the country back on its feet and assistance pledged by international donors. Yet for every gain made, a step back was taken elsewhere.

Remembering the dark days of the civil war, Afghans craved security more than anything, but requests to expand international peacekeepers outside the capital were repeatedly blocked by the Americans. Instead, many of the warlords and mujaheddin were allowed to creep back into power through either direct support or the turning of blind eyes. While there were intermittent factional fights across the north, the failure to properly control the south left the back door open for the return of the Taliban and the opium mafias. As the security situation there deteriorated reconstruction efforts ground to a halt, further alienating a Pashtun population wondering where their peace dividend had gone.

Despite the promises it soon became clear that Afghanistan was going to be an experiment in state-building on the cheap. America quickly became bored with Afghanistan and diverted its efforts and money towards

Taliban by Ahmed Rashid is the definitive history of the movement by a long-time observer of the Afghan scene, lifting the lid on regional power games, oil company manoeuvrings and radical Islamism.

| Operation Enduring Freedom defeats Taliban; Northern Alliance regains power | New constitution signed; Hamid Karzai elected president |

a new adventure in Iraq. The country received less than a third of the aid per head ploughed into reconstruction efforts in Bosnia, East Timor or Rwanda, and of that less than half went on long-term development programmes. A huge and expensive aid bureaucracy sprang up in parallel to the new Afghan government. Hamid Karzai's limited writ led him to be dubbed 'the Mayor of Kabul'. Unable to tackle the resurgent warlords, many of them were simply co-opted into government.

Afghanistan – The Mirage of Peace by Chris Johnson and Jolyon Leslie is the best book on the shelves to give a detailed analysis of the successes and failures of post-Taliban Afghanistan.

It wasn't all bad news. UN-led disarmament programmes had some impact on reducing the number of small and heavy weapons in the country. School enrolment numbers surged. Attempts to increase the international military footprint resulted in the formation of Provincial Reconstruction Teams (PRTs), with small military units combining security and reconstruction projects, albeit with extremely mixed success. In 2004 a new constitution was agreed upon, and presidential elections returned Karzai as leader. A year later, parliamentary elections took place, with reserved seats for women, although many were not only dismayed that known human rights abusers were not disbarred from standing, but that several even found their way into Karzai's cabinet – where they lobbied for immunity from prosecution for war crimes.

A fitful peace returned to most of the country, but international neglect of the south has been the worm in the bud. Pakistan has continued to play its own double-game, publicly signing up to the War on Terror while allowing safe haven to the Taliban leadership and fighters launching cross-border raids. In 2006 the growing insurgency resulted in widespread battles in Helmand and Kandahar Provinces and the bloodiest year since 2001. Suicide bombs, previously unknown in Afghanistan, have been imported from Iraq. Stuck in the death-grip of drugs and insurgency, south Afghanistan looks increasingly like a separate country. With the rest of the nation continuing along its unsteady path, Afghanistan's immediate future is hard to predict.

2005	2006
Parliamentary elections held	NATO takes responsibility for Afghan security; widespread violence across the south

The Culture

THE NATIONAL PSYCHE

Foreign writers have frequently turned to romantic clichés when writing about Afghans. They are portrayed as fiercely proud, lavishly hospitable to guests yet always ready to pick up their rifles to defend what is theirs, and with a streak of defiant independence that renders the country ungovernable. Like all clichés, these have some basis in fact, but the truth is more complex.

Afghans are a naturally conservative people, and deeply religious. Their independence comes from the harshness of the country, where arable land is at a premium and the difficulties of the terrain has promoted self-reliance and inhibited the formation of strong central governments. As a result, power has devolved down to the tribe, village and – central to Afghan life – the family. The household and the mosque are the cornerstones of community.

Travellers have always remarked on Afghan hospitality, derived from the tenets of Islam and tribal codes such as Pashtunwali (p44). Even today, showing hospitality to a guest is a point of honour, down to the poorest Afghan who will offer tea even if they can ill afford it. This is a manifestation of Islam that gets to the heart of traditional Afghan tolerance, and a world away from the insular and zealous strains of Islam imported into Afghanistan since the Soviet invasion.

The experience of war has greatly damaged Afghan society. Nearly a quarter of the population fled the country, where years in refugee camps in Pakistan, or in exile in other countries, has fractured traditions and ties to the land. Many recent returnees have headed for the cities in search of work, rather than return to their home villages. Civil war helped further split the country along ethnic lines, and post-conflict reconciliation continues to be a painfully slow process. Many warlords retain political power and sit in parliament, despite an official prohibition

> 'Here at last is Asia without an inferiority complex.'
> ROBERT BYRON, *THE ROAD TO OXIANA*

> *An Historical Guide to Afghanistan* (1977) by Nancy Hatch Dupree remains a classic tourist guide to pre-war Afghanistan. It's still a great read, and can be picked up in Kabul.

'THE BOOKSELLER OF KABUL'

The most successful of the flood of books on Afghanistan that followed the Taliban's ouster was *The Bookseller of Kabul* by Norwegian journalist Åsne Seierstad. It recounted her meeting with a Kabuli bookseller, Sultan Khan, who invited her to live with his family for several months. A pacy account of Afghan family life, in particular the drudge and horrors regularly inflicted on the women of the family, it became Norway's top-selling non-fiction book and was subsequently published in over 20 countries. It was here that the controversy began.

'Sultan Khan' was the thinly-disguised Shah Mohammed Rais, owner of the renowned Shah M bookshop (p84) in Kabul, who had had his books burned by the communists, the mujaheddin and the Taliban in turn. When given a copy of the book he was outraged, and claimed that Seierstad had abused his hospitality by revealing family secrets and writing slander, including allegations that female relatives had had boyfriends – a grave matter of honour once the book was translated into Dari and Pashto. Many Western critics also weighed in, questioning Seierstad's fictionalising of the thoughts of the characters when she had not met many of them, and spoke no Dari of her own. Seierstad herself appears nowhere in the book. Rais has repeatedly threatened a lawsuit for compensation, while in July 2006 his wife applied for asylum in Sweden claiming that the book had put her family's life in danger. On her part, Seierstad has openly regretted not consulting with Rais on the way his story should have been told. As the story rumbles on, this best-selling book has also become the most controversial.

during elections. Despite donning democratic clothes, many Afghans see this is as a sham: *'jangsalaran jangsalar hastand'* – warlords are and remain warlords.

LIFESTYLE

Afghan society is strictly segregated between the public and private domains. Women have always been seen as the symbols of family honour, and have traditionally been very restricted in their access to education and work. Since the 1970s, women's rights issues have made progress or been reversed according to the political and religious powers of the day (see p50).

The family is the bedrock of Afghan life, and family members only ever leave the home when they are married. Marriages are usually arranged between families by negotiation. The bride's mother and aunts usually hold the key to such discussions, although a matchmaker is sometimes used. The bride brings a dowry of jewellery and goods to set up her new house, while the groom's family pay a *mahr* (bride price) for the marriage. In some cases, poverty can force parents to 'sell' their daughters in marriage against their or her wishes. Marriage and family are so important to Afghans that they often cannot understand why Westerners travel unaccompanied by their family – particularly Western women.

An instantly recognisable manifestation of Afghan conservatism is dress. According to the Quran, modest dress is incumbent on men as well as women, although it is in women that this has taken its most extreme form (see boxed text, p46). Clothing must hide the shape of the body for both sexes, while for women the *hijab* (veil) is essential for covering the hair. Afghan men most commonly wear the *pirhan tonban* (traditional male clothes) of baggy pyjama trousers and long shirt, also called a *shalwar kameez*. Only in Kabul can you sometimes see men be so daring as to wear short-sleeved shirts.

Need to orient yourself? Afghan graves usually lie in a north-south direction, with the body laid on its right side so it faces Mecca in the west.

A *kozda* (engagement ceremony) marks the public announcement by both families of a betrothal, celebrated with gifts of flowers and sweets. In some cases, this party may be the first time the bride and groom have met.

EXILE AND RETURN   *Tamim Ansary*

Before 1978, Afghan exiles and émigrés numbered in the mere hundreds. Then, within four years, some six million fled the country. Most just dragged themselves to camps in Pakistan and Iran, but several hundred thousand went on to the West, accumulating mostly in Germany and the USA, and then in Australia, Denmark, Holland and Britain. Twenty years later, a whole generation of Afghans were coming of age in exile, longing volubly for a homeland they had never seen, a longing often expressed rhetorically as nostalgia for their own *khawk*.

What is *khawk*? English has no exact synonym. Soil, dust, land…all come close but none has the full resonance, for *khawk* connotes not just soil, but home, nation, ancestry, life, death, rooted permanence, the evanescence of all things, and purity. Yes, purity: Muslims must cleanse themselves for prayer but if water is unavailable, they may perform their ritual ablutions with *khawk*.

When I first returned to Afghanistan after the Taliban fled, my cousins took me to the places they assumed I most craved to see: my own *khawk*. In Kabul, this turned out to be my father's property, a concrete house squatting in a weed-choked yard, its roof all blown away, its crumbled walls scarred by grooves where guerrilla armies had ripped out the wiring to sell for cash.

In our ancestral village north of Kabul, my *khawk* was a patch of stony, featureless desert floor hemmed in by ditches running from a bombed-out, communal irrigation system that once provided this land 18 hours of water per week.

Finally they took me to my other *khawk*: the village graveyard where my father, uncles, grandparents and ancestors lay buried. A few graves had headstones, but most were unmarked mounds with no inscriptions – none were needed. In this village, everyone knew who was buried where.

While keen to preserve their traditions, Afghans are more than happy to engage with modernity and the West. Education is increasingly seen as essential for the country's development, while natural business acumen and links from years in exile makes Afghan businessmen well-placed to help their country, given enough political stability. And yet, modern business suits and mobile phones only go so far: tradition still rules, and anyone wanting to get on is still going to have to drink a lot of tea, the one unchanging facet of all Afghan society.

Afghans are traditionally pragmatic and wary of ideology, and often quick to switch political allegiances when the wind changes direction, hence the saying, 'You can't buy an Afghan, you can only rent him.'

ECONOMY

The Afghan economy is largely based on subsistence agriculture. The main crops are wheat and soft fruit, with a similar importance placed on raising livestock. At the end of 2001, the economy was at a standstill, wracked by several years of drought, and an international embargo against the Taliban. In the intervening years, a flood of aid money and investment has entered the country, prompting economic growth rates in double figures – a boom that was only just starting to slow as we went to press. Pakistan, Iran, India and the UAE are all important trading partners.

For all this, growth in the formal economy has been massively overshadowed by Afghanistan's production and export of opium. The country produces over 90% of heroin sold in the UK. Helmand and Badakhshan are the major poppy growing areas: if Helmand was a separate country, it would still be the biggest exporter of opium in the world (see boxed text, p196). Tackling opium production, which funds the resurgent Taliban and contributes to systematic corruption at all levels of government, remains a key issue in Afghan reconstruction.

Since the break-up of the Soviet Union, Afghanistan has been touted as a transit route for oil and natural gas pipelines from Central Asia to the Arabian Sea. Governments and oil companies have signed memoranda of understanding with a succession of regimes in Kabul (at one point

When the war burst out, my father stayed in Afghanistan because he didn't want to be buried in strange soil. When the Afghan exile community first burgeoned in the San Francisco Bay Area, they could get together on only one project: buying a bit of land to consecrate as an Afghan graveyard, a poor substitute for their native *khawk*. Now, with the Taliban gone, some of the exiles making the pilgrimage home are the dead. Yes, some Afghan families in America are now going to the extraordinary trouble and expense of flying their dead home for burial in their native *khawk*.

When I came home from Afghanistan – mine being the rootless soul of modern Western civilisation – I told my relatives I was thinking of giving my land away to the poor squatters living on it. Ripples of alarm ran through my clan. One cousin called me from Portland to plead, 'Don't do it, Tamim. That land is not just equity like your house here, that's the *khawk* your forefathers' wells have watered. Our ancestor Sheikh Sa'duddin is buried there. That *khawk* is your blood, your history, it's who you are. You can't give it away.'

Visitors to Afghanistan may see barren landscapes dotted with simple graves, but Afghan exiles returning here see something indefinably more. The Afghan poet Khalili once wrote:

The fountainhead of satisfaction is the company of those we love.
It's the distance from our friends that makes death difficult.
But all the friends gather in the khawk's heart in the end,
So in death as in life we are always in the company of friends.

Tamim Ansary is the author of West of Kabul, East of New York.

Love & War in Afghanistan is a deeply moving series of life stories told first-hand from ordinary Afghan men and women, collected by authors Alex Klaits and Gulchin Gulmamadova-Klaits.

Taliban representatives were even flown to Texas for talks) but continued instability keeps plans firmly on the drawing board. Afghanistan itself has small natural gas deposits in the north, which are yet to be fully exploited.

POPULATION

Afghanistan's rich mix of over 20 ethnic groups reflects its geographical and historical position as the crossroads of Asia. Successive waves of people have invaded and settled in the country, while others left to conquer or settle neighbouring countries. The result is a patchwork of nationalities that spills over Afghanistan's borders at every point, into Pakistan, Iran and Central Asia – relatively few ethnic groups are contained entirely inside Afghanistan.

While the concept of an Afghan nationality is a very real one, decades of war has enflamed ethnic divisions. Population flight in the form of the refugee crisis has further fractured traditional ethnic and power balances in the country. Reliable population data are hard to come by in Afghanistan, although a limited census was carried out in 2003 to aid planning reconstruction.

For an insight into the role that complex Pashtun tribal relations (and warlordism) have played in post-Taliban Afghanistan, read Sarah Chayes' *The Punishment of Virtue*.

Pashtuns

The Pashtuns are the largest ethnic group in Afghanistan. The oldest continuous inhabitants of the area, they are mentioned in ancient Aryan texts as the Paktua, and by the Greek historian Herodotus as the Paktues. The British called them Pathans, while Pashtuns have often simply referred to themselves historically as 'Afghans'. They claim descent from Qais, a companion of the Prophet Mohammed.

Pashtuns live mainly in east and southern Afghanistan, spreading into North West Frontier Province and Baluchistan in Pakistan. This whole area, straddling the contentious Durand Line, is often known as Pashtunistan. There are slight dialectical differences between the two populations – those speaking the 'softer' western dialect (Pashto) and the

---

THE PASHTUN CODE

Pashtunwali, the Pashtun moral code, has traditionally taken precedence over any external laws, acting as a constitution for Pashtun society. It has frequently been interpreted by the West as shorthand for tribal extremism, but it also provides a surprisingly open and democratic code for managing tribal affairs within the conservative and feudal nature of Pashtun society. Its key concepts are *siali* (individual equality), *nang* (honour) and *melmastia* (hospitality). Group decisions are made by a council of elders, or *jirga*.

Nang is central to a Pashtun's identity, most importantly that of the family (and women in particular). *Melmastia* is the showing of hospitality to all visitors without expectation of reward. This can even go as far as offering sanctuary to a criminal, and laying down one's life for a guest. From these two pillars flows the concept of *badal* – the obligation to avenge an insult of injustice to the individual, family or clan. Injustices can be those committed on the day or a century ago – a practice which readily leads to blood feuds, and is a major reason why many Pashtun villages look like collections of small forts. The vanquished in a fight may go to the victor in absolute submission for forgiveness. The winner is expected to show magnanimity to restore the balance of honour, a practice called *nanawatai*.

Like many tribal structures, Pashtunwali has been threatened and reinterpreted as a result of war, with tribal power in many cases shifting from the elders to the young men with guns. The rise of Islamism among Pashtuns, in great part due to the post-Taliban radicalisation of the Afghan–Pakistan border regions, continues to further undermine this ancient code.

'harder' eastern one (Pakhtu). Yet these differences are nothing compared to the stark clan lines that have traditionally divided Pashtun society. The two main clans are the southern Durranis and the eastern Ghilzais, each further divided into subclans, known as *khel*. The Durranis have provided Afghanistan's rulers since Ahmad Shah Durrani founded the Afghan kingdom in 1747 – Hamid Karzai is from the Popolzai subclan. The Ghilzais have always played second fiddle politically – a resentment exploited by Pakistan in the 1980s and '90s through its sponsorship of Ghilzai *jihadis,* including Gulbuddin Hekmatyar and the Taliban leadership.

Tajiks

Tajiks represent almost a quarter of the Afghan population. They are an Indo-European people, and blue eyes and sandy hair aren't uncommon. Until the 20th century, *taj* was shorthand for a Persian speaker, and the modern term Tajik encompasses a diverse group of settled peoples living in northern, western and northeastern Afghanistan, united by their language and adherence to Sunni Islam.

Tajiks are not as tribal as Pashtuns, with loyalties revolving around the family and village. Since Dari has remained the language of government for several hundred years, they have traditionally served as administrators, but with the reigns of power kept firmly from them by the Pashtuns. Only in the 20th century has this balance been undone, with the Bacha Saqao rebellion of 1929, the Tajik-dominated mujaheddin government in the 1990s and the Northern Alliance in post-Taliban Afghanistan. The continued strength of the Tajiks, exemplified by the near canonisation of Ahmad Shah Massoud, against the marginalisation of the Pashtuns remains a key political issue for the country.

Hazaras

The Hazaras occupy the mountain vastness of central Afghanistan known as the Hazarajat, and are the country's largest Shiite minority. This fact of religion has led to them being persecuted throughout history, largely viewed as a servant class by the ruling Pashtuns. Hazaras have distinct Mongoloid features, and they ascribe their ancestry to Genghis Khan's warriors – *hazar* being Dari for thousand, representing the Mongol hordes. It's more likely that the original Hazaras were Mongol farmers whose arrival in Afghanistan followed sometime after the great Khan. Modern Hazaras are also farmers, practising *lalmi* (rain-fed agriculture) in the marginal mountain environment. Aside from the Bamiyan region, there are large numbers of Hazaras in Kabul, Ghazni and Mazar-e Sharif. Hazara society is based on the power of the *mir* (local chief), with great stock placed on descent from the line of the Prophet Mohammed. Hazaras speak Hazaragi as well as Dari.

While traditionally marginalised, the Soviet invasion and civil war ironically gave an opportunity for the Hazaras to organise politically. Heavily supported by co-religionist Iran, the Hezb-e Wahdat party proved one of the most resilient of the mujaheddin groupings. The Hazaras fought and suffered bitterly in Kabul against Ahmad Shah Massoud's Tajiks, while the Taliban brought an ethnic fury to the Hazarajat in an attempt to bomb and starve the population into submission.

Uzbeks

The Uzbeks originally descended from Siberian nomads who settled in central Asia following the tumult of Genghis Khan. They became settled

Pashtun hospitality – and revenge – is legendary. One proverb says 'Help a Pashtun, and not only will he never forget it, he will repay you double. Hurt a Pashtun, and not only will he never forget it, he will repay you double.'

Naswar is Pashtun snuff, a chewing tobacco mixed with flavourings such as lime or juniper that gives users a mild buzz. But take care not to swallow the noxious green juice!

THE BURQA

Few symbols have been so closely and negatively tied to a country as Afghanistan and the burqa (*chaderi* in Dari). Afghan women are often seen as downtrodden creatures beneath the billowing folds of powder-blue burqas, faceless and voiceless. But the burqa isn't synonymous with women's rights, and shouldn't be seen as the only barometer of social change.

The burqa was once a symbol of urbanised Afghan women. Its impracticality was a sign that the wearer was free from the toil of the fields. Village women would only don burqas to visit towns, where they would be free from the gaze of unrelated men. In the 1920s, Queen Soraya famously scandalised much of Afghan society by being photographed in a sleeveless dress, and although Kabul of the 1970 and '80s was the fulcrum of women's rights, mini-skirted Afghan women were always a rarity.

War marked the big change. In the refugee camps, burqas were adopted as tented life increased the difficulties of keeping the private (female-dominated) and public spheres separate, and was enforced by the rise of the fundamentalist mujaheddin groups. When civil war broke out, the burqa became essential as a guarantee of anonymity and protection against harassment and rape. The Taliban merely formalised its wearing as the most visible symbol of their anti-women policies.

Many women in Afghanistan continue to wear the burqa for cultural reasons. Some women have always worn it and assert that they will continue to do so. The burqa can be seen as a tool to increase mobility and security, a nuance often missed in the outside world's image of the garment. Assuming that a burqa-clad woman is not empowered and in need of liberation is a naïve construct. The majority of Afghan women are more concerned with access to education and economic opportunities.

ETHNIC BREAKDOWN (2006 ESTIMATE)

Pashtun: 42%

Tajik: 27%

Hazara: 9%

Uzbek: 9%

Turkmen: 3%

Baluchi: 2%

Other: 8%

in the 15th century, when the Shaybanid khanates of modern Uzbekistan emerged to overthrow the decadent Timurid empire. Northern Afghanistan became a semi-independent network of Uzbek khanates, such as Balkh, Kunduz and Maimana, with the Uzbek population boosted in the late 19th and early 20th centuries following the Tsarist and Soviet upheavals in Central Asia. Primarily farmers, they are also known for their horses and skill at *buzkashi*. Most original Uzbek tribal affiliations have now been lost.

Uzbek men traditionally wear the *chapan,* a quilted silk coat tied with a sash, although this tends to be restricted to older generations and for celebrations. Modern Uzbeks are more recognised by their affiliation to their strongman leader, General Abdul Rashid Dostum (see p145). In the civil war, Dostum's Uzbek militias were greatly feared, particularly in Kabul where they were notorious for their looting and pillaging, and dubbed by others as *qilimjan* (carpet thieves).

Other Peoples

Nomadism still plays an important part in Afghan life. The largest group of nomads are the Kuchi, a Pashtun tribe. Many Kuchi have suffered greatly in recent years, losing much of their livestock to droughts, coupled with the effects of land mines on traditional grazing grounds. The exact number of Kuchi is unknown, but they possibly number up to three million, spread across the whole of the country. They are the only ethnic group to have reserved seats in parliament. Among the Dari speakers, the main nomads are the Aimaq in central and west Afghanistan who are of Turkic-Mongoloid stock. In the far northeast of the Pamirs and Wakhan, the Kyrgyz continue a nomadic lifestyle with their yaks, sheep and camels (see p171).

Of the settled nationalities, the next largest populations are the Turkmen and Baluchi. The Turkmen are found mainly in the northwest along the border with Turkmenistan, where they are mostly herders and farmers noted for their carpets and *karakol* (sheep) skin production. Like the Uzbeks, many Turkmen came to Afghanistan in the 19th and early 20th centuries. Politically they maintain close ties with the Uzbeks. The Baluchi span the southern border region with both Pakistan and Iran, where they are mainly herders and traders. In the eastern provinces of Nuristan and Kunar are the fair-skinned and blue-eyed Nuristanis. Afghanistan's last pagans, they were only converted to Islam in the late 19th century. Their oral history ascribes their European features to descent from the troops of Alexander the Great (see p186).

In the northwest, the farming Ismaili Wakhis share land and trade with the Kyrgyz. The other Shiite ethnic groups are the Farsiwan (often mistakenly labelled Tajiks) of Herat and the northwest, and the Turkic Qizilbash living in Kabul.

RELIGION
Islam
HISTORY
Islam has shared roots with the other great monotheistic faiths of the Middle East but is considerably younger, springing into being in AD 612, when the Prophet Mohammed received his revelations from God (Allah) in Mecca. The revelations incorporated elements of Judaism and Christianity, including a reverence for the same prophets such as Abraham (Ibrahim), Moses (Musa) and Jesus (Isa). While Jews and Christians have traditionally been respected as People of the Book (*Ahl al-Kitab*), Islam regards itself as the summation of these faiths, with Mohammed being the prophet who received Allah's final revelations to mankind. (Muslims reject the Christian belief in the divinity of Jesus as a misreading of the Bible – a mistake many Afghans will be happy to point out to you.) Mohammed's revelations were complied into the Quran, Islam's holiest book, while his collected sayings (the Hadith) are another important reference for Muslim scholars.

In 622, the Prophet Mohammed and his followers were forced to flee Mecca to Medina due to religious persecution (the Islamic calendar begins with this flight, known as Hejira). He returned in triumph eight years later at the head of an army, capturing the whole of Arabia, and starting one of the greatest political and religious revolutions in history. Within a century, Islam had spread as far west as Spain and east towards central Asia.

The word Islam translates loosely from Arabic as 'the peace that comes from total surrender to God'.

The Prophet died soon after retaking Mecca. Disputes over his succession boiled into violence between those who believed the new caliph should be chosen from Mohammed's most trusted followers and those who supported his heirs. In 661 the Prophet's son-in-law Ali was assassinated, prompting the split between the Shiite and Sunni sects. The Shiites were Ali's supporters, beaten by the Sunnis who supported the Prophet's brother-in-law, the governor of Syria, as caliph. The schism became irreconcilable in 680 when Ali's son Hussain and most of his male relatives were killed at Kerbala in Iraq by Sunni partisans.

Sunni Islam emphasises the traditions of the Prophet, while Shiite Islam places greater emphasis on the authorities of imams as a spiritually perfect elite chosen by Allah. Today, almost 90% of Muslims worldwide are Sunni, divided into four schools according to their interpretation of Sharia, or Islamic law. Around 85% of Afghans are Sunni, with Hazaras comprising most of the Shiite, along with the Farsiwans and Ismaili Wakhi community. Afghanistan follows the non-hierarchical Hanafi school of Sunni jurisprudence, although Shiite law was given equal status in the 2004 constitution.

ISLAM IN AFGHANISTAN

The village mosque is the centre of Afghan Islam, where the local mullah is the prime interpreter of the Quran for his traditionally non-literate flock. Many village mullahs cannot read either, so their knowledge of the holy book is often based on oral tradition, mixed with other Afghan codes, such as Pashtunwali, that remove them by some degrees from the Islam recognised by scholars. Afghans place much stock in their non-hierarchical society, and the same goes for religion. Tradition is vitally important, and while this has led to some insular practices (including common village strictures against women's education and being allowed to work), in many other areas it has led to the broadly tolerant nature of Afghan society. Belief in magic and *djinns* (invisible creatures made from fire mentioned in the Quran) is widespread.

Mohammed decreed all Muslims should pray facing the Kaaba in Mecca, the Black Stone supposedly given to Ibrahim by the archangel Gabriel.

Holy men have always been important in Afghan culture. *Pirs* (local saints) are revered while *sayids* (descendants of the Prophet Mohammed) are especially respected. In addition, wandering holy men called *malangs* are thought to be touched directly by Allah; these are rare individuals who leave the security of the family and village structures to follow the path of Sufism, Islam's mystical tradition. Many Sufi orders (*tariqa*) exist in Afghanistan, mostly of the Naqshbandi and Qadirriyah traditions, each following a charismatic leader. Sufism seek knowledge of Allah through direct personal contact, often through rituals of music or poetry aimed at inducing a trance-like state of rapture – a heresy to orthodox Muslims (although Sufis also pray in the traditional Muslim manner). Sufi *tariqa* have produced several Afghan leaders, and played a key early role in the Jihad against the Soviets.

Radical Islam played little part in Afghan culture until society started to fracture during the war. Fundamentalist groups like Gulbuddin Hekmatyar's Hezb-e Islami weren't popular with the majority of Afghans while the foreign fighters who followed the ultra-orthodox Wahhabist sect from Saudi Arabia frequently despised the Afghans they were fighting for their supposedly lax attitude to religion. The strain of Islam followed by the Taliban similarly ran counter to much of traditional Afghan belief.

The Taliban were the children of Pakistan's madrassas (Islamic colleges), which often offered the best chance of any education for those raised in the refugee camps. Here they were influenced by the austere Deoband creed, at once sympathetic to and influenced by the Pakistan Islamist parties, and Saudi Wahhabist who provided much of their funding. The madrassa-raised Taliban were free of the tribal strictures of

---

THE FIVE PILLARS OF ISLAM

Muslims express their faith through five core beliefs, named here in Dari:

- ◼ Kalimeh – the creed that 'There is no God but Allah, and Mohammed is the messenger of God'
- ◼ Namaz – praying five times a day at fixed times, prostrated towards the holy city of Mecca
- ◼ Zakat – the giving of alms, generally interpreted as 2.5% of a person's income
- ◼ Rouza – dawn-to-dusk fasting during the month of Ramazan
- ◼ Haj – performing the pilgrimage to Mecca at least once in one's lifetime, if able

---

ZIARATS

Ziarats (shrines) are of great importance in Afghan Islam. Although Islam does not traditionally recognise saints, the graves of *pirs,* or anyone thought to have achieved closeness to Allah, often attract local cults. People visit their *ziarats,* typically festooned with brightly coloured flags, to pray for the intercession of the *pir* for a particular favour. Women visit some for help conceiving, or to get a love-match in marriage. Other *ziarats* are renowned for their curative abilities. Caretakers often sell amulets containing earth from the grave or verses from the Quran to aid the fortunes of visitors.

The graves of *shahid* (martyrs who have died in battle) are regarded as particularly potent. In Khost, the graves of 38 Arab and Pakistani fighters killed by a US bomb in 2001 have become a famous *ziarat.* Their political beliefs are totally irrelevant – as *shahid* their graves are holy ground. Ironically, the ultra-orthodox foreign fighters who supported the Taliban would have scorned and punished such behaviour as idolatrous. Presumably as more visitors come to pray to them, they spin in their graves a little faster.

Pashtunwali and had an exile's lack of knowledge of Afghan and general Islamic history. Instead they preferred to deal with absolutes, shunning debate, moderation and the West. The radical laws they enacted once in power were far removed from most Afghans' concepts of Islam. In particular, their virulent anti-Shiism led to persecution of the Hazaras, and the banning of festivals like Nauroz that were perceived to be anti-Islamic.

Other Religions

Afghanistan has long hosted populations of Jews, Sikhs and Hindus, all of which have now dwindled. At the start of the 20th century, Afghan Jews numbered around 40,000, a number that has plummeted since the founding of Israel to just one man in Kabul, Zablon Simintov, who keeps an unobtrusive synagogue on Flower St.

Before the arrival of Islam, Kabul was a Hindu city, but most Afghan Hindus and Sikhs arrived in the country following the mid-19th century influx of Indian court musicians to Kabul. Around 1200 Hindu and Sikh families remain in Afghanistan, mostly merchants in Kabul, Kandahar, Ghazni and Jalalabad. Muslim occupation of Hindu and Sikh properties after years of war (particularly Hindu cremation grounds) has caused some tensions.

Christianity is a more controversial subject. Afghanistan's large Christian Armenian population was expelled in the 19th century after being accused of assisting the British, and it wasn't until 1933 that a church – a chapel inside the Italian embassy – was allowed to open, still Afghanistan's only officially sanctioned church. Afghans remain highly sensitive to Christianity taking a foothold in the country. In 2001 the Taliban arrested several international aid workers on charges of proselytising, and in 2006 there was an international furore when an Afghan Christian convert was tried and threatened with the death penalty for apostasy – he was later granted refugee status in Italy.

ARTS
Poetry

Both Dari and Pashto poetry plays an enormous role in Afghan culture, and a good Afghan education places as much emphasis on the writings of the great poets as on the Quran.

Afghanistan's greatest poets are Abdul Rahman Baba and Khushal Khan Khattak, who both wrote Pashto poetry in the 17th century, a time

WOMEN IN AFGHANISTAN *Lina Abirafeh*

Progress and social change in Afghanistan have long rested on the 'women question'. It is said that *zan, zar wa zameen* ('women, gold and land') have been the cause of conflict for centuries in Afghanistan. Afghan women's rights have always been highly politicised and gender politics, as much as geo-politics, has provided the impetus for conflicts. Throughout modern Afghan history, Afghan women have been used as the barometer to measure social change. Afghan women have repeatedly been caught between waves of enforced modernisation and conservative undercurrents. Today – several years after the Taliban – the 'women question' remains on shaky ground.

In the early 1970s, Afghan women's rights were included in the national constitution. Women – working as doctors and engineers – were seen on the streets of Kabul wearing skirts. By the end of that decade, Soviet occupation coupled with a conservative backlash would strip women of these hard-won rights. For the next 20 years, a variety of regimes exercised their influences on women's rights. The 'women question' continued to deteriorate.

Both Afghanistan and its women suffered in anonymity until the Taliban – and the activists who opposed them – gained international attention. Organisations such as the **Revolutionary Association of the Women of Afghanistan** (RAWA; www.rawa.org) brought Afghan women's rights to the forefront of the international women's agenda. RAWA's story is both romanticised and immortalised through their murdered leader Meena, who founded the organisation in 1977. RAWA's membership is large, and yet members often do not know each other due to the organisation's secret status.

Organisations like RAWA, operating clandestinely in Afghanistan and Pakistan, revealed the horrors inflicted by the Taliban upon women – including rapes, stonings and confinement. They bravely resisted oppression and persevered through home schools for girls, women's clinics and a network of underground operations providing support services for women and children.

Post-Conflict Progress?

In the immediate aftermath of the Taliban, Afghan women were hopeful and demonstrated their strength and determinaan by assuming professional roles, public positions and accessing education opportunities. Afghan women's rights are safeguarded in the new constitution that was approved by the Afghan constitutional loya jirga, or grand assembly, in January 2004. Afghanistan is also a party to CEDAW, the Convention on the Elimination of all Forms of Discrimination Against Women. While these rights exist on paper, the battle to bring them into practice is just beginning.

The parliament, formed in 2005, is 27% female. One outspoken member, Malalai Joya, gained international attention – and put her own life at risk – when she publicly denounced warlords in the 2003 constitutional loya jirga. She continues to fight for women's rights despite myriad death threats.

Despite select public accomplishments, conditions for women remain challenging. Post-Taliban Afghanistan remains a place where the lives of women's rights activists are increasingly threatened, where girls, schools are being burned, and where social indicators – for men and women – remain staggering. Afghanistan faces one of the highest illiteracy and maternal mortality rates in the world. Widows and female-headed households continue to live in dire poverty. Violence against women – particularly domestic violence – is increasing. Self-immolation is becoming a popular exit strategy for women whose lives show no alternative to living in despair. Women's rights activists are being brutally assassinated. The September 2006 assassination of women's rights activist Safia Amajan is a case in point. The head of the provincial women's affairs department in Kandahar, Amajan was murdered to send a message to women's rights advocates.

Today's Afghanistan might allow more opportunity for women – marginally, in urban areas – but fewer women appear to be accessing those opportunities. Both men and women are waiting to see how the relatively new parliament – and the proposed revival of the Department for the Promotion of Virtue and Prevention of Vice – will fare and what changes this will bring. Recent increases in insecurity in Afghanistan are taking a variety of forms and affecting all aspects of Afghans' lives. Afghan women and girls are particularly affected by the current climate of elevated lawlessness and violence.

Girls' Education

Once a highly touted accomplishment of the international community's reconstruction efforts, girls in school are now increasingly threatened. Schools continue to be burned, and teachers' lives put at risk. *Shabnameh* (Night Letters) are threatening letters left in public places or on the doors of individual homes at night, frequently claiming that those Afghans who are 'associating with infidels' are thereby 'betraying' Islam and Afghan culture and will be punished. This tactic was frequently employed during the parliamentary elections to intimidate female candidates and is now directed toward teachers who attempt to educate girls. Fear of violence has a profound effect on women both because they are targeted for violence and because of the stigma they face if they are victims. Groups opposed to girls' education have used threats of violence as a deterrent, keeping an increasing number of girls out of school every year. The forces against girls' education are stronger than the communities' will to resist them.

What Next for Afghan Women?

To better understand the situation of Afghan women, it is important to understand the socio-cultural context and the fluctuating history of women's rights in the country. Throughout modern Afghan history, women have repeatedly found themselves at the centre of conflicts between Western concepts of modernisation and Afghan codes of culture. The two are not incompatible. It is a question of approach, not content. Importing an agenda of 'liberation' is not the answer, particularly when indigenous roots for human rights and other so-called Western concepts already exist. Afghan women continue to make changes and act on their own behalf as they have always done. There is such a thing as Afghan feminism – it did not need to be imported.

Many Afghan women's groups are working to support women through programs such as rights training, vocational training, job placement, health care, literacy, etc. The **Afghan Women's Network** (AWN; www.afghanwomensnetwork.org) is one such example. AWN was created in 1996 and comprises 72 NGOs and 3000 individuals who work to 'empower women and ensure their equal participation in Afghan society'. Their efforts include advocacy, networking, and capacity building in issues such as gender-based violence, women's legal rights, civic education, leadership and communication. AWN and many other groups strive to offer women the tools with which they can achieve self-sufficiency, a choice, and a voice.

In the words of one Afghan woman: 'Tell [the world] that Afghan women are very strong and they will do anything for the future of their country and their children'.

For more information on women in Afghanistan, try the following books and websites:

- *Afghanistan, Where God Only Comes to Weep* by Siba Shakib
- *Kabul in Winter* by Ann Jones
- *Women's Resistance* by Cheryl Bernard
- *Veiled Threat: The Hidden Power of the Women of Afghanistan* by Sally Armstrong
- *With All Our Strength: The Revolutionary Association of the Women of Afghanistan* by Anne E Brodsky
- *Veiled Courage: Inside the Afghan Women's Resistance* by Cheryl Bernard
- *Women for Afghan Women: Shattering Myths and Claiming the Future* edited by Sunita Mehta
- *Lessons from Gender-focused International Aid in Post-Conflict Afghanistan… Learned?* by Lina Abirafeh (www.fes.org.af/AFGHANISTAN0905ABIRAFEHGENDER.pdf)
- *Burqa Politics: The Plights of Women in Afghanistan* by Lina Abirafeh (www.chronogram.com/issue/2004/10/news/burqa.php)
- *Afghanistan: Women Still under Attack – a Systematic Failure to Protect* (http://web.amnesty.org/library/Index/ENGASA110072005?open&of=ENG-AFG)
- Afghan Gender Café (www.afghangendercafé.org)
- Organization for Promoting Afghan Women's Capabilities (run by Malalai Joya; www.geocities.com/opawc)
- Afghan Women's Mission (www.afghanwomensmission.org)

LANDAYS

Pashtun women are typically thought of as being the most voiceless of all Afghan communities, but they are also composers of one the most vibrant forms of poetry in the country – the *landay*. *Landay* is the Pashto word for a small venomous snake, and these poems follow suit: short, but with a lot of bite.

Like haiku, *landay* is a stylised poetry with a set number of syllables. The authors are usually unknown, but in almost all examples the woman addresses the man. Touching on the universal themes of love and war, the *landays* reveal a strong thread of pride, passion, longing and anger from beneath the burqa. Unrequited love and illicit love affairs are used by the women to taunt the weakness and virility of their men, for it is the women alone who carry the risks and consequences of their love. Some *landays* have even reached into history, such as Malalai's taunt to her menfolk credited with inspiring a famous Afghan victory over the British army in 1880: 'My love! If you do not fall in the battle of Maiwand/Someone is saving you as a symbol of shame!' Here are some of our other favourites:

'My beloved returned unsuccessful from battle
I repent the kiss I gave him last night'

'May you turn into a riverside flower
So that I may come on the excuse of taking water and smell you'

'O passing traveller!
Are you satiated with my sight or should I turn my face again?'

'You started loving, not I
Now the scandal has come into the open you blame me'

'Call it romance, call it love, you did it
I am tired now, pull up the blanket for I want to sleep'

when Afghans were struggling against Mughal and Safavid rule. Abdul Rahman Baba was a mystic, whose poems meditated on the divine and the yearning of the soul to be reunited with its creator. Such longing is a classic feature of Sufi poetry, and Abdul Rahman Baba's work sits neatly alongside much of the Persian poetry written in Afghanistan and Iran at the time. His contemporary, Khushal Khan Khattak, also wrote on the divine, but his poems were more visceral, dealing with love and war in a more epic style. Khattak led tribal rebellions against the Mughals, and for many he continues to be the model of the Pashtun, at once a poet and warrior. His best poems shoot barbs at dictators and mullahs and sing paeans to the beauty of Pashtun women and (no false modesty here) his own glory as defender of his people. He wrote over 45,000 poems and in his own words 'gave the Pashto language much of beauty that it lacked before'. Pashtun poetry stills exists largely in his shadow.

> The Pashtun name spells honour and glory
>
> Without that what is the Afghan story?
>
> KHUSHAL KHAN KHATTAK

Writers in Dari (in this context usually referred to as classical Persian) have touched on many of the same themes as Abdul Rahman Baba, and form part of the same canon of Sufi poets from Iran. The classic poetic form is the *ghazal* (rhyming couplet) used almost exclusively on the subject of unattainable spiritual love, a subject rich in both secular and spiritual allegory. Best known to Western audiences is Rumi, born in Balkh in 1207. In Herat, the Sufi saint Ansari was a prolific composer of *ghazals* in the 11th century, while 400 years later Jami was a famed poet at the Timurid court. At this time Herat was so richly endowed with poets that Babur joked in his autobiography that you couldn't stick out your

leg in the city without kicking one. The tombs of both still attract many
visitors in modern Herat (see p138 and p139).

Afghanistan stakes a claim for the first woman to write classical Persian
poetry, Rabi'a Balki, who met a tragic end in 9th century Balkh (p157).
Afghans also lay claim to the Iranian national poet Firdausi, who composed his epic *Shah Nama* while court poet for the Ghaznavids in the
11th century. Iranian poets like Jami's contemporary Hafez are equally
loved.

Afghanistan's most celebrated 20th century poet is Khalilullah Khalili.
He died in 1987 and is buried in Peshawar, next to Abdul Rahman Baba.
An Assembly of Moths is the best known of his collections translated
into English.

Poetry hasn't been able to stand outside the currents of recent history.
Khalili was forced into exile after the Soviet invasion, and wrote poems
about the resistance. Poets were also targeted themselves – the critic
Professor Bahauddin Majrooh was assassinated by Hekmatyar's men
in Peshawar in 1988, while as recently as 2005 the popular female poet
Nadia Anjuman was murdered in Herat.

Carpets

Afghan carpets are the country's most famous folk art. An important
trade item, carpets also have a strong social meaning, and often com-
prise part of a bride's dowry. The number of carpets a family owns is a
significant indicator of wealth, even if they are a poor rural family who
can only afford a machine-made carpet from Pakistan.

Northwest Afghanistan and its Turkmen population has always been
the centre of carpet production. Carpets are hand-knotted, although
modern Belgian wool is preferred these days to that from local sheep.
Production is a home industry, mainly run by women who make them
when not working in the fields. The most common design is the Tekke,
with the rug divided into quarters containing stylised *gul* (flowers).
Deep reds and ochres are the primary palette. These carpets are also
known under the generic name Bukhara, the main place where they
were historically sold for export. The *filpai* (elephant's foot) is another

Rugs of War (http://sts-dev
.anu.edu.au/rugsofwar/)
is a great blog about
Afghan war rugs run by
art historians Nigel Len-
don and Tim Bonyhandy.

AFGHAN WAR RUGS

Carpet weaving isn't a folk art stuck in aspic, never veering from centuries-old patterns and traditions. Designs are regularly updated according the needs of the export market – in the 1960s and
'70s many designs were aimed specifically at the hippie and Peace Corps market. These variants
reached their apogee in the 1980s with the appearance of the Afghan war rug. Adapting the
Baluchi convention of depicting plants and animals on their carpets, refugees in Pakistan started
to weave in images of war – weapons, tanks and planes. These were sold in Peshawar, then awash
with aid workers, spies, arms dealers and lots of money. The rugs caused ripples in the international
carpet market, with some dealers decrying the corruption of a famous art form, others applauding
the Afghans' innovative adaptation to circumstance. Either way, the carpets were snapped up in
a flurry of dollars.

When the Soviets withdrew in 1989, carpets depicted the retreating military columns crossing
the border, but as the world lost interest in Afghanistan, so did the carpet dealers. No one wanted
to celebrate Mullah Omar in warp and weft. A resurgence only took place after the US routed the
Taliban. Shoppers on Chicken St were surprised to find this quickly commemorated in rugs, with
American flags and cruise missiles and – some were horrified to discover – depictions of the planes
flying into the World Trade Centre on 9/11. They're not to everyone's taste, but the Afghan war
rug continues to evolve.

instantly recognisable Afghan design, with its huge medallions that dominate the carpet.

Baluchi carpets frequently have stylised animals as well as flowers, and designs such as the tree of life. Baluchis also produce intricate *gilims*, woven rather than knotted.

The Foundation for Culture & Civil Society (www.afghanfccs.org) holds regular Afghan music concerts in Kabul – see p102.

Afghan carpet production moved wholesale to Pakistan during the war, instantly creating an industry for a country that had never before had one. Even now, a Pakistani carpet is very likely to have an Afghan origin. Now that carpet producers have returned, the success of the Pakistani brand has hampered the rebuilding of Afghan carpet exports.

Music

Afghan music is divided into two main strands – classical (also known as art music) and folk. In the 19th century court musicians were brought to Kabul from north India, bringing a tradition that still heavily influences Afghan music. The instruments used are similar to those found throughout the region and in the Arab and Turkish worlds. Foremost among these is the *rebab* (short-necked lute with waist), the national instrument and particularly associated with Pashtun music. The *dutar* (long-necked lute) from Herat is also prominent. Both instruments are played in the main classical music genre, the Kabuli *ghazal*, accompanying sung mystical poetry with harmonium and *tabla* (Indian tuned drums). Classical musicians train for years under *ustads* (masters), the most famed of whom was Ustad Mohammed Qasim Afghan in the 1920s – who was popularly called the father of Afghan music.

Three Women of Herat by Veronica Doubleday is an intimate portrait of the lives of female musicians in 1970s Afghanistan, a world now largely lost.

Folk music is divided into ethnic genres, but the one thing that unites them all is the *atan*, the so-called national dance performed by both sexes at any celebration. Rhythm is very important in folk music, and there are a number of drums such as the barrel-shaped *dohol*, the goblet-shaped *zirbaghali* and the flat-framed *daff* (or *daireh*). The latter is the only instrument women are meant to play, and is also used in many Sufi rituals.

AHMAD ZAHIR, THE AFGHAN ELVIS

Ask any Afghan to name a popular singer, and it's likely they'll say Ahmad Zahir. A strikingly handsome man with huge sideburns, he revolutionised Afghan popular song but died a tragically young death – characteristics that have led many to claim him as the Afghan Elvis Presley. And like the King, Ahmad Zahir continues to cast a long shadow from his grave.

Zahir was born in 1946, the son of a diplomat. A natural musical talent, he studied classical Afghan and Indian music, but was unusual in writing his own compositions. He was also influenced by Western styles, and was unafraid to mix electric guitars and saxophones with traditional instruments. Zahir's star rose at the right time, when national radio was increasing opportunities for musicians. His golden voice and new musical style touched a chord with Afghans, and as a Pashtun who sang in Dari he became a symbol for the whole country. His dynamic stage performances helped create Afghanistan's first modern celebrity. But he also used a poet's right to criticise power – having praised Daoud in 1973, he later raised his voice at the republic's empty promises, leading to a ban of some of his music. After the Saur Revolution, many of his songs had to be recorded in secret.

In July 1979 Zahir was killed in a traffic accident near the Salang Pass, aged 33. Many Afghans believe that he was actually assassinated by the communist regime. But his music has stood the test of time, and is one thing that a frequently divided country can happily agree on.

Music has suffered greatly in recent decades. Severe restrictions were placed on musicians in the refugee camps and later under the mujahed-din government, and they were often forbidden to play to respect the martyrs in a time of national calamity. The musician's quarter of Khara-bat in Kabul was levelled. This anticipated the total ban imposed by the Taliban, when unspooled cassettes fluttered at checkpoints, confiscated from taxi drivers, and musicians had their instruments smashed. Only chants celebrating *jihad* were allowed.

Modern Afghan pop is a genre that flourished in exile, with singers like Farhad Darya and Marwash, while many Afghans returned from exile sporting a love for Hindi pop.

Architecture

Afghan building has harnessed the vitality of the Central Asian steppe to the refinement of Persian culture to produce in its mosques and minarets some of the masterpieces of world architecture.

Much Islamic vernacular architecture tends to be flat and functional, with time and money dedicated instead to religious buildings. Exceptions where form and function blend successfully can be found in the Pashtun *qala* (fortified houses) of the east and south, where each building resembles a mini castle, as well as in the desert houses of the west, with their cooling domes and wind towers. Mud-brick is the building material of choice. The buildings are hard to date, and the viewer can sometimes be forgiven for wondering if a crumbling building was recently abandoned by its owner, or levelled by the Soviets or even Genghis Khan.

The mosque is the centre-point of Afghan architecture. The typical mosque consists of a courtyard, portico and prayer hall, facing Mecca. A minaret is usually attached for the call to prayer.

Afghan Islamic architecture really began to take off in the 10th and 11th centuries, with the rule of the Ghaznavids, who built in fired brick. Their successors, the Ghorids, took this to an artistic high with their construction of the Minaret of Jam (pp126-7) and Herat's Friday Mosque (pp136-7). Decoration was plain, and it wasn't until the rise of the Timurids, who drew in influences from across the whole Muslim world, that buildings started to sing with colour. The almost-totally-destroyed Musalla Complex (pp137-8) in Herat was the apogee of Timurid architecture, but even the citadel there was brightly decorated. The Timurids also loved high entrance portals and fat ribbed domes, such as that found at the Shrine of Khoja Abu Nasr Parsa (pp156-7) in Balkh.

Afghan architecture went into a general decline following the Timurid period, as the region's cultural centre shifted east with the Mughals. Until the modern period, most buildings were rather poor copies of Mughal originals. In the 20th century, the westernised King Amanullah tried to import central European classic design to the country with commissions such as Darulaman Palace – not an entirely successful enterprise.

Since then, the story of Afghan buildings has sadly been largely one of neglect and destruction through war. Afghanistan is currently undergoing a building boom, with new buildings hastily thrown up every day. Ugly and modern confections with lots of plate glass and fake columns, they bear little resemblance to any indigenous tradition, and seem more to do with the pretensions of the Afghan nouveau riche. They're often dubbed 'poppy palaces' for the basis of much of the wealth funding the boom.

The abandoned metal shipping container is the war's legacy to Afghan architecture: pressed into service everywhere as shops, workshops and temporary accommodation, often covered with mud-brick to insulate against the heat and cold.

Monuments of Central Asia by Edgar Knobloch puts Afghan architecture firmly in its regional context.

AFGHANISTAN'S ARCHITECTURAL HIGHLIGHTS

The following is our pick of the architectural highlights of Afghanistan. Of these, the Minaret of Jam has been made a World Heritage site by **Unesco** (www.unesco.org/afghanistan), while the Minarets of Ghazni and the No Gombad Mosque have all been listed as endangered by the **World Monuments Fund** (www.wmf.org).

- Friday Mosque (1200; in Herat) – an astounding Ghorid monument, with four huge portals covered in a blaze of modern mosaic

- Gazar Gah (1425; in Herat) – a Chinese-influenced Timurid decoration, with 30m-high entrance portal

- Musalla Complex (1417; in Herat) – the forlorn remains of a showcase of Timurid art and architecture

- Herat Citadel (1415; in Herat) – an imposing castle with impressive crenellations, huge views and decorative tilework

- Shrine of Khoja Abu Nasr Parsa (1460s; in Balkh) – a stunning blue Timurid ribbed dome and massive portal

- No Gombad Mosque (800–900; in Balkh) – Afghanistan's oldest surviving mosque, with delicate stucco decorations

- Shrine of Hazrat Ali (1480; in Mazar-e Sharif) – every square inch covered in dizzying blue tiles.

- Minaret of Jam (1194; in central Afghanistan) – as remote as you can get, this 65m spire stands as a lonely sentinel in the mountains

- Shah-e Doh Shamshira Mosque (1920; in Kabul) – a bizarre two-storey interpretation of Italian baroque, in lemon yellow

- Shah Jahan Mosque (1647; in Kabul) – an understated white marble mosque from the builder of the Taj Mahal

- Minarets of Ghazni (1099–1151; in Ghazni) – a pair of monumental octagonal-shafted victory towers

- Mausoleum of Ahmad Shah Durrani (1770s; in Kandahar) – a brightly decorated Mughal-style remembrance of modern Afghanistan's founder

Cinema

Afghans love the movies, in particular Hindi and Bollywood films. Afghan cinema itself began in 1951 with the film *Eshq wa Dosti* (Love and Friendship), but it wasn't until the late 1960s and '70s that filmmakers started producing films in any quantity. Although well regarded for such a young industry, local filmmaking was quickly stifled under the dead hand of Soviet censorship following the 1979 invasion, and didn't begin to recover until the turn of the century. The Taliban took to the national film archives with their usual zealous attentions, and only the bricking up of many films behind false walls prevented the country's entire film stock going up in flames.

Phil Grabsky's feature documentary, *The Boy Who Plays on the Buddhas of Bamiyan* (2004), is a touching account of a Hazara refugee family living in the shadow of the destroyed monuments.

The Iranian director Mohsen Makhmalbaf's *Kandahar* (2001) about an Afghan exile returning to the country to save her friend from suicide met such international acclaim that even George W Bush apparently saw it. Makhmalbaf and other Iranian filmmakers have been instrumental in assisting the revival of Afghan cinema, efforts that helped produce Afghanistan's first post-Taliban movie *Osama* (2003) by Siddiq Barmak – a heart-breaking story of a young girl who has to disguise herself as a boy to work in Taliban-era Kabul – that collected a sweep of prizes at international film festivals. The Afghan diaspora have similarly picked up the camera, with Jawed Wassel's *Firedancer* (2004) about Afghan-Americans, and Farid Faiz's *Ehsaas* (Emotion; 2006) about refugees in the UK.

Afghanistan has also recently found itself as the stage for several international films, including Samira Makhmalbaf's 2003 *At Five in the Afternoon* about a Kabuli girl dreaming of becoming president, and the Bollywood feature *Kabul Express* (2006) by Kabir Khan.

SPORT

Afghanistan's turbulent history hasn't bred a nation in love with the quiet pursuits of lawn bowls. Sport is as you might expect it – martial and unruly. If things can be fought, Afghans will fight with them, from dogs and birds to the more esoteric – kites (see boxed text, p58) and even eggs (where dyed and boiled eggs are smashed against each other in a test of strength). But no sport more closely captures the Afghan spirit than *buzkashi*, which is often cited as a metaphor for Afghan society and politics as a whole. The chance to see a match should never be passed up.

Buzkashi literally means 'goat grabbing', and is wild beyond belief. It's something akin to rugby on horseback, where the 'ball' is the headless carcass of a goat or calf, often soaked in water to toughen it up. The *boz* (carcass) is placed in a circle and surrounded by members of the two teams – any number of riders can participate. At the signal, a melée erupts as all try to grab the *boz* and lift it to their saddle, so they can carry it to the winning spot. Only *chapandazan* (master players) ever get the chance to manoeuvre the *boz* free, masterfully controlling their horses amid a thrashing of bodies, hooves and whips. The carefully trained horses are highly prized – 'better a bad rider on a good horse than a good rider on a bad horse'.

Traditional *buzkashi* is played on the north Afghan plains between the autumn ploughing and the spring planting seasons. A more formalised version was adopted by the Afghan Olympic Committee in the 1960s to bring it to Kabul, formalising the rules (banning knives among other things) and team sizes – this was sponsored by successive regimes as a form of patronage. *Tooi* (ceremonial matches) bring great prestige to the host who offer prizes to the most successful *chapandazan*. Mazar-e Sharif hosts the grandest *buzkashi* in Afghanistan, every Nauroz.

Wrestling and boxing are popular, and there is something of an obsession with bodybuilding studios. Many refugees brought a love of cricket back from their time in Pakistan. Football is naturally popular and was one of the few team sports tolerated by the Taliban, who weren't averse to the occasional public execution on the penalty spot as pre-match entertainment. One Pakistani team who played in Kandahar at the time were arrested for wearing shorts, had their heads shaved and were finally deported. Afghanistan has since rejoined FIFA, and played in the first qualifying match for the 2006 World Cup (where they were soundly thrashed by Turkmenistan).

MEDIA

Radio is the most important media in Afghanistan, where it plays an essential role in spreading news as well as entertainment. The national station, Radio TV Afghanistan, started broadcasting in the 1920s and has spent its life under pressure from the establishment of the day, pressure that continues from religious and political interests. The station faces strong competition from new broadcasters such as Arman FM, who mix

Afghanistan's unlikeliest cinematic outing is 1988's *Rambo III*. Sly Stallone goes *jihad,* joining the mujaheddin to sock it to the Russians, take in a game of *buzkashi* and generally save the day to a constant backdrop of explosions.

For the definitive guide to the Afghan national sport, read *Buzkashi: Game and Power in Afghanistan* by Whitney Azoy.

KITE FIGHTING

Of the Taliban's many prohibitions, the ban on kite flying seemed one of the most needlessly cruel. Any visitor to Afghanistan will soon become accustomed to seeing kites flapping above the streets. Kite flying is a favourite obsession of Afghan boys, one recently revealed to the outside world through Khaled Hosseini's haunting novel *The Kite Runner.*

The smallest kites are tiny affairs homemade from plastic or paper scraps and a wire frame. There's no tail to increase manoeuvrability, and fliers can get their kites aloft in the barest waft of air, with patient tugs of the line. Being Afghanistan of course, there's a martial element to the pursuit and kites are fought against each other for supremacy of the skies. In kite fighting (*gudiparan bazi*) the kites' strings are covered with a mix of paste and ground glass. As the kites fly together, the flier attempts to position his kite to rub against the string of his opponent, to cut the kite loose. As the vanquished kite flutters to earth, a mad race breaks out to claim the prize. Trees and power lines take their share of the winnings too. Winter, with its strong winds, is the most popular time for kite fighting, while Kabul hosts a kite-fighting festival around Nauroz (see p95).

Afghan Wire (www.afghan wire.com) provides a daily translation into English of top stories in the Afghan press.

chat with popular Afghan and Hindi pop music. For all this, the most listened-to broadcaster in Afghanistan consistently remains the BBC. Its long-running Dari and Pashto soap opera *New Home, New Life* has been used to tackle issues from health education and land mine safety, to domestic violence and explaining the new constitution. The programme is so popular that some warring factions would call local ceasefires so as to not to miss an episode.

Newspapers have mushroomed in recent years, and there are thought to be over 300 papers and magazines in circulation. Daily newspapers published in both Dari and Pashto include *Anis, Erada* and the popular weekly *Kilid.* Many newspapers are open in the support for one political faction or another, and truly independent journalism is still taking baby steps and is under pressure from many sides.

TV is popular wherever a generator can be found to power a satellite dish. The private station Tolo TV has been a big hit, with shows like *The 6.30 Report* carrying critical reportage, while *Hop* steals from MTV with a mix of chat and music videos. Religious and political conservatives aren't fans, however – criticism of women presenters led to the murder of Shaima Rezayee in 2005, and other reporters are regularly harassed.

Food & Drink

It's unsurprising that given Afghanistan's location its cuisine has been influenced by – and had an influence on – its neighbours. Dishes are simple but delicately flavoured with spices and dried fruit. When allowed, Afghan appetites are prodigious and meals are served with mountains of rice and bread, to be washed down with copious amounts of tea. Reliance on just a few standard dishes means that travellers aren't likely to remember Afghanistan for the food, but there are some brilliant exceptions worth hunting out.

STAPLES & SPECIALITIES
Bread

Fresh Afghan bread (nan) is rather delicious. Made from great sheets of lightly leavened wheat flour, it is baked quickly on the side of a *tandoor* (clay oven). A sprinkling of sesame seeds may also be added. Watching a bakery in full swing, with a finely honed team of bakers rolling dough, slapping it on the inside of the *tandoor* and fishing out the fresh loaves with a hook is a thing of real joy. Shoppers leave with sheaves of bread folded underarm, or draped over the handlebars of their bicycles.

As well as the major Afghan staple, bread is also used as a plate for serving dishes on, as well as cutlery for manoeuvring food to the mouth. The juice-soaked nan left at the end of a meal is called *sabuz*, often served to the poor at the end of the day.

In northern Afghanistan, bread comes in rounder loaves rather than the flat sheets found elsewhere, and shows the Central Asian influence of the Afghan Uzbeks. It's slightly heavier than traditional nan.

Main Dishes

While bread is the backbone of Afghan cuisine, it's closely followed by rice. Any visitor to Afghanistan will eat their fair share of *pulao* – long-grained rice cooked in a huge vat, piled high over a serving of meat and often with a bowl of *qorma* (vegetables) on the side. *Qabli pulao* (often mistakenly called *Kabuli*) is the national dish, flavoured with grated carrot, raisins and almonds. The simplest version is *chilau*, with nothing more than plain rice and meat. *Norinj pulao* has orange peel to add a slight tang. The side vegetables are usually *kachaloo* (potato), often cooked with more meat. If you're lucky you'll be offered *borani* – fried vegetables such as *banjan* (aubergine) served slathered in a yogurt sauce. Yogurt is an important feature of Afghan cooking, and is dried into balls of *krut*, which can be stored for long periods and later reconstituted into sauces. Yogurt sauce is also an accompaniment to *mantu*, a type of ravioli originating from north Afghanistan, which is stuffed with meat. A vegetarian version is *ashak*, filled with leek.

Soups are popular. *Shorwa* is a thin and often oily broth. You tear pieces of bread into the *shorwa* to soak, and then eat with your fingers. *Ash* is more substantial, with noodles, beans and vegetables added to the mix. Both *ash* and *shorwa* usually have small pieces of meat floating in them for flavour.

Lamb and mutton are the most widely eaten meats. The fat-bottomed sheep is possibly Afghanistan's most iconic animal, carrying a huge wobbling mass of fat on its buttocks that's highly prized and costs more

---

If you want to recreate your culinary Afghan adventure at home, look no further than the comprehensive *Noshe Djan: Afghan Food & Cookery* by Helen Saberi.

In 2006 the World Food Programme estimated that over six million Afghans did not meet their minimum food requirements, and provided food aid to over 1.7 million Afghans every month.

DOS & DON'TS

■ Afghan meals are usually eaten from a communal dish. Always eat, offer and accept food with your right hand – never your left.

■ Don't hesitate to ask for cutlery if you're having trouble getting rice from hand to mouth.

■ Always remove your shoes before entering the dining area in a private home, or sitting on the floor in a chaikhana (teahouse).

■ Don't point the soles of your feet at diners when seated on the floor.

■ Beware of accepting food from Afghans who may not be able to afford it – they may only be offering out of hospitality. If the offer is meaningful you'll be asked three times, at which point it's fine to accept, but try not to eat the choicest morsels on the dish.

■ Don't eat too quickly – as soon as you finish, your host will stop eating too. Putting your right hand on your heart indicates you've had your fill.

■ Never blow your nose during a meal (or in public if at all possible) as it's very rude.

---

than the animal's meat. You'll most commonly encounter it diced and squeezed between cubes of lean meat in a kebab. These *sikh kabab* are eaten alongside a *kofteh*, a kebab of ground meat. Both come served with bread and raw onion, and a sprinkling of spice. *Chapli kabab* is eaten in the east and south, and is something akin to a Pashtun hamburger.

Snacks

Street snacks are plentiful in Afghanistan, and if you're eating mostly local food they're a good way of breaking out of the standard routine of *pulao* and kebabs. They're sold from mobile stands run by sellers called *tabang wallah*. Tastiest and most filling of all is *boloni*, a fried pancake stuffed with finely chopped vegetables. The commonest filling is potato with onion or greens *(sabzi)*, although you can often find *kadu* (squash). Another popular dish is *shor nakhod*, stewed chickpeas with a mint sauce, samosas and falafel stuffed in nan with some salad. *Mantu* is also often sold by *tabang wallahs* as well as *mahi* (fish) deep-fried and sold in sheets of paper.

Desserts & Sweets

Afghans delight in their sweet tooth. Milk-based puddings like *firni* are popular, along with syrupy *jalebi* and a multitude of sticky pastries like *baklawa*.

Local handmade *bastani* (ice cream), flavoured with rosewater or pistachio is delicious, but can be a source of stomach problems (a factory making pasteurised ice cream recently opened in Herat).

Fruit

Fresh fruit is one of the delights of any visit to Afghanistan. Marco Polo was one of the first Westerners to rhapsodise about the joys of sweet and juicy Afghan *tarbuza* (melons) that are grown in vast quantities across the north. The *kharbuza* (watermelons) are just as good. Kandahar is famous for its fat *anaar* (pomegranates), Bamiyan for its *sib* (apples) and the Shomali Plain for its many varieties of *angur* (grape). *Tut* (Mulberries) are grown everywhere, and are often sold dried as an instant energy food. Nuts are also very popular. Fruit is seasonal and arrives in waves as summer and autumn progresses.

DRINKS

There are few things more Afghan than drinking tea, or chai. The national drink is *chai sabz* (green tea), followed closely by *chai siaa* (black tea), both served scaldingly hot in small glasses. Chai is sweetened with heaps of sugar, or is served with a small dish of sweets. In Herat and some other places, chai is sucked through a *ghand* (sugar cube) in a manner similar to that in Iran. Green tea may sometimes be flavoured with cardamom.

Bottled water is widely available, including locally bottled brands such as Zalal and Cristal. Although water from springs and pump boreholes is generally good, you should never otherwise assume that water is safe to drink unless treated. As a rule, Afghans drink very little water, believing that tea is better for them – in winter many shun it altogether, convinced that it's bad for their health. Fizzy drinks can also be found everywhere; Coca Cola opened a bottling plant in Kabul in 2006, a marker on Afghanistan's path to the globalised economy.

Fruit juices are very popular, including *kela* (banana) and *aam* (mango) when in season. These are often topped with cream and honey, and a few almonds. Alternatively, look for fresh lemonade, freshly pressed from tiny *limu* (lemons), and a sweetened spoonful of sugar.

The availability of alcohol is a contentious subject. In the 1960s and '70s there was small-scale local wine production using grapes from the Shomali Plain, but alcohol consumption has always been frowned upon. The Taliban crushed the contents of the Kabul Intercontinental Hotel's wine cellar under their tank tracks, and it remains illegal for Afghans to drink. However, alcohol has been widely available in Kabul for the international community since the fall of the Taliban. A clampdown was announced in 2006 and supplies dried up, but seemed to be flowing fairly freely again as we went to press. In the north, alcohol smuggling from Uzbekistan – vodka and Russian Baltica beer – is a big business.

WHERE TO EAT & DRINK

The chaikhana (teahouse) is the most common eatery in Afghanistan, in many cases doubling as a cheap sleeping house for travellers. There are usually only one or two dishes on offer; if you just stick to these places you'll quickly become tired of answering the '*pulao* or *kabab*?' question. In larger towns, more formal restaurants broaden the range of Afghan dishes, and there are fast food joints selling local versions of burgers, chips and pizza.

Kabul has a surprisingly broad range of international restaurants, offering everything from Thai and Italian to Croatian. Take care if asking directions to a Chinese restaurant, however – these have become synonymous with brothels.

VEGETARIANS & VEGANS

Afghanistan isn't a country designed for vegetarian travellers. Anyone who can afford to eat meat does, so the concept of voluntary vegetarianism is incomprehensible. Be prepared for a lot of self-catering, and enjoy the variety of Kabul's eating scene between trips further afield.

Dished served in chaikhanas will almost always include meat, whether it's buried under a *pulao* or hidden in a bowl of *qorma*. If you ask to skip the meat, you'll just get the same dish with the meat fished out. Eating street food brings a lot more variety, and you can usually find stalls selling *boloni*, vegetable-filled samosas and the like. Few Afghans eat meat every day, even those who can afford to, so eating at someone's house may bring up dishes like *borani* that are rarely served in restaurants. As an honoured guest however, you'll still usually be offered meat.

The Mughal emperor Babur loved Afghan melons so much that he regularly had them shipped to India packed in crates of ice.

The Russians introduced tea to Afghanistan in the 19th century – previously only curds were drunk. They also left the word *samovar* (hot water urn), still boiling away in the corner of every chaikhana.

EAT YOUR WORDS

Speaking some of the local lingo always helps and never more than when it's
time for a meal. Afghans will appreciate your efforts, even if your pronunciation is off the mark, and it might help you get beyond the default *kabab/pulao*
(rice with meat or vegetables) dining options. For more information about
pronunciation and other language phrases, see the Language chapter, p227.

Useful Phrases

DARI

I'd like ...	*... mikham*
I'd like what he's eating.	*man az ghazayi ke un mikhore mikham.*
I don't eat meat.	*gohst nemikhoram.*
The bill please.	*lotfan surat hesab biyarin.*

PASHTO

I'd like ...	*ghuarum che okherum ...*
I'd like what he's eating.	*da hagha khuakha zema khuakhada.*
I don't eat meat.	*ze ghuakha ne khurem.*
The bill, please.	*bill rawra.*

Food Glossary

Important food terms are presented below in Dari and Pashto, but be
aware that most Afghan dishes, from *kababs* to *mantu*, are the same in
both languages.

DARI

aam	mango
ab	water
ab-e mive	fruit juice
anaar	pomegranate
angabin	honey
anjir	fig
ash	soup
badam	almond
banjan	aubergine
banjan-e rumi	tomato
bastani	ice cream
berenj	rice
chai sabz	green tea
chai siaa	black tea
gerdu	walnut
ghawa	coffee
gosht	meat
gosht-e barre	lamb
gosht-e gau	beef
gosht-e gusfand	mutton
gosht-e shotor	camel meat
holu	peach
kachaloo	potato
kharbuza	watermelon
khorma	cherry
limu	lemon
lubiyaa	beans
mast	yogurt
moraba	jam

morgh	chicken
moz	banana
namak	salt
nan	bread
norinj	orange
panir	cheese
peste	pistachio
piyaz	onion
tarbuza	melon
tokhm	egg
sabz	vegetable
shukar	sugar
sib	apple
zaradalu	apricot

PASHTO

ashak	noodle soup
bolani	stuffed pancake
chai	tea
da sahar chai	breakfast
da gharmy dodai	lunch
da makham dodai	dinner
dal aw sabzi	lentils and vegetables
dodai	bread
dodai aw kabab	bread and kebab
dodai awe kecha ghuakh	bread with mutton
doreh/roti	food
ghata ghuakha	beef
ghuakha	meat
hagay	eggs
kecha ghuakha	mutton
khuraka feroshi	food stall
kouch	butter
maicha	noodles
manto	steamed meat ravioli
market	market
mashrubat	beverages
masta	yogurt
muraba	jam
polave	steamed rice
polave awe sabzi	rice pilaf and vegetables
qabilie	rice with dried fruits
qahwa khana	tea house
rasturan	restaurant
sabzi	vegetable
samosa	triangular shaped stuffed meat pie
shidy	milk
shorwa	soup
ubuh	water
wrigy	rice

Environment

THE LAND

Afghanistan's geography has played a key role in its history. It is divided into three main zones – the northern steppe, the southern desert plateau, and between them the massive spine of the Hindu Kush mountain range. The flat north and west open out to the grass plains of Central Asia and the Iranian plateau – well-trodden invasion routes throughout the centuries, this area was also part of the highway for goods and ideas that formed the Silk Road. The dry south has been a hinterland between empires from Persia and the Indian subcontinent, while the great craggy peaks that dominate the country have given refuge to its people, and made it hard for any power to conquer them completely.

The Hindu Kush mark the westernmost outpost of the Great Himalaya Range, caused by the ancient collision of the Indian and Asian tectonic plates. Two fault lines – the Chaman and Hari Rud – pass through Afghanistan, making it prone to earthquakes. In the northeast, the Hindu Kush rises in a massive knot where it meets the Pamirs, which are still slowly rising. Water from here drains into the Amu Darya to be ultimately lost in the dry reaches of Central Asia; most of the rivers in the Hindu Kush are on the Indian side of the continental watershed, destined to join the Indus in Pakistan and eventually the Arabian Sea. Mountain areas are very prone to flooding in winter and spring. Only the eastern provinces of Kunar and Laghman catch the dying breaths of the Indian monsoon, allowing rich forest to develop.

A key feature of the northern plains are the rounded hills of loess, a fine glacial dust blown in from China. This dust makes the plains extremely fertile, as shown by the annual explosion of plant life during the spring rains.

The south is a land of deserts *(dasht)*. Lack of water here is a perennial problem. Afghans have developed a sophisticated system of *kareez*, or underground irrigation canals, to carry water from the foothills, often over hundred of kilometres. Many *kareez* are several hundred years old. These were once far more extensive, allowing the Ghaznavid empire to flourish in the region in the 11th to 12th centuries. Genghis Khan did huge damage to this intricate irrigation system, and taken with the resulting depopulation, left an environmental scar that the south has arguably yet to recover from.

WILDLIFE

Afghanistan is home to a wide variety of wildlife. Its location means that it straddles both northern temperate and southern tropical zones, as well as being a key staging point for many migratory bird species. Unfortunately, war, habitat destruction and the easy availability of firearms have all conspired to wreak havoc on Afghan species.

Mammals

The most famous of Afghan animals is perhaps the Marco Polo sheep, named for the traveller who first described them to the west. Standing over a metre at the shoulder with a pale grey coat, the rams have tremendous spiral horns that curve up to 150cm in length. It is a mountain species, found in the Wakhan Corridor, but also in Tajikistan, Xinjiang in China, and northern Pakistan. Marco Polo noted that local herders made

'Together we started forward into those bitter cold mountainous parts, and never a road broader than the back of your hand.'

RUDYARD KIPLING, *THE MAN WHO WOULD BE KING*

The name Hindu Kush is supposed to mean 'killer of Indians', a definition first cited by the great traveller Ibn Battuta in 1334.

SNOW LEOPARDS

The snow leopard (Dari: *palang-e barfi*) is at once the loveliest and most elusive of Afghanistan's large mammals. It is restricted to the Pamir Knot and the high slopes of Badakhshan, possibly extending into Nuristan. It is a much bulkier animal than the common leopard, with large paws, thick grey spotted fur and a long tail that makes it supremely adapted to its mountain environment. Its preys ranges in size from marmots to ibex, although it is also fond of domestic livestock.

This fact is a key problem for the snow leopard's continued survival. Attacks on livestock enclosures often follow the 'fox in a chicken coop' template, with the animal killing more than it could eat. Hunting as a result of predation is the main cause of snow leopard death in the Wakhan. Pelts are generally sold to itinerant merchants, eventually finding their way to Kabuli fur traders. The trade is illegal, and although a hunting ban in the Wakhan appear to be respected by locals, enforcement of antipoaching laws for all species hunted for pelts (also including lynx, wolves and common leopard) remains a problem.

cairns of the horns and bones as landmarks along trails, something the Wakhi and Kyrgyz still do today. There are several other fine mountain sheep and goat species, now mostly confined to Badakhshan and other provinces bordering Pakistan. These include the markhor, with its corkscrew twisted horns, the urial sheep and the magnificent Siberian ibex. Until the war, these were all more widespread throughout the country. The desert-dwelling goitered gazelle – a favoured hunting quarry of the Mughal emperors – is close to extinction in the country.

Where there is prey, there are predators. The snow leopard (see above) is only the most renowned. The common leopard remains thinly spread across the country, in hill country, mountains and plains. Similar habitats also support the grey wolf, which exists in pairs or family groups rather than the more commonly imagined large packs, as well as jackals. The brown bear persists in Badakhshan and Nuristan, but its status is unknown. The related but smaller black bear stills hangs on in tiny numbers in Nuristan. Afghanistan once also supported populations of the Caspian tiger (now completely extinct) in the marshlands and forests along the Amu Darya, and Asiatic cheetah, used for hunting gazelle. Small numbers of striped hyena can still be found in the scrub and deserts of the south.

The rhesus macaque is the only primate in Afghanistan and is found in the forests of Nuristan.

'There are great quantities of wild sheep of huge size. Their horns grow to as much as six palms in length and are never less than three or four'.

MARCO POLO, IN THE AFGHAN PAMIR

Birds

There are over 460 species of bird recorded in Afghanistan, with nearly 200 of those breeding in the country. Species are mostly Palearctic, (from Europe, the Mediterranean and North Asia), with a significant number from the Indian subcontinent.

Commonly seen species include the mynah, rock dove, bulbul and buzzard. In the mountains, ravens and choughs are regularly seen. Large raptors include the black vulture and the huge lammergeier, both of which can be spotted in remote mountain areas. Birds of prey have commonly been seen as an important trade item for some groups, and are captured for hunting or selling on to Arabs.

Afghanistan forms an important corridor for migrating waterbirds, with the south traditionally serving as an over-wintering ground, and species flying north over the Salang Pass in spring and summer. These range in size from small ducks and waders up to storks, although the Siberian crane has not been seen for several years.

Plants

Much of Afghanistan is sparsely vegetated. The mountain slopes of the east are the greenest parts of the country, with a mix of oak, juniper, pistachio and pine forest. All of Afghanistan's forests are threatened; it's thought that in the last 25 years the amount of wooded area has tumbled six-fold to around 0.5% of the country's landmass.

The northern plains are dry and at first glance fairly lifeless, but they hide a fertility that springs into life every April and May with the rains turning the swathes of land a deep green sprinkled with colourful blooms of wild tulips and gentians. The deserts of the south on the other side of the mountains receive little of this water. Vegetation here seldom stretches beyond camel thorn, mimosa and sagebrush.

NATIONAL PARKS

On paper, Afghanistan initially appears to have a number of national parks and wildlife reserves. Facts on the ground are a little murkier. While several parks and reserves were listed in the late 1970s, no legal protection was ever granted, while any hope of control was gradually eroded by the years of war. These include the Band-e Amir National Park near Bamiyan; the waterfowl sanctuaries of Ab-i-Estada at Ghazni and Kol-e Hashmat Khan in Kabul; and the wildlife reserves of Ajar Valley (also near Bamiyan), the Big Pamir in the Wakhan Corridor, and Registan Desert Reserve in the south.

Band-e Amir, known for the unique geological features that make up its six mineral lakes, became Afghanistan's first national park in 1973. The influx of domestic tourists and their waste pose a particular problem for management of the area, as well as landmines along some approaches to the lakes, although when we visited both a national park office and gatehouse appeared to be under construction and the uncontrolled fishing on Band-e Haibat had largely disappeared.

Afghanistan contains some important wetlands, although these have been severely depleted by the persistent drought of the 1990s. Ab-i-Estada was a major stopping-off point for migratory waterfowl and Siberian cranes, as well as a nesting site for flamingo. On the edge of Kabul Kol-e Hashmat Khan was a large reed-covered lake that was a favourite waterfowl hunting spot for Afghan royalty and Kabulis alike, but it is now almost completely dry. In Nimroz, Hamoun-i-Pouzak Sanctuary sits on the border with Iran, where the Helmand river disappears into a number of shallow lakes – another major centre for waterfowl. At the time of going to press, Afghanistan was due to become a signatory of the Ramsar Convention on Wetlands.

In north Afghanistan, reserves have been proposed at Imam Sahib along the Amu Darya, and the areas of Herat and Badghis provinces bordering Turkmenistan. The latter area used to be home to a population of wild ass (almost certainly now locally extinct), and still harbours small numbers of urial sheep, goitered gazelle and leopard among its remnant juniper forests. Imam Sahib is home to wild boar, otter, jackal, porcupine and possibly Bukhara deer.

The New-York-based Wildlife Conservation Society (www.wcs.org) has been leading the way in the Afghan Pamirs, surveying wildlife, working with local communities on conservation issues and lobbying for protected status for the region.

ENVIRONMENTAL ISSUES

War has taken its toll on the Afghan environment, both through direct pressure on land, such as degradation and direct war damage, and through the complete breakdown of systems of resource management, from the village level up to the government. The environmental problems facing the country are myriad.

Perhaps the biggest problem has been the large scale clearing of Afghanistan's forests, most notably in the heavily wooded provinces of Nuristan, Kunar, Khost, Paktika and Paktia. While much damage has been done by local populations and passing refugees in need of firewood, clear-cutting by mujaheddin to smuggle timber into Pakistan has caused widespread deforestation, while the huge profits have entrenched criminality. This has made large swathes of these areas prone to soil erosion and flooding. In the northwest, the once productive pistachio forests have also been largely cleared, causing more long-term economic damage. Aid agencies have started reforestation programmes in many areas, but the scale of the problem is enormous, and government control in some of the most heavily logged areas along the eastern border remains sketchy.

Poaching and hunting remains an issue. Birds of prey in particular are caught and sold in the Gulf. The Taliban went as far as building an airstrip in the Registan to facilitate Arab sponsors who came to hunt houbara bustards – a popular pursuit of Osama Bin Laden.

Landmines continue to plague agricultural and urban environments. Pollution is an increasing problem, particularly in cities like Kabul with their growing populations and creaking infrastructure. Access to potable water and sewage systems are both hugely inadequate. The Afghan government, together with UN Environment Programme (UNEP), is attempting to address some of these issues, and has become a signatory to the Convention on Biological Diversity and the UN Convention to Combat Desertification, but there's a long way to go before real progress can be marked on the ground as well as on paper.

The 2003 *Afghanistan Post-Conflict Environmental Assessment Report* by the UN Environment Programme (http://postconflict.unep.ch/) is a key starting point for the investigating the current state of the Afghan environment.

Safety in Afghanistan

No visit to, or time spent in, Afghanistan occurs without risk. The risks are varied and omnipresent: from kidnapping to improvised explosive devices (IEDs), from suicide bombings to land mines, from diseases to highway robbery. The time of the Taliban saw brutal policies in the country that ensured excellent security and very little crime based on a culture of fear and absolute control. Since the fall of the Taliban in 2001 the prevailing security environment has worsened and remains extremely volatile and unpredictable: a complex mix of insurgency, narcotics, lack of governance, absence of the rule of law and cross-border influence. Large-scale clashes and terrorist attacks continue unabated in parts of the country; even after half a decade of the presence of tens of thousands of International Security Assistance Force (ISAF) and Coalition soldiers.

Despite on occasions being directly targeted and even killed, thousands of internationals have been working for Non-Governmental Organisations (NGOs), international organisations (IOs) and for contractors since that time. Of those, 80% are located in Kabul and less than 5% reside outside of the main regional centres. Few independent travellers make the trip to Afghanistan, most only taking in Kabul, Bamiyan and some of the northern areas.

It also needs to be recognised that even in the halcyon days of the Hippy Trail in the 1960s and '70s, work and travel in Afghanistan was not without risk due to the absence of a strong government, lack of rule of law and the challenges of moving in extremely remote areas lacking communications and medical services. The same can be said for the NGOs and IOs working for the Afghan people during the Jihad against the Russians and later on during the Civil War and the Taliban regime. The fact is, internationals have been working and travelling to Afghanistan throughout its turbulent past and continue to do so: it is how you prepare, present and conduct yourself that will keep you out of harm's way.

Those working for NGOs, IOs or contractors will be afforded some level of security support to them – support which differs greatly between organisations. This is in stark contrast to the independent traveller, who does not have ready access to these support mechanisms. You need to be acutely aware of this in your planning.

A simple equation that encapsulates this chapter is **risk = threat x vulnerability**. A threat is something that can harm you and a risk is the chance of being harmed by that threat and the greater or lesser your exposure to the threat is your vulnerability. There is little you will be able to do to change the threat environment around you. However, there is a great deal you can do to reduce your vulnerability, which can be as simple as not moving on foot at night.

WARNING!

You are the only one responsible for your security, and this should never be delegated to anyone else. This chapter is in no way a substitute for professional, relevant and current security advice, training and information. Moreover this should be a continual process that starts during your planning and is ongoing throughout your visit.

BEFORE TRAVELLING TO AFGHANISTAN

Preparation for working in or travelling to Afghanistan is critical. It is essential to take the time to learn about the country, culture and customs, which will help you ready yourself, not only with your packing, but mentally. For even the most seasoned, risk-savvy, independent traveller Afghanistan can be an assault on your norms. Your preparation will help to keep you out of trouble and allow you to hit the ground at least walking, without wandering around looking lost and vulnerable upon arrival. For example, the value of understanding cultural sensitivities (a matter of security if you get it wrong and end up insulting an Afghan) or learning some key Dari and Pashto words and phrases cannot be underestimated.

Turning to what you pack, assembling a quick run (or grab) bag is an extremely valuable addition to your luggage. This is to be kept with you should you have to leave in a hurry or lose everything else. The important thing is to think through what your essential items are in an emergency.

Anyone travelling to Afghanistan, regardless of the length of the visit, needs to arrange for comprehensive insurance for both medical and personal property. Not all insurers will insure for travel to Afghanistan and those that do may exclude or limit many essential items due to war/terrorism risks. For those working in Afghanistan ensure you check with your employer as to the extent of your coverage and take out additional insurance if required. Finally, make sure you read the fine print!

> Suggested things to put in your grab bag are: passport, personal documents, medications, water, small amount of food, Leatherman type multi-tool, warm covering, medical kit, mobile phone charger and toiletries.

Training Courses

For those planning to spend extended periods in Afghanistan and its remote areas a generic security training course is highly recommended. There are a wide range of courses available:

AKE Group (☎ +44 (0)1432 267111; www.akegroup.com) Their 'Surviving Hostile Regions' five-day course is broken down into four areas; Awareness, Medical, Self Sufficiency and Planning and are conducted in the UK, US, Australia and Sweden. The course fees are pricey at UK£1790, but can be offset by discount offered on insurance premiums following the completion of the course. AKE also offers a weekly comprehensive security information update on all provinces of Afghanistan on a subscription basis of UK£1200 annually.

Centurion Safety (☎ 44-1637 852 910; www.centuriansafety.net) Popular with journalists working in high-risk areas; conducts a three-day 'Hostile Environments and Emergency First Aid Training for Aid Agencies' in the UK and US. The course is a little pricey at UK£750, but that's an all-inclusive fee. The former UK Royal Marine instructors take students through topics including first aid, vehicle safety and convoy routines, radio procedures and mines, and booby traps.

RedR Australia (☎ 613-9329 1387; www.redr.org) Conducts a four-day 'Personal Security and Communications' course for AUD$800 for organisations and AUD$1000 for individuals. Topics covered include evacuation, hostage and arrest, culture and personal responsibility, and trauma and stress. Course fees are inclusive of food and accommodation. RedR International runs similar courses in the UK, US and areas where NGOs are operating, including Sudan and Sri Lanka – unfortunately not Afghanistan.

> The highly useful ECHO Generic Security Guide for Humanitarian Organisations can be downloaded from http://ec.europa.eu/echo/pdf_files/security/echo_generic_security_guide_en.pdf.

INFORMATION RESOURCES

Up-to-date, accurate information and analysis of the prevailing political and security environment is going to be your greatest asset for travelling or working within Afghanistan in order to remain situationally aware. Things on the ground are fluid and can change extremely quickly, so you always need to know, to the greatest possible extent, what could happen and what you are going to do if it does. It is good to augment your latest news with general, historical, humanitarian and reconstruction information, which will help you put things into perspective.

A list of good news sources can be found on p19. A shortwave radio is also recommended, and some stations such as the BBC World Service broadcast on FM in Kabul (see p84).

Most NGO and IO workers will receive daily security updates from their organisations' security advisors or from the Afghanistan NGO Safety Office (ANSO). To further enhance this it behoves you to establish a network of local security information wherever you are planning to work or travel, whether that be local staff or international colleagues.

Security briefings

Currently there are no organisations offering regular security briefings to independent travellers. For registered NGOs, there is a weekly security briefing in Kabul held by **ANSO** (coordinator@afgnso.org; briefing at Maple Leaf Inn ⊗ 3pm Thu). The **UN Mine Action Centre for Afghanistan** (UNMACA; ☎ 070 450027 Wazir Akbar Khan, Kabul) provides land mine and unexploded ordnance (UXO) safety briefings when requested to NGOs and contractors, where they also provide participants with extremely useful handouts.

THE AUTHORITIES

The Afghan National Security Forces are developing slowly, with the assistance of the international community. The Afghan National Police (ANP) are the most visible force; you will see them at check points, border crossings and airports. Corruption is a major issue within the ANP with many supplementing their meagre income of less than US$50 per month with criminal activities. Internationals have been targeted for *baksheesh* (bribes) after dark at check posts in the provincial centres however, they back down with a threat of a call to the Police HQ or an Embassy. Little should be expected in terms of assistance from the ANP. Their capability to investigate or prosecute crimes is extremely limited and they are preoccupied with fighting the insurgency.

Those working or travelling within Afghanistan may have an encounter with the Afghan National Army (ANA), often seen with the ISAF forces, being mentored by them. As with the ANP, corruption and involvement in the drugs trade is an issue. It must also be noted that both criminals and insurgents have been known to steal and wear ANA and ANP uniforms to conduct their operations; therefore, it is unwise to automatically assume that everyone in uniform is a legitimate member of the security forces.

In the past ISAF has supported both Afghan and international civilians with *in extremis* and medical support, including vehicle accidents and protection during riots. As an independent traveller you are unlikely to be able to contact them for assistance. Should they be mobilised they would not ignore a request for assistance but their own operational commitments and political caveats may preclude them from intervening.

COMMUNICATIONS

Communications underpin personal security management. As a minimum, anyone planning on working or travelling in Afghanistan should purchase a SIM card from a local provider or if possible set their international SIM to roam. This is a necessity not a luxury. Although the Afghan networks can be unreliable, with frequent call drop outs or inability to get a line out, they are the primary source of communication and as good as it gets. Coverage is improving continually with most provincial centres and main routes having access. It should also be noted that following a significant security incident such as a bombing, the network is swamped with people trying to locate others.

To make the best use of your communications ensure you develop a 'check in' schedule with your colleagues or fellow travellers. Also ensure you have the relevant emergency numbers for the areas you will be travelling in programmed into your phone.

TYPES OF RISK

The types of risk in Afghanistan are complex and overlap heavily. Many security incidents are also 'dressed up' to make them look like insurgent acts; however, many are perpetrated by criminals, warlords or narcolords to avoid the attention of the international military forces.

Insurgency

Despite the attempts of the government and international forces to break the back of the insurgency, some analysts conclude that capability and sophistication of the insurgents is at its highest point since 2001. The insurgency is by no means homogenous, with two main groups: indigenous Afghan insurgent traditionalist groups including the Taliban and Hezb-e Islami Gulbuddin (HIG); and global fundamentalist, Al Qaeda–inspired terrorist organisations with their roots outside Afghanistan. Their objectives are more or less aligned: to overthrow the elected government and return Afghanistan to an Islamic Emirate according to strict Sharia law, without foreign influence. There are clear links between them and the criminal and narco elements, as a means of supporting themselves and their operations.

The insurgency is extremely active in the Pashtun Belt; however, at times this spills over into Kabul. IEDs, BBIEDs, VBIEDs, rocketing, assassination, ambushes and propaganda are some of the tactics they are employing in their jihad – with a great deal of knowledge-sharing going on between groups in Iraq and Afghanistan. The challenge that is faced by both the government and the international community is that without reconstruction it is almost impossible to bring about enduring security and vice versa – currently both are eluding them.

Although independent travellers and NGO workers have been targeted by these groups on an extremely limited scale, it is clear that their primary target for the time being remains the Afghan Government, ISAF and Coalition forces. Some NGOs believe that there has been a blurring of lines between their humanitarian activities and the operations of the ISAF Provincial Reconstruction Teams (PRTs). They feel that with the invasion of the 'humanitarian space' by gunned-up army types building schools and digging wells their vulnerability has increased through the perception of NGOs in turn being involved with the military.

Mines and UXOs

With its war-torn past Afghanistan remains one of the countries in the world most highly contaminated with land mines; 32 of the 34 Afghan provinces are affected by mines. They are not the only explosive remnant of war that account for, on average, three Afghans a day being killed or injured: UXOs include any munition that has been fired or dropped and has failed to detonate, from a hand grenade to a missile. UXOs can be found anywhere from rooftops to backyards or the desert and are equally as lethal as land mines.

The economic and social cost of the mine and UXO problem in Afghanistan is massive. Large tracts of farming and grazing land are

Many NGOs will also operate a VHF and HF radio network; make sure you get training on how to use it. They also may operate Thuraya or Iridium satellite phones.

MORE ACRONYMS

IED – Improvised Explosive Device

BBIED – Body Borne IED (suicide vest)

VBIED – Vehicle Borne IED

SVBIED – Suicide VBIED

DBIED – Donkey Borne IED

unproductive due to the threat that lies beneath the topsoil, and provides a barrier to the land's reconstruction. Moreover, the direct cost of demining and associated activities runs at about US$100 million per annum. The sheer number of amputees in Afghanistan is a morbid reminder of the social cost of the problem, not forgetting the widows and orphans they create.

The Afghan NGO Organisation for Mine Clearance and Afghan Rehabilitation (OMAR) produces a series of guidelines for land-mine awareness and safety:

To learn more about land mines in Afghanistan, visit the OMAR Land Mine Museum in Kabul (p93).

- Stay away from areas such as military bases, battlefields, destroyed houses, unused roads and paths, wells, the banks of irrigation canals and culverts.
- When travelling by road, stay on the road even when taking a toilet break. If in doubt, turn back – land mines are laid to be invisible.
- Red and white marks indicate an area marked by a mine-action programme. Red marks show mined areas; white marks show that the area has been cleared and is safe.
- Talk to locals and observe local behaviour to find out about safe areas. Locals often develop their own signs for marking mined areas. These include rocks laid across a path, piles of stone or bundles of sticks.
- If you face a mine or UXO, stay calm. Turn back and slowly follow your footsteps to return to a safe area, shouting a warning to those with you. Mark the mined area with a line of rocks and inform the local authorities and/or demining agency.

Crime

With the majority of Afghans living in extreme poverty the security situation further impedes their ability to earn a basic living. The security forces are preoccupied with the insurgency and crime has flourished, aided by lack of capability and corruption within the ANP. The criminal threat is amplified by the questionable success of the DDR (Disarmament, Demobilization and Reintegration) programme, whose goal was to remove warlord power structures and weapons. Hundreds of what are now called 'illegally armed groups' operate freely across the country with arsenals of light and heavy weapons, therefore highway banditry, car jacking and protection rackets are rife.

When out and about don't dress extravagantly, keep your cash stashed, your jewellery covered and your mobile phones in your pocket.

By comparison to the local population, any international in Afghanistan is extremely affluent and is a potential target of at the very least petty crime.

KIDNAPPING

Kidnapping remains a threat for internationals in Afghanistan and is perpetrated by two groups: by criminals for ransom and by insurgents as part of their operations. Criminal groups have been known to sell hostages to the highest bidder, usually the insurgents.

Although numerous Turkish and Indian road construction and telecommunications engineers have been kidnapped, some later being beheaded by insurgents in the south, most other cases have been criminally inspired. An Italian NGO worker and three UN elections workers were kidnapped in Kabul and later released in 2005 – it was never confirmed if a ransom was paid.

Any kidnapping will be preceded by reconnaissance and planning. It is essential that you do not set patterns of movement and timings. This is particularly important for those working in Afghanistan, going to the office at 8am and returning to your guesthouse at 5pm on the same route everyday could indeed make you a target. Vary your movement and remain situationally aware.

Opium

The 2006 opium crop reinforced Afghanistan's infamous accolade of being the world's largest producer of opium; in fact, the country produced 92% of the global crop or a staggering 6100 metric tons. Some of it will be processed into heroin in Afghanistan, but most of the processing is done in neighbouring countries, and then trafficked all the way to the streets of Europe and Russia. It is Afghanistan's largest export and unfortunately, due to a lack of natural resources, the country's economy is reliant on its production. Expensive attempts at eradicating the crop have been made – in terms of financial resources expended and the deaths of Afghan security forces clashing with farmers – all with little impact. However, it is clear that on the opium issue, the insurgency, warlords and some government officials are happy to cooperate in the name of mutual gain.

Although the opium poppies look beautiful and many internationals would like to have their picture taken in a field, 'opium tourism' is a dangerous activity. Most fields are guarded by armed men to protect the crop when it is growing and being harvested. It may be a lethal case of mistaken identity if you are confused as potential poppy eradication surveyor earmarking annual earnings for destruction. Moreover anti-personnel mines are known to have been planted in fields to also disrupt eradicators. To learn more about opium in Afghanistan see the boxed text, p196.

MOVING AROUND

There is no doubt that you are most vulnerable in Afghanistan when you are moving around, with the majority of security incidents occurring when travelling by road. Therefore, your movement in Afghanistan should be planned, methodical and necessary.

Driving in Afghanistan requires nerves of steel in order to dodge the donkey carts, overloaded trucks and total absence of road rules. Accordingly it is advisable not to drive yourself; most NGOs employ drivers to not only drive but also maintain the vehicles. They have a distinct advantage when it comes to the language and local knowledge for navigation. However, like you, it is important your driver knows what to do in the event of an emergency.

Some NGOs prefer to use low profile, local-looking vehicles rather than large 4WDs plastered with their symbols – while others not only display their logos, but also fly their flag. The threat of the environment you are working in will often dictate which option to take, and what works in one province won't necessarily give you the same amount of protection in others.

Likewise your ability to use local transport, whether that is taxis, Millie buses or rickshaws will be influenced by the prevailing security situation. Ensure you travel in at least a pair and keep in regular contact with your colleagues or fellow travellers. The decision to transit through high-risk areas should not be taken lightly, like the Kabul–Herat run by bus, where insurgent and bandit check points are commonplace, and this reinforces the need for the latest information.

Even if you never leave Kabul, you will certainly encounter checkpoints, mostly manned by the ANP; however, ISAF and the ANA may also be present. Comply with their instructions, listen to what they

Afghan prisons have a growing foreigner population, almost exclusively of drug traffickers. Many are lured by the easy cash; however, increasingly, more are being intercepted by the authorities.

The ANP will usually arrest the drivers involved in a motor vehicle accident at the scene, regardless of how minor the damage is – it's the closest thing the not-at-fault driver gets to insurance.

want, don't argue or insult them and if possible stay in the vehicle. Using some Dari or Pashto usually works well to break the ice if there is a problem. If you are approaching a checkpoint at night make sure you dim your headlights and switch on the interior light so the security forces can see who is in the vehicle. Note also the money being palmed by officers from every other passing vehicle – the sort of corruption that dismays ordinary Afghans and helped pave the way for the Taliban in the 1990s.

It is extremely important that your vehicle does not come too close to any ISAF, ANP or ANA convoys. These conveys are often the targets of suicide car bombs using the modus operandi of ramming into their vehicles and detonating themselves. Therefore, after several verbal and visual warnings they will shoot into any vehicle moving too close to them with their large mounted machine guns. Do not attempt to overtake these convoys – regardless of how slow they are moving.

> When you check into your accommodation orientate yourself with the exits, bunker and fire fighting-equipment. Don't be afraid to move the bed away from the window either.

EMERGENCIES

Having a plan for what you will do in the event of an emergency is critical, whether that be a vehicle accident or being in an area when the security forces are attacked by a suicide bomber. Although you can never plan for every eventuality, you need to remember a few guiding principles. If you are involved in an incident, do what you can at the scene in the immediate aftermath to save loss of life and prevent injury. After the situation has stabilised and the security forces have taken charge pull back to a safe area and call your emergency contacts.

If you are not involved in the incident, do not rush to the area with your camera as a 'war tourist'. You are exposing yourself to extreme risk, not only with nervous security force personnel potentially shooting you, but also secondary attacks from insurgents such as bombs that are detonated to inflict casualties upon the responding forces. Stay away from these areas: ISAF and the Afghan Security Forces will handle the situa-

---

HOW TO UNDO ALL YOUR GOOD WORK IN A NIGHT

Good reputation and behaviour are serious considerations in a 'shame and honour' culture like Afghanistan. It continues to be one of the most conservative Islamic countries in the world, underpinned by an ancient tribal structure, with most of its population living in poverty. Although you will see Westernised Afghans in Kabul, they represent a tiny fraction of the population. The economic divide between expats and such Afghans and the majority of the population who live below the US$1-a-day poverty line consolidates the opinion of Afghans that expatriates earn excessively large amounts of money only to spend it on immoral pursuits that serve to corrupt their nation. Since the fall of the Taliban, Kabul has been flooded with influences from the West that are abhorrent to Afghan culture such as alcohol and prostitution. No one really knows how much was here before the influx of internationals – however the perception among Afghans is that they brought it with them. Afghans are not allowed to enter the expatriate restaurants in Kabul or purchase alcohol, and internationals are openly asked by Afghans 'Do you go there for whiskey and sex?' Although this is clearly not the case, it serves to reinforce the negative perceptions. The Kabul scene grows by the month fuelled by well-paid contractors, diplomats and UN workers. Behaviour such as drunkenness in public, insulting Afghan guards and continued support of Chinese restaurants, most of which are fronts for brothels, make it hard to insist that Western culture is not having a negative effect on the country. Most work in Afghanistan to do good, but as one Afghan commented, 'We know that you come a long way from your family and put yourself in danger to help us but why do you have to insult our culture while you are doing it?'

tion. The same applies if there is shooting, rocketing or armed clashes, which are more common at night; stay inside your accommodation and away from the windows. If you are working for an organisation, this is where you will have to comply with the security procedures – for example moving to the bunker. As outlined earlier, independent travellers do not have such support.

Medical Emergencies

The health services in Afghanistan are continually improving with the assistance of organisations such as the ICRC and Emergency. However as an independent traveller or worker, your aim should be to get stabilised and evacuated as soon as possible, whether to home, Islamabad, Delhi or Dubai, should something happen to you. Cleanliness, lack of medical supplies, intermittent power, out-of-date medication, over-prescribing and medicating for additional profit and the questionable credentials of some medical staff are all reasons why immediate evacuation is your best option. Those Afghans who can afford it also seek treatment in neighbouring countries. For more information see p221.

Working in Afghanistan

The fall of the Taliban saw a flood of international aid workers, contractors and business people come to Afghanistan. Most are based in Kabul, where there is a thriving expat scene. Numbers are more thinly spread elsewhere, with the international presence in the south and east continuing to shrink.

Particularly if you're working in the humanitarian sector, working in Afghanistan can be stressful. Hours are long (six-day weeks are usually the norm), and security concerns can restrict your movement. Each organisation has its own arrangements – UN agencies tend to have the tightest security, with blanket restrictions and regular 'lockdowns'; other agencies have a more flexible and nuanced response to local conditions. While it's important to take their security advice extremely seriously, don't let it make you paranoid. Either way, bring plenty of reading material, as nights can be long if you're not allowed out. See the Safety in Afghanistan chapter (p68) for more information relevant to those working in the country.

If you're working with an international organisation, check the training and orientation you'll receive prior to posting. The **Aid Workers Network** (www.aidworkers.net) is a useful resource, with a good forum and advice on everything from careers to training courses. The **British Agencies Afghani-**

ReliefWeb (www.relief web.int) and DevNet (www.devnetjobs.org) are good places to look for jobs in the development sector in Afghanistan.

REPORTING FROM AFGHANISTAN *Christina Lamb*

'Going inside' was what we called it in the old days. When the Russians were occupying Afghanistan back in the 1980s, most of us covering the war were based in the Pakistani city of Peshawar, divided from where we wanted to be by the jagged mountains of the Khyber Pass.

By foot, donkey or motorbike, we would travel back and forth across those mountains with the mujaheddin, dodging landmines and Soviet helicopter gun-ships. Sometimes we would darken our faces with dirt and a potassium mixture to blend in with the fighters; sometimes we would be disguised in burqas. We lived on stale *nan* (bread), occasionally supplemented by rice from some villagers or okra fried in diesel oil. When you were inside you longed to be out, but when you were out, you spent all your time trying to get back in.

There were no satellite phones then so it was impossible to file copy while inside Afghanistan and crossing the border meant being out of contact for weeks. Even when back in Pakistan, it was so hard to get an international phone line that most of the time the only way to file was through the telex operator in the Public Call Office who required regular *baksheesh* (tips) to keep him punching out all the holes in the ticker tape.

Once I got a visa from the communist regime to cover the war from the other side. That was little better. Copy had to be sent through the one-armed telex operator at Hotel Kabul who doubled, somewhat alarmingly, as the taxi driver, his one black-gloved hand swinging back and forth from the gear-stick to the steering wheel.

These days it's much easier. The major cities of Kabul, Herat, Kandahar and Jalalabad all have mobile phones and internet, and some guest houses such as the Gandamack Lodge even boast wi-fi.

But other aspects of reporting Afghanistan have got harder. For a start, journalists have become targets. Afghanistan has not reached anywhere near Iraq levels but there have been a number of kidnaps and murders of correspondents.

The new highways between Kabul and Kandahar and Kabul and Jalalabad have slashed journey times but roadblocks have once more become a feature. Some are Taliban looking for government sympathisers; others are bandits or even police demanding bribes. Some of us have started wearing burqas again on the road.

stan Group (www.baag.org.uk) has an excellent downloadable briefing pack for those working in Afghanistan.

Unfortunately the influx of foreign workers has had some negative consequences. For more on the attitudes of some Afghans to expats, see the boxes 'How To Undo All Your Good Work In A Night' (p74) and 'The Kabul Bubble' (p82).

TOP TIPS FOR WORKING IN AFGHANISTAN

The experience of living and working in Afghanistan can be a very personal one, so we asked a variety of expats to give us some hard-earned gems of advice:

> It's thought that there are currently around 7000 foreigners working in Afghanistan, plus 16,000 US Army personnel and 18,000 NATO forces.

- 'Learn about Afghan culture and society before you arrive. There is no substitute for respecting and understanding the context you work in. Do some homework to understand what will and won't work in Afghanistan. Listen to Afghans about what they want: this shouldn't be about us.'
  LA, Kabul

- 'Don't fall in the trap of getting stuck in Kabul, make sure you use some of your downtime to explore this amazing country.'
  Anonymous, Kandahar

- 'If you value your clothes, always self launder (plus it gives you something to do on the weekend!). But never use the local washing powder, although it makes a good toilet cleaner. Never blow your nose in public – it's considered very rude. Finally, always pack your iPod.'
  SC, Lashkar Gah

Reporting Afghanistan has also become more depressing. Back in the 1980s Afghanistan was a romantic story – the Spanish Civil War of my generation – a David and Goliath struggle by these men from the mountains with their plastic sandals and old Lee Enfields turning back the most powerful army on earth. That first soured in the early 1990s when the Russians had left and the mujaheddin all started fighting each other. The moment the last Soviet soldier stepped back across the Amu Darya, Afghanistan dropped off the news agenda anyway.

That all changed of course with 9/11. In the ensuing fight to oust the Taliban, it was once again easy to identify who were the good guys and who were the bad. The Taliban after all were one of the world's most repressive regimes and most of the world was on the other side. But five years on from BBC reporter John Simpson's infamous liberation of Kabul, much of the goodwill towards Westerners had already dissipated. In large swathes of southern Afghanistan, propaganda from the resurgent and newly media-savvy Taliban combined with some overenthusiastic NATO bombing, had convinced many to see peacekeeping forces from the US, Britain, Canada and elsewhere as the occupiers.

One thing that has not changed in 20 years of reporting Afghanistan is the difficulty in finding the truth. Afghans are a captivating people, with their noble stance, generous hospitality and proud history, and a love of beauty that has even the most brutal warlord tying plastic flowers to his Kalashnikov. But to say Afghans are prone to exaggeration is like saying the French quite like wine.

The number of times I would arrive at a mujaheddin camp in the late 1980s to be told that I'd just missed them winning a major battle or shooting down seven Soviet Migs. Strangely the wreckage was never anywhere to be found. Similarly in June 2006 I went with some British soldiers into a village in Helmand where they assured us there were no Taliban then directed us straight into an ambush.

People often ask if it's a problem being a female correspondent in Afghanistan. Strangely, it's not at all. Warlords and commanders generally seem to regard Western women journalists as some kind of asexual species. We also have a distinct advantage of being able to go and sit in the women's quarters, giving us access to half the population our male colleagues often miss.

Christina Lamb is the award-winning Foreign Affairs correspondent of the Sunday Times and author of The Sewing Circles of Herat: My Afghan Years.

■ 'Things to bring: a very warm duvet or sleeping bag for the winter, carbon monoxide detectors for heaters in the winter so you don't die in your sleep. Bring lots of intensive moisturiser, but not lightweight stuff – something like Elizabeth Arden Eight Hour Cream. In the summer, a pumice or equivalent for feet and especially heels which can get dry and cracked.'
JN, Kabul

■ 'Nothing is never what it seems in Afghanistan and if we (the visitor) can understand 20% of what is really going on in any one scene (politically, culturally and so on) we are doing pretty well. Instead, chill out and spend your first couple of months just listening and observing.'
Anonymous, Kabul

Essential Field Guide: Afghanistan by Edward Girardet and Jonathan Walter is an excellent primer for those staying long-term in Afghanistan.

■ 'Try to learn enough language to do the basic greetings at the very least. It takes down barriers quickly and serves to humanise you to Afghans. They love to hear you try and are very forgiving with their language. Lots of people bring great big clunky hiking boots as their main shoes. Try to remember to bring a lightweight pair of shoes that slip on and off easily. It makes it easier getting in and out of houses and offices.'
JK, Faizabad

■ 'The key tip is to approach Afghanistan mentally prepared for a truly surreal experience and adventure. You'll certainly get sensory overload here and it's normal to get depressed occasionally and ask the proverbial 'what the hell am I doing here?' question. It's vital to have a set of friends outside of the work field that you are involved in. Try to break out of the UN, USAID/American, NGO, security firm or French/Euro speaking cliques. Otherwise, you end up talking shop all the time and find it hard to let go.'
Anonymous, Kabul

■ 'Get out on the street to walk, see, feel, experience. The bazaars and streets have so much to offer, but many expats will never take the risk for fear of what might happen and never for a moment thinking what they might have missed.'
JV, Bamiyan

■ 'Try to make local friends and visit as many local restaurants and places as possible. Ask plenty of pertinent questions with your Afghan friends, but realise there is a huge cultural and economic gap. Just because someone speaks English well and dresses in Western clothes does not mean they share all of your values and beliefs.'
JR, Kabul

■ 'Don't bring too many things – pretty much any Western products are available. Shop locally instead of just going to the PX supermarkets. The only advantage they have is the alcohol they sell, and that's now restricted to International Security Assistance Force people.'
SKL, Kabul

Kabul كابل

When the Taliban fled Kabul in the face of the post-9/11 US bombing campaign, they left a city wrecked by years of war. Half the city consisted of rubble and no-one could remember the last time anything new had been built. It was a city on life-support.

Today, Kabul seems to change on an almost daily basis. Swathes of the city have been cleared, and new buildings are quickly thrown up as if in a steroid-powered building contest. The air is thick with the sound of mobile phones. New restaurants and busy bazaars cater to the nouveau riche Afghans surfing an economic boom and the sizeable international community helping with Afghanistan's reconstruction (or just making money out of it). While there's a long way to go before Kabul is restored to its position as a travellers' haunt, there's a whiff of its old cosmopolitan self in the air.

But it's not all roses and flashy new 4WD cars. Electricity and clean water remain a distant aspiration for the majority of the population, which has doubled since the end of 2001 with returning refugees. Plenty of Kabulis still live in bombed-out buildings or worse, and beggars, war widows and street children further swell the traffic jams that clog the city. Reconstruction for the poorest has been frustratingly slow.

Kabul today is a fascinating snapshot of the birth pangs of a new nation, and a city permanently on the cusp of change. As an introduction to Afghanistan it's exciting, frustrating, inspiring and shocking in equal measure.

HIGHLIGHTS

- Enjoy the green spaces and flowers of **Babur's Gardens** (p87), recently restored to their former glory
- Ponder the surviving exhibits at the **Kabul Museum** (p88), a frontline in Afghanistan's struggle to keep its heritage alive
- Climb above the **City Walls** (p90) for crisp air and mountain views over the city
- Visit the **OMAR Landmine Museum** (p93) to learn more about the silent killers still plaguing the country
- Haggle for carpets and lapis lazuli in **Chicken Street** (p102), home to Afghanistan's keenest souvenir sellers
- Experience the sights and smells of old Kabul at the traditional **Bird Market** (p90) of Ka Faroshi

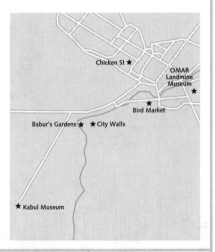

■ AREA CODE: 020　　■ POPULATION: 3 MILLION (ESTIMATED)　　■ ELEVATION: 1800M

KABUL

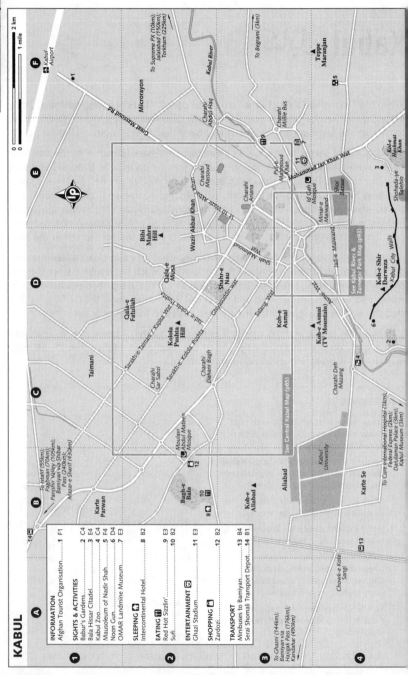

INFORMATION
Afghan Tourist Organisation......1 F1

SIGHTS & ACTIVITIES
Babur's Gardens...................2 C4
Bala Hissar Citadel...............3 E4
Kabul Zoo........................4 C4
Mausoleum of Nadir Shah..........5 F4
Noon Gun.........................6 D4
OMAR Landmine Museum.............7 E3

SLEEPING
Intercontinental Hotel............8 B2

EATING
Red Hot Sizzlin'..................9 E3
Sufi.............................10 B2

ENTERTAINMENT
Ghazi Stadium....................11 E3

SHOPPING
Zardozi..........................12 B2

TRANSPORT
Minibuses to Bamiyan.............13 B4
Serai Shomali Transport Depot....14 B1

HISTORY

Legendarily founded by Cain and Abel, Kabul is an ancient city, repeatedly fought over by all the region's great empires and religions. Known in antiquity as Kabura, it was an Achaemenid outpost 2500 years ago, later renamed Parapamisidae by the Bactrian Greeks who built a city here. In the centuries that followed, Kabul became a Buddhist city during the Kushan era, Hindu under the Indians and finally Muslim with the Arab expansion from the east. Kabul's first Afghan rulers were the Ghorids in the 12th century.

The whirlwind of destruction wreaked by Genghis Khan had largely blown itself out by the time he reached Kabul, and the city escaped the worst of the Mongol destruction. Kabul prospered under Timur in the 14th century, who even married the sister of one of Kabul's rulers, and used the city as the base for his conquest of India. In 1504 Kabul was captured by Babur, founder of the Mughal empire.

Babur loved Kabul, and had rhapsodised about its many delights. Even as his ambition drove him eastward to India he dreamed of the city, writing 'I have a longing beyond expression to return to Kabul. How can its delights ever be erased from my heart?'. His body was returned to Kabul for burial.

As Mughal interests became centred on India, Kabul's fortunes waned. A period of Safavid Persian interest was cut short by the meteoric rise to power of Ahmad Shah Durrani, who captured Kabul from his Kandahar base, forging the modern Afghan kingdom in the process. His son, Timur Shah, moved the Afghan capital to Kabul in 1772.

Kabul was never a secure throne. When Dost Mohammed became amir in the 1820s, he found himself squeezed not just by Afghan rivals, but by the British and Russian empires. Initially courted by both powers, the British eventually sent an army of occupation to Kabul in 1839, putting their own puppet on the throne. It was an early round of the Great Game that ended in disaster for the British – their resident hacked to pieces by a mob, and the Kabul garrison massacred as it tried to retreat from the city (see p32). The British sent an army of retribution to Kabul in 1842 and dynamited

(see p32)

RISK ASSESSMENT

As the capital and centre of the international presence in Afghanistan, Kabul is a target for anti-government elements, and 2006 saw the first suicide bombings in the city for several years. Security is generally tight, and at the time of research Kabul was quiet but unpredictable. The threat of future attacks against targets of 'high value' remains – these potentially include Afghan and international forces, areas around ministries, the airport and Jalalabad roads. Be aware that crime is also rising in Kabul – see p87 for more information.

see p87 for more information

the medieval covered bazaar, but also allowed Dost Mohammed to slip back in to the country and quietly regain his throne.

Incredibly, the British failed to learn their lesson, and were back again in 1878 trying to impose their rule. There was another massacre of British residents and another punitive army sent to Kabul (this time it was the Bala Hissar to be destroyed). At the end of the war, Amir Abdur Rahman Khan was left master of his kingdom.

At the start of the 20th century Kabul was the focus of an ambitious modernising program under King Amanullah. The model quarter of Darulaman was built on the southwest of the city, with tree-lined avenues and a European-style palace. Kabul boomed for the next 40 years. The USA and Soviet Union competed to provide vast amounts of aid, which helped pay for the paving of the city and the opening of Kabul University. The capital became a cosmopolitan place, and welcomed tourists from around the world.

Things started to change following the Soviet occupation in 1979. On the surface Kabul continued to prosper. Women made up nearly 40% of all governmental jobs, and the city's shops were well stocked. The population largely sat out the war that raged across the country, although resistance groups increasingly infiltrated Kabul's tight defences to carry out guerrilla attacks and bombings.

If a smooth change of power was expected following the withdrawal of the Red Army in 1989, events quickly proved otherwise. The victorious mujaheddin entered the capital in April 1992 and straight away fell into a murderous battle for control of the city. Kabul's residents slid into a nightmare.

Ahmad Shah Massoud's Tajiks nominally controlled the presidency and most of Kabul, but they were immediately attacked by the forces of Gulbuddin Hekmatyar, whose preferred military tactic was the mass shelling of the city. Also jostling for power were General Dostum's Uzbeks and the Hazara militias. At different times, all fought with or against each other, but the effects of these ever-changing allegiances held little meaning for Kabul's suffering population.

The factional fighting devastated Kabul, which was divided into a patchwork of competing fiefdoms. The west and south of the city were flattened under continuous bombardment, and countless atrocities were committed against civilians. Around 50,000 Kabulis lost their lives between 1992 and 1996, and a flood of refugees left the city.

The puritan Taliban might have been welcomed as a group that could return the rule of law, but they quickly disposed of this notion. Their first action on capturing Kabul in September 1996 was the public lynching of the former communist president Najibullah. The illiterate Taliban held a strong distrust of Kabul and its educated Persian-speaking population, and ruled the city with a harsh fist.

The Taliban's Vice and Virtue Police quickly squeezed the life out of Kabul, beating women for wearing high heels under their burqas, and imprisoning men whose beards were too short. Mullah Omar only visited Kabul once, and Afghanistan's capital effectively returned to Kandahar.

Under American bombardment, the Taliban fled Kabul in November 2001 and the Northern Alliance walked back in to power. Another army followed, this time of aid workers, contractors and returning refugees. Reconstruction continues, but it's a slow and often very frustrating process.

CLIMATE

Kabul's mountain location gives it a generally pleasant climate. Babur thought so too, noting that 'within a day's ride from Kabul it is possible to reach a place where snow never falls, but within two hours one can go where the snow never melts.' Summer temperatures reach a maximum of around 33°C in August, although the high altitude means that nights are cold enough to war-

THE KABUL BUBBLE

Since the fall of the Taliban, Kabul has seen a huge influx of aid money, foreign experts and returning Afghan exiles and refugees. Promises of reconstruction were made and expectations from a battered population were high. Compared to the rest of the country, Kabul was in a bubble of international attention with a booming economy. And yet in May 2006, a traffic accident involving the US army precipitated mass riots across the city, with anger vented at the international community and government alike. What went wrong?

In one respect, the expectations of Kabulis were too high. Kabul's infrastructure was not only shattered by war, but was originally designed for a much smaller city. Many refugees chose to return to the capital to seek work, rather than their home province, placing a massive burden on the city.

At the same time, many international organisations have proved ineffective at delivering services, either duplicating each other's work or inadequately consulting with locals on implementing projects. Of the scores of organisations that flooded into Kabul in 2002, many had little Afghan experience, and spent a lot of money on start-up costs or just reinventing the wheel. Landlords were quick to capitalise by hiking up their rents – a house in Wazir Akbar Khan costing US$200 a month in September 2001 was US$3000 six months later. With the white Landcruisers favoured by many NGOs such a visible symbol of the international presence, they have made an easy target for mullahs and politicians. The MP and former planning minister Bashar Dost created shockwaves when he called for the majority of international NGOs to be closed down, with many others agreeing with the Afghan proverb that derided them as 'cows that drink their own milk'.

The expat lifestyle has also been the target of popular ire. The free availability of alcohol to foreigners and the many Chinese restaurants that had opened purely as fronts for brothels were

rant wearing an extra layer and a blanket on your bed. Temperatures drop to just below freezing between December and February, when there can be heavy snow. Heavy rain and snowmelt can cause problems for Kabul's creaking infrastructure, and thick dust turns quickly to mud.

One drawback to Kabul's mountain-fringed location is that dust and pollution is easily trapped in the atmosphere, reducing the air quality considerably.

ORIENTATION

Kabul sits in a plain ringed by the mountains of the Hindu Kush at an elevation of 1800m.

Little remains of Kabul's old city. The mountains of Koh-e Shir Darwaza run south along the city, topped by the old city walls, and leading in the east to the royal citadel of Bala Hissar. The mountains of Koh-e Asmai (popularly known as TV Mountain) and Koh-e Aliabad loom in from the north, pinching Kabul in two.

The Kabul River flows between this gap in the mountains, and further divides the city. To the north is Shahr-e Nau (New City), centred on its eponymous park and Pashtunistan Sq (Charahi Pashtunistan). Near the edge of the park are the new glass landmark

---

KABUL'S STREET NAMES

Many Kabulis don't know the names of streets, and many addresses are given only relative to a major road or landmark. Formal street-naming plans have been mooted, but have been mired in controversy – many Kabulis have found the renaming of Great Massoud Rd in particular poor taste, given the destruction of Kabul by the mujaheddin.

Charahi (crossroads) are commonly used as landmarks, so it's useful to know the names of the major junctions when asking directions or catching a taxi.

---

buildings of the (blue) Kabul Business Centre and the (green) Kabul City Centre. East of this is the prosperous Wazir Akbar Khan district, home to many embassies.

The bustle of the city increases the closer you get to the river. Kabul's commercial heart beats at Mandayi Market around Pul-e Khishti Bridge, and Jad-e Maiwand, the most traditional areas of the city. Swathes of Jad-e Maiwand were flattened during the civil war, making it a popular subject for photojournalists. Unlike much of Kabul, it remains largely untouched by the recent pell-mell development.

---

among the first subjects of attention from the new Afghan parliament. Western journalists have hardly been able to resist either, finding easy stories amid the 'party scene' that has flourished as a response to tight security measures and six-day working weeks.

Popular frustration is also vented at those in power, with the government regularly derided as self-serving and corrupt. Several large-scale land-grabs took place following the formation of the interim government, with powerful ex-mujaheddin figures and others close to Hamid Karzai implicated in lining their pockets by illegally evicting residents. The construction boom, with myriad 'poppy palaces' sprouting across the city, has further highlighted the creation of an Afghan elite separate from the mass of Kabulis, who have seen few of the benefits of the economic boom. As their name suggests, many of these luxurious villas are the products of another sort of ill-gotten gain.

Kabul's exploding economy has been driven by the dollar, having an inflationary effect on the price of basic commodities. One side-effect of the influx of NGOs has been to draw qualified Afghans away from the public sector. A teacher earning US$40 a month could earn seven times that as a translator for an international organisation, weakening Afghan institutions. Not enough has been done to bolster the state, either by foreign donors refusing to disburse monies to the Afghan government in favour of funding NGOs, or by allowing NGOs to direct policy or become providers of services in place of the state. Capacity building still has some way to go.

Progress is being made, and there are many NGOs doing valuable work, and fostering strong ties to the communities they work in. But as the riots of 2006 demonstrated, wider discontent could cause the bubble to burst yet.

Also levelled in war was the model district of Darulaman in west Kabul, home of the former palace and the Kabul Museum.

Kabul International Airport lies northeast of the city at the end of Great Massoud (formerly Airport) Rd, near the Socialist-era apartment blocks of Microrayon.

Maps

Shops and street kids in the Chicken St area sell large maps of Kabul but these are copies of 1970s maps and very out of date.

Afir (Map p85; House 2, Street 3, Sarakh-e Taimani, Qala-e Fatullah; ☽ 3-8pm) Has a popular and useful Kabul map aimed primarily at expats.

AIMS (Map p85; ☎ 070 248827; www.aims.org.af; Salang Wat) Sells detailed city and country maps produced mainly for government and NGOs. Order in advance.

INFORMATION
Bookshops

In addition to the shops below, Zardozi (p102) has a large book-swap facility.

Habibi Bookstore (Map p85; Chicken St) Another well-stocked bookshop, also sells some international magazines.

Shah M Books (Map p85; Charahi Sadarat) Comprehensively stocked with Afghan-related titles – if they don't have it, it probably wasn't published. Wide range of postcards (with stamps). A mobile shop (Books & Rivers) was being launched as we went to press.

Cultural Centres

British Council (☎ 079 9000 101; www.britishcouncil .org/afghanistan.htm; House No 15-17 behind Nadirya High School, Kart-e-Parwan) Visiting Arts programme provides links between Afghan and UK artists; occasional events.

Centre Culturel Français (Map p93; ☎ 079 9304 351; www.ambafrance-af.org; Charahi Malik Asghar, next to Lycée Estiqlal) Occasional film showing and music concerts.

Goethe-Institut Kabul (Map p85; ☎ 070 274606; www.goethe.de/kabul; Shah Mahmoud Wat, Wazir Akbar Khan) Film showings most Saturdays.

Emergency

Afghan NGO Security Office (ANSO; ☎ 070 283320/ 079 9322 133; coordinator@afgnso.org)

Ambulance (☎ 020 112/079 9357 049)

ISAF (☎ 079 9512 904)

Kabul City Police (☎ 020 100/079 9046 714)

Kabul Fire Brigade (☎ 020 210 1333)

Internet Access

Internet places open and close with reckless abandon. Broadband is the standard, with fees around 40Afg to 70Afg per hour.

AM Internet Club (Map p85; Flower St)

Bakhtary Net Cafe (Map p85; Chicken St) In courtyard off main street.

New Haider Internet (Map p85; Charahi Haji Yaqub)

Park Net Cafe (Map p93; Mohammed Jan Khan Wat)

Internet Resources

Survival Guide to Kabul (www.kabulguide.net) Has a very useful bulletin board for news among the expat community.

What's On in Kabul (kabul.news@caritas.org) Weekly newsletter with news and listings.

Media
NEWSPAPERS & MAGAZINES

Kabul has a selection of English-language newspapers. The *Afghanistan Times*, *Kabul Times*, *Kabul Daily* and *Kabul Weekly* are the pick, all featuring a mix of local journalism and syndicated international news. Also look out for the military *ISAF News*, in English, Dari and Pashto.

Afghan Scene (www.afghanscene.com) Free glossy monthly magazine aimed at the international community, distributed widely across Kabul.

New Kabul/Les Nouvelles de Kaboul (www.ainaworld .org) A new magazine in English and French produced by media NGO Aina, launched as we were going to press.

RADIO

These radio stations broadcast on FM in Kabul (remember that news bulletins are on the half hour):

Arman FM (98.1FM) Afghan popular music.

BBC World Service (89.0FM)

Deutsche Weille (90.5FM) In English and German.

Kabul Armed Forces Network/National Public Radio (107.3FM) US radio.

Radio France Internationale (89.5FM) In English and French.

Medical Services

There are plenty of pharmacies in Kabul, but check drugs for expiry dates. Embassies can provide lists of recommended medical services, but the following hospitals are run to international standards:

Blossom Group Hospital (Map p85; ☎ 070 298397; www.blossom-group.org; Hanzala Mosque Rd, Shahr-e Nau; ☽ 24hr) Private Indian-run hospital with walk in general practice clinic and emergency treatment.

Cure International Hospital (Map p80; ☎ 079 9883 830; near Darulaman Palace, Jad-e Darulaman; ☽ 8am-3pm Sat-Wed, 8am-12pm Thu, closed Fri) General practice and surgery.

CENTRAL KABUL

0 — 0.5 miles
0 — 1 km

INFORMATION
Afghanistan International
Bank..................................1 E3
AIMS...................................2 C3
AM Internet Club...................3 D3
Anaar Travel........................4 C3
Bakhtary Net Cafe.................5 D3
Belgian Embassy....................6 E2
Blossom Group Hospital..........7 C2
Canadian Embassy..................8 E3
DHL.....................................9 D3
DK German Medical
Diagnostic Centre.............10 C3
Dunya Travels......................11 D3
Dutch Embassy.....................12 D3
Emergency Hospital...............13 D3
French Embassy.....................14 E3
German Embassy...................15 E3
Goethe Institut.....................16 D4
Habibi Bookstore..................17 D3
Indian Embassy.....................18 C3
Interior Central Passport
Department.....................19 C4
Iranian Embassy....................20 D3
Italian Embassy.....................21 E4
Japanese Embassy..................22 D3
Kabul Bank...........................23 D3
Moneychangers Offices........24 (see 28)
Net Café..............................(see 28)
New Haider Internet..............25 D2
Norwegian Embassy..............26 E2
Pakistani Embassy..................27 E3
Park Netcafe........................28 C3
Post Office............................29 D4
Shah M Books.......................30 D4
Sky Travel & Tours................31 E2
Standard Chartered Bank.......32 E2
Swedish Embassy...................33 E2
Swiss Embassy......................34 E2
Tajikistani Embassy................35 E3
TNT.....................................36 D4
Travel World........................37 C3
Turkish Embassy....................38 E3
Turkmenistani Embassy..........39 E2
UK Embassy..........................40 E3
US Embassy..........................41 F3
Uzbekistani Embassy.............42 E2

SIGHTS & ACTIVITIES
European Cemetery................43 D2
National Archives..................44 D4

SLEEPING
Assa 1..................................45 D3
Assa 2..................................46 D2
Assa 3..................................47 D3
B's Place...............................48 D1
Euro Guest House.................49 E2
Gandamack Lodge................50 D3
Golden Star Hotel.................51 D3
Heetal Heritage Hotel............52 E2
Insaf Hotel...........................(see 80)
Kabul Inn.............................53 C4
Kabul Lodge.........................54 C4
Le Monde Guest House.........55 C3
Maple Leaf Inn......................56 C3
Marco Polo Inn.....................57 C1
Mustafa Hotel......................58 D4
Naween Guest House............59 D2
Park Palace..........................60 C3
Rose Garden & Carwan..........61 D4
Sarai Hotel...........................(see 0)
Safi Landmark Hotel..............62 D3
Salsal Guest House................63 D3
Shahr-e Nau Guest House.......64 D3
Star Inn...............................(see 0)

EATING
Anaar...................................65 E2
Baku....................................66 E2
Carlitos................................(see 52)
Chelsea Supermarket.............67 D3
Chief Burger.........................68 D3
Delhi Darbar.........................69 D3
Everest Pizza.........................70 E2
Flower Street Café.................71 C1
French Bakery.......................72 D3
Golden Key Seafood..............73 E2
Herat...................................74 D3
Jaisalmer.............................75 D1
Khosha................................(see 51)
Kulba Afghan........................76 D2
La Cantina............................77 D2
Lai Thai................................78 E2
Le Bistro..............................79 D3
Popolano.............................80 C3
Samarqand...........................81 D2
Shamiana.............................(see 0)
Shandiz...............................82 E3
Street Food stalls/Juice
sellers..............................83 D3
Sufi 2...................................84 D2
Taverna du Liban...................85 E2
Vila Velebita.........................86 F2

DRINKING
Cabul Coffee House...............87 C1
Deutscher Hof......................88 D1
Hare & Hounds.....................(see 50)
L'Atmosphere.......................89 C1
Mustafa Hotel......................(see 58)

SHOPPING
Afghan Gallery......................90 C2
Afghan Handicrafts
Centre..............................(see 4)
Nomad Carpet Gallery...........91 C3
Tarsian & Blinkley..................92 D2
Zarif & Royah.......................93 D2

TRANSPORT
Air Arabia............................(see 11)
Ariana Afghan Airlines............94 E3
Azerbaijan Airlines.................95 C3
Indian Airlines.......................(see 4)
Iran Asseman Airlines.............96 F2
Kam Air...............................(see 0)
PIA.....................................97 E3

See Kabul River & Zumagar Park Map (p93)

KABUL

KABUL'S STREET CHILDREN

The UN estimates that around 60,000 school-age children work on the streets of Kabul. Contrary to popular belief, most of these children aren't orphans, they're just desperately poor. You'll see street children everywhere, cleaning shoes, collecting rubbish or burning *spandi* (a sort of aromatic herb) in tin cans and waving the smoke over people for good luck and a few afghanis. A good wage is 50Afg to 100Afg a day.

Many children have to support parents who are impoverished, disabled or widowed. Although the Afghan constitution makes primary education compulsory, economic necessity forces these children away from school. Many schools charge fees that are out of reach of the poorest Afghans, and while school registration has increased five-fold since the fall of the Taliban, around seven million children don't attend classes, over half the children in the country.

One highly regarded charity working with street children is **Aschiana** (www.aschiana.com). Meaning 'nest' in Dari, Aschiana recognises the problem of children being forced to work out of need, and provides basic literacy and numeracy education to the poorest children. Many children attend classes in the morning and receive a meal at lunch before going to work in the afternoon. Older children also receive vocational training once they can read and write. Based primarily in Kabul, Aschiana has recently started to expand to Herat and Mazar-e Sharif, as well as setting up outreach camps for returning refugees. It's an uphill struggle, but several hundred children a month are integrated into the education system through their work: one for every five kids working Kabul's streets.

DK German Medical Diagnostic Centre (Map p85; ☎ 079 9136 211; www.medical-kabul.com; Street 3, Charahi Ansari; treatment requires deposit of US$100/5000Afg against cost of treatment; ☯ 9am-5pm, closed Fri) Offers wide range of laboratory diagnostic tests, vaccinations and X-rays. Dental and gynaecological services were being introduced as we went to press.

Emergency Hospital (Map p85; ☎ 070 287519; Charahi Sherpur; ☯ 24 hr) Emergency surgical centre only.

Money

For exchange, ask at your hotel or guesthouse; banks aren't much help. Moneychangers are found at Charahi Torabaz Khan or in the market around Pul-e Khishti Mosque. Look for the small stands with piles of money. There are also some moneychangers around the taxi stands of Serai Shomali motor park.

Afghanistan International Bank (Map p85; behind Amani High School, Wazir Akbar Khan; ☯ 9am-5pm Sun-Thu, 9am-1pm Sat) ATM. Also has 24-hour ATMs at Kabul Airport, Intercontinental Hotel, Kabul City Centre, Chelsea Supermarket and Supreme PX. Issues dollars and afghanis.

Kabul Bank (Map p85; Jad-e Torabaz Khan) Also has a branch of Western Union.

Standard Chartered Bank (Map p85; Street 10, Wazir Akbar Khan; ☯ 9am-6pm) Issues dollars and afghanis.

Post

Central Post Office (Map p93; Deh Afghanan)
Post Office (Map p85; Interior Ministry Rd)

INTERNATIONAL COURIERS

DHL (Map p85; ☎ 070 276362/079 9750 750; Charahi Sherpur; ☯ 9am-6pm Sat-Thu)

Federal Express (Map p80; ☎ 020 2500525; Sarakh-e Khai, Karte Se; ☯ 8am-5pm Sat-Thu)

TNT (Map p85; ☎ 020 2200266; Charahi Torabaz Khan; ☯ 8am-5pm Sat-Thu)

Telephone

Kabul's phones are in a state of confusion (see p209). In addition to the new mobile phone networks, Kabul had some digital fixed lines installed in 2000 with seven-digit numbers, and a decrepit five-digit analogue network. Both can usually only call other local numbers.

It's possible to place calls at any of Kabul's post offices, but it's easier to go to any of the phone stands found on any street.

Tourist Information

Afghan Tourist Organisation Head office (Map p80; ☎ 020 2300 338; atokabul@yahoo.com; Great Massoud Rd); Asmai Wat (Map p93; ☎ 079 9304 516) The head office is the place to go for letters to extend visas. The Asmai Wat branch can organise drivers and translators. There are two largely ineffective sub-offices at the airport and Intercontinental Hotel.

TOURS

Two private tour operators run good quality city tours of Kabul, taking in the major sights, and can also arrange trips to Istalif, the Panjshir Valley and the like:

Afghan Logistics & Tours (☎ 070 277408/079 9391 462; www.afghanlogisticstours.com; full-day Kabul tour US$80)

Great Game Travel (☎ 079 9489 120/077 9489 120; www.greatgametravel.com; full-day Kabul tour US$80, US$60 per person if four people)

Travel Agencies
The following agents are reliable providers of international air tickets. Plenty more agents are clustered around Charahi Ansari.

Anaar Travel (Map p85; ☎ 079 9308 303; www.anaar travels.com; opposite Indian Embassy, Interior Ministry Rd) General sales agent for Indian Airlines.

Dunya Travels (Map p85; ☎ 079 9386 921/070 238700; www.dunyatravels.com; Charahi Ansari)

Sky Travel & Tours (Map p85; ☎ 020 210 4410/079 9484 848; www.skytravel.com; Street 15, Wazir Akbar Khan)

Travel World (Map p85; ☎ 020 2203453; Charahi Ansari)

DANGERS & ANNOYANCES
Security in Kabul is now handled primarily by the Afghan police and army – the ISAF military patrols that were such a common sight until recently have largely taken a back seat. Although the situation can change incredibly quickly, Kabul is generally a calm city, with the greatest risk to personal safety being the insane traffic.

It's essential to keep in touch with the news, and to talk to locals and other foreigners to gauge the popular mood, as well as getting security briefings where possible. That said, the riots that shook Kabul in 2006 took almost everyone by surprise. At such times, visibly Western buildings or interests can be targets.

There have been several incidents of street crime against foreigners, mainly bag-snatching. A vehicular version of this has been the 'broken car' ruse – your vehicle is flagged down by a local claiming his car has broken and needs assistance. When your attention is drawn, his accomplices rob your vehicle. We recommend keeping all doors locked when driving in Kabul.

We don't recommend walking in Kabul after dark. Aside from the crime risk, there are very few streetlights, so broken pavements present a genuine accident risk. Many international organisations maintain curfews for their staff.

There have been kidnapping attempts (successful and unsuccessful) against foreigners by criminal gangs. For more on kidnapping, and other security concerns, see the Safety in Afghanistan chapter, p68.

One environmental hazard you'll quickly become aware of is the terrible quality of Kabul's air, thick with pollution from the traffic, thousands of generators and the endless dust. Anyone staying in the city for any length of time is liable to pick up the 'Kabul cough' – seeking fresh air outside the city is the best remedy. In winter and spring, the dust can quickly turn streets into mud slicks.

SIGHTS
Babur's Gardens
Laid out by the Mughal ruler Babur in the early 16th century, and the site of his tomb, these **gardens** (Bagh-e Babur; Map p80; admission 100Afg; ☺ 7am-sunset) are the loveliest spot in Kabul. At 11 hectares, they are also the largest public green space in the city. Left to ruins during the war, they have been spectacularly restored by the Aga Khan Trust for Culture (AKTC).

The garden was laid out in the classical *charbagh* (four garden) pattern, with a series of quartered rising terraces split by a central watercourse. The garden was used as a pleasure spot by repeated Mughal rulers, but fell into disrepair after the dynasty lost control of Kabul. Abdur Rahman Khan restored much of the grounds at the turn of the 20th century. Public access was allowed in the 1930s, but the gardens were despoiled and many trees cut for firewood in the anarchy that swept through Kabul during the civil war.

The garden is surrounded by high walls, rebuilt by the local community. Visitors are greeted by a large traditional caravanserai which is planned to open as a visitors centre, showing many of the finds excavated in the archaeological dig that preceded the restoration. Although modern, it stands on the footprint of an older building of the same plan built as a refuge for the poor in the 1640s. From the caravanserai the eye is immediately swept up the terraces, following the line of the white marble watercourse. On either side the grounds are deeply planted with herbaceous beds and saplings. Many species chosen for replanting are specifically mentioned in the *Baburnama*, including walnut, cherry, quince, mulberry and apricot trees. In the centre of the garden is a pavilion built by Abdur Rahman Khan, with a series of information boards on the restoration programme.

Above this there's a delicate white marble mosque built in 1647 by Shah Jahan, who commissioned the Taj Mahal. While on a much smaller scale, the similarities in style are evident in the clean carving of the stone.

Overlooking the whole of the garden from the top terrace is Babur's tomb, inside a simple enclosure. Babur wished to be buried under the open sky so his grave is uncovered, surrounded by a simple marble screen. The headstone says it was erected for 'the light-garden of the God-forgiven angel king whose rest is in the garden of Heaven'. Given the near-miraculous resurrection of the grounds, it's an easy poetic sentiment to agree with.

Kabul Museum

The **Kabul Museum** (Map p80; Darulaman; admission 20Afg, camera 100Afg; 8am-3.30pm) was once one of the greatest museums in the world. Its exhibits, ranging from Hellenistic gold coins to Buddhist statuary and Islamic bronzes, testified to Afghanistan's location at the crossroads of Asia. After years of abuse during the civil war, help from the international community and the peerless dedication of its staff means the museum is slowly rising from the ashes.

The museum opened in 1919, and was almost entirely stocked with items excavated in Afghanistan. As the fall of communist Kabul became apparent with the Soviet withdrawal, many of the most valuable pieces were moved into secure storage, but the majority of exhibits remained in situ. Unfortunately the museum quickly found itself on the frontline of the mujaheddin's terrible fight for Kabul. Between 1992 and '94 the museum was used as a mujaheddin base. During this period the museum was massively looted – not just ransacked – but with care taken to select the most valuable pieces for resale on the illicit antique market (the museum's library and inventory was also lost at this time, to hamper efforts to trace the provenance of stolen goods). Among the priceless treasures lost include many of the Bagram Ivories (see p109), the Kunduz Hoard of Graeco-Bactrian coins (see boxed text p163) and unique Gandharan statues of Buddha. During this looting, the museum was further damaged by a rocket attack that destroyed its upper floor. When the Rabbani government regained control of the area, soldiers posted to guard the site continued ad hoc looting of their own.

On capturing Kabul in 1996 the Taliban vowed to protect what remained, but it was a short-lived promise. In March 2001, as the giant Buddhas at Bamiyan were being levelled, soldiers entered the museum with hammers and smashed what statues and other image-bearing exhibits they could

---

BABUR, THE FIRST MUGHAL

Born in 1483 to the ruler of the Ferghana Valley in modern Uzbekistan, Zahiruddin Babur inherited his father's kingdom before he was even a teenager. His early career was less than brilliant. By the age of 20 the young king (a descendant of Timur on his father's side and Genghis Khan on his mother's side) had repeatedly captured and lost his beloved Samarkand, only to be driven out of the Ferghana by Uzbek warlords.

This misfortune sent him to Afghanistan, where he took Kabul in 1504. Here he prospered, visiting Herat during its last days of Timurid rule, capturing Kandahar and campaigning in the Hazarajat. Afghanistan also became the springboard for his ultimate conquest of India, where he founded the Mughal dynasty ('Mughal' being a corruption of 'Mongol' – local parlance for anyone from Central Asia).

But Babur wasn't just an empire builder. He recorded his memoirs in the *Baburnama*, Islamic literature's first autobiography, relating everything from his military campaigns to the after effects of his drinking parties and the choosing of plants for his formal gardens. Babur's intimate character sketches of generals and poets bring his court to life in rich detail, and reveal a great love for Afghanistan and a distaste for the climate of his new Indian empire. Babur died in 1530.

THE BACTRIAN GOLD

In 1978 a hoard of Kushan gold was excavated by Soviet archaeologists near Shiberghan. Dubbed the 'Bactrian Gold', it was a trove to rival Tutankhamen's tomb in Egypt, but decades of war have kept it hidden from the world.

The find had barely been catalogued by the time the Russian tanks rolled in, and the treasure was never publicly displayed. Over the years, stories grew up around it – it had been spirited to Moscow, looted by the mujaheddin, sold by the Taliban or just plain lost. In 2004 the Afghan government revealed its location to the world, safely stored in the national bank vaults, using power tools to open the safes as the keys had long disappeared.

The gold revealed inside was astounding. A crown made of thousands of leaves of yellow metal, curly-haired cupids riding dolphins, clasps showing Persian gods, and a sensual brooch of the Greek goddess Aphrodite with Bactrian wings and an Indian face. All rich evidence of the cultural melting pot of 1st century Afghanistan.

The Bactrian Gold has yet to be exhibited in Kabul as security still isn't good enough to put it on public display. But at the end of 2006 it formed the centrepiece of a special exhibition at the Musée Guimet in Paris, appropriately titled 'Afghanistan: Rediscovered Treasures'. Several of the remaining Bagram Ivories also featured in the exhibition, alongside Kushan glass goblets and material from Ai Khanoum. It's hoped that before too long the Afghan people will be able to enjoy their heritage in Kabul for themselves.

find. The oxymoronically-titled Minister for Culture led the destruction.

That a museum still stands is little short of a marvel. Less than a third of the collection survives, but there's a surprising amount on display. In the entrance hall is a 15th-century black marble basin from Kandahar, known colloquially as the Buddha's Begging Bowl because of the carved lotus at its base. To the left is a large Greek inscription from Ai Khanoum and to the right is the Rabatak Tablet found near Pul-e Khumri in 1993, covered with yet-to-be deciphered Bactrian script.

Further on, a pair of glass cases display Graeco-Bactrian Buddha statues from the 3rd and 4th centuries AD in limestone and schist, the few to escape the Taliban's rage. Other treasures downstairs include a lovely carved marble door from Kabul, and a reconstructed stucco section of a 12th-century mosque from Lashkar Gah. Exhibits are interspersed with photos of looted items and the half-demolished museum.

The highlight of the museum is the Nuristani gallery upstairs. It is filled with huge wooden deities and ancestor figures, carved before the 1890s when the region was still pagan. Goddesses ride mountain goats, warriors sit astride horses and loving couples are carved on posts for the marital bed. As works of art they're radically different to anything from elsewhere in Afghanistan; the flat mask-like faces seem more Central African than Central Asian. The statues were chopped up by the Taliban, but have been magnificently restored.

Security is tight at the museum, with bag checks as you exit as well as on entering. While you wait, take a moment to read the plaque outside the front door: 'a nation stays alive when its culture stays alive'.

The old **royal palace of Darulaman** sits opposite the Kabul Museum. Built by Amanullah in the 1920s, in grand European style, the palace is now little more than an empty shell. Don't explore the palace too closely as there are still unexploded ordnances (UXOs) in the area. Between the two look out for the rusting steam train, more evidence of Amanullah's ill-fated experiment in modernity – only a few miles of track were ever laid.

European Cemetery

This **cemetery** (Map p85; Kabre Ghora, Shahabuddin Wat; admission by donation; ☒ 8am-4pm) was built in 1879 by the British army for the dead of the Second Anglo-Afghan War.

The cemetery contains around 150 graves. Most are from members of Kabul's international community from before the war. Only a few of the original British Army headstones remain, now mounted in the south wall. They have been joined by newer memorial stones added by the British, Canadian, German and Italian ISAF contingents.

The cemetery's most famous resident is Aurel Stein, the acclaimed Silk Road archaeologist of the early 20th century. Stein spent much of his career obsessed by Alexander's campaigns in the east, but his British citizenship meant that the Afghan authorities always refused him permission to dig in the country. In 1943 he got the go-ahead at the age of 82, only to catch the flu and die a few days after arriving in Kabul. His grave is marked with a large cross and frequently a wreath. More recently, the cemetery saw the burial of the French aid worker Bettina Goislard, murdered in Ghazni in 2003.

The cemetery has been maintained since the 1980s by Rahimullah, supported by a small stipend from the British Embassy. His story of meeting a disapproving Mullah Omar (the Taliban had a guesthouse next door) is worth the hearing, and always popular with journalists.

Ka Faroshi Bird Market

Entering Kabul's **bird market** (Map p93; Kucha-ye Ka Faroshi; ☿ Sat-Thu) is like stepping back in time a hundred years, to a corner of the city untouched by war or modernisation. Also known as the Alley of Straw Sellers, it's a narrow lane tucked away behind the Pul-e Khishti Mosque, lined with stalls and booths selling birds by the dozen, plus the occasional rabbit.

King of all the birds on sale is the *kowk* (fighting partridge). These are prized by their owners who lavish great care on them, and keep them in domed wicker cages that are almost works of art in themselves. *Kowk* are fought on Friday mornings in quick bouts of strength (the birds are too valuable to allow them to be seriously harmed), with spectators gambling on the result. Their highly territorial nature also lets them act as decoys for hunters, attracting potential rivals who end up in the pot.

Similar to the *kowk* is the *budana*, a small lark-like bird. These are also fought, especially among Kandaharis. Unbelievably, their small size means that their owner frequently keeps them tucked in his trousers, bringing them out for contest and display. More benign are the myriad canaries and finches, kept simply for their song.

At the far end of the bazaar are the *kaftar* (doves), a common sight in Kabul's late afternoon skies (see boxed text below) .

Bala Hissar & the City Walls

The old seat of royal power, a fortress has stood on the site of the Bala Hissar since the 5th century AD, and quite possibly before. It sits at the foot of the Koh-e Shir Darwaza mountains, guarding the southwestern approaches to Kabul.

The **citadel** (Map p80) as it stands today was built at the end of the 19th century. The previous fortress was destroyed by the vengeful British army at the end of the Second Anglo-Afghan War. Now, as then, it is used by the army and closed to visitors. However, the old city walls snake out from its towers along the mountain ridges and make a fantastic walk, raising you high above the dirty air of the city to give some breathtaking views of the capital.

The starting point is at the foot of the huge cemetery of Shohada-ye Salehin. Most approaches will take you past Jad-e Maiwand and the ruined Shor Bazaar, a traditional centre for Kabul's musicians, and the place where 'Bukhara' Burnes was killed by the mob in 1841. The road brings you along the southern foot of Bala Hissar, with good views up to its ramparts. Start the walk around 1km after the citadel.

DOVE CHARMING

Flying doves is almost as much a national sport as *buzkashi*. It even has its trademark bird, the white-bodied and grey-winged *amiree*. Owners keep their flocks in rooftop cages and fly them every night. It looks like a peaceful pastime but is actually fiercely competitive. As a flock circles in the sky, a rival flock may be released by another owner to fly amongst it. Battle joined, the new flock attempts to charm birds away from its companions, and to return with them to its new owner, who scoops them up with a net. The owner, or *kaftar baz*, uses whistles, calls and food to manoeuvre his birds to carry out the deception. If a friend's dove is captured, it can be requested back by an appropriate show of contrition. Otherwise, the new owner adds it to his flock or sells it in the bazaar. The best quality doves can sell for up to 2500Afg in the Ka Faroshi market.

There are two routes leading up the slopes to the mountain's ridge. A longer path on a gentler gradient takes you to an obvious pass between two peaks. To the left was territory held by Hekmatyar during the civil war, with Massoud's men to the right. A better alternative is to keep to the right and head steeply uphill straight away. A 40-minute hike brings you to a high ridge from where you can look east to the Bala Hissar, and north to central Kabul – Shahr-e Nau Park, Jad-e Maiwand and the Pul-e Khishti Mosque are good monuments to take your bearings from. Boys quite often fly kites here. At this point you're already higher than Koh-e Asmai (TV Mountain) opposite.

Continue west along the ridge. Almost straight away you meet the old walls, several metres thick in places. Although the path is clear and well-beaten, it's possible to find plenty of spent ammunition here, so resist the temptation to nose around any of the foxholes near the walls. As you slowly ascend the ridge curves north, revealing splendid views of west Kabul and Darulaman.

After half an hour of walking you'll near the end of the ridge and a final view – this time straight down to Babur's Gardens and Kabul Zoo. With views to all sides, this is the best spot in Kabul for understanding the city's geography, especially the narrow strategic gap where Koh-e Shir Darwaza and Koh-e Asmai almost meet – known as the Shir Darwaza (Lion's Gate) – with the Kabul Valley stretching far in either direction. Also look out for the platform of the **Noon Gun**, and follow the path downhill towards it.

The Noon Gun is in fact two cannons dating from Abdur Rahman's reign. They were fired daily, and to mark the end of the Ramazan feast, but only the barrels now remain. From here, follow the paths through the local houses to emerge near Babur's Gardens.

The walk should take three or four hours in total. Take a sun hat and plenty of water. Although there aren't any red rocks designating mines, we'd still advise you to stick to the worn trail.

Kabul Zoo

The **zoo** (Map p80; Charahi Deh Mazang; admission 100Afg; ⏲ 8am-sunset) is a popular place for Kabulis in need of recreation. Western animal lovers might find it more than a little depressing.

Visitors are greeted by a bronze statue of Marjan the lion, the zoo's most celebrated animal. A present from West Germany in the 1960s, Marjan survived life on the front-line and a Taliban grenade attack, only to expire soon after Kabul's 2001 liberation. He has since been replaced by a pair of lions presented by China. A couple of sloth bears can be seen in a pit, pacing like asylum inmates. Some wolves do the same nearby, next to a cage of grumpy-looking black vultures. Only the colony of macaques look happy with their surroundings, with the young diving pell-mell into their moat (this could be an illusion though – one effected an escape during our visit, and was rounded up by visitors using the time-honoured method of throwing chairs at it).

The zoo sits on the Deh Mazang roundabout, in front of the newly rebuilt Traffic Police headquarters (until recently one of the most spectacularly smashed buildings in Kabul). The Minar-e Abdul Wakil Khan stands in the centre of the roundabout, erected for a Nuristani general who fought against Bacha Saqao's rebellion in 1929.

National Gallery

The **National Gallery** (Map p93; Asmai Wat; admission 250Afg; ⏲ 8am-4pm) contains a mix of historic pictures and paintings by modern Afghan artists. Like Kabul's other cultural institutions, it didn't escape the Taliban's zealous attentions, as the cabinet displaying ripped up watercolour portraits attests. Amazingly, however, the gallery's staff fought back as only artists could. Knowing the Taliban's juncture against images of living things, many of the exhibits were over-painted with watercolours, hiding a horse behind a tree, or turning a person into a mountain view. Over 120 paintings were saved from destruction in this way when the zealots came with their knives.

Some of the most poignant paintings are relatively recent, including a moving picture of Kabul in rubble by Dr M Yousef Asefi, with a ruined well and bloodied slippers picked out against the rubble. Upstairs, visitors are greeted first by a copy of the famous *Remnants of an Army* by the Victorian painter Lady Elizabeth Butler, showing the last survivor of the British retreat from Kabul limping into camp. There are some quite lovely watercolours of Kabul life in the next room, plus views of some of the key moments of Afghan history, including the crowning of Ahmad Shah Durrani, and the slaying of Genghis Khan's grandson at Shahr-e Zohak.

At the end of the upstairs gallery is a room dedicated to Afghan leaders. Medieval amirs sit next to mujaheddin leaders like Abdul Haq. The modernisers Amanullah (here looking like an unfortunate cross between Hitler and Hirohito) and Nadir Shah look across from the opposite wall. One particularly striking portrait hangs in the corridor just outside, a sister of King Zahir Shah's wife (date and artist unknown) in a red traditional dress, looking out at the view with such an arresting gaze it would have driven the Taliban to apoplexy.

Outside the gallery is a long display room showing modern pictures for sale. Many of them were painted by the gallery's staff, who also give good guided tours.

Sultani Museum

This private **museum** (Map p93; Asmai Wat; admission 200Afg; ⊗ 8am-4pm) in the same grounds as the National Gallery is something of a curiosity. It was set up in 2004 by Ahmad Shah Sultani, a gold trader and sometime antiques dealer, who spent much of the civil war in exile in London. Here he collected a large collection of Afghan antiquities, aiming to preserve them for the country. Much of his collection is of looted or smuggled items, but those recognisably from the Kabul Museum have been returned. His collection has yet to be properly catalogued, but is thought to contain over 3000 pieces. Sultani's ultimate plan is to donate his collection to the state.

The museum is heavily locked, and on issuing your ticket the *chowkidar* (caretaker) goes through the laborious process of disabling the security alarms. The first room is full of Islamic-era manuscripts and some beautiful Qurans in just about every conceivable calligraphic script.

The following rooms are a treasure-trove of Afghan history, with artefacts from all periods jostling for space on the crowded shelves. Wooden stamps for stuccowork in mosques sit next to a delicate and stunning gold coronet, possibly of Kushan origin. There's a large display of coins – Graeco-Bactrian, Kushan, Sodgian and even Roman. Opposite are rare examples of Ghaznavid and Ghorid pottery, nearly 1000 years old and Nuristani wood carvings.

Poor labelling lets the exhibition down, often leaving you wondering exactly what you're looking at, and thirsting for more information (the 'cookie mud' from which many finds seem to have been dug remains a mystery). It's frustrating, but an oddly appropriate metaphor for the troubled state of Afghanistan's heritage.

National Archive

Holding over 15,000 documents, the **National Archive** (Map p85; Salang Wat; admission free; ⊗ 8am-5pm Sat-Thu) is housed in a palace built at the end of the 19th century by Abdur Rahman Khan for his son.

Important documents are on display (although some are copies, with the original too valuable to show) including the treaty with the British Empire in 1919 that finally gave Afghanistan full independence. Accompanying this is a host of newspapers, period photos and old banknotes, although most labelling is in Dari. Older documents are present too, including a 14th-century letter written by Timur, and several Qurans dating from the Durrani period.

Although scholars will get the most out of a visit, the archive is still worth visiting for the building, with it's attractive painted ceiling and carved woodwork. It's a slightly incongruous sight among the metal workshops that line this section of Salang Wat.

Mausoleum of Nadir Shah

King Nadir Shah was assassinated in 1933 the time-honoured way that most Afghan leaders meet their fate. His monumental **tomb** (Map p80) sits overlooking east Kabul at Teppe Maranjan. It has suffered considerably in war.

The mausoleum is of imposing black marble, with monumental columns topped by a huge metal dome. Even if the facings weren't cracked and the dome punctured, the building gives the distinct impression that this was a man who'd rather have been feared than loved. The plinth in the centre of the mausoleum is symbolic; the royal graves are in a locked chamber beneath the building (look through the gate). The most recent addition is that of the wife of Zahir Shah, who died shortly before she could return from exile after the Taliban's fall.

Smashed steps lead downhill past more graves to the tomb of Sultan Mohammed Telai, Nadir Shah's great-great grandfather. Its arches are decorated in Italianate stucco, but the tomb itself is badly damaged and graffitied. The strategic location of the hill is readily apparent from here, and was much fought over in the 1990s.

Teppe Maranjan is thought to be the oldest continually inhabited part of Kabul, with excavations revealing coins and statuary from the Kushan period in the 4th century AD. One statue from this period, of Bodhisattva in meditation, is on display in the Kabul Museum (p88), clearly showing the fusion of Greek and Indian artistic traditions. Smashed by the Taliban, its restoration is a small triumph.

Kite-flying is a popular pursuit at Teppe Maranjan, which is the location for a large kite festival at Nauroz (see p95).

Mausoleum of Abdur Rahman Khan

The **tomb** (Map p93) of the 'Iron Amir' sits in Zarnegar Park. Originally a palace, the building has a bulbous red dome atop a whitewashed drum, and fussy decorative minarets. The park is surrounded by market traders but can be a good place to escape from the nearby bustle and traffic. The mausoleum itself is closed to visitors. On the opposite side of the park a huge new mosque was under construction when we visited, named for its private benefactor – confusingly called Haji Abdul Rahman (no relation to the amir).

OMAR Land Mine Museum

This is a **museum** (Map80; ☎ 079 9349; www.landmineclearance.org; bottom of Teppe Maranjan; admission by donation, camera fee US$5, video US$50; ⌚ Sun-Thu) that only a country like Afghanistan could host. Run by the Organisation for Mine clearance and Afghan Rehabilitation (OMAR), it acts as a training and education centre for land mine and UXO clearance.

The exhibit holds more than 60 types of mine that still litter the countryside, from small anti-personnel mines to those the size of dinner plates aimed at vehicles. There are mines made by almost any country you care to think of, except Afghanistan itself.

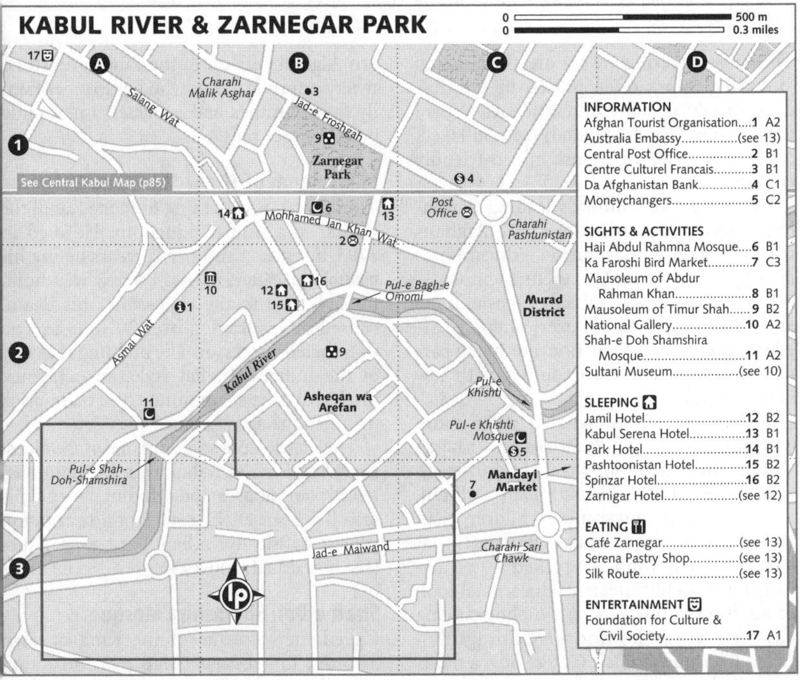
KABUL RIVER & ZARNEGAR PARK
0 500 m
0 0.3 miles
A
B
C
D
1
2
3
Charahi Malik Asghar
Salang Wat
Jad-e Froshgah
Zarnegar Park
See Central Kabul Map (p85)
Mohhamed Jan Khan Wat
Post Office
Charahi Pashtunistan
Pul-e Bagh-e Omomi
Murad District
Asmai Wat
Kabul River
Asheqan wa Arefan
Pul-e Khishti
Pul-e Khishti Mosque
Pul-e Shah-Doh-Shamshira
Mandayi Market
Jad-e Maiwand
Charahi Sari Chawk
INFORMATION
Afghan Tourist Organisation....1 A2
Australia Embassy................(see 13)
Central Post Office..................2 B1
Centre Culturel Francais...........3 B1
Da Afghanistan Bank...............4 C1
Moneychangers.......................5 C2
SIGHTS & ACTIVITIES
Haji Abdul Rahmna Mosque....6 B1
Ka Faroshi Bird Market............7 C3
Mausoleum of Abdur Rahman Khan......................8 B1
Mausoleum of Timur Shah......9 B2
National Gallery....................10 A2
Shah-e Doh Shamshira Mosque............................11 A2
Sultani Museum...................(see 10)
SLEEPING
Jamil Hotel...........................12 B2
Kabul Serena Hotel................13 B1
Park Hotel............................14 B1
Pashtoonistan Hotel...............15 B2
Spinzar Hotel........................16 B2
Zarnigar Hotel.....................(see 12)
EATING
Café Zarnegar......................(see 13)
Serena Pastry Shop..............(see 13)
Silk Route...........................(see 13)
ENTERTAINMENT
Foundation for Culture & Civil Society.......................17 A1

RESTORING OLD KABUL

Precious little remains of old Kabul. Even before the war, ill-conceived Soviet town planners had started to tear down whole areas in favour of shabby concrete developments. Following the bombs and rockets, demolition has continued as the value of land has soared, and new buildings (concrete with lots of glass and fake pillars this time) are thrown up on a daily basis. Two organisations have been working with local communities to try to preserve as much of the traditional fabric of Kabul as possible.

The **Turquoise Mountain Foundation** (www.turquoisemountain.org) is working in the Murad Khane district, the oldest settlement on the north bank of the Kabul river, and just a stone's throw from the Serena Hotel. An oasis of traditional architecture, it also highlights some of the key challenges in saving old Kabul. The oldest areas are often poorest, with houses lacking basic services and streets clogged with detritus. At the same time, the riverside has some of the highest commercial value areas in Kabul, with a huge attendant pressure from developers. The Murad Khane project works closely with the local community, who lobbied the government in support of it. One of the first tasks was simply the removal of rubbish – in some places just doing this lowered the street level by over 2m. Next, the Foundation has started working with landlords to adopt valued buildings to restore them, co-funding the venture. Turquoise Mountain has set up a school in the Karte Parwan district, with Afghan masters teaching traditional woodwork, plaster, tiling and masonry techniques.

South of the river, the **Aga Khan Trust for Culture** (www.akdn.org/agency/aktc.html) has been working in the Asheqan wa Arefan district around the Mausoleum of Timur Shah. By creating local employment, improving local water supplies and removing waste, the Trust has built a strong foundation for restoring the physical structure of the neighbourhood – from the delicate wooden latticework windows to rebuilding in mud-brick and plaster. Importantly, both projects demonstrate that restoration of old buildings can bring significant improvements to the quality of life of their residents, as well as raise awareness within the communities of the value of their heritage.

The most sobering by far are the Russian 'butterfly' mines often picked up by children mistaking them for plastic toys. Where most mines are deliberately camouflaged, these come in a range of bright, kid-friendly colours.

OMAR is the country's leading demining organisation, with over 500 Afghans working in mine-clearance. Education is an important second facet to their work. Murals and posters depicting types of mine and UXO can be found everywhere in Afghanistan – visual education aids being particularly important in a country with low literacy levels.

OMAR is also working in partnership with the UK charity **No Strings** (www.nostrings .org.uk), which uses puppet theatre to teach land mine safety information to children. Mines kill and injure more children than adults, and the use of story to illustrate what happens when a mine is picked up or disturbed is a highly effective educational tool. In addition to the theatre, a mobile cinema has been set up showing a No Strings film called *Chuche the Little Carpet Boy*, a mod-ern Afghan version of the Pinocchio story where a grandmother who has lost her family to land mines makes herself a new child out of carpet rags.

Mausoleum of Timur Shah

Timur Shah was the first to make Kabul the capital of a unified kingdom. He died in 1793, but it was another 23 years before his **mausoleum** (Map p93; Mandayi market) was built possibly due to the chaos after his death caused by his leaving over 20 sons and no nominated successor. The building is a copy of the Indian Mughal style, an octagonal brick structure surmounted by a plain brick drum and shallow dome.

The mausoleum stands in one of the oldest surviving parts of Kabul, with its traditional street plan, houses and winding lanes. This area has been at the centre of a restoration project by the Aga Khan Trust for Culture (see boxed text, above).

Shah-e Doh Shamshira Mosque

Called the 'Mosque of the King of Two Swords', this **mosque** (Map p93) on Kabul

River must be one of the most unusual in Islam. Built in the 1920s during Amanullah's drive for modernisation, it looks like it would be more at home in Versailles or Vienna. The facades are all Italianate baroque with stucco detailing, picked out in white against a lurid lemon yellow paint-job. That it has two storeys is even more peculiar, and only the tiny minarets disclose the building's true purpose.

The mosque's name is derived from a far older story than Amanullah's strange architectural tastes. In the 7th century Kabul was a Hindu city, besieged by an Arab army. The Arab king was beheaded, but was so inspired by Allah that he continued fighting, leading his men to victory at the point of his two scimitars.

The mosque underwent large-scale restoration in 2002, and is a major focus for Kabul's Ashura commemorations. The attractive two-storey riverfront buildings stretching away from the mosque are unique in Kabul, and in urgent need of restoration.

Bibi Mahru Hill

Also called Teppe Bemaru, this low **hill** (Map p85) overlooks Wazir Akbar Khan. It's popular with some expats living in the district for walking, and has reasonable views. At the top there's an Olympic-size swimming pool built by the Russians that's barely been full since it was built due to the difficulties of pumping water uphill. During the war the diving board was notorious as an execution spot.

The pool sits on the spot where Babur got his first views of Kabul. Nearly 350 years later, it was the site of an important turning point in the First Anglo-Afghan War. An ill-led British force was soundly defeated in battle here, a rout that paved the way for the disastrous retreat from Kabul.

FESTIVALS & EVENTS

Security can be very tight in Kabul on public holidays and anniversaries such as Massoud Day (9 September). Despite official exhortations, Victory Day (28 April) is a low-key affair, as it celebrates the mujaheddin capture of Kabul in 1992. Many Kabulis prefer to mark this as the start of the slide into the anarchy and chaos that destroyed their city – a day of tragedy rather than celebration.

Nauroz

The Afghan new year, Nauroz (above) is celebrated across Kabul. Festivities are concentrated in two main areas. The shrine of Karata-e Sakhi at the base of Koh-e Asmai is a traditional point of celebration, where flags are raised to mark the new year. There's more of a spectacle around the Mausoleum of Nadir Shah at Teppe Maranjan, which hosts a Fighting Kite Festival on the day. When this was held in 2005 for the first time in 30 years it attracted over 150,000 attendees, Kabul's most festive day out in years.

Concerts are held across the city – check with the FCCS (p84). Ghazi Stadium is also used to host special events, including a farmer's parade of livestock, and the last *buzkashi* of the season.

Barf-e Awal

The first snowfall of winter is called *Barf-e Awal*. Many Kabulis play surprise games (*barfi*) on their friends at this time, sending them riddles in an Afghan variant of trick-or-treat. Whoever receives their riddle first, must treat the sender to a meal. The riddles are traditionally sent to the home (so many people won't answer their door on this day), but in modern Afghanistan look for people sending joke text messages to their friends with the first flurry of snow.

SLEEPING

Most accommodation in Kabul is based in Shahr-e Nau, close to Chicken St or Shahr-e Nau Park. Guesthouses extend into Wazir Akbar Khan, jostling for space alongside the embassies. For those staying in Kabul long-term, room rates are usually negotiable. Unless noted, all guesthouses have secure parking. Prices exclude 10% tax.

Budget

Park Hotel (Map p93; ☎ 020 2103 355; Mohammad Jan Khan Wat; r US$6) This hotel sits above an arcade of electronics shops. One step up from a chaikhana, it has simple cell-like rooms with grubby walls, and a large communal area full of local men lounging over endless pots of tea. Don't expect too much of the shared bathrooms.

Salsal Guest House (Map p85; ☎ 079 9734 202; Jade Torabaz Khan; s/d US$10/20) This is a great new addition to the budget hotel scene, and the pick of the ultra-cheapies. Carpeted rooms

KABUL

are small but on the cosy side, with a fan and decent bedding. Shared bathrooms are pretty clean with hot water, and the management is helpful.

Spinzar Hotel (Map p93; ☎ 020 22891; Pul-e Bagh-e Omomi; s/d $20/40, s/d with shower US$40/50) Popular with Afghan businessmen, this tall greenish building has commanding views over the river. Rooms and shared bathrooms alike are drab but clean. The 4th-floor restaurant is worth visiting for non-guests, for both the views and decent Afghan food.

Mustafa Hotel (Map p85; ☎ 070 276021; www .mustafahotel.com; Charahi Sadarat; s/d from US$35/50, half-board supplement US$10; 🖳) Truly a Kabul institution, the Mustafa was the main post-Taliban hang-out for journos, 'security consultants' and other would-be adventurers. If the high-rolling days have passed slightly with the death of its irrepressible manager, Wais Faizi, it's still a good place to stay, with small comfy rooms, hot water and satellite TV in the lounge. There's a special 'backpacker' rate of US$20 per day including internet for those booking in advance online.

Star Inn (Map p85; ☎ 079 9143 252; Flower St; s/d incl breakfast US$35/45) This tidy little hotel has a good central location. Rooms have attached bathrooms and TV, although some are a bit on the poky side. Communal areas are nicely decorated with Afghan textiles giving a friendly air, and the place is scrubbed spotless.

The hotels listed below were popular with backpackers until recently, when the police banned them from accepting foreign guests. We've listed them in the hope that improved security will allow travellers to return in the future.

Pashtoonistan Hotel (Map p93; Pul-e Bagh-e Omomi; US$10) Signed only in Dari, this place has a flat rate for its rooms, each containing between three and five beds. The communal bathroom is pretty basic, but par for the course for this rock-bottom choice.

Zarnigar Hotel (Map p93; ☎ 020 2100 980; zarnigar _afghanistan@hotmail.com; Mohammad Jan Khan Wat; s/d US$10/15) A few doors down from the Jamil, this can be a good choice. The rooms are simple but clean, with shared bathrooms. The hotel also has a decent restaurant overlooking the street, a good place to watch the world go past over a plate of *pulao* (rice dish).

Jamil Hotel (Map p93; ☎ 079 3212 128; Mohammad Jan Khan Wat; s/d US$10/20) Rooms have en suite, and although there is sometimes a problem with the water, the management should keep you supplied with buckets. The hotel isn't brilliantly signed – it's next to Al-Miraj Electronics.

Midrange

Euro Guest House (Map p85; ☎ 070 197220/079 9342 705; hamidwl@netscape.net; Street 15, Wazir Akbar Khan; r incl breakfast from US$40; 🈯 🖳) Tangerine walls on the main street through Wazir Akbar Khan make the Euro hard to miss. There are a selection of different rooms (up to US$100), but the cheaper end are the best value. Service is good, and as with most guesthouses, the Euro can arrange drivers and the like.

Insaf Hotel (Map p85; ☎ 070 286384; Charahi Ansari; r US$50) Close to the action around Shahr-e Nau Park, this modern hotel has en suite rooms that are simply but decently decorated. There's one price for one or two beds. Next to Popolano restaurant, part of the hotel also acts as a wedding hall, so weekends are potentially noisy affairs.

Park Residence (Map p85; ☎ 070 225038; park _residence@hotmail.com; Charahi Ansari; r incl breakfast US$50; 🈯 🖳) Look twice for the entrance to this place facing the park – security is tight but unobtrusive. Modern rooms have en suites and are positively cosy, with a fridge and satellite TV; there's also a small bookshop and a pleasant garden.

Marco Polo Inn (Map p85; ☎ 070 274542; Street 3, Qala-e Fatullah; r US$50; 🖳 🈯) This new guesthouse run by an Afghan-German is a great deal. Rooms, with attached bathroom, are very nicely furnished with lots of dark wood giving the place an almost Bavarian feel. There's a restaurant too, and a neat garden to relax in.

Assa 1 (Map p85; ☎ 079 9555 666; info@assa.com.af; off Flower St; r US$50; 🖳) Another long-standing favourite, this medium-sized guesthouse has a selection of well-turned out rooms, favoured by long-term guests. Worth a look, there is also Assa 2 and Assa 3 just around the corner, offering more of the same for the same price.

Rose Garden & Carwan Sarai Hotel (Map p85; ☎ 079 9013 055; carwan_sarai@yahoo.com; Interior Ministry Rd; s/d US$50/60, r with bathroom US$66; 🖳) Formerly named the Karwansara Guesthouse, this place is a lovely old merchant's house set in a large and leafy garden. Some of the rooms are a little small, but they're all turned out well enough for comfort. The restaurant has good Afghan and international dishes.

Park Palace (Map p85; ☎ 070 656561; parkpalace kabul@hotmail.com; Ghiyassudin Wat, Kolola Pushta; r incl breakfast US$55; 🔀 🖵) A deservedly popular hotel with consultants and long-term stays, the Park Palace has good quality en suite rooms with service to match. The buffet breakfast is something of a treat – look for people rushing it down while their Landcruisers queue outside the gate to whisk them off to the office.

Le Monde Guest House (Map p85; ☎ 079 9614 872; lemondegh@hotmail.com; Herati Mosque St, Shahr-e Nau; r US$60; 🖵) This is a traditional Kabul home turned into a cosy, well-run guesthouse. Generous rooms are well set up, and there's a lovely garden. Given that the manager is a chef, the food is excellent.

Naween Guesthouse (Map p85; ☎ 079 9016 644; naweenguesthouse@yahoo.com; Ghiyassudin Wat, Kolola Pushta; r incl breakfast US$60; 🖵) Another well-run guesthouse popular with contractors and UN workers, the Naween offers a high level of comfort and security. All rooms are en suite.

B's Place (Map p85; ☎ 070 283968; bs_place _rg@yahoo.com; Street 2, Qali-e Fatullah; r US$60) One of the first of the post-Taliban guesthouses, B's Place has six rooms with shared bathrooms, decorated in traditional Afghan style. There's a pleasant garden, and an Italian restaurant, but the place feels a little worn out by the competition from all the new hotels. A bit of a mixed bag.

Shahr-e Nau Guesthouse (Map p85; ☎ 070 267814; off Flower St; r incl breakfast US$60-80) Easily spotted by its pink external walls, the Shahr-e Nau Guesthouse is a decent place. Rooms come in a variety of shapes and sizes, with up to three beds, making this a good deal if there's a few of you, but less so for solo travellers. All are en suite.

Kabul Inn (Map p85; ☎ 079 9359 355; kabul _inn@hotmail.com; near Zargona High School, Qala-e Fatullah; r incl breakfast US$64; 🔀 🖵) Behind high walls on the main road, this Tajik-run place is bright, modern and clean. Rooms have satellite TV and bathrooms, all kept spotless. Even the grass on the lawn is clipped to within an inch of its life. Very good value, although the restaurant food is a little dull.

Kabul Lodge (Map p85; ☎ 079 9423 562/070 282643; kabullodge@yahoo.com; Passport Lane, off Interior Ministry Rd; r incl breakfast US$75; 🔀 🖵) A well-established guesthouse, the Kabul Lodge is impeccably run with helpful and efficient management. Rooms are large (with en

suite) and there's a great restaurant, open to non-guests from 6pm.

Top End

Heetal Heritage Hotel (Map p85; ☎ 079 9159 697; heetalkabul@yahoo.com; Street 14, Wazir Akbar Khan; s/d from US$85/89; 🖵 🔀) At the edge of Wazir Akbar Khan, and in the lee of Bibi Mahru Hill, the Heetal gets cleaner air than many places in the city. Perhaps that's why it flags itself as Kabul's first eco-friendly boutique hotel. No one could venture another reason when we asked. It's nicely laid out though, in a decent approximation of a caravanserai. Rooms could be bigger, but there's a good restaurant serving everything from Tex-Mex to Indian and a weekly film night to keep you entertained. Discounts are frequently available.

Maple Leaf Inn (Map p85; ☎ 079 9321 401/070 203412; mapleleafinnkabul@yahoo.ca; Street 3, left off Charahi Haji Yaqub; r US$80; 🔀 🖵 🔊) Formerly called Ottawa Resorts, the motto here is 'blending serenity and efficiency'. Management is certainly efficient, while rooms match the standard of a business-class hotel anywhere you might think of. A popular venue for business breakfasts and lunches, people-spot for the movers and shakers here. Stays over a month bring the price down to US$70 a day.

Gandamack Lodge (Map p85; ☎ 070 276937/079 9569 904; www.gandamacklodge.co.uk; next to UNHCR, Charahi Sherpur; US$90-$160; 🔀 🖵) A perennially popular option with visiting media, the Gandamack Lodge is run by Peter Jouvenal, the acclaimed cameraman and Afghan expert. Now in larger premises with a nice garden, rooms are comfy and tastefully decorated in colonial fashion. The restaurant is excellent, and worth visiting for the full English cooked breakfast (US$12)

KABUL

alone, plus there's the Hare & Hounds pub in the cellar. At the entrance there's a simple memorial to peace activist–aid worker Marla Ruzicka.

Intercontinental Hotel (Map p80; ☎ 020 2201 320; reservations@intercontinentalkabul.com; Bagh-e Bala, Karte Parwan; s/d from US$90/100; 🖳 🖀) This venerable institution was Afghanistan's first international luxury hotel. It's a 20-minute drive from the centre of town if the traffic allows, but the hilltop location gives great views of Kabul. The recent refit has lifted the rooms considerably. ATO and Ariana have offices here. There's also a gym, much needed after sampling the fare of the three restaurants. The pool sometimes has water, but don't bother looking for the bikini-clad swimmers still sunning themselves in the old 1970s adverts.

Kabul Serena Hotel (Map p93; ☎ 079 9654 000; www.serenahotels.com; Jad-e Froshgah; s/d US$120/140; 🖀 🖳) Formerly the Kabul Hotel, the Serena is now owned by the Aga Khan and has undergone a massive renovation to transform it into Kabul's swankiest hotel by some stretch. The public areas are all light and space, while rooms have all mod-cons and a sprinkling of traditional Afghan decor. Security on the door is unsurprisingly strict, while the pastry shop's brunch (p101) was the place to be when we dropped in. As we went to press, they'd just cut the ribbon on the hotel spa.

Golden Star Hotel (Map p85; ☎ 075 2004 787; goldenstar_hotel@yahoo.com; Charahi Haji Yaqub; s/d US$100/140, ste US$200; 🖀) One of Kabul's newest hotels, this literally towers above all others from its vantage point attached to the Kabul Business Centre. Rooms are exceedingly comfortable and well-appointed with all facilities. The deluxe suites even come with their own sauna, surely a first for Afghanistan. The Khosha restaurant and bar (opposite) sits on the top floor, overlooking Shahr-e Nau. Generous discounts can bring this easily into the midrange bracket.

Safi Landmark Hotel (Map p85; ☎ 020 2203 131; safilandmarkhotel@yahoo.com; Charahi Ansari; s/d US$200/250; 🖳) You can't miss the Safi, part of the Kabul City Centre tower block in bright green glass. The lobby speaks of understated service and a glass elevator whisks you to your room, many of which overlook the shopping mall. Everything is laid on, but for the money the rooms are a bit small and cramped. A 50% winter discount make things better value, although at that time you'll miss out on the rooftop coffee shop.

EATING

Kabul has the best range of restaurant in the country by some degree, with eve rything on offer from traditional Afghan meals to Thai and Croatian food. Many restaurants aimed primarily at the expa community open and close on a regular basis so we can't hope to be comprehen sive – check *Afghan Scene* magazine or the *What's On in Kabul* newsletter for the lat est developments. In addition, many of the guesthouses and hotels listed above have attached restaurants worth checking out.

Restaurants serving alcohol are noted i text, but see the Drinking section on p10 for possible legal complications.

Restaurants
AFGHAN

Herat (Map p85; Cinema Zainab Rd, Shahr-e Nau; meal 60-150Afg; 🕙 10am-10pm) A really great Afghan place which positively bursts at lunchtimes as half of Kabul appears to eat here. The *mantu* (steamed meat dumplings) will se you back 80Afg, but save some room for the sticky sweets at the end with your tea.

Kulba Afghan (Map p85; ☎ 079 9210 143; Muslim St Shahr-e Nau; mains from 200Afg; 🕙 10am-10pm) This restaurant is almost two in one, as it sit on the third floor above the also popula Rose Restaurant. What makes this more o a draw is the live Afghan music from 6pm to 10pm, and booths with cushions to tuck yourself into. Stuff yourself with the huge Kulba special (300Afg) which has a bit o everything – *pulao*, kebabs, *mantu*, chips *qorma* (stewed vegetables), plus salad, yo gurt and a soft drink.

Sufi 2 (Map p85; ☎ 070 210651; Muslim St, Shahr-e Nau; dishes from US$4; 🕙 10am-10pm) A sister branch to the original Sufi, this was just opening during research. With the decor and serv ice borrowed from its sibling, lunch is big thing here, with lots of delicious dishe like pumpkin *boloni* (stuffed pancakes), sa mosas and some great sweets like *gosh-e fi* (elephant's ear) pastries.

Sufi (Map p80; ☎ 070 210651; near Aryub Cinema Bagh-e Bala, Karte Parwan; meals US$5-11; 🕙 11am 10pm) Sufi is a little way out of town, nestle beneath the Intercontinental Hotel, but it' worth the trip. Beautifully decorated with prints and fabrics, guests eat Afghan style, seated on cushions and carpets around low tables (though there are some tables and chairs too). There's a wide variety of Afghan dishes, nicely served up – we particularly enjoyed the *kofte chalau* (minced kebabs with dried fruit and saffron).

Khosha (Map p85; ☎ 079 9888 999; in Golden Star Hotel, Charahi Haji Yaqub; dishes from US$6; ⏲ 11am-9.30pm, 6-11pm) This place was freshly minted when we visited and looked a treat. The rooftop setting gives great views over Kabul, while the interior is decorated with Kuchi textiles. As well as Afghan favourites, there are some good vegetable dishes normally found only in the home, like *banjan borani* (aubergine with tomatoes and yogurt), plus a great lamb *qorma* with chickpeas.

ASIAN

Alcohol is served at all the restaurants following.

Delhi Darbar (Map p85; ☎ 079 9324 899; Cinema Zainab Rd; mains from US$5; ⏲ 10am-10pm) A popular choice for Indian food, and successful enough to create a mini-franchise, with branches in Mazar-e Sharif (p153) and even Tajikistan. The focus is on north Indian cuisine, plus some fiery curries and lots of vegetarian options. The one-dish-fits-all *thalis* remain a prize attraction, washed down with a cold lager.

Samarqand (Map p85; ☎ 079 9234 646; near Pan-Ipina, Qala-e Musa; dishes from US$6; ⏲ 10am-10pm) This relaxed restaurant was one of the most popular in town when we dropped in, serving a mix of Central Asian food – beautifully flavoured rice and meat options – and international dishes. The regular theme nights liven things up, with Chinese food on Friday, and salsa dancing on Wednesday and Saturday.

Jaisalmer (Map p85; ☎ 079 9200 570; Street 1, Qala-e Fatullah; mains from US$7; ⏲ 11am-10pm) Another good Indian restaurant, with great and highly spiced tandoori dishes. It's slightly hidden away and not brilliantly signed, but don't despair: they offer a home delivery service.

Lai Thai (Map p85; ☎ 070 297557; Street 15, Wazir Akbar Khan; mains from US$7; ⏲ 11am-11pm) Is there an expat left in Kabul who hasn't eaten here? We doubt it. With wonderful food in a traditional Thai setting, the owner has made a

habit of opening in war-torn areas – there are sister outfits in Kosovo and East Timor. Tasty spring rolls and satay are US$4 each.

Baku (Map p85; ☎ 079 9083 918; Lane 5, Street 15, Wazir Akbar Khan; meals from US$7; ⏲ 11am-10pm) What do you eat in an Azeri restaurant? It turns out to be a mix of Afghan and Turkish food, with hearty *shashlik* (kebabs) and *plov* (*pulao*) balanced out by *dolma* (stuffed leaves) and other treats. With regular flights from Baku to Kabul, it makes sense to give this place a try.

Silk Route (Map p93; ☎ 079 9654 000, ext 4554; Kabul Serena Hotel, Jad-e Froshgah; meals from US$8; ⏲ 6-10pm) Southeast Asian food mightn't be quite what you were expecting at the Serena Hotel's flagship restaurant, but it delivers with some aplomb, with a variety of tasty Thai, Vietnamese and Indonesian dishes – however incongruous. The setting is immaculate, so dressing smartly is a good idea.

Shamiana (Map p85; ☎ 020 220 3131; Kabul City Centre; meals from US$8; ⏲ 7am-11pm) The Safi Landmark's rooftop restaurant tries its hand at a bit of everything Indian, Chinese and Afghan, plus a dash of Italian and anything else you can think of. It mostly works, and its plush surroundings means that you'll be dining next to some extremely rich Afghans at the next table.

Anaar (Map p85; ☎ 079 9567 291; Lane 3, Street 14, Wazir Akbar Khan; mains from US$8; ⏲ 11am-10pm) Recently relocated to new premises, Anaar remains one of Kabul's lovelier restaurants. There's a wide selection of Thai, Indian and Chinese dishes with vegetarians particularly well-catered for. Thankfully, the new premises still feature a lantern-hung garden for al fresco dining, otherwise withdraw to the cosy interior, decorated with traditional Afghan crafts.

Golden Key Seafood (Map p80; ☎ 079 9002 800; Street 10, Wazir Akbar Khan; meals from US$8; ⏲ 10am-9pm) Of the Chinese restaurants, this is our favourite, despite the old adage of never eating seafood in a land-locked country. Flown in from Dubai, the fish and shellfish (and meat dishes) are actually excellent, and come with as many noodle and rice options as you could wish for.

MIDDLE EASTERN

Taverna du Liban (Map p85; ☎ 070 210651; Lane 3, Street 14, Wazir Akbar Khan; mezze from US$3, mains from US$8; ⏲ 11am-10pm) Several Lebanese restaurants have come and gone in Kabul; this one has stayed the course. Tables are easily laden with mezze like *houmous*, *tabouleh* and Lebanese salad, making it easy to fill up before hitting the grill for your main. At the end of your meal, you can relax by smoking a *shisha*, perfect in the garden in the warmer months.

Shandiz (Map p80; ☎ 07079 9342 928; Street 10, Wazir Akbar Khan; meals from US$4; ✆ 10am-9pm) Opposite the domestic Ariana office, Shandiz serves Iranian food in pleasant surrounds. The *chelo morgh* (chicken and rice with berries) is as good as in any Persian restaurant.

Haji Baba (Map p85; Charahi Torabaz Khan, Shahr-e Nau; meals from US$7; ✆ 11am-9pm) Run by a genial Afghan, the food here bridges the gap between Persian and Herati food. The surroundings are brisk and simple, not that the many locals passing through seem to mind. They're here for bowls of thick chicken *shorwa* (soup) and plates of moist kebabs, king of which is *maheecha*, a sublime oven-baked leg of lamb. Be sure to leave room for dessert.

WESTERN

Popolano (Map p85; ☎ 070 288116; Charahi Ansari; meals from US$5; ✆ 9am-10pm) Popolano offered Kabul's first post-Taliban pizza, and is still going strong. The fickle expat dining scene means it hasn't been trendy for several years and it gets a correspondingly decent Afghan crowd, but we still like its strong blend of pizza and pasta, served in something approaching a bistro.

La Cantina (Map p85; ☎ 079 8271 915; off Butcher St, Shahr-e Nau; dishes from 330Afg; ✆ 11.30am-3pm, 6pm-late Tue-Sun, closed winter) There's a full range of Tex-Mex food on offer here, with great plates of nachos, burritos and bowls of chilli – tick off your choices on the menu sheet and present it to the waiter to order. Dining is al fresco, with the traditional Afghan courtyard garden pressed into service as a half-decent pueblo substitute (hence the dining season is restricted to the warmer months). Alcohol is served.

Le Bistro (Map p85; ☎ 079 9598 852; off Chicken St; mains US$5-12; ✆ 8am-10pm) In a pleasant Kabuli house, this French restaurant has its own bakery attached, making the continental breakfast (US$10) a treat of bread, pastry and croissants. Evening meals are good, even if the servings are a little on the small side. Carpets and paintings festoon

the walls, and there are regular art shows and sales on site.

Vila Velebita (Map p85; ☎ 079 9160 368; Street 10, Wazir Akbar Khan; pizzas from US$8, mains from US$12; ✆ 10am-10pm) The name of this restaurant seems to confound many Afghans, but it's actually named for a famous Croatian nationalist song. The quality of the food is high, with wood-oven pizzas, and a mix of pasta, steak and seafood, but the price tag is equally steep, especially if you throw in a bottle of Croatian wine.

Red Hot Sizzlin' (Map p80; ☎ 079 9838 646; ARC Yuksel Camp, Old Microrayon; meals from US$9; ✆ 11am-9pm) Slightly out of the way, this restaurant is the place to go if you are after a steak American-style. It's all Tex-Mex here, with juicy T-bones, piles of fries and a cold one to wash it all down.

Carlitos (Map p85; ☎ 079 9159 697; Heetal Hotel, Street 15, Wazir Akbar Khan; buffet US$12; ✆ 10am-10pm) Carlitos touts itself as Kabul's best Mexican restaurant, and not happy with that crown it then goes on to attempt Lebanese, Indian and anything else it can think of. It's at its best in the summer, when the Thursday and Friday buffet and barbeque comes into play. With a bar attached, it's deservedly popular.

Café Zarnegar (Map p93; ☎ 079 9654 000, ext 4553; Kabul Serena Hotel, Jad-e Froshgah; brunch US$31; ✆ 6.30am-10pm) If you're in need of a splurge, come here from 11am for Friday brunch. There's a huge buffet with everything from tremendous salads and burgers through to sushi (yes, sushi), plus some Afghan dishes to remind you what country you're in if the surrounding glitz makes you forget.

Quick Eats

Any chaikhana you visit will be able to serve you up *pulao* or a plate of kebabs for less than 80Afg. There are plenty of good meat and chicken kebab-style places between Shahr-e Nau Park and Charahi Haji Yaqub interspersed with ice cream and juice bars. More fun still is to explore the mobile street food stalls that spring up on busy market streets – there are good clusters on the western edge of Shahr-e Nau Park, and in the markets around Pul-e Khishti bridge. For less than 50Afg you can fill up on a pile of *bolani*, samosas and bowls of *shor nakhod* (chickpeas with mint).

Serena Pastry Shop (Map p93; ☎ 079 9654 000, ext 560; Kabul Serena Hotel, Jad-e Froshgah; ✆ 7am-10pm) All the delicious pastries you could ever want are here, in plush and polished surroundings. If your great aunt ever comes to Kabul, bring her here.

French Bakery (Map p85; Jad-e Torabaz Khan; cakes from 25Afg) A tiny shop opposite the Kabul Bank, this is a great place for a mid-morning bite, with some heavenly banana cakes and brownies. They're a little dry by the end of the day; we're not sure if this is a product of the genuine 'Frenchised' baking process advertised.

Chief Burger (Map p85; Cinema Zainab Rd, opposite Shahr-e Nau Park; meals from 80Afg; ✆ 9am-9pm) Western fast food, Afghan-style. This place is heaving at lunchtime, with local workers and students (there's a 'family lounge' for women). There are burgers, pizzas and a great tandoori chicken, served on nan with fries. Quick, tasty and filling.

Flower Street Café (Map p80; ☎ 070 293124; Street 7, Qala-e Fatullah; snacks from US$4; ✆ 8am-5pm) The name is momentarily confusing, as this café is nowhere near Flower St. It's worth finding though, as it does some great sandwiches and burgers served in a flowery garden, with cake for afters. Alternatively they'll deliver your lunch to your door, but that means you'll miss out on the great smoothies and cappuccinos.

Everest Pizza (Map p80; ☎ 079 9317 979; Street 13 Wazir Akbar Khan; pizzas from US$5; ✆ 9am-9pm) There's some argument about the best pizza in Kabul, but this place consistently turns out the goods. Tasty sauce, a good variety of toppings and the all important takeaway/home delivery option.

Markets & Self-Catering

For fresh produce, the best place to go is the Mandayi Market around Pul-e Khishti mosque (Map p93) – either side of the river you'll find endless stalls selling fruit, vegetables, bread and even wheelbarrows full of cows' hooves. Around Shahr-e Nau, you're more restricted to the always-moving handcarts, piled high with fruit and veg, but there are plenty of corner shops for dried goods.

Flower Street (Map p85) Where the souvenir shops of Chicken St end, the grocery stores of Flower St begin, piled high with everything you might need from cornflakes to maple syrup. Interspersed with these there are some lovely bakeries, places selling pirated DVDs, and the flower shops that give the street its name – most likely piling the petals on to highly-decorated wedding cars.

Chelsea Supermarket (Map p85; Jad-e Torabaz Khan) The biggest (and dare we say most expensive?) supermarket selling imported food and toiletries in Kabul. It's handy though, and has just installed an ATM. Who can argue with its proud motto over the door: 'Be happy all the time'?

Supreme PX (Jalalabad Rd, ✆ 8.30am-5pm) The best established of the military PX stores, every expat winds up here from time to time. There is a huge range of imported goods and food, hidden behind the most extreme security you have ever seen at a supermarket.

DRINKING
Bars

The availability of alcohol is a perennial topic of discussion in Kabul. During research it was officially 'banned', leading to its disappearance from the PX stores, and a price hike for all the places serving it. The authorities seemed happy enough with this clampdown, but be aware that changing domestic politics could quickly lead to the bars and restaurants we've listed here running very dry.

L'Atmosphere (Map p85; ☎ 079 9300 264; Street 4, Qala-e Fatullah; ✆ 10am-late; ⊜) It's a restaurant, but not so many people come to 'Latmo' for the food. Especially in the summer when the pool is full, this is a bar pure and simple, and the most popular expat joint in town. On Thursday nights you could be forgiven for thinking you're back at the university bar, as the place fills up with the young and beautiful (and single) side of the aid worker scene. It's certainly fun, but we're not sure if it's Afghanistan at all, and it'll leave your head spinning in more ways than one.

Hare & Hounds (Map p85; in the Gandamack Lodge, Charahi Sherpur; ✆ 6pm-late) This bar gives you a geographic jolt in a completely different way: an English pub shipped lock, stock and barrel to Kabul, all the way down to the beer mats and dart board. It's as cosy as you'd hope; if it had real ale on tap, we'd be in heaven.

Deutscher Hof (Map p85; ☎ 079 9322 582; Street 3, Qala-e Fatullah; ⏱ 11am-11pm) Doubling up as a German restaurant and catering college, the high walls here hide steins of Bavarian lager, and regular events like Kabul's Oktoberfest.

Mustafa Hotel (Map p85; Charahi Sadarat; ⏱ 6pm-late) Made notorious by the company it's kept in the past, you can almost count the journalists who haven't written a piece on the Mustafa bar on one hand. At it's best, it's a funky mix of Rick's Bar in *Casablanca* with the alien cantina in *Star Wars*, populated by security contractors, backpackers and other unusual types.

Cafés

There's a chaikhana on just about every corner in Kabul if all you're after is a pot of tea – yours for 20Afg with a blaring Bollywood video thrown in for free. Our favourites are those along Jad-e Maiwand and Mohammed Jan Khan Wat, where you can grab a first-floor window seat and watch the world go by. Alternatively, the juice bars around Shahr-e Nau Park are great places to refuel with banana, carrot and mango juices and more, for less than 50Afg.

Chaila (Map p80; Karte Se; coffee from 50Afg, milkshakes from 100Afg; ⏱ 8:30am-6pm Sat-Tue, 8:30am-8pm Wed-Thu, noon-6pm Fri) Ever popular with the large number of expats who live in west Kabul, Chaila is a joint Afghan-American enterprise. They serve brick-oven pizzas and quiche, as well as sandwiches and home-made ice cream, but they're best known for their milkshakes and superb coffee – the cappuccinos and espressos are simply fantastic. It's all tastefully decorated, and they have wi-fi and cable TV to boot.

Cabul Coffee House (Map p85; ☎ 070 293124; Street 7, Qala-e Fatullah; juices/coffee from 100Afg; ⏱ 8am-5pm) With funky paintings on the wall and some mellow jazz on the stereo, this is a great addition to the Kabul scene. As befits its name, the coffee is great, as are the juices. Grab a paper or something from the bookswap and chill out in the garden. The menu has sandwiches (from 300Afg), burgers and the like.

ENTERTAINMENT
Music

Most live music in Kabul is played at weddings. Should you get an invitation, they can be brilliant affairs. Several of the cultural centres (see p84) host concerts. The most notable one is the **Foundation for Culture & Civil Society** (FCCS; Map p93; ☎ 070 292322; www.afghanfccs.org; opposite National Archive, Salang Wat), which hold regular open-air concerts of traditional Afghan music during the warmer months, and exhibitions by local artists.

Sport

Kabul's sporting options tend to be ad hoc, with the most popular pursuits being kite fighting (p58) and pigeon-flying (p90). On early Friday mornings impromptu gatherings of men appear to gamble on partridge and dog fights.

Afghan Scene and *What's On in Kabul* regularly contain adverts for gyms and expat sporting get-togethers. A slightly out-of-town alternative is a round at Kabul Golf Course (p109).

Ghazi Stadium (Map p80; Mohammed Jan Khan Wat; foreigner 250Afg) Kabul's main stadium hosts football matches most Friday afternoons. In the winter months and at Nauroz there are occasional *buzkashi* matches.

Cinema

The Goethe-Institute (p84) has regular film showings, and the Maple Leaf Inn (p97) shows movies in its private theatre on Fridays.

Aina Media Centre (Map p85; ☎ 070 224983; Shah Mahmud Wat) Weekly outdoor films showing during the summer months.

Shahr-e Nau Cinema (Map p85; Shahr-e Nau Park) Afghanistan's first cinema, almost exclusively Bollywood (and male audience).

SHOPPING

Kabul's shopping scene has seen some ups and downs, from the destruction of its covered bazaar in 1842 and Jad-e Maiwand in the 1990s, to the glitzy glass mall of the new Kabul City Centre. In the 1960s there was even a branch of the British high street icon Marks & Spencer.

Chicken Street (Map p85; Shahr-e Nau) This famed street has been a focus for Afghanistan's tourists since the days of the Hippy Trail. All kinds of handicrafts are available here, from jewellery to carpets, 'antique' muskets to lapis lazuli. Good times ebb and flow with the number of international workers in the city (in Taliban-era Kabul shop owners once chased us down the street, begging to open their shops for us), but starting prices are always high, so don't be afraid to haggle.

Afghan Gallery (Map p80; ☎ 079 9712 442; afghan _gallery@afghangallery.com.af; Sarakh-e Kolola Pushta) This gallery sells well-made handicrafts, including embroidery, pottery and jewellery. There is also a wide selection of carpets woven to traditional designs, knotted by a local women's carpet cooperative.

Zardozi (Map p80; ☎ 070 287963; opposite Moulavi Abdul Mateen Mosque, near old British Embassy, Karte Parwan) Formerly the DACAAR Sewing Centre, Zardozi is an income-generating project working with female refugees and traditional artisans. The showroom has some lovely embroidery including clothes, and some miniburqas just the right size to slip over a bottle of booze.

Tarsian & Blinkley (Map p85; ☎ 070 223286; www.tarsian.com; Muslim St; ⌚ by appointment) Afghan women's fashion doesn't begin and end with the burqa. Tarsian & Blinkley has chic women's clothes immaculately cut and sewn by a team of over 50 Afghan women and run by an Afghan-American designer – a business venture that scooped it a Global Social Venture prize to boot.

PARSA (☎ 070 288233; www.parsa-afghanistan.org; Paiko-e Naswar, Kart-e Ariana) A shop run by the NGO PARSA as an income-generating project for Afghan women, with plenty of tempting goodies, like scarves, purses covered with delicate needlework and other pocket-sized trinkets.

Nomad Carpet Gallery (Map p85; ☎ 079 9328 632; near Unica, Charahi Ansari) Chicken St doesn't have a monopoly on Kabul's carpet market. Nomad has a wide selection of rugs, and has taken the innovative step of commissioning modern designs along with the traditional, to great effect.

Zarif & Royah (Map p85; ☎ 070 195677; www.zarif-royah.com; Lane 3 off Butcher St, Shahr-e Nau; ⌚ call ahead) Kabul's other fashion house (along with Tarsian & Blinkley), Zarif & Royah recently hosted Kabul's first fashion show. Elegantly cut women's clothes in traditional Afghan fabrics wouldn't look out of place in Milan or Paris.

Afghan Handicrafts Centre (Map p85; Interior Ministry Rd) A government-run set of units and shops, selling everything from carpets to woodwork and jewellery. There's less scope to haggle, but you can sometimes get to see craftsmen at their trade.

GETTING THERE & AWAY

Kabul is the main gateway to Afghanistan, and has the country's only international airport (Map p80; ☎ 020 2300 016; Great Massoud Rd). For more information on international flight connections, see p212. For details of connections served by humanitarian flight services, see p212.

Ariana has daily connections to Herat (3200Afg, one hour), as well as three times a week to Mazar-e Sharif (2500Afg, 30 minutes), Faizabad (2500Afg, one hour) and Kandahar (2200Afg, 30 minutes). In theory there are also flights on at least a weekly basis to Shiberghan, Kunduz and Maimana, but Ariana couldn't vouch for these when asked.

Kam Air flies daily to Herat (3250Afg, one hour), and Mazar-e Sharif (2500Afg, 30 minutes). Services to Kandahar and Faizabad were being mooted as we went to press. As with all domestic flights in Afghanistan, schedules can be extremely flexible.

Air
AIRLINE OFFICES

Air Arabia (Map p85; ☎ 079 9700 095; www.airarabia .com; Charahi Ansari)

Ariana Afghan Airlines (Map p85; ☎ 020 2100 271, domestic flights 020 2301 339; www.flyariana.com; Street 10, Wazir Akbar Khan)

Azerbaijan Airlines (Map p85; ☎ 070 296914; Charahi Ansari)

ICRC Air Operations (International Committee of the Red Cross; ☎ 070 285948; kabul.kab@icrc.org; Charahi Haji Yaqub)

Indian Airlines (Map p85; ☎ 079 9308 303; www .indian-airlines.nic.in; Interior Ministry Rd) Inside Anaar travel agent.

Iran Asseman Airlines (Map p85; ☎ 079 9324 006; www.iaa.ir; Street 10, Wazir Akbar Khan)

Kam Air (Map p85; ☎ 020 2301 753; www.flykamair .com, Kabul Business Centre, Shahr-e Nau)

Pactec (☎ 070 282679/079 9300 837; bookingkbl@pactec.net; Street 15, Right Lane 1, House 12, Wazir Akbar Khan)

PIA (Map p85; ☎ 020 2203500; www.piac.com.pk; btwn Streets 10 & 15, Wazir Akbar Khan)

UNHAS (United Nations Humanitarian Air Service; ☎ 070 284070/282559; kabul.unhas@wfp.org; WFP Compound, btwn Charahi Zambak & Charahi Ariana, Shahr-e Nau) UNHAS uses the UNAMA terminal at Kabul airport for all its domestic flights plus the Islamabad and Dushanbe flights. Kabul-Dubai flights depart from the main international terminal.

Bus & Minibus

Several terminals serve Kabul, in reality little more than massed ranks of vehicles with drivers shouting out the destinations. There are no timetables – vehicles depart as soon as they're full. If you do have to wait, there's always somewhere to get tea or juice and a plate of kebabs.

Minibuses to Jalalabad (200Afg, three hours) and the Pakistan border at Torkham (300Afg, 4½ hours) leave Begrami Motor Park on the outskirts of Kabul on the Jalalabad Rd (150Afg by taxi from Shahr-e Nau). A few vehicles also leave early just after dawn from Pul-e Mahmoud Khan, close to the Id Gah Mosque, but note that all transport coming to Kabul from the east terminates at Begrami, and isn't allowed into central Kabul for security reasons. The fastest way to get to the border is to hire a taxi outright for 2500Afg.

Transport heading north through the Salang Tunnel departs from Serai Shomali Transport Depot (Map p80), a 20-minute taxi ride to the Khair Khana district on the edge of Kabul. Minibuses from here travel to Mazar-e Sharif (500Afg, eight hours), Pul-e Khumri (200Afg, four hours), Samangan (300Afg, five hours), Kunduz (400Afg, 10 hours), and Faizabad (800Afg, 1½ days). Serai Shomali is also the place for more local transport to Istalif (30Afg, 1½ hours), Paghman (30Afg, 30 minutes) and Charikar (40Afg, 30 minutes).

To travel to Bamiyan, catch a minibus from Kote Sangi (sometimes called Pul-e Socta) in west Kabul (400Afg, nine to 11 hours). Transport from here usually takes the southern route through the Hajigak and Unai Passes – see p114 for security information before considering this route. At the time of writing the northern route via Shibar was preferred for security reasons. This may mean hiring a vehicle outright, or paying a supplement to the driver to use the alternate route.

Kote Sangi is also the terminal for minibuses south to Ghazni, Kandahar and on to Herat, but this road is extremely dangerous for foreigners and we strongly advise against it.

Prices and times given here are for 16-seater HiAce minibuses. Smaller TownAces fill up (and leave) quicker, and are slightly more expensive. Faster shared taxis also depart from the same terminals, and cost up to a third more. It's not possible to arrange seats in advance. Long distance transport can start leaving from 5am or before, so arrive early.

GETTING AROUND

While Taliban-era Kabul was largely a city of bicycles, traffic jams are an unwelcome side effect of progress. Getting around can be a nightmare at any time of day, with frequent road closures for unexpected security measures. Travel between Shahr-e Nau, Wazir Akbar Khan and the airport can be notably tiresome due to the large numbers of concrete roadblocks outside embassies that turn the roads into obstacle courses.

To/From the Airport

A taxi between the airport and the centre of Kabul should cost 200Afg, a 20-minute trip in good traffic (but allow for longer). Security at the airport is extremely tight. Access is divided into three zones. Zone A, immediately outside the airport doors, is reserved for VIPs and anyone lingering here will be swiftly moved on. Zone B, 50m to the right when facing the airport entrance, is for accredited cars, while Zone 3 just beyond this is for taxis and everyone else. All vehicles are subject to a security check on arrival and all luggage is searched so factor in time for this.

Car

A couple of companies offer secure radio controlled taxi services in Kabul, aimed at the expat community. Both operate 24-hour services, and also rent cars and 4WDs with drivers for short and long-term hire.

Afghan Logistics & Tours (☎ 079 9391 462/070 479435; www.afghanlogisticstours.com; midnight-6pm US$7, 6pm-midnight US$5, full-day within/outside Kabul US$40/80, airport transfer US$20)

Safe Trip Kabul (☎ 079 9041 130; www.safetripkabul .com; according to time of day US$6-13, full-day within/outside Kabul US$80/90, airport transfer US$25)

Local Transport

Old buses operated by Afghan Millie Bus trundle the routes across Kabul, but they are slow with standing room only. Destinations aren't marked, so shout out where you want to go when the bus stops. If you're not in a rush, fares cost around 3Afg. A similar network of minibuses also criss-cross the city, usually stopping to pick up passengers at roundabouts and major junctions. Look for the vehicles with a young lad hanging out of the door barking out the destination.

There are over 40,000 registered yellow taxis in Kabul, forming the bulk of the city's traffic. Shared taxis run the main roads, linking the districts. If you flag one down you'll need to know the nearest landmark or major junction to your destination. Most taxi drivers assume that a foreigner will want to hire the whole vehicle, so make this clear when you get in. Shared taxis have a minimum fare of 20Afg.

Finding an empty taxi to hire can sometimes be a challenge, though they'll often veer towards a walking foreigner. Drivers almost always ask for 100Afg for a fare, although short hops should give you change from 70Afg. Women should be wary of taking taxis alone.

Around Kabul
اطراف کابل

Many short-term visitors to Afghanistan tend to arrive in Kabul and then leave as soon as they can, attracted by the better-known attractions of Bamiyan and Herat. That's a shame, because there's still plenty to see within a couple of hours' drive of the capital.

North of Kabul is the wide expanse of the Shomali Plain, a richly fertile region renowned for its fruit, and framed by the Koh Daman mountains of the Hindu Kush. Once a much-contested battlefield, the Shomali Plain is home to the ancient village of Istalif, at the foothills of the peaks, a popular recreation spot for centuries and home to Afghanistan's most recognisable pottery.

The highway continues across the plain until it starts to rise towards the mountains, offering the traveller a choice of destinations. Straight ahead and up takes you along a series of dizzying switchbacks to the Salang Pass, the gateway to northern Afghanistan. A second road tempts you towards a narrow gorge with a rushing river that opens out into the spectacular Panjshir Valley. This is one of the country's most beautiful spots, and the last resting place of one of its national heroes.

Closer to Kabul you can find activities both Afghan and Western in taste. Kabulis take their families to the green surrounds of Paghman for weekend picnics, while at Qargha Lake you might find yourself unexpectedly shouting 'Fore!' at Kabul Golf Club – surely Afghanistan's most peculiar sporting venue.

HIGHLIGHTS

- Shop for traditional pottery in the historic village of **Istalif** (opposite), overlooking the Shomali Plain
- Watch out for unexpected bunkers at the **Kabul Golf Club** (p109) at Qargha Lake
- Visit the tomb of Ahmad Shah Massoud in the sublime **Panjshir Valley** (p110)
- Cross the **Salang Pass** (p112), the mountain gateway to northern Afghanistan

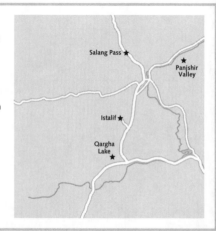

For sake of this chapter, we've only considered destinations that make easy day trips north of Kabul. Other potential excursions from the capital include Jalalabad (p182) and Ghazni (p196). Both are subject to particular security issues – check the relevant sections for more details.

ISTALIF   استالف

The mountain village of Istalif has enchanted travellers for centuries. Babur waxed lyrical about the wine parties held in its gardens, while British officers enjoyed its shady slopes during their first occupation of Kabul. Today it is a popular spot for weekend daytrips for Kabulis and expats alike, coming for the tremendous scenery

and the famous blue pottery made in the village.

Istalif clings to the slopes of the Koh Daman mountains north of Kabul, giving splendid views across the Shomali Plain. This fertile region has traditionally been the breadbasket of Kabul, or perhaps its fruit bowl, for the villages are renowned for their grapes, cherries, figs and mulberries. The Shomali Plain suffered grievously in the recent years of war. Its wide spaces are ideal for armoured warfare, and dead tanks still litter the landscape. The Taliban took particular trouble to subdue the plain and its mainly Tajik population. In 1999 a scorched earth campaign displaced around 140,000 residents, destroying houses and

AROUND KABUL

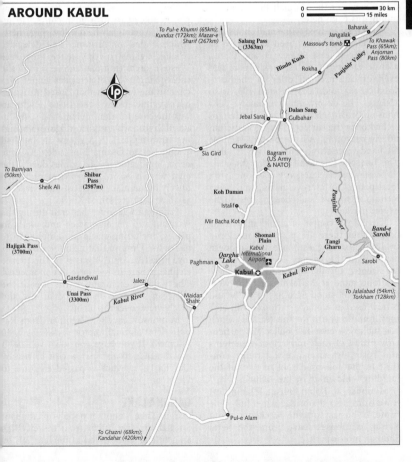

AROUND KABUL

0   30 km
0   15 miles

To Pul-e Khumri (65km); Kunduz (172km); Mazar-e Sharif (267km)

Baharak
Jangalak
Massoud's tomb
To Khawak Pass (65km); Anjoman Pass (80km)
Salang Pass (3363m)
Hindu Kush
Rokha
Panjshir Valley
Dalan Sang
Jebal Saraj
Gulbahar
Charikar
Bagram (US Army & NATO)
Sia Gird
Koh Daman
To Bamiyan (50km)
Shibar Pass (2987m)
Sheik Ali
Istalif
Panjshir River
Mir Bacha Kot
Band-e Sarobi
Shomali Plain
Tangi Gharu
Hajigak Pass (3700m)
Qargha Lake
Kabul International Airport
Paghman
Kabul
Kabul River
Sarobi
Gardandiwal
Jalez
To Jalalabad (54km); Torkham (128km)
Unai Pass (3300m)
Kabul River
Maidan Shahr

Pul-e Alam

To Ghazni (68km); Kandahar (420km)

irrigation canals, and rooting out thousands of acres of vines and fruit trees. The plain is still heavily mined, (so always stick to the beaten track), but since 2001, the vineyards have made an amazing recovery. In summer the main road through the plain is lined with stalls selling grapes by the boxload, from sweet seedless ones the size of your fingernail to larger juicier varieties.

The mountains rise up dramatically on either side of the plain, and about 55km north of Kabul a side road bears west and starts climbing towards Istalif. The road curls around the slopes through orchards and poplars, and crosses a small river to emerge in the main bazaar. At the far end of the bazaar is a small mosque with an unusual hexagonal minaret. There are wonderful views of the Shomali Plain and the mountains from here.

The bazaar is lined with small shops selling pottery. Istalif has been known for its pottery for at least 500 years, and there's a large variety of plates, bowls, pots and even candlesticks on offer. A medium-sized bowl should cost around 100Afg to 150Afg. The decoration is usually a deep blue or brown glaze with simple designs etched onto the surface. They're rustic but utterly charming. All the pottery is made on hand-wheels and fired in wood kilns. The **Turquoise Mountain Foundation** (www.turquoisemountain.org) is currently working with local potters to improve glazing and firing techniques to give Istalif better access to the export market.

There are a couple of chaikhanas in the bazaar, but there are plans to develop a traditional-style guesthouse with modern facilities in the village, as well as a visitor's centre. On the road into Istalif, there is a food stand at the **Takht**, set amid plane trees. A hotel stood here in the 1970s and is now used as a police station – with luck they'll allow you onto the terrace, which has sublime views. The police are particularly proud of their nursery of geraniums and roses, which make a strange contrast to the collapsed roof of part of the building – blown up by the Taliban.

Minibuses to Kabul (30Afg, 90 minutes) leave from near the bridge when full – the route is busiest on the weekend. From Kabul, minibuses leave from the Serai Shomali motor park.

> **WARNING**
>
> As we were going to press there were reports of anti-government elements operating in Paghman and the surrounding districts. Take trusted security advice before considering a trip to Paghman.

PAGHMAN   پغمان

King Amanullah built Paghman in the 1920s as a showcase for his ideas on modernising Afghanistan. It was decorated with pleasure gardens and ornate buildings, including a Victory Arch freely copied from the Arc de Triomphe, celebrating Afghan independence in 1919. Its gardens have since been a popular picnic spot for Kabulis.

Despite its model status, Paghman has played a key part in Afghan conservatism. In 1928 Amanullah held a loya jirga here which ended in turmoil. The delegates rebelled against his insistence they wear Western dress (top hats, no less), and the subsequent arrests of delegates helped precipitate the rebellion that closed Amanullah's regime. During the 1980s, Paghman was the base for the fundamentalist Abdul Rasul Sayyaf, who was a key figure in bringing Arab fighters to Afghanistan and had strong ties to Osama Bin Laden. Despite being implicated in war crimes during the civil war in Kabul, Sayyaf has remained hugely influential in the post-Taliban scene as an advisor to Hamid Karzai.

Paghman was much battered during the war, but still remains green and pretty in places, including the grass amphitheatre of Bagh-e Umumi that held the disastrous loya jirga (Amanullah was even said to race elephants here in his more idle moments). The Bahar Restaurant at the top of the village has simple dishes and drinks, and lovely views over the plains.

Minibuses leave for Paghman from Kabul's Serai Shomali motor park (25Afg, 30 minutes). If you have your own vehicle, it makes sense to also pay a visit to nearby Qargha Lake, which is passed en route to Paghman.

QARGHA LAKE   بند قرغه

Qargha Lake is another popular picnic spot for Kabulis, just 10km from the city. It's an artificial lake created in the late '50s by

President Daoud as a recreation facility for Kabul, and the clear air and cool waters make a great respite from the dust and fumes of the city. On Fridays the area throngs with families, and there are plenty of tea and food stalls and children running around to make quite a festive atmosphere.

Qargha Lake is also home to the **Kabul Golf Club** (☎ 079 9226 327/9029 011; www.kabulgolf club.com; greens fee 750Afg, club rental 250Afg, caddie fee 250Afg; ☺ 7am-dusk), which must be one of the most unusual courses in the world. King Habibullah introduced golf to Afghanistan in 1919, and is even buried on Jalalabad's municipal course (p183). The Kabul course reopened in 2004 after 26 years' closure. Its reconstruction was led by Muhammad Afzal Abdul, who was the club's last pro in 1978. The club is at the end of the dam.

The course is nine holes, with the back nine played off different tees. The greens are actually 'browns', a mix of sand and engine oil brushed to make a smooth putting surface. Unsurprisingly, the roughs are pretty tough, but even the fairways would challenge Tiger Woods. The club guidelines make interesting reading. Comparing the course to St Andrews', players are advised 'don't even ask for the stroke index because this is Afghanistan and they're all tough.' A second caddie is recommended, to go ahead of your shot to spot your ball. At the end of the round, the branded accessories (even golf towels) make unusual souvenirs.

Every August, the club hosts the Kabul Desert Classic tournament, a fundraising match organised by expats, with proceeds going to local charities.

Spojmai Lakeview Café (☎ 079 9003 333; spojmai@ gmail.com; fee for non-members incl one drink 100Afg, mains from 500Afg) is a members club overlooking the lake. Cushions are strewn on the terrace and roof for lounging around in and catching the sun and breeze. Barbeques are a speciality, especially the *chupan kabab* (grilled mutton). Sports on offer include tennis, jet skiing and horse riding.

A return taxi to Qargha Lake from Kabul should cost around 1000Afg. Minibuses (25Afg, 30 minutes) run on the weekend from Serai Shomali.

BAGRAM بگرام

The site of both an ancient city and a modern airbase, Bagram is 50km northwest of Kabul, near the town of Charikar. Modern Bagram was built by the Soviets, and was a key supply route during their occupation. Its possession was much contested between the Northern Alliance and the Taliban, and at the time of the American-led war in 2001 the two armies controlled opposite ends of the base. Bagram is now home to around 10,000 international military personnel, mainly American.

The site's history as a military camp is far more ancient. Alexander the Great founded the town, naming it Alexandria-ad-Caucasum, and used it as a base for his invasion of India. It was a major Graeco-Bactrian city and became the summer capital of the Kushan empire in the early centuries AD. Then known as Kapisa, it was one of the most important stops on the Silk Road. Kapisa was a cultural melting pot, its many Buddhist monasteries displaying art influenced

AROUND KABUL

THE BAGRAM IVORIES

The treasures excavated at Bagram illustrate the rich tastes of Kushan Kapisa. Glass from Alexandria, lacquer from China and Greek bronzes have all been discovered. The greatest of these are probably the Bagram Ivories.

Dating from the 2nd century AD, the ivories are a series of intricately carved panels, originally used for decorating thrones and boxes. Their style is instantly recognisable as Indian. Female figures are shown with full bosoms and wide hips, wrapped in transparent veils. Parrots and elephants decorate floral scenes, all carved in painstaking relief. Coupled with the rest of the Bagram finds, they contribute to a uniquely Afghan, yet international culture.

The current fate of all the ivories is unknown. Following the looting of Kabul Museum in the 1990s they disappeared from view. Several pieces have turned up on the international underground art markets, with price tags in the hundreds of thousands of dollars – one was famously bought by a Pakistani army general. The Kabul Museum managed to save some of the ivories from the looters, but they remain hidden in safekeeping. For more on the Kabul Museum, see p88.

by India, their coffers rich from trade with China and Rome. Any echoes of Kapisa have long been muffled by the sound of military aircraft.

Since the war, Bagram has acquired a black name. It is the site of a notorious detention facility in the 'War on Terror', used as a way station for the US prison at Guantánamo Bay. Amnesty International and Human Rights Watch have accused the authorities of torture and widespread prisoner abuse at Bagram, allegations denied by the US army, despite their admission of the assault and homicides of several Afghans in custody.

The small town of Bagram on the edge of the airbase has an interesting bazaar (busiest on Friday) selling US army goods and supplies that have been 'lost', sold or otherwise disappeared from the base – anything from army-issue sunglasses to ration packs. A scandal hit the base in 2006 when computer hard drives on sale were found to contain sensitive military information.

Minibuses run to Bagram from Kabul's Serai Shomali motor park (50Afg, 45 minutes). Alternatively, travel to Charikar (40Afg, 30 minutes) and change there. Charikar is famous for its handmade knives, and there are several chaikhanas on the main town roundabout. The big unnamed place on the southwest corner of the roundabout does a heaving trade – as well as kebabs and pulao it has great peppery *shorwa* (soup), and some divine almond ice cream.

PANJSHIR VALLEY   دره پنجشیر

The stunning Panjshir Valley has become one of the most celebrated places in Afghanistan. Its charging river and fields and orchards made it a popular tourist destination in the 1970s, but a decade later it became known as a symbol of resistance to the Soviets, the unconquerable redoubt of the mujaheddin leader Ahmad Shah Massoud. Having fought for over 20 years, Massoud was killed by Al-Qaeda in September 2001, and his tomb halfway up the valley, near his home village of Jangalak, is a must-see for any visitor.

The name Panjshir means 'Five Lions', for five brothers from the valley who miraculously dammed a river for Sultan Mahmoud of Ghazni in the 10th century AD. A *ziarat* (shrine) to them stands near the mouth of the valley.

Panjshir is possibly the most beautiful valley in Afghanistan. Starting at Dalan Sang, the narrow gorge that forms its mouth, the road proceeds up the valley, which gradually widens to reveal carefully irrigated fields of wheat and maize dotted with villages and walnut and mulberry groves. The Panjshir River itself is rich with fish. It's quite common to see men thigh-deep in the water casting nets and the catch is often for sale cooked at roadside stalls. In late spring, snowmelt turns the river into a torrent, but even in late summer there are plenty of rapids. A few enterprising expats have even managed to take advantage of the fast flowing waters by bringing their own kayaks.

The Panjshir has always been an important highway. Nearly 100km long, it leads to two passes over the Hindu Kush – the Khawak Pass (3848m) leading to the northern plains, and the Anjoman Pass (4430m) that crosses into Badakhshan – used by the armies of Alexander the Great and Timur. The Red Army had some of its darkest days in Afghanistan here.

Panjshir was ideally located for guerrilla attacks on Bagram and the supply convoys crossing the Salang Pass. As the Soviets learned to their cost, it was also brilliantly defensible. In the first three years of the war, there were six major offensives against the Panjshir, all of which ended in defeat for the Russians. Armoured columns could be easily attacked from the mountain walls, and the road easily cut by the mujaheddin. Destroyed tanks still litter the valley floor. Several times Massoud ordered the entire evacuation of the civilian population, to reduce casualties caused by high-altitude bombing. In total there were ten failed assaults on the Panjshir, causing the Russians to call a ceasefire with Massoud, unheard of during the war.

As well as a place of hiding, Panjshir was a source of income for Massoud. Medieval Panjshir had been famous for its silver mines, but repeated Soviet bombing

---

WARNING – UXO

The Panjshir Valley remains heavily affected by unexploded ordnances (UXOs), with local hospitals regularly reporting casualties. Always stick to the well-worn paths.

CROSSING THE KHAWAK PASS

In the winter of 329 BC, Alexander the Great was pursuing the remnant army of the Persian empire across Afghanistan, final victory always one step ahead of him. The Bactrian warlord Bessus had claimed the throne and retreated north of the Hindu Kush, razing the ground behind him, safe in the knowledge that no army could cross the mountains without supplies in winter.

Alexander had a different idea. He led his army up the Panjshir to push across the Khawak Pass, still deep in snow. Local villagers had buried their winter food, so the army had to carry all they ate. They ran out of food and slaughtered the pack animals, eating them raw due to a lack of firewood. Alexander, himself sick with fatigue and altitude sickness rode up and down the great column, driving his men on. The epic crossing took 17 days, when the exhausted army descended to bountiful villages on the northern plains. Incredulous at the feat, Bessus panicked and fled towards the Amu Darya, where he was cornered and executed, the last gasp of the mighty Persian empire.

Today, the Khawak Pass can still only be passed on foot. Locals ascribe the cairns at the summit to the Greek soldiers who fell on the march. 2300 years later, Ahmad Shah Massoud used the pass as a supply corridor to the Panjshir, to harry the soldiers of another superpower.

revealed seams of emeralds in the mountain walls that were mined and smuggled to Pakistan. The emeralds are of extremely high quality, but the mining technique still favoured – using old military munitions in barely-controlled explosions – frequently cracks the gems, reducing their value.

Massoud's Tomb

Ahmad Shah Massoud's tomb is about 30km from the mouth of the valley, high on a promontory with a splendid view across the Panjshir.

A modest and attractive whitewashed tomb with a green dome was built soon after Massoud's funeral, but when we most recently visited this was being replaced with a far more grandiose structure, a strange hybrid of ancient and modern. The traditional dome and tiles clash with the overblown 21st-century vernacular, all plate glass and fake columns. It's not a particularly happy collision. Only the actual tomb chamber inside, with the simple grave strewn with wild flowers seems to reflect the character of the slain leader.

In comparison, the half-destroyed Russian armoured vehicles next to the grave offer a starker reminder of Massoud's legacy. There's a small kiosk next door selling cards and books about Massoud, but nothing in English.

Almost the entire (male) population of the Panjshir attended Massoud's funeral in September 2001, and thousands of mourners still visit the grave on the anniversary of his death. Official commemorations are held in Kabul on 9 September, moving to Panjshir the following day. It's an emotional scene, held under tight security.

Despite his death, Massoud maintains a powerful presence in the valley. His portrait is everywhere, even on the windshields of vehicles. While other Afghans may hold mixed feelings about the man, Panjshiris are proud of their most famous son. In the immediate post-Taliban period, the Panjshiri faction of the Northern Alliance held all the main reins of power, and immediately upgraded the valley to full provincial status.

Getting There & Away

Minibuses to Panjshir run from Kabul (100Afg, 2½ hours) every day, via Jebal Saraj. Ask for Rokha or Baharak, the nearest villages to Massoud's Tomb. A return trip in a taxi should cost around US$50. The road through the valley is paved.

Security is tight in the valley, and all vehicles are stopped at a checkpoint just past Dalan Sang. It's advisable to bring your passport, and if travelling by private vehicle, a driver who has been to the valley before. Permission from the *amniyat* (security officers) is needed to travel past Massoud's Tomb.

In theory it is possible to continue up the valley to cross the Anjoman Pass (p166). It is essential you check in with the *amniyat* if trying this, as they will probably insist on your being accompanied by a soldier (and paying for it). Failure to do so would almost certainly result in arrest.

There is a **Governor's Guesthouse** (r US$20) in Rokha (sometimes known as the Royal Guesthouse or Massoud's Guesthouse). To stay overnight, visit the Governor's office in Rokha for written permission.

SALANG PASS   كوتل سالنگ

All road traffic between Kabul and north Afghanistan must cross the **Salang Pass** (3363m). One of three main passes across the Hindu Kush, the Salang was pierced in 1964 by the construction of a huge tunnel. Before then, the two halves of the country were effectively cut off from each other by the first snows of winter.

The Salang Tunnel is a marvel of Soviet engineering, and its military importance became apparent as soon as Russian tanks rumbled through en route to Kabul. In the 1980s Massoud's fighters regularly ambushed convoys from his nearby Panjshiri stronghold, while General Dostum's control of the tunnel gave him the keys to northern Afghanistan for several years. Since the fall of the Taliban, the pass more prosaically claims to be the site of the world's highest mobile phone tower.

The road to the Salang starts to rise into the mountains at **Jebal Saraj**. The centre of town is marked by a small white palace on a rise, which reputedly belonged to the Tajik rebel Bacha Saqao, who claimed the Afghan throne in 1929. The road splits here, with a spur leading northeast to the Panjshir Valley. Chaikhanas in Jebal Saraj double up as popular carwashes – look for the many fountains of water shooting into the air,

powered from the mountain streams above. The same waters powered Afghanistan's first hydroelectric station here during Habibullah's reign.

From Jebal Saraj, the road is a climbing procession of switchbacks, passing tiny villages clinging to the slopes, and groves of mulberry and cherry trees alongside the river. In several places, the swift waters have been dammed to make pools, which locals populate with wooden duck decoys for hunting.

Around 35km from Jebal Saraj, look out for a large and recently rebuilt *ziarat*. In the 1970s a terrible accident was prevented when a conductor – the brakes of his bus having failed – threw himself under the wheels of the vehicle to stop it careering to its doom. It's a popular place to stop for prayers and, after experiencing the way many drivers treat the Salang as an alpine racecourse, you may wish to do the same.

The pass itself is 12km from the *ziarat*. A series of covered galleries mark the approach, protecting the road from landslides. The mouth of the tunnel yawns into the side of the mountains. Nearly 3km long, claustrophobes won't enjoy the trip, which is gloomily lit and thick with traffic fumes. Delays at the tunnel are not uncommon, with traffic frequently held up to allow one way passage only. These delays can become even more severe with the snows of deep winter, and although the pass is kept open all year, it's sensible to bring some supplies and clothes against the weather when traversing at this time.

Bamiyan & Central Afghanistan

بامیان و افغانستان مرکزی

The massed peaks of the Hindu Kush form a huge tangled knot in the centre of the country, aptly known as the Koh-e Baba – the Grandfather of Mountains. It's also the Hazarajat, the home of the country's minority Hazara population. Today it's a remote and marginal area, but was once the crucible for some of Afghanistan's greatest cultural achievements.

Buddhism flowered in the green Bamiyan valley 1500 years ago; a centre of art and pilgrimage that reached its apogee in the creation of the giant statues of Buddha, which overlooked the town until their cruel destruction by the Taliban in 2001. Even deeper into the mountains, the fabulous Minaret of Jam still stands as a testament to the glories of later Muslim dynasties.

But the scenery is the real star of central Afghanistan – an unending procession of rocky mountaintops, deep gorges and verdant river valleys. The bright light and crisp mountain air makes the landscape sing, not least the incredible blue lakes of Band-e Amir.

The roads can be as bad as the views are spectacular, and visitors should prepare for bumpy travel and some chilly nights at high altitude. You'll need to time your trip for the warmer months: many communities become cut off once the snows of winter arrive, with roads impassable until after the spring melt.

BAMIYAN & CENTRAL AFGHANISTAN

HIGHLIGHTS

- Stand in awe beneath the giant empty Buddha niches of **Bamiyan** (p114)
- Dip your toes in the sapphire-blue lakes of the **Band-e Amir** (p122)
- Climb the ancient ruined citadel of **Shahr-e Zohak** (p119), guardian of the Bamiyan valley
- Bump along the remote and spectacular back-roads of Afghanistan's **central route** (p124)
- Scale the lost **Minaret of Jam** (p126), hidden in the folds of the Hindu Kush

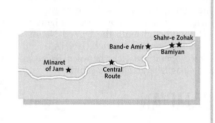

> **RISK ASSESSMENT**
>
> Bamiyan has consistently remained one of the calmest provinces in Afghanistan, with no major security incidents. Travellers are advised to avoid the southern route to Bamiyan from Kabul via the Hajigak Pass and Maidan Shahr in Wardak Province due to poor security, where there have been repeated abduction threats made against internationals.
>
> The central route is reasonably secure but very remote. There have been regular reports of robberies against private vehicles in the Chist-e Sharif and Obey areas.

CLIMATE

Dominated by the crags of the Koh-e Baba and Hindu Kush, central Afghanistan has a dry mountainous climate. In summer, days are warm (up to 28°C) while high altitudes mean that nights can be cold even in the middle of August. Warm clothes are essential. Temperatures drop considerably from November, skirting around freezing point. The region sees heavy snow from this point onwards, which can persist until March or even April, cutting off swathes of the region (although Bamiyan remains connected to Kabul year-round).

GETTING THERE & AWAY

Central Afghanistan's isolation is felt in its poor transport links to the rest of the country. Two punishing roads lead slowly from Bamiyan to Kabul, via either the northern Shibar Pass, or the Hajigak Pass to the south. Roads are similarly poor leaving the Hazarajat across the central route to Herat – a trip of several days in the summer, frequently impassable during the winter snows and merely treacherous during the spring melt. There are no commercial flights to Kabul, although both the United Nations Humanitarian Air Service (UNHAS) and Pactec operate services between Bamiyan and Chaghcheran and the capital.

BAMIYAN بامیان

Bamiyan sits at the heart of the Hazarajat in a wide valley braided with mountain rivers and is one of the poorest yet most beautiful parts of Afghanistan. Once a major centre for Buddhist pilgrimage, modern Bamiyan is now more closely associated with the destruction visited on Afghanistan's culture by war. The two giant statues of Buddha that once dominated the valley now lie in rubble, victims of the Taliban's iconoclastic rage. Despite this, the Bamiyan valley still holds a powerful draw over the imagination. It was made a World Heritage site in 2003 for its cultural landscape and is a must-see for any visitor to Afghanistan.

While isolated today, it wasn't always so. Bamiyan was once an important way station on the Silk Road. Trade and pilgrims flocked to its temples and in return Bamiyan exported its art – a synthesis of Greek, Persian and Indian art that had a major influence on Buddhist iconography as far afield as China. Centuries later, Bamiyan became the focus of Afghanistan's nascent tourist industry, as visitors came to rediscover its past glories and gaze in awe at the monumental Buddha statues carved from its cliffs.

War brought an end to that. Initially isolated from the fighting, Bamiyan suffered terribly under the ideological fervour of the Taliban, whose anti-Shiite doctrines drove ethnic massacres as well as the smashing of idols.

Since the Taliban's defeat, Bamiyan has returned to the peace of earlier years and is currently home to a New Zealand–led Provincial Reconstruction Team (PRT). It has consistently been one of Afghanistan's real oases of calm, although locals grumble about the slow pace of reconstruction.

For many, Bamiyan can best be experienced at sunset from the hills overlooking the valley. The niches of the Buddhas evoke a particular power at this hour and as the light of the day changes so does the colour of the cliffs, from honey to pink, ochre to magenta.

HISTORY

Bamiyan's place in Afghan history begins with the emergence of the Kushan empire in the 1st century AD. As a halfway point between Balkh and the Kushan capital at Kapisa (near modern Bagram, see p109), it grew rich from the trade along the Silk Road between Rome and the Han Chinese.

The nomadic Kushans quickly took to Buddhism and were instrumental in fusing astern art with the Hellenistic tradition eft by the Greeks. This Graeco-Buddhic rt flowered in Bamiyan, which quickly became a major centre of culture and religion where monasteries flourished.

Kushan power waned, but Bamiyan remained a cultural centre. Another wave of invaders, the White Huns, were assimilated in the 4th century and went on to create two giant statues of Buddha, carved out of the sandstone cliffs of the valley walls, bedecked with jewels and gilt. Bamiyan became one of the most important Buddhist pilgrimage sites in the world.

Events in the east threatened Bamiyan's pre-eminence and in the 7th century, Afghanistan felt the eastward thrust of Islam.

High in the mountains, Bamiyan clung on to its Buddhist traditions for another 400 years, until the ascendant Ghaznavids finally brought Islam to the valley for good.

A series of smaller dynasties held sway over Bamiyan until the beginning of the 13th century. The Shansabani kings briefly made the valley the capital of a realm stretching as far north as Balkh and Badakhshan, until they were swept away in the Mongol tidal wave in 1222.

Genghis Khan initially sent his favourite grandson to deal with the Shansabani kings and they responded by slaying the young general. As revenge, Genghis sent his warriors to storm the citadels. Every living thing in the valley was slaughtered.

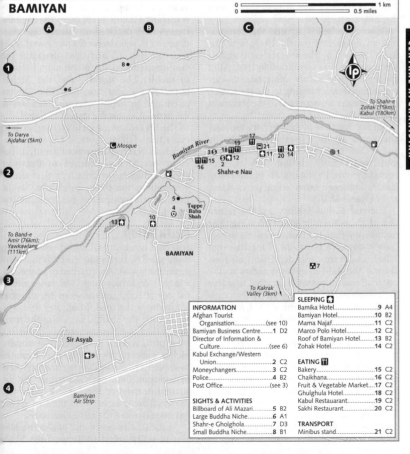

BAMIYAN

INFORMATION	
Afghan Tourist Organisation	(see 10)
Bamiyan Business Centre	1 D2
Director of Information & Culture	(see 6)
Kabul Exchange/Western Union	2 C2
Moneychangers	3 C2
Police	4 B2
Post Office	(see 3)

SIGHTS & ACTIVITIES	
Billboard of Ali Mazari	5 B2
Large Buddha Niche	6 A1
Shahr-e Gholghola	7 D3
Small Buddha Niche	8 B1

SLEEPING	
Bamika Hotel	9 A4
Bamiyan Hotel	10 B2
Mama Najaf	11 C2
Marco Polo Hotel	12 C2
Roof of Bamiyan Hotel	13 B2
Zohak Hotel	14 C2

EATING	
Bakery	15 C2
Chaikhana	16 C2
Fruit & Vegetable Market	17 C2
Ghulghula Hotel	18 C2
Kabul Restauarant	19 C2
Sakhi Restaurant	20 C2

TRANSPORT	
Minibus stand	21 C2

BAMIYAN & CENTRAL AFGHANISTAN

Bamiyan never fully recovered from the Mongol devastation. While the Hazaras now claim descent from the Mongol invaders, they spent the next 600 years independent but isolated from Afghan history. The Hazaras' adherence to Shiite Islam meant they were further distrusted by the Afghan mainstream.

In the 1890s Abdur Rahman Khan led a military campaign to bring Bamiyan and the Hazarajat under the control of the Afghan state. He declared a jihad against the Hazaras, taking many into slavery and giving their land to Pashtun farmers. Ironically, the Hazaras were allowed to return when the newcomers found it impossible to raise crops in Bamiyan's marginal environment. The area remained the most underdeveloped part of Afghanistan throughout the 20th century.

Bamiyan rebelled against the communist government in early 1979, with the town inspired by the success of Ayatollah Khomeini's Shiite revolution in Iran. After the Soviet invasion, the mountainous surroundings were a blessing to the resistance, who drove the Russians out of the Hazarajat by 1981.

For the first time in their history the Hazaras could organise themselves politically and militarily. Bamiyan was ruled by the mujaheddin party Hezb-e Wahdat, supported by Iran. By the middle of the 1990s, Hazara influence extended as far as Kabul and Mazar-e Sharif.

The rise of the Taliban saw the return of anti-Hazara sentiments. Following their capture of Kabul, the Pashtun militia immediately started a blockade of the Bamiyan valley. The region was dependent on food aid but the Taliban refused access to the international community, in a bid to starve their enemies. By the time the Taliban captured Bamiyan in September 1998, much of the population had fled to the mountains. In an echo of Abdur Rahman Khan's policies, the Taliban tried to encourage Pashtun's nomads to settle on the Hazaras' land.

Almost immediately, the Taliban threatened to blow up the giant Buddhas, but backed down in the face of international outrage. Mullah Omar even went as far as declaring that they should be protected to encourage a future return of tourism to Afghanistan.

WHO'S THAT MAN?

You'll be hard-pressed to find pictures of Ahmad Shah Massoud in Bamiyan: locals still remember his 1995 shelling of Hazara civilians in Kabul. Instead, pictures of the late Hezb-e Wahdat leader Abdul Ali Mazari are prominently displayed, including a large billboard overlooking the town. Mazari was mysteriously killed by the Taliban in 1995 after trying to form an alliance with them against the mujaheddin government in Kabul and the Hazaras are now led by Karim Khalili – another favourite on the walls of Bamiyan.

Such ideals didn't last long. With UN sanctions biting, and faced with a newly resurgent Hazara resistance, the Buddha statues were declared un-Islamic and their destruction was decreed. Over two days in the beginning of March 2001, dynamite and tank-fire reduced the monumental statues to rubble. The world – and the Afghan population – was horrified. The Taliban celebrated by selling picture calendars of the demolition on the streets of Kabul.

The US-led campaign in November 2001 saw a final Taliban spate of killing and destruction before Bamiyan's liberation. But peace has finally returned to Bamiyan, even producing the country's first female governor in the figure of Habiba Sorabi. Economic development has been slower to follow.

ORIENTATION

Bamiyan is set in a wide and pretty valley, dominated by the sandstone cliffs that form its northern wall. Approached from the east, a large sign misleadingly welcomes you to the city of Bamiyan; the town lies a further 15km down the road. Minibuses drop you off outside the chaikhanas along the main bazaar (Shahr-e Nau), where you'll also find most of Bamiyan's amenities. The Buddha niches, a short walk over the river from the town centre, are visible from everywhere in Bamiyan. Bamiyan's old bazaar lies destroyed in front of the Large Buddha and much of the area between the two niches has been marked for mine clearance.

At the southwestern end of Shahr-e Nau a road leads uphill to Teppe Baba Shah which offers the best scenic views of the valley, as well as being the location for many NGO offices. As it curls uphill, the road splits left towards Shahr-e Gholghola. From Teppe Baba Shah, continue south to the airstrip and the village of Sir Asyab, where you will find some more sleeping options (a taxi from Shahr-e Nau will cost around 80Afg).

INFORMATION
Internet Access
Bamiyan Business Centre (Shahr-e Nau; per hr 60Afg; ☺ 2.30-7pm) Well run with fast internet connections.

Money
There are plenty of moneychangers' offices along Bamiyan's main bazaar.
Kabul Exchange (Shahr-e Nau, next to Marco Polo Hotel) Has a branch of Western Union, but keeps erratic business hours.

Post & Telephone
At the time of research, only Roshan offered mobile phone coverage in Bamiyan. There are PCOs along the main bazaar.
Post office (Shahr-e Nau) Look for the hand-painted 'Post' sign on the door, but it's more reliable to send mail from Kabul.

Tourist Information
An excellent guide to the valley is the recent reprint of Nancy Dupree's *Bamiyan*, but frustratingly this is only available in Kabul.
Afghan Tourist Organization (Bamiyan Hotel, Teppe Baba Shah) Has little tourist information, but can organise cars and drivers.

SIGHTS
The Buddha Niches
The empty niches of the Buddha statues dominate the Bamiyan valley. Carved in the 6th century, the two statues, standing 38m and 55m respectively, were the tallest standing statues of Buddha ever made. Now gone, the emptiness of the spaces the statues have left behind nevertheless inspires awe and quiet contemplation in equal measure. The bases of the niches are fenced off and although it is quite possible to view them for free from some distance, a ticket from the office of the **Director of Information and Culture** (in front of Large Buddha niche; 160Afg, ticket also valid for Shahr-e Gholghola & Shahr-e Zohak; ☺ 8am-5pm) allows further access to the site.

Next to the director's office is a large shed containing the salvaged remains of the **Large Buddha**, which give an insight into the construction of the statues. They weren't simply carved out of the sandstone cliffs – rough figures were instead hewn from the rock, which was then covered in mud and straw to create the intricate folds of the robes, before being plastered and painted. The Large Buddha was painted with red robes, while the Small Buddha was clothed in red. Their faces were covered in gilded masks, although all traces of these disappeared in antiquity. The Chinese monk Xuan Zang visited Bamiyan at the height of its glory in the 7th century, writing of the statues that 'the golden hues sparkle on every side, and its precious ornaments dazzle the eye by their brightness'. As a devout pilgrim, Xuan Zang may have looked back on the statues' ultimate destruction

---

THE RECLINING BUDDHA OF BAMIYAN

The Chinese pilgrim Xuan Zang, who visited the valley in the 7th century, is our best chronicler of Bamiyan. After accurately describing the two standing Buddhas, he left a description of a third to entice later generations of archaeologists: 'In the monastery situated two or three li to the east of the city, there is an image of the Buddha recumbent, more than one thousand feet long, in the posture of entering Nirvana.' If true, this Buddha would be as long as the Eiffel Tower is tall – but what happened to it?

Since the fall of the Taliban, a team led by the Afghan archaeologist Professor Zemaryali Tarzi has been searching for it, believing it to have been buried under rubble from an earthquake. In an area southeast of the Small Buddha, he believes he may have found part of the toe of this Reclining Buddha. A major problem is that the statue is thought to have been made of mud bricks, and so would have been highly susceptible to erosion. However, Professor Tarzi's excavations have uncovered several small Buddha statues and carved heads, which have been presented to the Kabul Museum. The fate of the Reclining Buddha may never be known, but the search continues.

as reflecting a central teaching of the Buddha: nothing is permanent and everything changes.

The remaining chunks of statue are a small fraction of the total – the Taliban sold much of what was not simply destroyed to Pakistani antique dealers in Peshawar.

The view from the base of the niche to its ceiling is dizzying. The ceiling and walls were once covered with frescoes, using symbolism borrowed from Greek, Indian and Sassanid (Persian) art. The fusion of these traditions gave the Buddhist art of Bamiyan its vitality, which would later spread to India and China.

The cliffs surrounding each Buddha are honeycombed with monastic cells and grottoes, and your entrance ticket allows a guided tour. When we visited, the guides were enthusiastic but didn't have much English (or information), although a proper training programme is now reportedly in place. When exploring the cells and passages, good shoes are recommended, as well as a torch. Hard hats are provided – less for the fear of falling rocks than the inevitability of banging your head on the low ceilings.

The Large Buddha's grottoes are relatively few in number. You enter them by climbing almost around the back of the Buddha, cutting up some way to the left. The path here is marked with white rocks to show recent demining. The cells were originally decorated with frescoes displaying Buddhas and Bodhisattvas, all now lost in this section. In total, it is estimated that around 85% of the paintings disappeared during the war, through neglect, theft or deliberate destruction.

As you follow the passages you eventually emerge above the head of the Large Buddha. The views are amazing, unless you suffer from vertigo. The top of the niche has been braced with scaffolding to prevent subsidence. As with the cells, the ceiling was once elaborately painted.

The **Small Buddha** niche stands 500m to the east. The intervening section of cliff is honeycombed with cells, sanctuaries and passages tunnelled into the rock. Now long gone, a series of stupas and monasteries at the foot of the cliff further served the Buddhist complex. Xuan Zang noted 10 convents and over a 1000 priests and at its peak, Bamiyan is thought to have contained around 50 temples. Halfway between the two Buddhas is a smaller third niche high on the cliff, which would have held a free-standing Buddha statue. In the aftermath of the Taliban's ouster, many of these caves were occupied by Hazara internally displaced people (IDPs).

The grottoes of the Small Buddha are far more extensive and rewarding than those at the Large Buddha, in part because this site is nearly a century older. You enter via stairs at the base of the niche – these stairs encircle the niche, allowing the faithful to circumambulate the Buddha, an important ritual. Although almost all of the frescoes have been lost, a few glimpses remain in a couple of places. The so-called assembly hall on the west side has bright blue and maroon fragments of a huge lotus on its cup-

---

REBUILDING THE BUDDHAS?

Mullah Omar may have said that all he was doing was 'breaking stones' when he ordered the destruction of the Buddhas, but he was being disingenuous. Bamiyan was once the jewel in Afghanistan's tourism crown and many locals believe that rebuilding the statues will encourage foreign tourism and boost the region's economy, as well as being an act of cultural healing.

Hamid Karzai and Bamiyan governor Habiba Sorabi have both given vocal support. Unesco have been more ambivalent, claiming a mandate to preserve rather than rebuild and that general reconstruction of the town should take priority. Nevertheless proposals have been put forward by several sources, including an Afghan sculptor and a consortium headed by a Swiss museum. Costs are estimated at US$30 to US$50 million – big money in a town lacking mains electricity. Equally fanciful has been the plan by a Californian artist to project multiple lasers onto the empty niches to recreate the statues.

Meanwhile, the only actual rebuilding of the Buddhas has been in China, where replicas have been constructed in a theme park in Sichuan. The empty niches seem likely to exert their mournful auras over the Bamiyan valley for the foreseeable future.

ola, surrounded by a red band decorated with delicate white flowers. It's just enough to give a tantalising idea of how the whole might have looked. Near this hall is a vestibule looking out to the valley, which still retains its original façade, with the stone carved to resemble jutting wood beams.

The grottoes continue on the east side of the niche, with rooms containing carved lantern-roof ceilings and wall niches for Buddha statues.

Bamiyan's heyday as a Buddhist pilgrimage site barely lasted a handful of centuries. After a brief period of coexistence with its expanding Muslim neighbours, it slipped into terminal decline around the 10th century, when many statues and temples were destroyed. Memories of the Buddhist past faded and locals began to suppose that the statues were of pagan kings. Amazingly, Genghis Khan left them standing – about the only thing he did leave intact in Bamiyan. Greater damage was done in the 17th century when the Mughal emperor Aurangzeb smashed their faces. A hundred years later the legs of the Larg e Buddha were cut off by the Persian Nadir Shah.

During the civil war, the niches and caves were often used as ammunition dumps, with some soldiers occasionally using the statues for target practice. The final, terrible, indignity came with their complete demolition by the Taliban in March 2001, leaving behind an indelible testament to Afghanistan's many cultural losses in recent wars.

Shahr-e Gholghola

A 20-minute walk from Bamiyan stands the remains of Ghorid Bamiyan's last stand against the Mongol hordes. Shahr-e Gholghola was reputedly the best defended of Bamiyan's royal citadels and was captured by intrigue rather than force of arms.

Bamiyan's ruler Jalaludin held strong under Genghis Khan's siege, but he didn't reckon on the treachery of his daughter. She had quit her widowed father's castle in a fit of pique over his remarrying a princess from Ghazni. She betrayed the castle's secret entrance, expecting to be rewarded through her own betrothal to the Mongol ruler. But he put her to the sword anyway and slaughtered the rest of the defenders. The noise of the furious violence gave the citadel's modern name – 'City of Screams'.

To get to the citadel, follow the road up Teppe Baba Shah, but veer left at the first junction. The walk, curving past wheat and potato fields, is a pleasant one, particularly in late summer when you can watch the grain being threshed by yoked oxen. The road skirts the base of the citadel, with a path leading up an area cleared for parking. The ruins were mined during the war, and although there are no red or white rocks visible, it is still strongly advised that you keep only to the worn path to the summit. There is a small police post at the top, where you'll be asked to produce a ticket – the same one covering the Buddha Niches and Shahr-e Zohak (see p117).

The views over the valley to the cliff walls are gorgeous. Looking south, the view extends to the **Kakrak Valley**, which once held a 6.5m standing Buddha (the niche in the cliff is just visible with the naked eye) and some important frescoes, all now lost. It's a good couple of hours' walk, again through pretty farmland. Between the citadel and this valley are the remains of Qala-e Dokhtar (the Daughter's Castle), once home to Jalaludin's duplicitous offspring.

Shahr-e Zohak

The imposing ruins of Shahr-e Zohak guard the entrance to the Bamiyan valley, perched high on the cliffs at the confluence of the Bamiyan and Kalu rivers. Built by the Ghorids, they stand on foundations dating back to the 6th century. Genghis Khan's grandson was killed here, bringing down his murderous fury on the whole Bamiyan valley as a result. The colloquial name Zohak is taken from the legendary serpent-haired king of Persian literature.

The towers of the citadel are some of the most dramatic in Afghanistan. Made of mud-brick on stone foundations, they wrap around the side of the cliff, with geometric patterns built into their crenellations for decoration. The towers had no doors, but were accessed by ladders that the defenders pulled up behind them.

Passing the towers, a path leads up through a rock tunnel and the main gateway of the fortress, before switching back up the hill, past ruined barracks and storerooms. Take extreme care here – the route is marked with red rocks for landmines (many of then faded or peeling), so don't stray from the well-worn path. The path quickly steepens and becomes increasingly exposed to strong crosswinds. A rusting anti-aircraft gun and abandoned soldier's post market the summit.

The views over the confluence of the two rivers are awesome, with their thin strips of cultivated green providing a stark contrast to the dry pink and tan of the mountains. The location's strategic value is immediately apparent, and the heights seemingly impregnable to all except Genghis.

Shahr-e Zohak is around 9km from Bamiyan. To get there take any westbound transport out of Bamiyan. As the confluence of the Bamiyan and Kalu rivers is where the roads from the Shibar and Hajigak Passes meet, any transport should be able to drop you there. Ask to be let out at Tupchi village (40Afg, 25 minutes) or the checkpoint at Shashpul half a kilometre after it, which is next to the confluence. The soldiers here will check you have a ticket from the Director of Information and Culture in Bamiyan (see p117). From here, walk about 1km following the Kalu, until you can see a simple wood-and-earth bridge, roughly level with the last of the citadel's towers (if your vehicle is going in the Hajigak Pass direction – the nearest villages to ask for are Dahane Khushkak, Paymuri or Sawzaw – you can be dropped at this point). A short walk along the edge of a field brings you to a pass leading up to the towers.

Hiring a vehicle from Bamiyan will cost around 1100Afg return, depending on your haggling skills.

Darya Ajdahar

Five kilometres west of Bamiyan lies Darya Ajdahar, or Valley of the Dragon, where you'll find the petrified remains of a monstrous creature that once terrorised the region.

The dragon took up residence in Bamiyan in pagan times, and fed daily on a diet of virgins and camels provided by the browbeaten population. All attempts to slay it ended in a fiery end. Only Ali, the Prophet Mohammed's son-in-law, fresh from creating the Band-e Amir lakes (see p123), could manage the task. The dragon's burning breath turned to tulip petals as they licked around the hero, whereupon he drew his great sword Zulfiqar and cleaved the monster in two.

The dragon can clearly be seen and only those lacking poetry would remark that its body is merely a vast whaleback of volcanic rock split by an ancient earthquake. Others would point instead to the 2m-high horns and the two springs at its head – one running clear with the dragon's tears, the other red with its blood. The springs run the length of the great fissure and bending quietly down next to it, you can sometimes hear the groan of the dead beast echoing through the rock. At the far end of the dragon is a simple shrine dedicated to Ali.

The new village of Ajdahar lies at the head of the valley, built by the UN for Hazara returnees from Iran and Pakistan. It's a grim place, with barely a scrap of greenery, but the villagers are trying hard to make a living. The dragon lies at the valley's far end – look for the white smear on the rock and the spur of the dragon's horn on the north slope. Wear decent footwear for the short climb.

A round trip from Bamiyan to Darya Ajdahar in a private vehicle will cost around 500Afg. Transport leaves erratically to Ajdahar village (30Afg, 20 minutes).

SLEEPING

Marco Polo Hotel (Shahr-e Nau; dm 70Afg) More a chaikhana than a proper hotel, this is a real shoestring option – everyone squeezes into a small room on the ground floor, or retires upstairs to sleep in the restaurant. As with many chaikhanas, there's no bathroom so you'll quickly become familiar with Bamiyan's hammam (20Afg per person).

Mama Najaf (☎ 079 9426 250; Shahr-e Nau; dm 300Afg) Two communal rooms sit above a chaikhana up some extremely rickety wooden stairs. There's a simple bathroom and toilet, but for hot water you'll need to head for the hammam (20Afg per person) across the street .

Zohak Hotel (☎ 079 9235 298; Shahr-e Nau; s/d/tr US$20/40/50) Bamiyan's best budget option by some degree. The old upstairs dorm has been turned into a restaurant, while the addition of the rooftop shower with piping hot water is very welcome. Rooms are compact and basic, but clean. Food is good, with large plates of rice, vegetables and meat for around 150Afg.

Bamiyan Hotel (☎ 079 9212 543; Teppe Baba Shah; US$30, yurts US$40) This is Bamiyan's oldest hotel and one of the few still run by the ATO.

he luxury yurts the hotel boasted in the 970s have been rebuilt, offering one of fghanistan's most novel accommodation ptions. Standard rooms in the main hotel ave shared bathrooms. There's a pleasant arden, although the high perimeter walls lock great views across the valley. The res-aurant is Bamiyan's best eating choice; a ree-course meal with soup and fruit costs round 200Afg.

Bamika Hotel (☎ 079 9398 162; Sir Asyab; r US$40) his pleasant hotel suffers from poor sign-ng – it's some way into Sir Asyab village, 00m past the ICRC compound. Once there, 's both spacious and spotless. Rooms are arge and, unusually for Bamiyan, en suite with hot-water heater.)

Roof of Bamiyan Hotel (☎ 079 9235 292; Sir syab; r US$40-60) If it's location you're after, ead here – this hotel offers fantastic views ver the Bamiyan valley. Clean bathrooms re shared, with the cheaper rooms in a eparate annexe. There's a restaurant, plus a eries of yurts that were under construction vhen we visited. The manager, an Afghan eteran of the hippy trail, can organise reli-ble vehicle hire and the like.

ATING

across Afghanistan, Bamiyan is known or two things – potatoes and *krut*. *Krut* is ried yoghurt made into balls, which can be econstituted into a sauce, or sucked on as snack when travelling or working. It's an cquired taste. The potatoes make a pleas-nt change from rice, however, particularly vhen made into chips.

Bamiyan only has a few restaurants, all long the main bazaar in Shahr-e Nau, and ll offering standard chaikhana fare for 0Afg to 70Afg: kebabs, *pulao* and *shorwa* soup). None stand out over any others; ry the Ghulghula Hotel, the Kabul Restau-ant or the Sakhi Restaurant. All are 1st-loor affairs, with steps leading up from the treet, making window space a good place o watch the world go by.

The restaurants at the Zohak, Bamiyan nd Roof of Bamiyan Hotels offer more va-iety, although you'll need to give advance otice when you want to eat.

The shops along Shahr-e Nau bazaar are tocked with food staples and a few treats. he fruit and vegetable market runs parallel o the main street, one block to the north.

GETTING THERE & AWAY

Minibuses depart from the area around Mama Najaf hotel. Transport to Kabul (400Afg, nine to 11 hours), leaves around 4am to 5am, so it's important to check what's available the day before travel. Note that Kabul transport generally takes the south-erly road via the Hajigak and Unai Passes, which at the time of research was not con-sidered safe for travel for foreigners since it passes through restive Wardak Province. The northern road, via the Shibar Pass, is the more secure (and picturesque) option, but get up-to-date advice before travelling. Both roads are very poor quality – something of a political issue in the province.

Direct minibuses to Band-e Amir (150Afg, three hours) tend to be restricted to Thursday, Friday and Saturday. A large Millie bus also runs this route every Friday morning (40Afg, 3½ hours).

Heading west, minibuses travel most days to Yawkawlang (200Afg, five hours) according to demand, but transport beyond Yawkawlang is hard to find unless you're prepared to hire your own vehicle. Snowfall and floods can make the road west from Bamiyan extremely difficult from Novem-ber to as late as May. For more on travelling this route see p124.

There's no public transport heading north from Bamiyan, making it easier (and quicker) to go to via Kabul and the Salang Tunnel. With your own transport, the di-rect road is slow and remote, albeit with good mountain views. From Bamiyan, take the Shibar Pass road and turn north where the road splits at Shikari. The road passes the ruined ramparts of Sar Khoshak (de-stroyed by Genghis Khan) and the entrance

BAMIYAN & CENTRAL AFGHANISTAN

THE SHIBAR PASS

As the narrow road bumps over the Shibar Pass (2960m) spare a thought for Alexander the Great's soldiers who slogged over it in the winter of 327 BC. Cold and tired, they didn't know (or probably care) that they were crossing a continental watershed, where the Indian subcontinent is divided from Central Asia. Rivers to the east of the Shibar Pass ultimately join the Indus river system, while those on the west flow to-wards the Amu Darya.

to the Ajar Valley at Doab before eventually turning east to follow the Surkhab river to Doshi, where the road joins the main Kabul–Mazar-e Sharif highway. Allow a day's solid driving for this route. Should the Salang Tunnel be closed for maintenance, traffic is often diverted along this back road. If this happens, minibuses can take up to 36 hours to travel from Kabul to Mazar-e Sharif.

Vehicle hire in Bamiyan tends to cost around US$50 to US$100 for a half/full day for a 4WD.

Flights from Kabul with UNHAS or Pactec take around 25 minutes. It's a dramatic approach by air, swooping down the length of the valley.

AROUND BAMIYAN
Band-e Amir   بند امیر

The glittering lakes of Band-e Amir must rank as Afghanistan's most astounding natural sight, hidden in the Koh-e Baba at an altitude of 2900m. A series of six linked lakes, their deep blue waters sparkle like otherworldly jewels against the dusty mountains that surround them.

The lakes' high mineral content gives them their colour, and in the case of the most accessible lake, Band-e Haibat (the suitably named Dam of Awe), these minerals have been deposited along its shore to produce a huge curtain wall over 12m high, streaked with sulphur and containing its waters high above 'ground' level. It's a

weird and stupendous sight, and it's nc surprising that locals should far prefer mythic, rather than geological, explanatio for the lakes' formation (see the boxed tex opposite). The lakes are reputed to contai great healing powers and pilgrims still vis to take the waters.

Approaching Band-e Amir, the first hir you have of their striking qualities is a brigl flash of lapis lazuli as the largest lake, Banc e Zulfiqar appears briefly to your righ Soon after, the road starts to descend fror a plateau immediately above the flat mirrc of Band-e Haibat. Its deep blue waters an white dams fringed with vegetation are rude shock when set against the cream an pink mountains – a sight to draw breat from even the most jaded travellers.

Arriving at the floor of the valley, vehi cles stop a five-minute walk away from th dam walls, near a cluster of chaikhanas an kiosks. On Fridays and Saturdays, the are absolutely throngs with Afghan day-trip pers, providing a rare echo of Afghanistan tourist heyday.

At the lakeshore, it's possible to hir pedalos (75Afg per 15 minutes), shape like swans, to take onto the water. They'r slightly kitsch, but are a great way of see ing the lake, particularly if you've got th stamina to pedal all the way to the end an back – a good couple of hours. Alternativel a boat (the 'Donald Duck') carries up to 1 people for trips around the lake and bac for 50Afg a head.

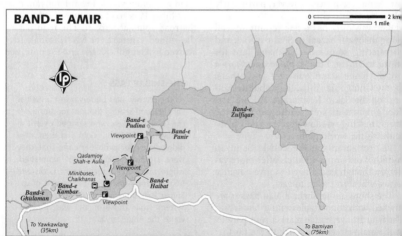

BAND-E AMIR

On a more spiritual level, a small shrine, nown locally as Qadamjoy Shah-e Aulia The place where Ali stood'), overlooks the ke here. Built in the 1920s on the site of an lder tomb, its doors are covered with small adlocks left as votive tokens, particularly rom women offering prayers for love nd fertility.

AND-E AMIR WALKING TOUR

. walk around the edges of the lakes is the est way to appreciate their scale, and the liff-top walk offers a succession of sublime istas. The summer sun can be very fierce t this altitude, so take a hat and plenty f water.

Follow the rough path up from the haikhanas to quickly find yourself looking own on **Band-e Haibat**. After about 15 min- tes the path reaches a promontory with great view, looking across the lake, and own into the first of a series of coves with nviting shallows. Continuing along the ath, you have to cut inland for about 20 ninutes, through some very dusty scrubby errain, occasionally veering back toward ne water. An hour after setting out you nd yourself looking over the far shore of ne lake and across to **Band-e Panir** (Dam of Cheese) This is the prettiest of the lakes, al- nost a perfect triangle of bright turquoise, ringed with a white beach. The lake sits lightly above Band-e Haibat bound by a vhite calcium travertine dam, and above nis again is the tiny **Band-e Pudina** (Dam of Mint), almost completely overgrown with egetation. Curving to the northwest, and igher still, the waters of the largest lake, and-e Zulfiqar (Dam of Ali's Sword), are just isible. The lakes are linked by a series of ascades, each feeding the one below.

Carrying on the walk for another 30 ninutes, the cliffs descend and allow you reach the shores of Band-e Pudina and and-e Panir. Few people get this far, and neir relative seclusion makes them great pots to take a dip. Band-e Panir in particu- ar is relatively shallow and not as cold as ne icy waters on the other lakes. Women nould take absolute care that there are no ocals around before plunging in.

Returning to Band-e Haibat, it is possible walk the perimeter of the dam walls. Algal rowths make it slippery in places. At the ar end are several tents, erected for the few

THE MIRACLES OF ALI

An infidel king called Babar ruled the Hindu Kush with a terrible fury. He was particularly frustrated by his inability to control a rag- ing river near his capital. Ali, the Prophet Mohammed's son-in-law, was travelling through the region, and, disguised as a slave, was brought to the king. Babar laughed at the captive and challenged him to perform a series of miracles. This Ali did – he hurled down rocks at the river to form Band-e Haibat, and sliced the top off a mountain with his sword to create Band-e Zulfiqar. His groom dammed Band-e Kambar and inspired by Ali, the king's own slaves made Band-e Ghulaman. Band-e Panir and Band-e Pudina were made with the help of a nomad woman, a piece of cheese and a sprig of mint. To top off the day's work, Ali killed a dragon that had been terrorising the region. Babar was so amazed with these feats that he converted to Islam on the spot.

pilgrims who come to Band-e Amir for the reportedly curative powers of the mineral waters. The walls terminate at the cliff, al- though there is a rough and precipitous path that can take you to the top. This follows the cliff edge past several chimney-like rock formations. After an hour, the path descends to the eastern shore of Band-e Pudina (also accessible if you have your own vehicle).

Two further lakes lie to the west of Band- e Haibat. The first, **Band-e Kambar** (Dam of the Groom) has almost completely dried up and is little more than a series of puddles. The shore of **Band-e Ghulaman** (Dam of the Slaves) is a further kilometre west. This has the lowest mineral content, and its shallows are thick with reedbeds. There is also plenty of bird-life here, giving it a much differ- ent character to the other lakes. The green shores are an ideal place for a picnic.

SLEEPING & EATING

In the past couple of years, a small 'street' has grown up to the side of Band-e Haibat, with half a dozen simple chaikhanas offer- ing the usual *pulao*, kebabs and an occas- ional omelette and chips for around 60Afg. Although you may see people fishing with lines on the lake, the *mohi* (fish) themselves rarely end up on the menu.

A few of the chaikhanas are little more than pitched tents, where for the price of dinner (or 100Afg, according to the manager's whim) you can stay for the night. Bring warm clothes and ask for an extra blanket. A short walk from the tents is a latrine block, dubbed the 'Taliban House' by local wags.

GETTING THERE & AWAY

There are direct minibuses to the lakes from Bamiyan on Thursday, Friday and Saturday mornings (150Afg, three hours), as well as a large bus every Friday morning (40Afg, 3½ hours). Hiring a vehicle from Bamiyan should cost around US$60. Public transport sometimes stops at the hamlet of Qarghanatu, two-thirds of the way from Bamiyan, for breakfast. The chaikhanas here serve *kimak*, a type of dried salty sheep's cheese.

Band-e Amir is a further 15km after the turn-off from the Bamiyan–Yawkawlang route: note that there are several stretches where the verges of this road are mined, although not in the immediate vicinity of the lakes. Band-e Amir is largely inaccessible during the winter, although the frozen lakes would be a tremendous sight.

BAMIYAN & CENTRAL AFGHANISTAN

THE CENTRAL ROUTE

راه مرکزی

Crossing the centre of the country along the spine of the Hindu Kush is one of the most remote and adventurous journeys it's possible to do in Afghanistan, but one that rewards travellers with a continuous parade of stunning mountain scenery. Travelling from Bamiyan, the route travels through the Hazarajat over a series of high mountain passes to the heart of the medieval Ghorid empire. This is a land of tiny villages, marginal agriculture, and nomad caravans with their camels and yurts. At its centre lies the fabled Minaret of Jam, hidden from foreign eyes for centuries, and even now is accessible to only the hardiest of travellers.

PRACTICALITIES

Some commercially available maps of Afghanistan mark the road from Bamiyan to Herat as a highway, a classification to b taken with a large pinch of salt. The roa quality ranges from poor to painfully bac all plied by seemingly indestructible HiAce and Kamaz trucks.

Public transport runs the length of th central route, although connections can b erratic and there are several bottleneck The two trickiest sections for onward trans port are west from Yawkawlang (opposite and travelling onward from the Minaret c Jam (p128). Squeezing into public trans port on long journeys can be particularl uncomfortable on this route, so one popu lar option is to buy two spaces instead c one. Expect to get out and walk some stee stretches, or put rocks under the vehicle' wheels to help it ford rivers.

With nonstop travelling, perfect con nections and no problems, it's just possibl to travel across the centre from Kabul t Herat in four days, although you'd nee a week in bed afterwards to get over it. I practice, allowing around six or seven day is more realistic.

Hiring a vehicle allows you to make th trip in something approaching comfort, a well as allowing stops for the myriad phot opportunities you will find along the way Expect to pay around US$100 to US$12 per day for a 4WD. Prices depend on you starting point: Herat is the most expensiv place to hire vehicles for this route, wit Chaghcheran the cheapest. A 4WD is es sential, although in 2003 we did meet Citroen 2CV that had somehow made th traverse having driven all the way fron Paris! If there are only a couple of you i the vehicle, don't be surprised if the drive stops to load rocks into the back as extr weight ballast. When making your plan: be explicit as to whether fuel is include and whether you are hiring the vehicl for a set period of time, or just to get t a certain destination. Politics and recen history can also play a part: Hazara driv ers in Bamiyan we talked to were reluctan to drive all the way past Jam, as it mean them returning on their own throug non-Hazara areas. That said, a local drive who knows the region is almost always th best option.

Between Bamiyan and Herat, fuel i available at Yawkawlang, Lal-o-Sar Jangal Chaghcheran, Chist-e Sharif and Obey.

AN AMERICAN PRINCE OF GHOR

Britain and Russia were the main drivers of the Great Game, but there were plenty of lesser-known actors on the stage, often playing for their own stakes. One of the most notable was the American adventurer Josiah Harlan, the probable inspiration for Kipling's classic story *The Man Who Would Be King*. Born in Pennsylvania in 1799, Harlan fled to India after being jilted by his fiancée. After working as a surgeon for the British East India Company he made a brief journey to Afghanistan before finding service with the Maharajah of Punjab, Ranjit Singh, in 1829. Seven years later he switched allegiances to the Sikh's great rival on the Afghan throne, Dost Mohammed. In 1838, Harlan led Dost Mohammed's army from Kabul via Bamiyan to campaign against the Uzbek warlord and slaver Murad Beg. As they breasted the Hajigak Pass, he became the first American to fly the Stars and Stripes on the Hindu Kush. On the march, Harlan became close friends with the Hazara ruler, Mohammad Reffee Beg, who crowned Harlan the Prince of Ghor in perpetuity.

Soon after the campaign, Dost Mohammed was swept up in the upheaval of the First Anglo-Afghan War and Harlan was ejected by the British. Having immersed himself in the Afghan culture, Harlan became a fierce critic of British policy in the region, and published a fiery memoir that was quickly banned in London.

Returning to the USA, Harlan later served as a Union colonel in the American Civil War and died in 1871 en route to China, in search of one last adventure.

The central route can normally only be tackled between May to October, although bear in mind that early snow or a late-spring melt can still cause problems outside these dates. Local transport tends to start winding down for the winter in November, when the high passes start to close. Babur recorded making the trip in the winter of 1506 – but only just, recording snow reaching past the stirrups of his horse.

In terms of facilities along the central route, only Jam's new guesthouse offers any form of comfort or modern amenities. Accommodation is at chaikhanas throughout, with their limited washing and toilet facilities. Diet is equally restricted and we found even rice hard to find in some places, until descending to the Herat floodplain. Chaghcheran, as the regional centre, is the only place west of Bamiyan with any kind of phone coverage until you reach Obey. If you need to stay in touch a Thuraya phone is essential.

BAMIYAN TO CHAGHCHERAN
Yawkawlang   يكاولنگ

Travelling west from Bamiyan past Band-e Amir, the land becomes increasingly barren until you reach the small town of Yawkawlang, where a river becomes bound with splashes of green irrigated land, leading to a tidy and newly built main bazaar.

It's almost too new and tidy. Possession of Yawkawlang was regularly contested

between the Taliban and Hezb-e Wahdat, with the local population being the main losers. In January 2001, after a final attempt by the Hazara to hold the town, the Taliban massacred over 170 of Yawkawlang's male residents and destroyed the bazaar.

There are two chaikhanas posing as hotels in Yawkawlang, standing opposite each other: the Pak Hotel and the Newab Hotel (west end of bazaar, 100Afg). Neither are great and both lack bathrooms, but the former at least has a private room for sleeping.

Yawkawlang tends to be the final terminus for transport from Bamiyan (200Afg, five hours), and westbound transport can sometimes be tricky to arrange. Hi-Aces only go irregularly to Chaghcheran (650Afg, one day), so usually the best option is to take a minibus to Panjao (Panjab on some maps; 100Afg, 2½ hours), which leave most mornings. Panjao is at the junction of the road going west to Chaghcheran, and east to Kabul via the Unai Pass, and has more plentiful transport connections. Read the risk assessment box (p114) before considering continuing to Kabul this way. Yawkawlang has an airstrip, used by regular Pactec flights.

Lal-o-Sar Jangal   لعل و سر جنگل

The road from Yawkawlang climbs steadily as it heads west, through a series of passes. After nearly three hours it crosses the grandest in the mountain chain, the Shahtu Pass

BAMIYAN & CENTRAL AFGHANISTAN

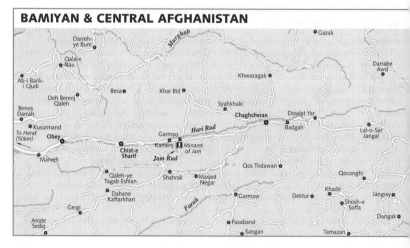

(3350m), en route to Panjao. The views, over the pastel-brown mountains topped with rocky crags, are wonderful. There are plenty of herds of goats and sheep here, and a succession of pretty valleys threaded with shallow rivers to be forded. Five hours after leaving Yawkawlang, the road reaches the bazaar town of Lal-o-Sar Jangal.

Lal (as it's locally known) is the traditional limit of Hazara territory, and sits below the Kirmin Pass (3110m), the watershed between the Helmand river system, flowing south, and the Hari Rud, which the road follows until it reaches Herat.

Lal's bazaar is well stocked and is overlooked by a ruined fort. There are several chaikhanas – the Sdaqat Hotel (near the fuel station, 70Afg) on the southern edge of town is adequate. Minibuses leave in the morning to Chaghcheran (500Afg, eight hours) and Panjao (100Afg, two hours).

CHAGHCHERAN TO HERAT
Chaghcheran   چغچران
At Chaghcheran the dense mountains the road has been winding through appear to recede, as the road climbs to a wide and largely barren plateau. A large sprawl of low buildings strung along the banks of the Hari Rud, Chaghcheran is the capital of Ghor province and its size comes as something of a shock after so many tiny villages.

Although the town has a mixed population, it sits at the heart of Aimaq territory. A seminomadic Turkic people, Aimaq camps

are easily spotted by their distinctive yurts These are in contrast to the black felt tent of the Kuchi, who also live in the regio in sizable numbers. It's not uncommon t see Kuchi camel caravans travelling to an from Chaghcheran to sell livestock. Th town also hosts a Lithuanian-led PRT.

Despite its size, sleeping options in Chagh cheran are restricted to chaikhanas, whicl are found in a cluster south of the river turn west at the red-and-white roundabou None are signed in English, and all are de pressingly basic. The Koswar Hotel (100Afg at least has the advantage of a toilet cubicl and a couple of private rooms.

Chaghcheran is the regional transpor hub, all arranged from the non-descrip transport office (next to Farvaden Phar macy) near the chaikhanas – look for the small painted with a bus and truck. HiAce run daily to Herat (800Afg, 1½ days) and Lal-o-Sar Jangal (500Afg, eight hours), anc occasionally to Yawkawlang (650Afg, on day) and Kabul (via Panjao, 900Afg, 1½ days). The office also has 4WDs – we wer quoted US$200 for a two-day trip to Hera via the Minaret of Jam. There is a smal airstrip on the eastern edge of town, witl regular UNHAS and Pactec flights to Kabu (via Bamiyan) and Herat.

The Minaret of Jam   منار جام
Reaching a dizzying height of 65m, the **Min aret of Jam** (Minar-e Jam; ticket US$5, still/video camer US$5/10, vehicle US$10, translator US$15) stands as a

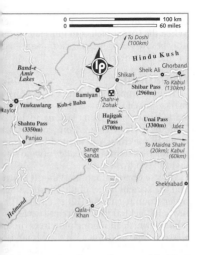

lait brick decoration. Interlocking chains, polygons and medallions wind delicately around the shaft, interspersed with text from the Quran.

At the neck of the first section, a band of Kufic text spells out Ghiyasuddin's name in glazed turquoise, the only colour on the minaret. Above this are spars from the original wooden scaffold and brick buttresses that would originally have supported a balcony. The second and third shafts are more restrained in their decoration, surmounted by a final lantern gallery with pinched and pointed arches. Few muezzins have ever had such a stage for their call to prayer.

At the time of its construction, the minaret was the tallest in the world and until the 20th century only the Qutb Minar in Delhi was taller. For many years, archaeologists were mystified as to its purpose. Its isolated location begs the same question from every visitor: why here? Given the lack of associated buildings, it was assumed by many to be part of a concurrent Central Asian trend for raising single massive towers as statements of political power, possibly marking victory over a pagan populace. Jam is now recognised to be the site of the lost city of Firuzkoh, the Ghorids' capital destroyed by the Mongols (see the boxed text, below).

It's possible to climb the minaret and the views are amazing. A ladder allows you to crawl through a narrow entrance hole to the interior. There are two staircases, winding around each other like a DNA double-helix. Care should be taken on the narrow steps and a torch isn't a bad idea. The stairs end in an open chamber, from where you

lonely sentinel at the confluence of the Hari Rud and Jam Rud rivers, the greatest surviving monument of the medieval Ghorid empire. Forgotten by the outside world until the mid-20th century, it remains a holy grail for many travellers to Afghanistan. The first view of the minaret as it looms suddenly and unexpectedly from the folds of the mountains is worth all the rough roads it takes to get there.

The minaret was built in 1194 for Sultan Ghiyasuddin, the grandest of the Ghorid rulers, and marks the highpoint of their fired-brick architecture (Ghiyasuddin also commissioned Herat's Friday Mosque at this time). Three tapering cylindrical storeys rise from an octagonal base, the whole completely covered in intricate *café-au-*

FIRUZKOH – THE TURQUOISE MOUNTAIN

Unlike the majority of Afghan empires that arose from the plains, the Ghorids were born of the mountain fastness of the Hindu Kush. Even so, the decision to build their capital Firuzkoh ('The Turquoise Mountain') in such an inaccessible place – far from the trade routes, with barely a square metre of flat arable land – seems an act of almost wilful perversity. Until recently, archaeologists were reluctant to accept Jam as the site of the lost city.

Post-Taliban surveys have forced a change of mind. In the immediate vicinity of the minaret, several courtyards and pavements of baked brick have been uncovered (possibly the minaret's mosque), along with the remains of other buildings. If the Ghorids' own chronicles are to be believed, the mortar for these was mixed with the blood of prisoners taken from recently conquered Ghazni. A Jewish cemetery was also recorded at the site before the war, while the watchtowers on the slopes to the west of the minaret were probably part of Firuzkoh's larger defences. Smaller looted artefacts have included carved doors, coins and pottery from as far as Iran and China. Archaeologists continue to survey the site.

can look out over the confluence of the rivers. A second staircase continues from here up to the lantern gallery, although the climb feels more than a little precarious.

In 2002, the Minaret of Jam became Afghanistan's first World Heritage site, simultaneously being placed on the list of World Heritage sites in danger. It's easy to see why. Sat on the confluence of the Hari Rud and Jam Rud rivers, erosion of the foundations has been a constant worry, and gabion walls have been built to reinforce the structure. Even so, the minaret still lists at a worrying angle. Illegal looting, which ironically reached its peak after the fall of the Taliban, has also damaged the site, and robber holes can easily be spotted in the area.

SLEEPING & EATING

There is a small government-run **guesthouse** (r US$30; dinner US$10, breakfast US$5) next to the minaret. Rooms are simple, but the mattresses are comfortable and the shower is one of the most welcome you'll take in the country. Meals are hearty. In Garmao, the nearest village 15km away up the Jam Rud, the Hotel Jam (70Afg) offers the usual chaikhana deal of a space on the floor for the price of dinner.

GETTING THERE & AWAY

No public transport goes to Jam. The best option is to take transport between Chaghcheran and Herat and get off at Garmao, where several locals act as motorbike taxis to the minaret (500Afg, two hours). The road is little more than a track, and is the roughest on the central route. Onward transport options from Garmao can be tricky, as vehicles are usually full when they drive through the village, but HiAces usually pass through en route to Chaghcheran (400Afg, five hours) around dawn, or to Herat (500Afg, one day, staying overnight at Darya Takht) in the afternoon. The road west, with its villages and orchards, is very picturesque.

With your own vehicle, Jam can be reached from Chaghcheran in seven hours, or from Herat in about 15 hours. There are two equally dramatic routes from Chaghcheran – the southerly main road via Garmao, or the northern road via Ghar-e Payon. The latter brings you to the minaret from the opposite bank of the Jam Rud. There is no bridge and the river can only

be forded by vehicles in the late summer. When the spring melt is in full spate, it can only be crossed by means of a zip wire – not for the faint-hearted!

Chist-e Sharif چشت شریف

Travelling from the centre, Chist-e Sharif marks the end of the high peaks and the start of the wide plains leading to Herat. Building styles change, from rough square mountain architecture to mud-brick compounds with domes and *badgirs* (wind towers) to keep them cool.

Chist-e Sharif is another Ghorid centre and the ancient home of the Chistiyah Sufi order, founded in the 12th century. The order left behind two fine **domed tombs** (*gombads*), which sit among pine trees on the western edge of town. Like the Minaret of Jam, they are decorated with intricate raised fired brick, although are in considerably poorer repair. The Chistiyah were noted for their use of music in their devotions, which brought them into conflict with the orthodoxies of the day. The main centre for the order is now in Ajmer, Rajasthan, although Afghans still visit the tomb of the 12th-century leader Maulana Mauduc Chishti for blessings. The tomb, rebuilt in the last century, is on the western side of the pines, picturesquely looking down the main bazaar street.

Chist-e Sharif has a busy bazaar and several chaikhanas for eating and sleeping. The **Eqbal Hotel** (Main bazaar; 70Afg) is the pick of the bunch, with decent food, ice-cold drinks and airy rooms. The **Chist Hotel** (Herat Rd), a kilometre out of town, is a large white modern building built in the aftermath of the Taliban's ouster, but has yet to open its doors to customers.

Heading west, the road dramatically improves after Chist-e Sharif. There are regular minibuses to Herat (180Afg, four hours) stopping at Obey (100Afg, two hours). Transport to Chaghcheran is not frequent so take whatever is available – minibuses to Chaghcheran from Herat usually stop for the night in Darya Takht, 40km away.

Obey وبی

Compared to the rest of the central route, Obey feels like civilisation – the main streets are paved and the bazaar is busy. Burqas, which have been largely absent nce Bamiyan, reappear in large numbers. he Hari Rud, a rushing river since Chagh- heran, becomes tamed and lazy, anticipat- ng its eventual dissipation in the deserts of urkmenistan.

Obey is known for its **hot springs**, which re actually 10km to the west of town, where road off the highway curves up into the ills. There is a bathhouse with grubby tubs nd an older building with a deep pool. A *howkidar* (caretaker) will let you in and ex- ect a tip of around 50Afg. If you follow the ath along the river for an hour, following he right fork where it splits, there is an-

other spring, used by local villagers. There's a simple pool covered with thatch and with a sandy bottom – it's a much more pleasurable experience, although the water is ferociously hot. As women come here to wash and do laundry, it's best to go with a trusted local who knows the way.

Minibuses and yellow taxis travel through- out the day to Herat (80Afg, two hours) from the road with the large square pigeon towers. Transport west is best arranged from Herat – also a more preferable option for sleeping, although there are several chaikhanas along Obey's main bazaar street.

Herat & Northwestern Afghanistan

هرات و شمال غرب افغانستان

'Khorasan is the oyster shell of the world, and Herat is its pearl', says an old proverb referring to this Afghan city's pre-eminence in a region that covered much of medieval Iran and Turkmenistan. It's a saying that still holds much truth, for Herat still shines as the cultural centre of Afghanistan, a seat of poetry, learning and architecture. Invaders from Genghis Khan to the Russians have all taken turns at flattening it, but Herat still manages to hold its head high, offer its visitors tea and suggest they sample its attractions. And there's much to take in, from the Citadel that towers over the Old City to its glorious Friday Mosque and many shrines. Those coming from Kabul will be equally amazed by the efficiency of its infrastructure, not least the electricity supply.

From this ancient Silk Road oasis, the road crosses the Safed Koh mountains – the last outpost of the Hindu Kush – to reach the northwest. Here the land flattens out to form part of the Central Asian steppe, a semidesert that's home to Kuchi nomads and Turkmen and Uzbek farmers. This is the main centre for the greatest of the country's folk arts, the Afghan carpet, and the bright swatches of knotted wool contrast sharply with the dusty landscape that produces them.

HIGHLIGHTS

- Gaze in awe at the dazzling mosaic tiling of the **Friday Mosque** (p136) in Herat
- Contemplate poetry with the Sufis at **Gazar Gah** (p138), one of Afghanistan's holiest sites
- Climb the battlements of Herat's **Citadel** (p137) for sweeping views across the city
- Haggle for carpets at the bazaar in **Andkhoi** (p144), the northwest's most traditional market town

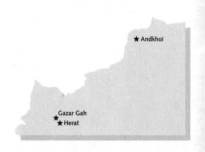

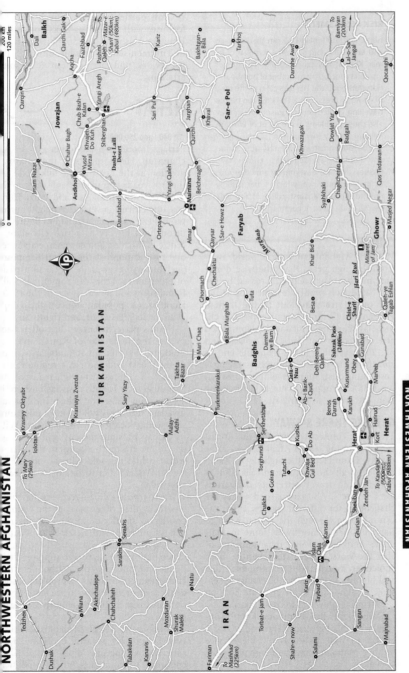

RISK ASSESSMENT

Herat has traditionally been an area of peace and prosperity, but since the removal of Is-mail Khan it has exhibited regular signs of instability, including a number of bombs and riots. Although the city was calm at the time of going to press, check the situation before travelling. Iranian penetration of the city may also cause problems in the event of Western military activity towards Iran.

The route northwest from Herat to Maim-ana should be avoided due to chronic law-lessness and anti-government armed groups in Badghis province, which is particularly remote. Attacks against police in the Bala Murghab district are common.

CLIMATE

Western Afghanistan feels a world away from the high peaks that otherwise domi-nate much of the country. Crossed by the low Safed Koh mountains, the land is flat and open, stretching out to the Iranian Plateau and Central Asian steppe. The cli-mate is accordingly hot and dry, dominated around Herat by the *Bad-e Sad o Bist* (Wind of 120 Days) that blows from the end of spring to the start of autumn, carrying a desiccating dust. Summer temperatures can reach 38°C, dropping to just below freezing from December to February.

GETTING THERE & AWAY

Transport connections around the north-west and to the rest of Afghanistan can be patchy. From Herat, the highway to Kabul runs through the restive south via Kanda-har, making travel extremely dangerous for foreigners. Alternative road routes are challenging for different reasons: either the central route through the Hindu Kush to Bamiyan, or the northwest route to Mai-mana, Andkhoi and Shiberghan along prob-ably the worst road in the country. Both choices are rough and uncomfortable rides, and highly susceptible to the changing sea-sons. Andkhoi and Shiberghan are both on the tarmac highway to Mazar-e Sharif.

Daily flights link Herat and Kabul, with regular flights between Herat and Mazar-e Sharif, as well as a less reliable service linking Maimana and Shiberghan to the capital.

Cross-border travel is relatively straigh▮ forward, with direct bus links connectin▮ Herat to Mashhad in Iran. Onward trave▮ to Turkmenistan is possible, although th▮ paperwork and permits can take som▮ arranging.

HERAT   هرات

☎ 040 / pop 250,000

Perhaps more than any other city in A▮ ghanistan, Herat speaks of the country▮ position at the heart of the Silk Road. A▮ the crossroads of trade routes leading to th▮ Middle East, Central Asia and India, Hera▮ has often been coveted by neighbourin▮ powers as a valuable prize. It has flourishe▮ throughout history as a rich city-state, ▮ centre of learning and commerce and eve▮ one-time capital of the Timurid empir▮ Such history has given the city a cultured a▮ of independence that can sometimes mak▮ Kabul seem a long way away. In the 1970▮ Herat was a popular stop on the Hipp▮ Trail for its relaxed air, and rightly so.

Herat's place in history has often bee▮ overlooked in favour of Samarkand an▮ Bukhara, but its inhabitants are prou▮ of their past and the city's reputation a▮ a place of culture. Although many of th▮ monuments to Herat's glorious past are i▮ a sorry state, ruined by British and Russia▮ invaders, the city is still the most rewardin▮ sightseeing location in Afghanistan. Wit▮ its Friday Mosque the city still possesse▮ one of the greatest buildings in the Islami▮ world, while the Old City is one of th▮ few in Afghanistan to retain its medieva▮ street plan.

Herat's post-Taliban recovery has bee▮ less rocky than other parts of the country▮ due in no small part to the customs rev▮ enues from trade with nearby Iran. Visitor▮ coming from Kabul will instantly notice th▮ difference: a reliable power supply, stree▮ lights and public parks. Although stree▮ crime can occasionally be a problem, it sud▮ denly seems remarkable to see families ou▮ on the streets at 10pm going to ice-crear▮ parlours.

Things haven't been a bed of roses, how▮ ever. Despite his removal by Hamid Kar▮ zai, Herat's longtime 'amir' Ismail Kha▮ continues to dominate the city's politica▮

HERAT

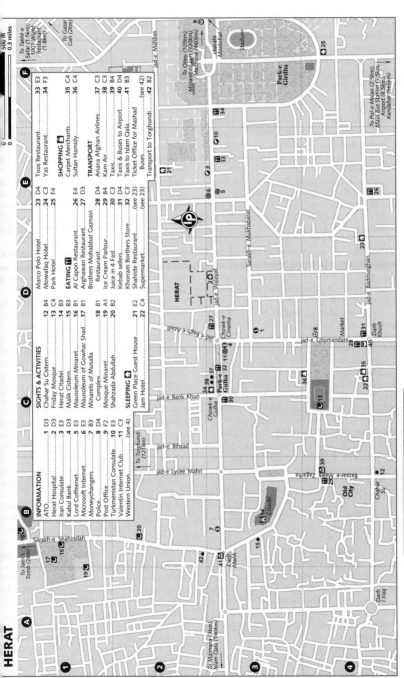

INFORMATION
ATO..1 D3
Heral Hospital.........................2 D3
Iran Consulate........................3 E3
Kabul Bank.............................4 D3
Lord Coffeenet........................5 E3
Microsoft Internet....................6 E3
Moneychangers........................7 B3
Police....................................8 D4
Post Office..............................9 F2
Turkmenistan Consulate.........10 E3
Valentin Internet Club............11 C3
Western Union.....................(see 4)

SIGHTS & ACTIVITIES
Chahar Su Cistern..................12 B4
Friday Mosque.......................13 C4
Herat Citadel.........................14 B3
Malik Cistern.........................15 B3
Mausoleum Minaret................16 B1
Mausoleum of Gowhar Shad....17 B1
Minarets of Musalla
  Complex..............................18 B1
Mosque Minaret.....................19 A1
Shahzada Abdullah.................20 B2

SLEEPING 🛏
Green Place Guest House.........21 E2
Jam Hotel..............................22 C4

Marco Polo Hotel....................23 D4
Mowafaq Hotel.......................24 C3
Park Hotel.............................25 F4

EATING 🍴
Al Capon Restaurant................26 E4
Arghwan Restaurant................27 D3
Brothers Mohabbat Gaznavi
  Restaurant...........................28 D4
Ice Cream Parlour...................29 B4
Juice in 4 Fasl........................30 C3
Kebab sellers.........................31 D4
Khorram Borthers Store............32 C3
Shahiste Restaurant............(see 23)
Supermarket......................(see 23)

Toos Restaurant.....................33 E3
Yas Restaurant.......................34 F3

SHOPPING 🛍
Carpet Merchants....................35 C4
Sultan Hamidy........................36 C4

TRANSPORT
Ariana Afghan Airlines..............37 C3
Kam Air.................................38 C3
Taxis....................................39 B4
Taxis to Airport.......................40 D4
Taxis to Islam Qala..................41 B3
Ticket Office for Mashad
  Buses.............................(see 42)
Transport to Torghundi.............42 B2

HERAT & NORTHWESTERN AFGHANISTAN

and economic scene, and the city's links to neighbouring Iran play an important role. The insecurity along the Herat–Kandahar highway occasionally ripples back to the city, although the presence of an Italian-led PRT has generally been well received.

HISTORY

Herat's history begins as Aria, an outpost of the Achaemenid empire, overrun in Alexander the Great's eastward expansion. In typical fashion he renamed it Alexander Arian in his own honour. The city grew and reaped the benefits of the new Silk Road under the Kushans and Sassanids and into the Islamic era.

Herat's expansion was checked by the visitations of Genghis Khan in 1221, who characteristically levelled the place, killing all but 40 of the populace after they rebelled against his power. But this just proved to be the preface for the city's greatest period, as a new power thundered out of the steppe 150 years later.

Timur founded his empire at Samarkand, but following his death in 1405, the capital moved southwest to Herat. Under Timur's son, Shah Rukh, Herat became one of the greatest centres of medieval Islamic culture and learning. A patron of the arts, Shah Rukh packed his court with scholars, poets and painters. Jami composed his greatest poems here and Bihzad's refined miniature painting would later go on to influence Indian art. The ruler's wife, the extraordinary Gowhar Shad (see boxed text, p138), commissioned many fine buildings from mosques to madrassas.

Such glory couldn't last. After Shah Rukh's death, there was a debilitating squabble for succession and Timurid power started to wane. Sultan Baiqara provided one last hurrah at the start of the 16th century, but the rot had set in. The future Mughal emperor Babur visited Herat at this time and left a lively description of the city, joking that you only had to stretch your leg to kick a poet, and complaining of the royal court's drunkenness. In fact, Baiqara so preferred to drink wine rather than exercise power that Timur's empire soon fell under the arrows of Uzbek invaders.

Herat spent the next centuries being fought over by the Mughals and Safavids. It finally regained its independence only

to find itself swept up in the superpowe rivalry of the Great Game.

The Persians were the first to make move on the city, laying siege to it in 1837 Russian officers aided the Persian army while a single British officer, Eldred Pot tinger, rallied Herat's defenders. The Af ghans held the day, but the siege influence British policy for the remainder of the 19th century. Herat was dubbed the 'Gateway to India' and the British were insistent i should stay in their realm of influence – an out of Russian hands.

Dost Mohammed incorporated Herat into the Afghan kingdom in 1863, but trou ble was never far away. Russian expansio towards the border in 1885 nearly brough the imperial powers to war. The British ordered Herat be prepared for an attac and many of Gowhar Shad's buildings wer demolished to allow a clear line of artiller fire for the defenders, although war wa ultimately averted.

After this, Herat's population were happ to be left alone for most of the 20th cen tury, but still resented Kabul's influence. I declared support for the rebel Bacha Saqa when he seized the throne from Amanul lah in 1929 and increasingly resented th communist influence from the capital in th 1970s. Events came to a head in March 197 when the city rose in open revolt. Led by loca mullahs and a mutinous army garrison com manded by Ismail Khan, around 100 Russia advisors were killed with their families. Th Russians helped the government quell th rebellion – by carpet-bombing the Old City Around 20,000 civilians were killed.

Following invasion, the mujaheddin har ried the Russians, in one of the most hidde corners of the war. Iran provided crucial sup port. After the Russian withdrawal in 1989 the city quickly fell to the mujaheddin, with Ismail Khan installed as Herat's ruler.

Nothing could save the city from the as cendant Taliban, however. In 1995 the city' army crumbled in the teeth of a Taliban advance and Herat was captured without fight. Ismail Khan himself was taken pris oner, but later escaped to Iran.

The educated Heratis chafed under th occupation and Iran closed its borders Herat's population swelled with an influ of internally displaced people (IDPs) flee ing drought.

Ismail Khan returned at the end of 2001 as the Taliban were swept from power. Increasingly conservative with age, he retained his own army and a version of the Taliban's Vice and Virtue Police, styling himself as the Emir of Herat. The city, however, boomed on customs revenues from trade with Iran, once again becoming a quasi-independent city-state, as it has been for much of its history.

Central control over Herat (and its taxes) finally came in late 2004 with Ismail Khan's replacement as governor, an event accompanied with much rioting. Local politics have trodden a sometimes uneasy path since, but the city still remains a beacon of progress compared with much of the country.

ORIENTATION

Herat sits in a wide plain, watered by the Hari Rud. To the north the ridges of the Safed Koh mark the boundary with the Central Asian steppe; to the south the road leads to Kandahar and the Indian subcontinent.

Only the core of Herat's Old City remains, around the crossroads of Chahar Su and the Friday Mosque. The Citadel dominates the northern edge of the Old City, looking out to the minarets of the ruined Musalla Complex. West of this is the wasteland created by Soviet carpet-bombing. Much of this area is undergoing a boom of new building, with glass-fronted villas sprouting up almost daily.

The New Town (Shahr-e Nau) is east and north of the walled city, home to the majority of government and NGO offices. The streets are lined with tall pine trees and decorated with parks, considerably improving the urban environment. Watch out for the working traffic lights – almost unheard of in Afghanistan.

Herat's airport is 8km south of the city. If arriving overland from Iran, Herat's minarets make a ready landmark. Most road transport leaves from the area south of the minarets, near Darb Malik on the edge of the Old City.

INFORMATION
Emergency
Ambulance (☎ 040 223413)
NSO West (☎ 070 405 697/079 9322 192)
Fire Brigade (☎ 040 445721)
SAF (☎ 079 9885 181)
Police (☎ 040 222200; Jad-e Ghomandani, opposite the Friday Mosque)

Internet
Prices are around 50Afg per hour.
Lord Coffeenet (Jad-e Walayat)
Microsoft Internet (Jad-e Walayat)
Valentin Internet Club (cnr of Park-e Gulha & Jad-e Ghomandi)

Medical Services
The area around the main hospital has plenty of pharmacies.
Herat Hospital (☎ 040 223412; Jad-e Walayat)

Money
Street moneychangers remain the best option in Herat: there are stands between Darb Malik and Chowk-e Gulha.
Kabul Bank (cnr of Park-e Gulha & Jad-e Ghomandi) Has a branch of Western Union inside.

Post & Telephone
Phone stands and PCOs are everywhere in Herat.
FedEx (☎ 040 220301; charahi Haji Ayoub)
Post Office (charahi Mostofiat)

Tourist Information
ATO (Afghan Tourist Organisation; ☎ 040 223210; Sarakh-e Mukharabat) Can provide drivers and guides for US$40 a day each (US$20 for half a day) and also arrange transport to the Minaret of Jam.

DANGERS & ANNOYANCES
Since Ismail Khan left Herat, security has decreased slightly. Political problems have occasionally spilled onto the streets, usually in the form of quick-to-fire demonstrations. As always, keep an ear very close to the ground. In 2006, violence also flared between Sunni and Shiite groups during Ashura.

Crime has reportedly become more of a problem in Herat, with an increase in street robberies. Several female international workers have reported severe harassment, bordering on violence, so particular care should be taken when walking in the city.

SIGHTS
Old City
Herat's Old City, measuring approximately 1200 sq metres, is the most complete traditional medieval city in Afghanistan. Four main streets branch out from the bazaar of Chahar Su (literally 'four directions'), quartering the city and leading to the old gates that once pierced the city walls (they

were pulled down in the 1950s). Characteristic of medieval urban design, the Old City has three focuses – the commercial centre (Chahar Su), the Royal Centre (the Citadel, opposite) and the Religious Centre (the Friday Mosque, right).

The four main roads leading from **Chahar Su** are lined with booths and shops. Until the 1930s, these roads were covered, with Chahar Su itself crowned with a large dome. Only small portions of the old vaulting survive, in the southeast corner of the city. Behind the shops there are plenty of serais – enclosures for caravans that served as warehouses and inns for traders and craftsmen.

Away from the main thoroughfares, the streets turn into a labyrinth of unpaved lanes, hiding the city's houses behind high mud walls. Wandering the streets and serais is one of the best ways to get a taste of traditional Herati – and Afghan – urban life.

That the Old City survived the Soviet carpet-bombing of Herat is a miracle, but its fabric is now under threat from the city's construction boom. Unlike Kabul, where an official ban on new construction in the Old City prevails, Herat's historic quarter is undergoing 'redevelopment' on an unprecedented scale. In the absence of building controls, owners are demolishing historic properties to rebuild in the popular modern glass-and-concrete style, with little thought for the city's character.

The Aga Khan Trust for Culture (AKTC) is currently working with Herat's government to rescue buildings and create a sustainable development plan for the Old City. Using a mix of satellite imagery and door-to-door surveys, they produced the first detailed map of the Old City, showing over 15,000 buildings with 62,000 residents, but with old buildings being lost on a weekly basis. AKTC has launched a conservation programme for several historic houses that promotes traditional building techniques, encourages self-built repairs and shows the potential for improving living conditions within traditional city homes.

AKTC has also helped restore Herat's traditional cisterns. The **Chahar Su Cistern**, at the centre of the Old City, and the **Malik Cistern**, opposite the western gate of the Citadel, are what remain of Herat's medieval water-supply system. Filled by aqueducts,

they provided year-round clean water fo the city's residents, even during the Persia siege of 1837–8. They only ran dry durin the 1980s. Both have gorgeous brick vaulte ceilings, with the octagonal Chahar Su Cis tern having a span of over 20m. Surrounde by bazaars and mosques, the cistern's resto ration should hopefully provide a focus fo further economic regeneration in the Ol City, although at the time of writing thei exact future use was under discussion wit community leaders.

Friday Mosque

Over 800 hundred years old, Herat's **Frida Mosque** (Masjid-e Jami; ☿ closed to non-Muslims du ing Fri prayers) is Afghanistan's finest Islami building, and one of the greatest in Centra Asia. A master class in the art of tile mosaic its bright colours and intricate detailing ar an exuberant hymn in praise of Allah.

Most visitors enter the mosque via th park on its eastern side, which leads u to a huge and richly tiled façade. The en trance corridors are to either side of this but they are frequently locked outside th main prayer hours, forcing visitors to gai access to the mosque proper via the sma street entrance on its northern wall. This i actually a more atmospheric choice, as th cool dark of the entrance corridor suddenl gives way to a bright sunburst of colour a you enter the main courtyard. Don't forge to remove your shoes at this point.

The mosque is laid out in a classical pla of four *iwans* (barrel-vaulted halls) wit arcaded walls around a central courtyar nearly 100m long. Two huge minarets flan the main *iwan*. Almost every square centre i covered in breathtaking mosaic, surrounde by blue bands of Quranic script. Only th simple whitewash of the *iwans* adds a note o modesty. The minarets, with their repeate bands of stylised flowers, arabesques an geometric patterns are simply dizzying.

The mosque was originally laid out b the Ghorid Sultan Ghiyasuddin in 1200 Originally it would have had quite a differ ent appearance, as the Ghorids preferre plain brick and stucco decoration. Th Timurids restored the mosque in the 15th century and introduced the bright mosaic but by the early 20th century so much o this had been lost that visitors remarked on the mosque's dullness.

The lavish tiling that now covers the mosque is the product of the mosque's tile workshop, an ongoing restoration project since the 1940s. While many of the mosaics are based on Timurid originals, the workshop has also introduced its own designs, colours and calligraphy. This traditional-meets-modern approach has led to the creation one of the gems of contemporary Islamic abstract expressionism.

The workshop is in a courtyard to the left of the main portal entrance in the garden – ask to visit it at the small office of the Ministry of Information, Culture and Tourism, just inside. The courtyard also contains one of the few remnants of the original Ghorid decoration, overlaid with Timurid tiling – a demonstration of the continuum of artistic styles that the mosque has witnessed. The craftsmen are normally happy to show off their work, from glazing the raw tiles to laying out the intricate mosaics.

It's normally not a problem to take photos in the mosque, but this should be avoided during prayer times. Early morning is the best time to catch the light on the tiles. Donations for the mosque's upkeep can be placed in the ceremonial bronze cauldron in the eastern arcade. Cast in the 13th century, it would have originally been filled with sweet drinks for worshippers on religious holidays.

Herat Citadel

Towering over the Old City, the **Herat Citadel** (Qala-ye Ikhtiyaruddin; admission 250Afg; ☉ 8am-5pm) has watched over Herat's successes and setbacks with its imposing gaze for centuries. The oldest building in Herat, it is believed to stand on the foundations of a fort built by Alexander the Great. It has served as a seat of power, military garrison and prison since its construction until 2005, when the Afghan army presented it to the Ministry of Information, Culture and Tourism, opening its doors to outsiders for the first time.

The Citadel is built on an artificial mound and stretches 250m east to west. Its 18 towers rise over 30m above street level, with walls 2m thick. A moat once completed the defences, although this was drained in 2003 to lay out a public park in the grounds. The present structure was largely built by Shah Rukh in 1415, after Timur trashed what little Genghis Khan had left standing. At

this time, the exterior was covered with the monumental Kufic script of a poem proclaiming the castle's grandeur, 'never to be altered by the tremors of encircling time'. Sadly, most of this tiling has been lost bar a small section on the northwest wall, the so-called 'Timurid Tower'.

Time's tremors inevitably did great damage to the Citadel. Repeated conquerors pillaged the Citadel, with locals prizing the valuable roof-beams and baked bricks. The greatest indignity came in 1953 when Herat's army commander ordered its complete demolition in order to move his military base on the outskirts of the city. Only the direct intervention of King Zahir Shah halted the destruction. Subsequent neglect caused several sections to collapse. An extensive renovation programme was launched in the 1970s, completed just two months before the Soviet invasion.

Visitors enter through the modern western entrance to the Citadel's lower enclosure. Most of this section is currently closed, so you are instead led through an imposing wooden gate and atrium to the upper enclosure. This is the most heavily fortified part of the Citadel and has its own wells, which were used to allow defenders to withstand sieges. Archaeological excavations are still ongoing in the main courtyard. To the left, there is a small hammam with beautifully painted but damaged walls, showing flowers and peacocks.

The biggest attraction is the Citadel's huge curtain wall topped with battlements. These offer tremendous views over Herat, looking south towards Chahar Su, and north to the minarets of the Musalla Complex. It's also possible to make out the last remains of the Old City walls.

Leaving by the western gate there is a small museum, which is planned to open in 2007.

Musalla Complex & Minarets

Herat's Musalla was Gowhar Shad's masterpiece, comprising a mosque, madrassa, mausoleum and over 20 minarets. At its height, it rivalled any of the great showpieces of Islamic architecture from Samarkand to Esfahan. Today, only five minarets and Gowhar Shad's mausoleum remain. The loss of the rest is a testament to the sorrier type of imperial meddling in Afghan politics.

HERAT & NORTHWESTERN AFGHANISTAN

The **Mausoleum of Gowhar Shad** (Bagh-e Gowhar Shad; admission free; ☉ 8am-sunset) sits in a small park, currently undergoing extensive re-planting. It's a textbook example of Timurid architecture, with its square box topped with a high drum and ribbed melon dome, albeit one largely denuded of its turquoise tiling. The door to Gowhar Shad's tombstone is normally locked, but the *chowkidar (caretaker)* can unlock it for you. The inside dome is beautifully painted in blue and rust-red. Shah Rukh was also originally buried here, until Ulughbek removed his body to Samarkand. Also inside are the broken remains of the mosaic that covered the exterior, mostly knocked off by Soviet shelling. The building next door holds the tomb of Mir Ali Shir Nawai, Sultan Baiqara's prime minister.

The mausoleum is at the heart of the old complex. By the park entrance is the sole standing minaret of her madrassa, tilting at a worrying angle and braced with steel cables. The tiling, a series of blue lozenges filled with flowers, only survives on its one side, where it is protected against Herat's abrasive wind. There are two balconies – just below the lower storey, mortar has taken a horrible bite out of the minaret.

On the southern edge of the park, the stump of another minaret is the only sign of Gowhar Shad's mosque. It was destroyed by Soviet artillery. Tantalising fragments remain of the beautiful mosaic and its white marble facings. Noting that minarets are usually the simplest parts of a building, Robert Byron was so moved by its fine decoration to write 'if the mosaic on the rest of the Musalla surpassed or even equalled what survives today, there was never such a mosque before or since.'

The loss of the complex rivals the destruction of the Bamiyan Buddhas for deliberate cultural vandalism. In 1885, when the British feared a Russian invasion of Afghanistan, they persuaded Abdur Rahman Khan to prepare Herat for defence. In a matter of days, British engineers dynamited almost the entire complex, to give a free line of fire for artillery. The invasion never came, but the damage was done. Two further minarets fell to earthquakes in the early 20th century, while the Soviets turned the whole area into a free-fire zone in the 1980s.

Opposite the park, four huge minarets mark the corners of Baiqara's long-gone madrassa. The minarets were covered in a delicate blue mosaic framed in white and set with flowers. Some tiling remains – war and abrasive wind has wiped out the rest. The towers now lean like drunken factory chimneys and exert a particularly mournful air at sunset. A road between the minarets still allows traffic to trundle past, the vibrations damaging the fragile foundations. Several tombstones lie abandoned in the area, including an exquisite yet eroded black marble tombstone, carved in the intricate Haft Qalam (Seven Pens) style. Long abandoned to the elements, a better-cared-for example can be seen at Gazar Gah (below).

Gazar Gah

This shrine, 5km northwest of Herat, is one of Afghanistan's holiest sites, dedicated to the 11th-century saint and poet Khoja Abdullah Ansari. Run by Sufis from the Qadirriyah order, it receives hundreds of pilgrims from across Afghanistan daily; Gazar Gah's name means 'the Bleaching Ground', a Sufi allusion to the cleansing of one's soul before Allah.

GOWHAR SHAD

The wife of Shah Rukh, Gowhar Shad, was one of the most remarkable women in Afghanistan's history. Although her name meant 'joyful jewel', she was anything but the trophy wife her name suggests. She was a great patron of the arts and commissioned some of Islam's finest buildings, including Herat's Musalla Complex and the Great Mosque in Mashhad (Iran). She also paid an active part in politics. Her son, Ulughbek, was made the viceroy of Samarkand and following her husband's death, she was heavily involved in the manoeuvrings over his succession. Her other son, Baisanghor, drank himself to death, so Gowhar Shad planned to make Ulughbek the ruler of Herat. Years of disputes followed, with her various sons and grandsons fighting for power, ultimately sowing the seeds of the empire's downfall. She finally met her end at the ripe age of 80, murdered by a rival after plotting to install her great-grandson on Herat's throne. Her gravestone reads she was 'the Bilqis [Queen of Sheba] of the time'.

The shrine is the most complete Timurid building in Herat and is dominated by its 0m-high entrance portal, decorated with estraint with blue tiles on plain brick. More iling fills the inside, much of it showing a distinctly Chinese influence – possibly a by-product of the embassies that Shah Rukh who commissioned the shrine in 1425) xchanged with the emperor of China. The ourtyard is filled with the gravestones of he many of Herat's old ruling families.

The saint's tomb is at the far end beneath a large ilex tree. An intricately carved m-high white marble pillar also stands guardian, contained behind a glass case. t's fascinating to sit and watch men and women offering prayers to the tomb before turning around to perform the full prayer itual facing Mecca. Prayers are also tied n rags to the ilex tree, usually by women having problems conceiving.

There are several other graves worth noting in the shrine. Amir Dost Mohammed, that great survivor of the First Anglo-Afghan War, is buried to the left of Ansari's tomb, having died soon after capturing Herat in 1863. His grave is surrounded by a white balustrade and marked with another marble pillar. One of Sultan Baiqara's sons also lies here. His tombstone s an incredible example of the Haft Qalam style of carving – interlaced flowers and arabesques painstakingly carved into seven ayers of relief. The tombstone is kept in a ocked side room, so you'll have to ask to be shown it.

There are more graves outside the portal entrance. Look for the much worn statue of a dog immediately outside. Local tradition ascribes this to the grave of Gazar Gah's architect, who wished to sit humbly before the Sufi master into the next life.

Slightly to the southwest of the main shrine is the **Zarnegar Khana** ('Golden Pavilion'). Built during Baiqara's time, it is a retreat for the shrine's Sufi adherents, who hold their *zikr* rituals inside. The interior has a fine domed ceiling, painted in blue and red, and picked out in gold leaf. The Zarnegar Khana was closed for restoration at the time of research. The grounds of the shrine also contain a second domed building, the Namakdan pavilion, and a cistern containing water from the holy Zam Zam spring at Mecca.

There's no entrance fee at Gazar Gah, but the Sufis who tend the shrine will welcome a small donation. Don't forget to remove your shoes on entering.

Buses run regularly to Gazar Gah from Chowk-e Cinema (5Afg, 15 minutes). A taxi costs around 50Afg.

Jami's Tomb

Mawlana Abdur Rahman Jami was Herat's greatest poet and one of the greatest Sufi poets who wrote in Persian. He was a regular at the court of Sultan Baiqara, where he composed many treatises on the soul's meditation of the divine. He died in 1492 and is still revered by modern Heratis, who can often quote from his greatest work, *Haft Awrang* (Seven Thrones), and regularly visit his **grave** (Sarakh-e Tanki Mawlawi; donation welcome, ☼ sunrise-sunset).

The tomb is a quiet and contemplative place, inside a modest enclosure under a pistachio tree, with a finely carved headstone. A large pole is hung with green banners and has had many nails hammered into it as prayer offerings. The tomb is visited by both men and women, who sit either side of the grave, in prayer or meditation. It's commonplace to walk around the grave and to take a pinch of earth as a blessing. There is also a small donation box here.

A larger mosque stands adjacent to the grave. Both are modern, rebuilt after being severely damaged by Soviet shelling in 1984. A taxi ride from the centre of Herat costs 80Afg.

Shahzada Abdullah

Two shrines sit on the main road just south of the Musalla Complex. Built in the late 15th century, they contain the tombs of two princes, Abdullah and Qasim, who died in the 8th century. Abdullah's tomb is the one nearer the road. The exteriors are plain fired brick with ogee portal arches, while the interiors are richly decorated with tiling – probably the best surviving tilework from medieval Herat.

Even a couple of years ago, the tombs were clearly visible from the road, but they have now been largely obscured by Herat's construction boom. The tombs' guardians, who also tend the many pigeons outside, appreciate a small donation from visitors.

Takht-e Safar

Spread across a hill 5km north of Herat, Takht-e Safar is a popular place for picnics. Built as a pleasure garden for Sultan Baiqara in the 14th century, it's an oasis of green, with good views to the city. It's a popular place for picnics and to catch the sunset (when cars full of wedding parties often descend on the scene).

At the bottom of the hill is a small theme park, complete with rides and a giant concrete pigeon. As you go up the hill, you pass a large swimming pool, popular with men species in the summer months. There's a small café offering drinks and ice cream. Further up the hill is a wedding club, backed by a large mural of Ismail Khan with Ahmad Shah Massoud. Climbing these steps provides the best views of Herat.

Pul-e Malan

This fine old 22-arched bridge is a few kilometres south of the city, visible from the road when driving from the airport. Believed to have been constructed by the Seljuks in the early 12th century, it has survived the floods that have washed away countless other bridges on the Hari Rud. According to legend, two sisters, Bibi Nur and Bibi Hur, collected egg shells to mix with the clay of the bricks, making the structure stronger than steel. It's no longer used for motor traffic, but is worth a visit for its picturesque setting.

SLEEPING

Sleeping options should change dramatically in Herat during the life of this book, with the opening of the city's first five-star hotel under construction on the outskirts near Takht-e Safar.

Jam Hotel (☎ 040 223477; Darb Khosh; s/d 300/600Afg) Tucked away in the Old City, this is Herat's best budget option. The rooms are basic, but have had a bit of a spruce-up since we last visited, making them good value for the price. The shared bathrooms are very simple and there's a restaurant for *pulao* (a rice dish) and kebabs. Rooms at the back have a great view of the Old City, overlooking the Friday Mosque.

Park Hotel (☎ 040 223010; Park-e Girdha; r US$20) Built in the 1930s, the Park is Herat's oldest hotel – Robert Byron stayed here while writing *The Road to Oxiana*. It's a caver-

ous, colonial-style place complete with creaky beds and overstuffed chairs, and surrounded by pine trees. All rooms are en suite. The hotel was being used mainly as a wedding hall when we visited. Full of potential, it just needs a little love (and money) spent on its upkeep.

Mowafaq Hotel (☎ 040 223503; Chowk-e Gulha with bathroom s/d US$20/30) Currently Herat's largest hotel, the Mowafaq is a trusty standby and conveniently located between the Old City and the New Town. The good-sized rooms are clean but everything feels a bit tired and dusty. The pool hasn't seen water in years. Get a room looking out to the minarets if you can.

Marco Polo Hotel (☎ 040 221944; heratmarcopolo@yahoo.com; Jad-e Badmurghan; s/d from US$41/51, with bathroom US$72/82; 🔀 🖳) This friendly and ever-expanding hotel is a great option. The rooms aren't elaborate, but there's 24-hour hot water, free internet, and helpful staff. The more expensive rooms also come with a free (nonalcoholic) minibar and laundry. Breakfast is included – a huge spread of bread, cheese, yogurt, eggs and fruit.

Green Place Guest House (☎ 070 405905; Jad-e Mahbas, lane 2; r US$50; 🔀 🖳) A small family-run guesthouse with a friendly atmosphere the Green Place (there is a garden) is a pleasant escape from the city. There are half a dozen rooms, all spotlessly clean and with shared bathroom. Prices include breakfast – dinner is available on request.

EATING & DRINKING

The Persian influence on Herati culture can easily be seen when you go out for a meal. Iranian-style rice (steamed and topped with sour sumac berries) is served as much as Afghan *pulao*. Locals also have a preference for black tea (sucked through a sugar-cube) over the green tea drunk in the rest of Afghanistan.

Arghawan Restaurant (☎ 040 221919; Chowk-e Cinema; kebab meal 200Afg; ⏱ 10am-10pm) Popular with middle-class Heratis and internationals alike, the attraction here isn't so much the formal dining room as the outside seating area, strewn with bolsters to slump against for shade from the daytime. The set meals are excellent value, comprising soup, salad, bread, rice, kebabs, tea and a soft drink.

Yas Restaurant (Park-e Girdha; menu from 60-200Afg) One of the few places we found n Herat serving *mantu* (a type of ravioli), Yas also has a decent range of kebabs with rice, salad and yogurt. The pizzas are disappointing in comparison. The restaurant always seems to be busy – its success has allowed it to buy what could be Herat's largest TV.

Shahiste Restaurant (Jad-e Badmurghan; meals 00Afg) On the 1st floor of the Marco Polo Hotel, this restaurant offers good Iranian-style food. The menu often only has a couple of dishes, but makes up for this with generous plates of salad, pickled vegetables and yogurt.

Brothers Mohabbat Gaznavi Restaurant (Darb Khosh; meals from 50Afg) One of the better large kebab joints, busy at any time of day or night. It serves up an endless procession of kebabs, *pulao* and chai. Female travellers may find themselves directed upstairs to the family dining room.

Al Capon Restaurant (Jad-e Badmurghan; meals from 00Afg) According to the sign, 'Al Capon' was a cowboy, but he rustles up a decent plate of rice and kebabs. Salads and a few Western-style fast-food items fill out the menu.

Toos Restaurant (Jad-e Walayat; pizzas 150Afg) Good for those wanting a break from Afghan fare, this place does a good imitation of Western fast food. Tasty pizzas are eat-in or takeaway, along with a few interesting variations on the hamburger theme.

Ice cream parlour (Bazaar-e Malek Zagarha; ice cream from 40Afg) This is the best place for ice cream in the Old City. With its low ceiling, wall carpets and Bollywood posters, it's a cosy place to tuck into a bowl of rosewater and pistachio ice cream. Afghan women eat here too.

Juice in 4 Fasl (Chowk-e Gulha; juice from 20Afg) Bright and shiny, this juice bar has wonderful juices and smoothies, from thick banana to tart pomegranate. There's ice cream too, lathered with mango puree, and an upstairs seating area that's perfect for watching Herat go about its business.

Khorram Brothers Store (Park e-Gulha; snacks from 0Afg) In the small park by Chowk-e Gulha, this snack bar sells a few kebabs plus hot and cold drinks including, unusually, coffee. It's almost worth visiting just for the fountain opposite – a concrete kitsch masterpiece of towering bears, goats and waterbirds.

Kebab sellers (Darb Khosh) Calling these places chaikhanas would be far too grand –

there's hardly room to sit down – but these hole-in-the-wall joints are perfect if you're in need of a quick kebab.

Itinerant fruit sellers push carts around the Old City and there's also a market next to the Friday Mosque. If you're after imported goods, there's a good **supermarket** (Jad-e Badmurghan) near the Marco Polo Hotel. It even has its own shopping trolleys.

SHOPPING

Herat is famous for its blue glass, handmade in a rough and chunky style. If you're lucky enough for it to survive Afghanistan's roads, it makes a great souvenir.

Sultan Hamidy (north side of Friday Mosque) Sultan Hamidy (or Ahmad) and his family have been making Herati glass for generations. The tiny factory is two doors down from the shop, with glass-blowing every couple of days. The shop itself is an Aladdin's Cave, with everything from glass and metalwork to rugs, beads and embroidery, all displayed as an anarchic explosion of stock. Prepare to spend hours looking for antiques, both old and new.

Carpet Merchants (Darb Khosh) One of the best places to buy carpets from the region is direct from the wholesale merchants who occupy this serai on Darb Khosh. Carpets and *gilims* festoon the balconies and courtyard, indicating that you're in the right place. Herati carpets are usually deep red, although the merchants buy from across the west and northwest as well as eastern Iran – Baluchi styles are also sold in large numbers.

GETTING THERE & AWAY

Kam Air (☎ 040 228951; Park-e Gulha) flies daily to Kabul (3250Afg, one hour), and every Monday and Thursday to Mazar-e Sharif (2500Afg, 50 minutes). **Ariana Afghan Airlines** (☎ 040 222315; Park-e Gulha) also has a daily service to Kabul (3200Afg).

At the bottom of Sarakh-e Shahzada, there are large buses to Kabul (600Afg, one day), which continue onto Mazar-e Sharif (1000Afg, two days). Note, however, that these travel to the extremely dangerous southern highway through Kandahar and cannot be recommended. In the same area you'll also find transport offices with buses to Iran, with daily departures to Mashhad (270Afg, seven hours) and Tehran (700Afg, two days).

Transport to Maimana is found 3km west of Herat's centre on Sarakh-e Fargha. HiAces leave daily at around 4am (1100Afg, two days). For more on this route, see right.

Minibuses to Obey (80Afg, two hours), Chist-e Sharif (180Afg, four hours) and Chaghcheran (800Afg, 1½ days) leave from the bus station 3km south of Herat on the road to the airport. This is also the general transport depot for HiAces to most other destinations from Herat.

Transport for Torghundi on the Turkmenistan border leaves on an ad hoc basis from the same area as the Mashhad buses. For more information see p216.

GETTING AROUND

Millie buses leave irregularly from Darb Khosh to the airport (6Afg, 50 minutes), although shared taxis (50Afg) from the same spot can be a better bet. The whole taxi should cost 300Afg or less.

Most taxi rides in Herat will cost between 50Afg and 80Afg. Until the last couple of years, a highly enjoyable way of seeing Herat was to hire a *gari* (horse-drawn buggy). The drivers take great pride in decorating their carriages, dressing their horses with bells and red pom-poms, but they are disappearing fast: on our most recent visit we only spotted a couple, having been largely replaced by scores of autorickshaws. Both cost around a third less than a taxi over the same distance.

Millie buses also ply the streets on set routes, which can be hard to fathom. Stops are on the main roundabouts, with tickets usually costing about 3Afg.

THE NORTHWEST

Where Herat looks toward the Iranian Plateau, northwest Afghanistan turns its face to the dry semi-desert landscapes of Central Asia. Skirting the length of the Turkmenistan border, it's a place of oases, seasonal rivers and dusty brown hills that sprout into life at the hint of rain. The same rains can make travel near impossible at these times – even gravel roads are largely an aspiration and you're just as likely to find yourself bumping along dry riverbeds and over sand dunes.

> **WARNING**
>
> At the time of going to press, Badghis province was considered too dangerous for travel, due to activity of criminal and anti-government elements. Travellers are currently advised to fly between Herat and Mazar-e Sharif (p141).

There's a small international presence in the northwest, but Badghis province in particular remains a wild area. Once in Faryab province security is generally better, handled by General Dostum's Uzbeks.

HERAT TO MAIMANA ہرات الی میمنه

While scenically dramatic, travelling this route through the northwest is not a trip to be taken lightly. The road is probably the worst in Afghanistan, and there's some stiff competition. A 4WD is essential, as there are large stretches of off-road driving and fording of rivers. In spring, rains can make this route almost impossible as swathes of the track turn to mud; in winter snow on the Sabzak Pass near Herat can cause its own problems. In the best of conditions it's a drive of two very long days. By public transport, it's well worth buying an extra seat in the vehicle for comfort.

On top of this, Badghis has a poor reputation for lawlessness, with a low police presence. Banditry against vehicles and NGOs is not uncommon, as well as tension between the Tajik and minority Pashtun populations that sometimes spills into violence. The stretch of road between Qala-e Nau and Bala Murghab (where public transport overnights in both directions) is the worst for lawlessness. When we took this route we were made to sleep in a local police station for security reasons. Checking the security situation with reliable sources is essential before planning a trip. Qala-e Nau is currently the only place on this road with mobile phone reception, making a Thuraya a good idea for staying in touch.

If all this sounds too much, take heart that there's a Kam Air service between Herat and Mazar-e Sharif twice a week.

Qala-e Nau قلعه نو

From Herat, the road heads north over the Safed Koh mountains, zigzagging its way over the Sabzak Pass (2400m). The landscape is harsh but dramatic, all rough peaks and escarpments studded with low trees. As you descend, the country becomes drier and drier until you reach Qala-e Nau, about seven hours from Herat.

Qala-e Nau is the capital of Badghis, big enough to have a roundabout and some fancy Victoriana street lights that at least show an aspiration towards electricity. Most public transport stops for a meal break in the town and there are some decent chaikhanas, with low barrel-vaulted ceilings. Bizarrely, several claimed to serve spaghetti alongside the usual *pulao*-shaped offerings.

There's a Spanish-led PRT on the southern outskirts of Qala-e Nau. The road between Herat and Qala-e Nau is currently being upgraded, but at the time of research the tarmac finished about 80km after leaving Herat.

Bala Murghab   بالا مرغاب

All transport between Herat and Maimana stops overnight in this small farming town, a full day's drive from both. It's an anomaly in the area in having a mainly Pashtun population, due to Abdur Rahman Khan's experiments in population movement in the 1880s. The town itself has little to draw visitors, but the surrounding farmland along the Murghab river is green and attractive.

There are a couple of chaikhanas on the town square, but police are unlikely to let foreigners sleep in them for security reasons. Instead, you're likely to be redirected to the Governor's Hotel – also known as the police compound. There are a couple of rooms, otherwise you bed down under the stars with whoever's on night-watch. It's not great, but it's fairly secure. Prices seem to vary according to whim: some people haven't been charged, others hit for dollars in double-figures.

As with much of this region, the landscape is dominated by rounded hills of loess – the fertile dust blown from Central Asia. Arid for most of the year, they suddenly turn green with the onset of the spring rains. At other times, Kuchi caravans are liable to provide the only colour in the landscape.

MAIMANA   میمنه

The capital of Faryab, the largely Uzbek town of Maimana has an easy-going provincial air. Horse-drawn taxis are the order of the day as much as cars, bumping along the rough roads and throwing up plumes of dust. Respite only comes with the spring rains, when the streets become a mess of sticky mud.

According to early Arab accounts, Maimana was founded by Israelites exiled from Jerusalem by Nebuchadnezzar, although archaeological digs have uncovered Neolithic beads in the area indicating much older habitation. The city grew and prospered, even taking the obligatory levelling by Genghis Khan in its stride.

Maimana rose again to become a powerful khanate, which spent much of its time playing off the rivalry between Kabul and Bukhara to its own advantage. It was a thorn in the side of Afghan amirs throughout the century, only being forced into the Afghan state at the end of a gun wielded by Abdur Rahman Khan in 1884, the last of the independent Uzbek city states.

Modern Maimana is a lot more relaxed now. The town is centred on a large park surrounded by pines, once the site of Maimana's Citadel. The main bazaar areas are to the north, between the park and the Maimana river. Monday and Thursday are the busiest bazaar days. Look out for the bright *chapans* and *gilims* for sale. A Norwegian PRT is based on the east side of the park.

Sleeping & Eating
At the time of research, police were only allowing foreigners to stay in one hotel in Maimana, although in theory there are several chaikhanas with private rooms on offer.

Maimana Municipal Hotel (☎ 079 915 8353; south of Maimana park; s/d 500/1000Afg) is a dusty 1930s edifice, with reasonable rooms filled with creaking furniture. The hotel is woefully low on bathrooms – just two for nearly 20 bedrooms. If it's full (it was block-booked with Indian and Chinese construction workers when we visited), the management is usually happy to let you stay in the plush conference room, which has surprisingly comfy sofas. Some locals know it as the Daulat Hotel.

Aside from the chaikhanas in the bazaar, **Turkestan Restaurant** (northeast cnr of park) is the only sit-down option for eating. The

---

THE DASHT-E LAILI

The Dasht-e Laili desert takes its name from the story of Majnun and Layla, the Romeo and Juliet of Persian literature. Their love forbidden by Layla's father, Majnun wandered the desert alone until he lost his mind. Layla was forced to marry another. Years later, following her death, Majnun made a pilgrimage to her grave, whereupon he lay down next to her and expired. The two lovers were finally reunited in the afterlife.

Every spring, the Dasht-e Laili springs briefly into life with the rains, turning an electric green and studded with flowers. Its name may also be a spin on *laleh*, the Dari word for the tulips that bloom so brightly here at this time.

---

breeze-block architecture lends the place a certain awkward ambience, and although the menu promises a choice of dishes, you'll end up with kebabs whatever you go for. Not signed in English, look for the glass kiosk outside with the brazier, next to the UNHCR compound.

There are several snack and juice stalls clustered around the south gate of the park; if you're lucky they'll be selling *boloni* and *mantu*.

Getting There & Away

Ariana operates an erratic flight to Kabul: check at the office on the northeast corner of the park, although it's frequently closed.

Minibuses to Shiberghan (300Afg, six hours) and Mazar-e Sharif (400Afg, eight hours) leave every morning from a stand by the river, 500m north of the main square near the police station. The road follows the direct route via Daulatabad and the Dasht-e Laili desert. Transport to Andkhoi (280Afg, five hours) leaves from the same area, but is less frequent.

HiAces make the epic trip to Herat (1000Afg, two days) daily at around 4am, leaving from the Sadam Yush depot, near the Municipal Hotel.

ANDKHOI   اندخوی

Visiting Andkhoi feels a little like stepping back in time to a part of Central Asia that no longer exists. It's a modest place given its history – it thrived in the medieval era and

Timur visited in 1380 where he receive an omen to conquer Herat. Now a mixe Turkmen and Uzbek farming communit on the edge of the Dasht-e Laili it feels fa removed from the bustle of most Afgha towns, and a long way from anywhere The old street plan is yet to be despoile by the ugly glass-and-concrete building so popular elsewhere in Afghanistan an there's barely a scrap of Western clothin in evidence. You'll never have seen so man people wearing *chapans* (robes).

Bazaar days (Monday and Thursday) ar the best time to visit. The main bazaar are is between the streets west and north of th town square. Huge piles of melons line th streets when in season, competing for spac amid the blacksmiths, dried goods and te stalls. Although there's no animal market it can still sometimes feel like the town ha more donkeys and camels than motor veh cles. The real reason to come here howeve is for the carpets and textiles.

Andkhoi has been a carpet centre sinc the 1920s, when floods of Turkmen refugee fleeing from the aftershocks of the Russia Revolution, entered north Afghanistar The flocks of karakul sheep they brough with them transformed the local economy producing high-quality skins and rugs.

The main road west from the tow square, surrounded by shops selling woo is where you'll find most of the carpets Dealers from Kabul and Mazar-e Sharif bu and commission much of their stock fror here. Watching the traders make a deal i a fascinating process. Although the carpe sellers are mainly wholesale, they're alway happy to make a sale and the prices ar considerably less than you'll find elsewhere Tucked amid the carpets, you'll also fin people selling textiles – hand-woven silk *suzanis* (spreads embroidered with silk o wool) and clothes. The haggling is about a laidback as it comes and if you can throv in a few words of Uzbek or Turkmen, don be surprised if your purchase comes with a invitation home for dinner.

Sleeping & Eating

The only hotel in town is the **Andkhoi Hote** (Muncipal Hotel; Main square; r 500Afg), a big pink and-blue building on the northeast corne of the square. Rooms are basic but big, wit simple shared bathrooms. Staff are friendl

nd usually surprised to see any foreigners
itching up.

There are plenty of chaikhanas in the
>azaar – the height of Andkhoi's dining
xperience.

Getting There & Away

A smooth tarmac highway leads to Shiber-
han (70Afg, one hour) and Mazar-e Sharif
150Afg, 3½ hours). HiAces and shared
axis leave throughout the day from a stand
>n the road, east of the town square. Head-
ng south, HiAces leave most mornings to
Maimana (280Afg, five hours) on a poor
desert road. In theory it should be possible
to cross into Turkmenistan from here via
he border town of Imam Nazar, although
he border is currently under dispute and
to transport was running when we visited
for more see p216).

SHIBERGHAN   شبرغان

Another of the old khanates that ran across
he north like knots on a string, the city of
Shiberghan is the centre of Uzbek power
n Afghanistan and the hometown of Gen-
ral Abdul Rashid Dostum (see boxed text,
below). A nondescript sort of a place, its
owslung appearance belies its history. Shi-
>erghan was part of ancient Bactria, the
great range of steppe that hosted the war-
ing city states of the Greeks and later, the
Kushans. In 1978 archaeologists working at

Tillya Teppe outside the city uncovered a
major Kushan gravesite containing a wealth
of gold artefacts – the so-called 'Bactrian
Gold' (see p89).

Other visitors commented on a different
sort of treasure. When Marco Polo stopped
in Shiberghan he noted that 'here are found
the best melons in the world in very great
quantity.' Modern travellers may well agree.
In addition to farming, Shiberghan's economy is now boosted by its natural gas fields –
the pipeline to Mazar-e Sharif follows the
main highway. The city has many Turkish
NGO offices, evidence of Dostum's period
in exile there in the late 1990s. Posters of
the big man himself are everywhere.

There's not much to see in Shiberghan
itself and although you might spend a night
here if you've come from Maimana, it's just
as easy to push on to Mazar-e Sharif. The
small Turkmen town of **Aqcha** lies 50km to
the east off the main highway and has an
interesting traditional bazaar every Monday and Thursday, with carpet and jewellery sellers.

Sleeping & Eating

If you need to stay the night, the **Shibirghan
Hotel** (Main Square; r US$20) is the best option. It's
on the northern edge of the main square –
look for the phone towers and football
pitch. Rooms are adequate, but nothing
fancy.

GENERAL DOSTUM

In the towns of the northwest, Ahmad Shah Massoud posters have been replaced with pictures of
a stocky bullish man with a heavy moustache. This is General Abdul Rashid Dostum, undisputed
heavyweight of Afghanistan's Uzbeks.

Dostum was a paratrooper for the Afghan army when the Soviets invaded and commanded
a large Uzbek militia that fought the mujaheddin across the north. In 1992, he sensed the wind
was changing and switched sides – a defection that precipitated Najibullah's ultimate downfall.
Dostum helped Massoud capture Kabul, but once in the capital the Uzbek militias became feared
for their orgies of rape and pillage. Within two years he switched sides again and teamed up with
Hekmatyar to bombard the city with heavy artillery.

Dostum's control of the Salang Pass meant almost total control of the north, which he ran like
a private fiefdom, printing his own money and even running his own airline, Balkh Air. Newly
independent Uzbekistan provided much backing until Dostum's world collapsed with the Taliban
capture of Mazar-e Sharif in 1997.

In 2001, Dostum became just another warlord back on the make after the Taliban's collapse,
but has had to share the northern spoils with more powerful Tajik rivals. He's not a man taken to
polite sharing either – a prodigious vodka-drinker, his cruelty is famous. In one notorious incident
he ordered the killing of a convicted thief by strapping him to the tracks of a moving tank. At the
time of writing he was Chief of Staff of the Afghan army, personally appointed by Hamid Karzai.

There are several cheap restaurants and chaikhanas immediately to the south and east of the main square, serving kebabs, *pulao* and *mantu*.

Getting There & Away

There should be a weekly flight to Kabul, provided Ariana wants to operate it – it was out of action when we asked around. The airport is 10km east of the city.

Minibuses to Mazar-e Sharif (100Afg, tw hours) fill up quickly from a small termina on the eastern edge of Shiberghan – loo for the brick factories nearby. Transpor to Aqcha (40Afg, 30 minutes) also leave from here.

Andkhoi transport (70Afg, one hour leaves from west of the square, past on of Dostum's gauche terracotta-and-lobster pink palaces.

Mazar-e Sharif & Northeastern Afghanistan

مزار شریف و شمال شرق افغانستان

Travel north of the Hindu Kush and you'll find a quite different Afghanistan. The Central Asian steppe starts here, a wide grassy plain that stretches all the way to Russia. For much of its history, the Afghan city-states of the north looked across the Amu Darya towards Bukhara and Samarkand for their interests instead of to Kabul. Indeed, until the Salang Tunnel through the Hindu Kush was completed in the mid-1960s this was a totally isolated part of the country, accessible only by traversing the highest part of the mountains north of Kabul, or making a long desert crossing via Herat.

Travellers should head first for Mazar-e Sharif, home to the shimmering blue domes of the Shrine of Hazrat Ali. Nearby lies the far more ancient town of Balkh, where Zoroastrianism was born and Alexander the Great took his wife. His footprints can also be detected near the town of Kunduz at the ruins of Ai Khanoum, the easternmost Greek city in the world.

Continuing further east, the big mountains start to rise from the plains again in the province of Badakhshan. One of the remotest corners of the country, roads here become lost in the tangle of peaks where the Hindu Kush meet the Pamirs. The best way to get around is by foot, or with the yaks of the nomadic Kyrgyz who live in the thin tongue of land of the Wakhan Corridor, an area bursting with potential as a future trekking destination.

HIGHLIGHTS

- Join the pilgrims at the blue **Shrine of Hazrat Ali** (p152) in Mazar-e Sharif
- Head to **Balkh** (p155) to find the ruins of an ancient citadel and Afghanistan's oldest mosque
- Discover the unusual Buddhist temple and caves of **Takht-e Rostam** (p158) in Samangan
- Look for the remains of ancient Greeks at **Ai Khanoum** (p162) on the Tajikistan border
- Trek with yaks in the high altitude splendour of the **Wakhan Corridor** (p167)

CLIMATE

The northern plains see extremes of temperature. Baking summers (up to 43°C) and freezing winters (occasionally down to -10°C) lead Mazar-e Sharif's citizens to joke about their *paka o posteen* ('fan or furcoat') climate. Spring and autumn are thankfully more temperate. Faizabad has a more moderate climate, although winter snows make travel in Badakhshan problematic between October/November and March/April. The high altitude Wakhan Corridor has warm days and near freezing nights even at the height of summer in July, while early snow effectively cuts the region off from the rest of Afghanistan from late September.

GETTING THERE & AWAY

Regular flights with Ariana and Kam Air link Mazar-e Sharif to Kabul. Kam Air also operates a twice-weekly flight to Herat. Ariana runs an erratic schedule for Kabul services to Kunduz and Faizabad.

The Salang Tunnel connects the northern and southern halves of the country. The main highway from Kabul to Mazar-e Sharif and on as far as Andkhoi is excellent, as i the road from the Pul-e Khumri junctio to Kunduz and Taloqan. A 4WD is recom mended for travel to Faizabad, and is es sential further into Badakhshan. There ar two border crossings between Afghanista and Tajikistan, at Shir Khan Bandar (nea Kunduz) and Ishkashim (in Badakhshan The border with Uzbekistan at Termez i open, and with sufficient paperwork it's jus about possible to trek from Badakhshan int Pakistan over the Dilisang Pass.

MAZAR-E SHARIF
مزار شریف

☎ 050 / pop 800,000

Mazar-e Sharif is north Afghanistan's sprawl ing urban centre, a relatively modern cit standing on the wide steppes near the bor der with Uzbekistan. Compared to som of the neighbouring towns it's a relativ youngster, and was long overshadowed by the power and prestige of its neighbou

NORTHEASTERN AFGHANISTAN

Balkh. It took the dreams of a group of 2th century noblemen to change that, when they claimed to have found the hidden tomb of Ali, the Prophet Mohammed's son-in-law, buried in a local village. Balkh declined and Mazar-e Sharif grew as a place of pilgrimage. Its shrine today is the focus of the national Nauroz celebrations. For travellers, it has plenty of amenities, and is a good base for the sights of Balkh (p155) and Samangan (p158).

Mazar-e Sharif is a mixed city, with large populations of Tajiks, Uzbeks and Hazaras (many Pashtuns fled after reprisals following the collapse of the Taliban). This cultural mix is represented in the city's culture, in everything from the Central Asian flavours on the menu in restaurants, to the comparatively liberal attitudes to women's education. Mazar-e Sharif is even the centre for a women's musical college – something unthinkable elsewhere in the country.

The city's location also means that it is a great centre for that true Afghan sport of the plains, *buzkashi*. Games can be seen most weekends throughout the winter until

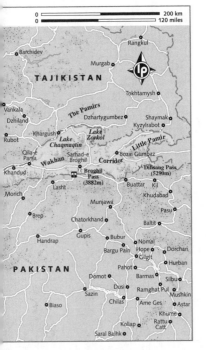

the Afghan New Year. Mazar-e Sharif becomes flooded with visitors at this time, for the annual Nauroz celebrations (see boxed text, p152). Nauroz coincides with the Gul-e Surkh festival, named for the red tulips that flower on the steppe, which are associated with prosperity and fertility.

Mazar-e Sharif mostly sat out the recent wars that afflicted Afghanistan, but its outward prosperity masks deeper political problems. In the post-Taliban environment, the city became a case study of Afghanistan's warlord problem, with rival Uzbek and Tajik strongmen jostling for power and control of revenues from natural gas reserves and the cross-border trade with Uzbekistan. At the time of writing, the situation was stable, but political competition still occasionally sparks into violence. The presence of a NATO Provincial Reconstruction Team (PRT; led by the UK and now Sweden) has helped calm tensions.

HISTORY

Mazar-e Sharif was the nondescript village of Khairan in the shadow of Balkh until the miraculous dream that revealed the location of Ali's tomb. A town quickly grew around the shrine, attracting many pilgrims until the Mongol's Year Zero levelled the area, pushing it to the margins of Afghan history for several hundred years. Mazar-e Sharif only regained its status when Ali's shrine was rebuilt in the last years of the Timurid empire. Since then, the town grew steadily until it

MAZAR-E SHARIF

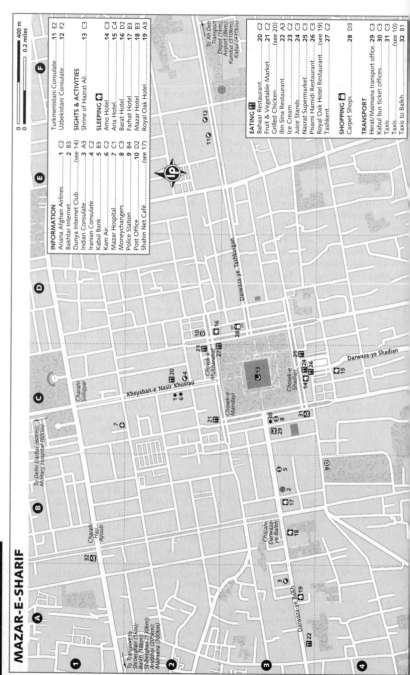

INFORMATION	
Ariana Afghan Airlines............	1 C2
Bakhtar Internet......................	2 B3
Dunya Internet Club..............	(see 14)
Indian Consulate....................	3 A3
Iranian Consulate...................	4 C2
Kabul Bank.............................	5 B3
Kam Air...................................	6 B3
Mazar Hospital.......................	7 C1
Moneychangers......................	8 C3
Police Station.........................	9 B4
Post Office..............................	10 D2
Shahin Net Café.....................	(see 17)

Turkmenistani Consulate.........	11 E2
Uzbekistani Consulate.............	12 F2

SIGHTS & ACTIVITIES	
Shrine of Hazrat Ali.................	13 C3

SLEEPING	
Amo Hotel...............................	14 C3
Aria Hotel...............................	15 C4
Barat Hotel..............................	16 D2
Farhat Hotel............................	17 B3
Mazar Hotel............................	18 B3
Royal Oak Hotel.....................	19 A3

EATING	
Bahaar Restaurant...................	20 C2
Fruit & Vegetable Market.........	21 C2
Grilled Chicken.......................	(see 20)
Ibn Sina Restaurant................	22 A3
Ice Cream................................	23 C2
Juice Stands............................	24 C3
Nasrat Supermarket................	25 C3
Pisarni Hamidi Restaurant.......	26 C3
Royal Oak Hotel Restaurant....	(see 19)
Tashkent.................................	27 C2

SHOPPING	
Carpet Shops..........................	28 D3

TRANSPORT	
Herat/Maimana transport office.	29 C3
Kabul bus ticket offices...........	30 C3
Taxis.......................................	31 C3
Taxis.......................................	(see 10)
Taxis to Balkh.........................	32 B1

ventually eclipsed Balkh, and was declared he capital of Afghan Turkestan in 1866.

Although Mazar-e Sharif was one of the irthplaces for the political parties that vould eventually form the Northern Alli-nce, it was a Soviet stronghold during the 980s. The flat plains surrounding the city nade it easily defensible, and the shops and arrisons were well stocked with goods from cross the Soviet border, only 60km away.

After the Russians pulled out, the defence f Mazar-e Sharif was entrusted to the semi-utonomous Uzbek militias led by General Abdul Rashid Dostum (p145). When Dos-um mutinied against the government in 992, setting up shop as the local power roker, he quickly gained control over most f north Afghanistan and prompted the fall f Kabul in the bargain.

Mazar-e Sharif was the capital of Dostum's rivate kingdom, bankrolled by the north's as reserves and with a line of credit from newly independent Uzbekistan. He only eft to play kingmaker in Kabul, and then helled it when his plans came to naught. Mazar-e Sharif remained an oasis of peace n the anarchy of the 1990s. By mid-decade ts population had swelled to nearly two million by refugees from other parts of the country, as well as those fleeing the civil var in nearby Tajikistan. Balkh University ppened, soon the only university offering higher education to women.

The Taliban were soon knocking on the loor. They cut a secret deal with one of Dos-um's generals and swept into the city in May 1997. This event triggered the Taliban's in-ernational recognition as the legitimate gov-ernment of Afghanistan by Pakistan, Saudi Arabia and the UAE. But just a day later the population (led largely by Hazara militia) rose in revolt and drove them out. Having sat out nearly 20 years of war, Mazar-e Sharif started to slide into chaos. The Taliban were back within the year with revenge on their minds. Hazaras were rounded up and sum-marily executed; their bodies were left lying in the street for five days to be eaten by dogs. Around 5000 people were killed.

Mazar-e Sharif was the first city to be abandoned by the Taliban in the US-led at-tacks of November 2001. Dostum returned again, this time on the US payroll. His old fort on the outskirts of the city, Qala-e Jangi, was the site of a notorious Taliban

prisoner revolt. In response, his troops packed subsequent Taliban prisoners into shipping containers, asphyxiating as many as 3000 men.

But years in exile had returned a dimin-ished figure in Dostum. Mazar-e Sharif was parcelled up by the resurgent Northern Al-liance, and it soon became clear that the Tajiks had the upper hand. Dostum has now ceded control of the city and province to the Tajik governor, Atta Mohammed.

ORIENTATION

Sitting in a large park in the centre of the city, the Shrine of Hazrat Ali dominates Mazar-e Sharif. Four main roads radiate out from the shrine to the cardinal points. Most amenities for travellers can be found within a kilometre of the shrine. Mazar-e Sharif has no historic quarter to speak of; the old bazaars that surrounded the shrine were torn down in the 1960s when the area was redeveloped.

The airport is 10km east of Mazar-e Sharif. Transport to Kabul and all points south and east leave from the Ah Deh depot 3km east of the centre. Transport west de-parts from a series of smaller stands on the road to Balkh.

INFORMATION
Emergency
ANSO North (☎ 070 030 064/079 9404 617)
Fire Brigade (☎ 079 9202 420)
ISAF (☎ 079 9639 135)
Police (☎ 079 9255 000)

Internet
Expect to pay around 60Afg per hour.
Bakhtar Net (Darwaza-ye Balkh)
Dunya Internet Club (Chowk-e Shadian) In same build-ing as Amo Hotel.
Shahin Net Café (behind Farhat Hotel, Darwaza-ye Balkh) Very high-speed connection.

Medical Services
Mazar Hospital (☎ 070 503 600; Charahi Sidiqyar)
Military Hospital (☎ 070 501 881; Dosad Bistar)

Money
There are moneychangers' stalls along the street west of the shrine. Currencies for all Afghanistan's neighbours are available.
Kabul Bank (Darwaza-ye Balkh) Has a branch of Western Union inside.

Post & Telephone

There are plenty of phone stands and PCOs on the four main streets surrounding the shrine.

Post Office (Chowk-e Mukharabat)

DANGERS & ANNOYANCES

Although Atta Mohammed has gained a firm hand on Mazar-e Sharif, factional disputes do occasionally break into outbursts of violence, so it's essential to keep your ear to the ground.

SIGHTS

Shrine of Hazrat Ali

The twin blue domes of the **Shrine of Hazrat Ali** (☼ dawn-dusk, Wed women only) are one of Afghanistan's most iconic sights, and pilgrims come from across the country to pay their respects at the tomb contained inside. Although non-Muslims are forbidden entry to the shrine building itself, views of the building are to be much enjoyed from the pleasant park that surrounds the complex.

Popular Muslim tradition contends that the Ali is buried in Najaf in Iraq, near the site where he was murdered in 661AD. Afghans typically tell another story. Instead, Ali's followers reputedly took his body to be secretly buried near Balkh. The burial was carried out in secret for fear of reprisals from Ali's enemies, and its location was lost until the 12th century when Ali appeared simultaneously in the dreams of 400 nobles from Balkh to reveal the tomb's exact position. A nearby hill was excavated, to dis-

cover a tomb chamber behind a steel door Ali's body lay behind it, his mortal wound as fresh as they day he received them.

The Seljuk Sultan Sanjar immediately buil a large shrine above the tomb, but it wa razed a century later by Genghis Khan. Wit Balkh's population decimated and scattered memories of Ali's tomb faded until revive by the Timurids in the 15th century. Sulta Baiqara rebuilt the shrine that still stand today.

The rich blue tiling that covers every sur face of the shrine is modern. The Timuri decoration fell into disrepair and the build ing was covered with a simple whitewas until the 1860s when it was restored by She Ali Khan, the amir swept away by the star of the Second Anglo-Afghan War.

Sher Ali Khan's tomb is to the west o the main shrine door. A larger tomb nex door is that of the other great scourge o the British, Wazir Akbar Khan, who die three years after driving the British Arm out of the country in their disastrous retrea from Kabul in 1842. On the east side of th shrine is a tall minaret-like pigeon tower The doves in the shrine complex are famou across Afghanistan. Every seventh pigeon is said to contain a spirit, and the site is s holy that if a grey pigeon flies here it turn white within 40 days.

There is no entrance fee to the shrin complex, although guards on the southern gate sometimes ask for a spurious 'camer fee'. Beggars and mendicants flock to th site, equally demanding of your attention.

NAUROZ IN MAZAR-E SHARIF

The Shrine of Hazrat Ali is the centre of Afghanistan's Nauroz celebrations, and people have traditionally converged on the city from across the country for the holiday. Banned by the Taliban as being unIslamic, over a million people attended the first Nauroz in 2002 following their overthrow. Numbers have since dwindled to a more manageable 100,000.

On the morning of 21 March, huge numbers of people converge on the shrine to witness the raising of the *janda*, a large religious banner. It flies for 40 days, with people crowding to touch it for blessings. Tradition holds that the seriously ill can be cured by praying at the shrine during Nauroz. In the afternoon the provincial government hosts a *buzkashi* match, on the *meidan* (plain) on the southern outskirts of the city.

Since 2004 the **Foundation for Culture & Civil Society** (www.afghanfccs.org) has hosted the Gul-e Sorkh International Music Festival in Mazar-e Sharif, with free music concerts across the city featuring musicians from across Afghanistan and its neighbours.

The crowds are huge and although security is tight you should watch out for pickpockets. Accommodation is at a premium and should be reserved well in advance, but if you can get a room, Nauroz is a fantastically exciting time to be in Mazar-e Sharif.

SLEEPING

Although there is a host of cheap hotels in Mazar-e Sharif, particularly on the western side of the shrine, at the time of research they were not allowed to take foreign guests.

Amo Hotel (☎ 050 2478; Chowk-e Shadian; s/d/tr US$10/20/30) This is a well-located cheapie, directly opposite the south entrance to the shrine: many of the rooms have great views across the domes. The rooms need a lick of paint, and the hot showers never seem to be more than lukewarm, but it's the best budget choice in town.

Aria Hotel (☎ 070 509 945; Darwaza-ye Shadian; s/d US$10/20) Just around the corner from the Amo, the decor here seems even more peeling. The shared bathrooms (squat toilet only) leave something to be desired, but the rooms themselves are light and airy. It's poorly signed – look for the sign on the corner of the building, although the entrance is actually upstairs from the main street.

Barat Hotel (☎ 070 502 235; Chowk-e Mukharabat; US$30-50; 🗙) A much more modern hotel, with carpeted rooms, squashy beds and decent furniture. Bathrooms are shared but are kept spotlessly clean and have lashings of hot water. Rooms on the upper floors are nicer, and are more expensive; management also ask for more if you want a view of the shrine. There's no restaurant, but food can be delivered to your room from nearby chaikhanas.

Mazar Hotel (☎ 050 2703/070 159 483; Darwaza-ye Balkh; r US$30-50; 🗙 🏊) This is a hotel in 1930s style, all high ceilings, grand dining rooms and monolithic pillars. It's a little dusty, giving the impression that it doesn't see all that many guests, but the swimming pool is popular with local lads in the summer. En suite rooms are a flat price for single or double occupancy, and have the novelty of a bath as well as shower.

Farhat Hotel (☎ 070 503177; Darwaza-ye Balkh; US$50; 🗙) Staff instruct you to leave your shoes at the front door; inside it's all over-stuffed furniture, bright carpets and fake sunflowers, trying their best to dispel the slightly gloomy post-Soviet atmosphere. Rooms are good nonetheless, all en suite, and there's a fast internet café next door.

Royal Oak Hotel (☎ 0799383127; sebroad3@hotmail .com; next to Governor's house, Darwaza-ye Balkh; s/d US$50-70/90, s/d with bathroom US$80/100; 🗙 💻) In the style of a Kabul guesthouse, the Royal Oak is aimed squarely at the international contractor market. High security walls contain a cosy house with annexe, comfortable decent-sized rooms, plus a large lounge and dining area. It's all run with great efficiency and has a good restaurant.

EATING & DRINKING

Mantu (steamed meat dumplings) are popular in Mazar-e Sharif, so take a break from kebabs and *pulao*. The vegetarian option, *ashak*, is also available. Central Asian influences are also apparent in the bread, which comes in heavy round loaves rather than the usual flat nan.

Delhi Darbar (☎ 070 505 417; Dosad Bistar; mains from US$4; 🕙 11am-10pm) This trusty Indian restaurant is something of an institution among Mazar-e Sharif's expats. The menu is mainly north Indian cuisine, with a refreshing choice of vegetable dishes. The meat/vegetarian *thalis* (South Indian all-you-can-eat meal) are excellent at US$6. Eat inside, or in the walled garden in summer, enjoying a cold beer at the same time. There's a sister branch in Kabul.

Pisarni Hamidi Restaurant (Darwaza-ye Shadian; dishes from 50Afg) One of the better chaikhanas near the shrine, this basic place has good *mantu* amid the expected piles of meat and rice – a reliable standard.

Ibn Sina Restaurant (Near Royal Oak Hotel, Darwaza-ye Balkh; dishes from 60Afg; 🕙 10.30am-11pm) An Afghan place worth making the effort to get to, the Ibn Sina has a well-stocked menu including *mantu*, *ashak* and a variety of soups and *qorma*. The white tiles give it a canteen appearance, but you can spread out on the *takhts* (raised seats) as well as sitting at tables. The restaurant's sign is fairly inconspicuous, so look out for the big tree outside the entrance.

Bahaar Restaurant (Kheyaban-e Nasir Khusrau; dishes from 70Afg) There aren't so many surprises at this restaurant in terms of the menu, but it's better quality than most, with several interesting *pulao* and *qorma* on offer. With the restaurant on three glitzy storeys above its own supermarket, this is about as fancy as Afghan dining gets in Mazar-e Sharif.

Grilled Chicken (Kheyaban-e Nasir Khusrau; meals from 70Afg) A seemingly endless round of kebabs and *pulao* can get pretty boring at times, something this place addresses wonderfully, with great chunks of delicious barbecued chicken. Next to the Bahaar Supermarket, there's a small off-street seating area hidden behind a wicker screen where you can tuck in.

Royal Oak Hotel Restaurant (☎ 079 9383 127; next to Governor's house, Darwaza-ye Balkh; dishes from US$8) Worth a splurge if you're missing some home comforts, this guesthouse restaurant has a changing daily menu, with anything from lasagne and risotto to some generous club sandwiches. Alcohol is served, and there's even a full English breakfast for US$10, complete with sausages and marmalade. Non-guests are advised to call before arriving.

Tashkent (Chowk-e Mukharabat; dishes from 100Afg) In the middle of the divided road, this is an Afghan fast-food place that delivers exactly what is promises. The pizzas (200Afg) aren't bad, but the burgers (110Afg) are tastier, served with a handful of chips.

Ice cream shops (Chowk-e Mukharabat; bowl of ice cream from 20Afg) If you're hankering for dessert, head here for a bowl of thick hand-churned ice cream, piled high in tiny bowls. There are a couple of un-named shops – several locals claimed that the one with the flame decor serves the best ice cream in the north.

Juice stands (Chowk-e Shadian; juice from 20Afg) This cluster of juice stands are a great refreshment stop. The banana or mango smoothies with cream and chopped almonds make a breakfast in themselves, while the sharp lemonade will cool you down on a scorching summer day.

The perimeter of the shrine usually has plenty of stalls selling street snacks – look out for those cooking up tasty boloni (stuffed vegetable pancakes) and falafel. You can fill yourself for less than 30Afg. Self-caterers will find fresh produce in the market on the northwest corner of the shrine, around Chowk-e Mandawi. **Nasrat Supermarket** (Chowk-e Shadian) is well stocked for imported goods.

SHOPPING

Mazar-e Sharif is an excellent place to pick up gilims (woven carpets) and needlework, the traditional handicrafts of north Afghanistan. Most of these are Uzbek, while the carpets tend to be made by Turkmen. Suzanis (spreads embroidered with

either silk or wool) make particularly goo souvenirs.

There is a line of carpet shops along th east side of the shrine, stocked high wit rugs, embroidery, lapis lazuli, and antique (old and new). Prices are slightly cheape than Kabul and the sell isn't so hard.

GETTING THERE & AWAY

Both airline offices are opposite the Ira nian consulate. **Ariana Afghan Airlines** (☎ 07 5010 075; Kheyaban-e Nasir Khusrau) flies to Kabu (2500Afg, 40 minutes) on Tuesday, Frida and Sunday. **Kam Air** (☎ 070 513 030; Kheyaban-Nasir Khusrau) were starting a service to matc at the time of writing, but also fly betwee Mazar-e Sharif and Herat (2500Afg, 5 minutes) every Monday and Thursday.

Transport for all points south and eas leaves from the Ah Deh depot on the easter outskirts of the city. Minibuses leave from early morning throughout the day to Kabu (500Afg, eight hours), Samangan (120Afg two hours), Pul-e Khumri (200Afg, 3½ hours) and Kunduz (350Afg, five hours) Shared taxis are equally plentiful. Trans port also leaves from here to the Uzbe border at Hairatan – for more informatio see p217.

Transport offices on Darwaza-ye Balk near the shrine sell tickets for large buse to Kabul (400Afg, nine hours). The vehicle aren't as fancy as advertised. The service continue to Herat (1000Afg, two days) but as these travel via Kandahar and th southern highway warzone they shoul be avoided.

Shared taxis to Balkh (30Afg, 30 min utes) depart from Charahi Haji Ayoub Minibuses and shared taxis to Shiberghan (100Afg, two hours), Andkhoi (150Afg, 3½ hours) and Maimana (400Afg, eight hours leave from near the Kefayat Wedding Club in the west of Mazar-e Sharif.

It's possible to travel to Herat via Mai mana in a three-day burst, but this is onl for the most hardcore and is subject to serious security concerns – see p142 fo more details. An office on the east sid of the shrine sells seats for the three-da Landcruiser trip for 1400Afg. The un marked office can be hard to find – it's on the corner, on the 1st floor on the left – ask at the offices selling the big buses to Kabul As the road effectively finishes two hours

om Mazar-e Sharif at Shiberghan, break-
ng the journey at Maimana is strongly
ecommended.

ETTING AROUND

here is no public transport to the airport.
he 15-minute taxi ride costs 200Afg. As
Mazar-e Sharif is a compact city, and you're
nlikely to stray too far on foot from the
eneral vicinity of the shrine complex, a taxi
o most destinations within the city should
eigh in at around 80Afg.

AROUND
MAZAR-E SHARIF

BALKH   بلخ

Today little more than a provincial market
own, Balkh was once of such stature that
he Arabs dubbed it the 'Mother of Cities'.
Nowhere in Afghanistan has such a glo-
ious history as Balkh, and its remaining
ights are well worth the short trip from
Mazar-e Sharif.

The town is possibly the oldest recorded
n the country. Some Islamic traditions
ave Balkh being founded by Noah after
he great flood, but it is better recognised
s the birthplace of Zoroaster, founder of
he world's first monotheistic religion. The
ecord is hazy here – the best estimates have
im being born around the 6th century BC.
The town of Bactra was established enough
o be a satrapy of the Achaemenid empire

by the time Alexander the Great took on the
Persians two centuries later.

Balkh was the scene of Persia's last stand
against the Greeks, with the Bactrian ruler
Bessus claiming the Achaemenid crown
from the fleeing Darius, only to be killed
in turn by Alexander in 329. Alexander's
men were horrified by Balkh – Zoroastrian
beliefs forbade burial or cremation to avoid
polluting the earth, so the Greeks took control of a city roaming with packs of 'de-
vourer dogs' who disposed of the recent
dead. Balkh served as the forward base for
Alexander's Central Asian campaigns, and
it was here that he married Roxane, adding
Afghan blood to the royal lineage, as well as
declaring his own divinity.

After Alexander, Balkh was the centre of
a succession of Graeco-Bactrian dynasties
who held sway over the region until falling
to the nomadic Kushans. Balkh prospered
as a way station on the new Silk Road, with
its people turning to Buddhism.

When the Arabs brought Islam to Afghanistan, Balkh was rich. They, and the
Bukharans after them endowed it with fine
mosques and palaces, and the city enjoyed
a reputation as one of the great centres of
Islamic learning.

Rumi, one of the most celebrated of Sufi
saints, was born in Balkh, although fled the
city in the face of the Mongol onslaught of
1220. When Marco Polo passed through 50
years later he still found the city 'despoiled
and ruined'. Balkh never recovered its glory,
despite a brief hurrah under Timurid rule.

BALKH AND THE WEED

What Helmand Province is to opium poppies, Balkh Province is to cannabis. The distinctive plants
can be seen growing everywhere, and are particularly visible on the road between Balkh and Mazar-e
Sharif, often grown as a thick hedge around the cotton fields. Baba Koo-i Mastan ('the divine mad-
man'), a pre-Islamic holy man from Bactria, is credited with being the first to refine hashish, and his
tomb near Balkh is still visited by locals and tended by a dope-smoking *malang* (holy man).

The smoking of *charas* (cannabis) has a long tradition in Afghanistan, and although illegal the
drug is widely available. An especially potent variety called *shirac* is produced only in Balkh. It needs
little irrigation, making it ideal for the dry province, and although farmers earn roughly a quarter of
what they would if they grew poppies, it has a short growing season and harvesting is less labour
intensive. And of course, it's a lot more profitable than growing regular crops.

The Taliban banned the cultivation and smoking of *charas* but since the end of 2001, farmers
have returned to it in a big way, taking advantage of the lack of governmental control, and the
West's preoccupation with opium. The provincial authorities are occasionally prompted by Kabul
to eradicate cannabis, but these efforts seem tokenistic at best. With such a long tradition behind
him, Baba Koo-i Mastan can sleep soundly in his grave for the foreseeable future.

As nearby Mazar-e Sharif prospered, Balkh struggled through the centuries until cholera and malaria forced a large-scale abandonment in the mid-19th century.

Orientation

The main road from Mazar-e Sharif turns right into Balkh through the old city walls. Opposite the intersection are two large mounds, Takht-e Rostam and Teppe Rostam, ancient Buddhist stupas, probably from around the 4th century AD. The former once held a tooth of the Buddha; the latter now has a tank parked atop it. There are shops and a taxi stand at the junction.

The centre of Balkh is 2km north past the ancient walls, where the unpaved road

meets a large park containing the Shrine of Khoja Abu Nasr Parsa. The Bala Hissar i beyond this. The No Gombad Mosque sit in farmland 1.5km south of the junction.

Sights

SHRINE OF KHOJA ABU NASR PARSA

Standing proud in Balkh's central park, thi shrine ('Khoja Parsa' for short) is a classi example of Timurid architecture, as we as a symbol of Balkh's final flourish befor sliding into permanent decline.

It was built in the 1460s and dedicated t a famous theologian at the court of Sulta Baiqara who had retired to Balkh. The shrin is dominated by its monumental portal en trance, flanked with twisted cable pillars an

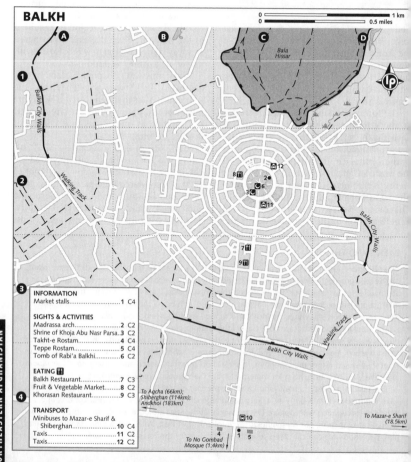

INFORMATION
Market stalls.............................1 C4

SIGHTS & ACTIVITIES
Madrassa arch...........................2 C2
Shrine of Khoja Abu Nasr Parsa..3 C2
Takht-e Rostam.........................4 C4
Teppe Rostam............................5 C4
Tomb of Rabi'a Balkhi................6 C2

EATING
Balkh Restaurant.......................7 C3
Fruit & Vegetable Market.........8 C2
Khorasan Restaurant.................9 C3

TRANSPORT
Minibuses to Mazar-e Sharif &
    Shiberghan...........................10 C4
Taxis...11 C2
Taxis...12 C2

decorated in blue mosaic. The stumps of two minarets stand behind the facade. The shrine s topped with a turquoise ribbed melon dome sitting on a high drum decorated with Quranic verses. Although much of the tile-work is damaged, the building as a whole remains quite astounding.

The door is normally kept locked, but t's worth getting inside if possible. The inner dome stands 29m high above a breath-taking octagonal chamber, supported with internal arches. Light filters through screen windows in the dome's drum, picking out he subtle rust-red and blue decoration.

Attached to the right of the shrine is a modern madrassa (islamic school). The shrine was damaged in an earthquake in he 1990s and has recently undergone re-pair to the dome.

On the northeast edge of the park, and argely hidden by trees, is an impressive rch, all that remains of the 17th century Madrassa of Sayid Subhna Quli Khan. Much uined, it still has traces of blue Timurid-nfluenced tiling on the interior. The park is a pleasant place to sit and people-watch.

TOMB OF RABI'A BALKHI
Opposite the shrine of Khoja Abu Nasr Parsa s the small yellow-tiled tomb of Rabi'a Balkhi. Born in 9th century Balkh, she is credited as he first (and greatest) woman to write po-try in Persian. Her verses are read for their mystical and often erotic undertones. Rabi'a Balkhi fell in love with her slave, and was punished by her brother by being bricked up in a dungeon. She slashed her wrists and wrote her most famous poem – a bitter testa-ment to doomed love – in her own blood on he walls of the prison.

The tomb was rediscovered in 1964, and s a popular place to visit for young women with romantic designs.

BALA HISSAR & CITY WALLS
The massive ramparts of the fortress of Bala Hissar stand guard on the northern edge of he city. The current fort was built by the Timurid in the 15th century on the site of an older citadel. The eroding mud-brick gives he place a much more ancient atmosphere. t's easy to imagine this as the location of Alexander's wedding feast to Roxane, or the ort's luckless defenders being swept away by Genghis Khan's hordes.

Others have had similar thoughts, and the fort is an uneven moonscape of robber holes, dug by locals looking for treasure. Small potsherds, many brightly painted are littered everywhere. There is some nominal protection, but farmers still dig every win-ter in the area, hoping for some old glass beads or Graeco-Bactrian coins to sell to dealers in Mazar-e Sharif and supplement their meagre incomes.

The ramparts give an interesting view across Balkh, with its repeated series of walled compounds. One surprise is how green Balkh appears from above. The tow-ering dome of Khoja Parsa is barely visible through the tops of the trees in the park.

The city walls, 12km around, can also be appreciated from this height, snaking to-wards the highway. The footpaths following the line of the walls are worth exploring.

NO GOMBAD MOSQUE
This ruined 9th-century mosque is thought to be the oldest in Afghanistan. The name refers to its originally nine-domed struc-ture, an unusual design rarely encountered in Islamic architecture. It's also known lo-cally as Masjid-e Haji Piyada ('Mosque of the Walking Pilgrim'), for a local pilgrim.

Today, little more than the mosque's ar-cade piers remain, the columns and arches standing free from a raised earth floor that has never been excavated. The decoration is a delight of carved stucco, the whole cov-ered with arabesques, scrolls and abstract geometric designs. The style shows the in-fluence of similar buildings in Samarra in Iraq, presumably a reflection of recently converted Balkh's connections with the rul-ing caliphate.

The whole site is in need of consolida-tion, and is covered with a metal canopy and surrounded by a perimeter mud-brick wall. The mosque is still used by local vil-lagers for prayers and sermons on Fridays, so try to avoid visiting at this time. There is a friendly *chowkidar* (caretaker) on site who appreciates a small donation, and will show off his prize pigeons given half the chance.

The mosque lies a 1.5km walk south of the intersection for Balkh on the road from Mazar-e Sharif. The metal canopy is easily spotted from the path, rising clear from the fields of marijuana that surround the site (see boxed text, p155).

MAZAR-E SHARIF & NORTHEASTERN AFGHANISTAN

Sleeping & Eating

There are no hotels in Balkh, which is close enough to Mazar-e Sharif to make a day trip the best option. There are a few chaikhanas on the main road from the highway to the park: the Balkh Restaurant and Khorasan Restaurant offer *pulao*, *shorwa* (soup) and kebabs. For the desperate, there would probably be a space on the floor to sleep for the price of dinner.

There's a fruit and vegetable market on the northern edge of the main park.

Getting There & Around

Share taxis run throughout the day to Balkh from Mazar-e Sharif (30Afg, 30 minutes), and leave in the opposite direction from either a stand on the main highway or one on the eastern edge of the park. Hiring a taxi for the return trip (including sightseeing) should cost 300Afg to 400Afg.

Balkh is small enough to explore by foot, although there are horse-drawn *garis* should the mood take you.

MAZAR-E SHARIF TO BADAKHSHAN

مزار شریف الی بدخشان

The road from Mazar-e Sharif to Badakhshan performs a large V, heading south past Tashkurgan and Samangan to the junction town of Pul-e Khumri. Here it switches north towards Kunduz before leaving the plains and climbing into the mountains of the far northeast.

TASHKURGAN تاشقرغان

The old bazaar town of Tashkurgan, 60km from Mazar-e Sharif, would once have been a key stopping-off point for any traveller to Afghanistan. Sometimes also known by its old name of Khulm, Tashkurgan was the site of the last traditional covered bazaar in the country, a wonderful maze of mud-brick streets and stalls that put visitors firmly in touch with Marco Polo and the Silk Road. The bazaar was levelled during the war, another sad testament to the recent destruction visited on Afghanistan's culture. Little remains for the modern traveller to see, except a small palace built by Abdur

Rahman Khan in the late 19th century i Indian colonial style.

Maps show a road heading due eas from Tashkurgan to Kunduz, but this i not used, being in complete disrepair an reportedly mined. All traffic heads sou instead. The highway passes through th stupendous gorge of Tangi Tashkurga where the mountains suddenly loom fro the plains and enclose the road in shee walls 300m high. In summer, watch out fo the impromptu fruit stalls here – the loca pomegranates and figs are delicious.

SAMANGAN (AIBAK) سمنگان(ایبک)

Samangan is an ancient town in a valley c rich farmland where the Hindu Kush start to meet the Central Asian steppe. It was al ready well known when the Arabs and Mongols vis ited, having been a major Buddhist centr under the Kushans in the 4th and 5th cen turies AD. The remains of this site, Takht-Rostam, sit on a hill above the town.

The town was a medieval caravan sto known as Aibak, a name many locals sti use today. Samangan still holds a sizeabl weekly market every Thursday and is note for its craftsmen who make traditional Af ghan musical instruments such as the *duta* (two-stringed lute) and *zirbaghali* (a drun made from pottery). Ask for the Bazaar-Danbora Faroshi (Lute-Sellers' bazaar).

Samangan's bread is equally renowned round Uzbek loaves that are sold by th roadside to vehicles travelling betwee Mazar-e Sharif and Kabul. There is a larg Uzbek population in the town, and you ca see pictures of General Dostum on displa

The town sits just west of the main high way, with the road into town leading to th main square and bazaar. Takht-e Rostar is 3km to the southwest, a 100Afg ride i an autorickshaw. There are no decent ho tels in town, but it's an easy day trip fron Mazar-e Sharif.

Takht-e Rostam

The remains of this **Buddhist stupa and mon astery** (entry 250Afg) are one of the most un expected sights in Afghanistan. On a hi above Samangan, they offer a commandin view of the valley below.

High on the rise is a well-preserve stupa – one of the earliest forms of Bud dhist architecture, simple mounds raised t

---

THE LEGEND OF ROSTAM

Rostam is one of the great heroes of Persian literature, immortalised in the epic *Shah Nama* (Book of Kings) by the Ghaznavid court poet Firdausi in the 10th century. Something of a giant, Rostam was born by caesarean section overseen by a mythical bird, and performed many great feats in his life accompanied by his equally heroic horse Rakhsh, including the slaying of a terrible dragon. But like a Shakespearean hero, Rostam's story is tinged with tragedy. His son Sohrab, who was born in Samangan, grew up alone and only met his father on the field of battle, where Rostam killed him in a case of mistaken identity. Rostam himself died at the hands of his treacherous brother Shaghad.

Many unusual rock formations in Afghanistan are accredited as the sites of the hero's achievements – look out for other Takht-e Rostams elsewhere in the country.

---

ontain relics of the Buddha. What makes Takht-e Rostam highly unusual is that instead of being built up, the 28m stupa has been carved out of the rock so is completely below ground level. The trench that surrounds the bowl of rock is around 8m deep, giving some sense of the scale of the work involved chiselling it out.

On top of the stupa is a carved stone building, a *harmika* that would have held the site's relics. The roof has a hole dug into it to hold a ceremonial umbrella. Since the passing of Buddhism, folklore has dubbed this the Takht-e Rostam – the Throne of Rostam. The legendary king (see above) reportedly married his bride Tahmina here, daughter of the king of Samangan. The hole of the roof allegedly held the wine for the wedding feast. Tahmina later went on to bear Rostam's doomed son, Sohrab. An information board adds more information, including the vital nugget that the site was built 'in the early years of Christmas'.

A path leads down to a cave entrance to the bottom of the stupa, allowing visitors to circumambulate the stupa (clockwise, according to Buddhist tradition).

Below the stupa is a series of five caves, again excavated from the rock. They're reminiscent of the monks' cells in Bamiyan, but on a much grander scale. The first cave has a 12m-high domed ceiling, carved with a huge lotus flower partially hidden by soot. This is followed by a wider cave with two long galleries with vaulted ceilings. There are individual cells that were used as retreats for meditation; the light filtering in through the carved windows does indeed give it a serene atmosphere.

The third cave is the largest in scope and finest in execution. An antechamber leads into an immense domed room. Roughly square, each wall has a niche that would have contained a Buddha statue, and topped with a carved column. The corners of the room have carved arches to support the great dome, as in a modern mosque. A hole in the ceiling bathes the room in a gentle light.

The fourth cave is a series of small rooms with a carved pool, thought to be a bathhouse. The final cave next to it is most likely a toilet, and is filled with rubble.

Getting There & Away

Samangan's transport depot is on the junction with the Kabul-Mazar-e Sharif highway. There are plenty of minibuses and shared taxis throughout the day to Mazar-e Sharif (110Afg, two hours), Pul-e Khumri (80Afg, 1½ hours) and Kabul (300Afg, five hours).

PUL-E KHUMRI   پلخمری

All travellers in northern Afghanistan will pass through Pul-e Khumri at least once. It's a large (and largely nondescript) town on a wide flood plain perfect for agriculture. There's not much reason to stop in the town itself, although in winter people occasionally get stranded here if the Salang Pass is closed. The Russian-built cement factory is the town's major attraction. Around 12km north of Pul-e Khumri is the Kushan Buddhist site of Surkh Kotal (see boxed text, p160).

There are no decent hotels in Pul-e Khumri, although the Zadran Hotel would do in a pinch. For onward transport, minibuses and taxis to Mazar-e Sharif (200Afg, 3½ hours) and Kunduz (100Afg, 1½ hours) depart from a depot where the highway

SURKH KOTAL

The acropolis of Surkh Kotal was built around AD 130 for the Kushan ruler Kanishka; it comprised a series of terraces built into the hillside overlooking the Anderab river. Kanishka was the greatest of Kushan kings, ruling from his capital in Kapisa (modern day Bagram) as far as Gujarat in southern India. He was a Buddhist king who traded with Rome and China, and whose art was influenced by Persia and ancient Greece.

Excavated in the 1950s, little now remains at Surkh Kotal of the marble staircase and fluted columns found at the site, lost to war and looters. Archaeology buffs will get the most out of a visit, although the views over the valley remain tremendous. Two important relics from Surkh Kotal can be seen at the Kabul Museum (p88): the remains of a statue of Kanishka, smashed by the Taliban but now restored, and a large tablet inscribed in Greek that would have been part of a temple sanctuary.

splits in the three major directions. Vehicles to Kabul (200Afg, four hours) leave from a depot on the southern outskirts of town.

A further 40km south of Pul-e Khumri is the small town of Doshi on the Anderab river, where the back road from Bamiyan joins the main highway. This stretch of road is particularly attractive in summer, with the green farmland following the river until the road snakes up into the Koh-e Daman mountains, heading for the Salang Pass (p112).

KUNDUZ   کندز

The largely Uzbek and Tajik town of Kunduz lies amid rich agricultural land, and is one of Afghanistan's most stable and thriving towns. The well-watered plains that surround it are ideal for growing rice, while the dusty loess hills to the north near the Tajikistan border turn emerald green at the first hint of the spring rains. Although there are few attractions to see in the town, it's a relaxing place to rest up on the road and a useful hub for those aiming for Badakhshan or Tajikistan.

Not all travellers' reports have been so favourable. In *The Road to Oxiana*, Robert Byron approvingly quotes a proverb of the time stating that 'a visit to Kunduz is tantamount to suicide'. When north Afghanistan fractured into city-states in the early 19th century, Kunduz was ruled by the slave-raiding Murad Beg. He was the most powerful and murderous of the northern khans, dealing with Kabul and Bukhara as equals. And if the slavers didn't get you, the fever-ridden marshes probably would. Malaria remains a problem in the area today.

Many settlers didn't come to Kunduz by choice either. The town has a large Pashtun minority, Ghilzais from the east who were forcibly relocated here in the 1890s as part of Abdur Rahman Khan's plans to weaken his tribal enemies. Thirty years later the population exploded again with an influx of Uzbek and Tajiks fleeing the expanding Soviet presence in Central Asia.

Kunduz was the scene of fierce resistance by the Taliban in November 2001 and was the first base for the International Security Assistance Forces (ISAF) mandate outside Kabul, with a German-run Provincial Reconstruction Team (PRT). Although largely peaceful today, the Hezb-e Islami party has a sizeable presence in the area – Gulbuddin Hekmatyar (p186) was born in the province and there have been occasional incidents involving anti-government violence.

Information

Haqkhawa Internet (Sarakh-e Iman Sahib; per hr 60Afg) On first floor of building.

Kabul Bank (cnr of Jad-e Haji Ghani) Has a branch of Western Union.

Moneychangers (Chowk-e Kunduz) Several moneychangers' stalls are just north of the main square.

Sights

The remains of Murad Beg's **fort**, the Bala Hissar, are on the outskirts of town off the main road heading north. Nothing remains inside, but the walls give decent views over the town. Also of interest are the grounds of the **Takharistan Madrassa**, west of the square on Sarakh-e Spinzar. The large mosque inside has recently been restored, and respectful visitors are usually welcomed. The land around Kunduz is ideal for raising horses, so it's no surprise that from late autumn to spring, *buzkashi* is popular in the town.

Sleeping & Eating

At the time of writing, chaikhana owners were banned by the police from taking foreigners as guests in Kunduz.

Ariana Hotel (☎ 070 274712; Jad-e Mahareif; s/d/tr US$10/20/30) This basic hotel is the best cheap option in Kunduz. All rooms have attached bathrooms, which are kept reasonably clean, although many of the fixtures are pretty ragged. Rooms look onto a busy central courtyard, and there's an attached wedding hall that could potentially make this a noisy option for light sleepers.

Kunduz Hotel (☎ 075 5505 702; kunduz_hotel@yahoo.com; Jad-e Dosti Afghan Aiman; s/d US$50/60; ✷) If you're after a solid Afghan business-class

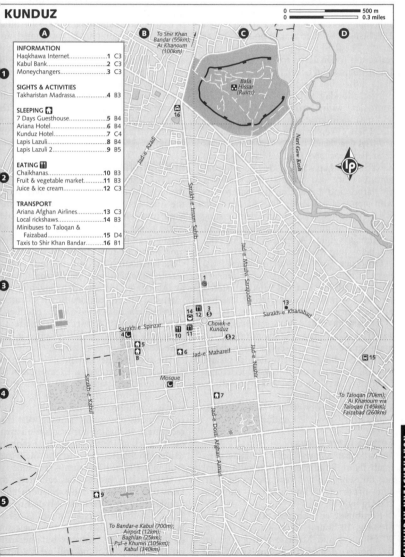

KUNDUZ

0	500 m
0	0.3 miles

INFORMATION
Haqkhawa Internet..................**1** C3
Kabul Bank............................**2** C3
Moneychangers.....................**3** C3

SIGHTS & ACTIVITIES
Takharistan Madrassa..............**4** B3

SLEEPING
7 Days Guesthouse..................**5** B4
Ariana Hotel..........................**6** B4
Kunduz Hotel.........................**7** C4
Lapis Lazuli............................**8** B4
Lapis Lazuli 2.........................**9** B5

EATING
Chaikhanas............................**10** B3
Fruit & vegetable market.........**11** B3
Juice & ice cream....................**12** C3

TRANSPORT
Ariana Afghan Airlines.............**13** C3
Local rickshaws......................**14** B3
Minibuses to Taloqan &
  Faizabad.............................**15** D4
Taxis to Shir Khan Bandar........**16** B1

To Shir Khan Bandar (55km); Ai Khanoum (100km)

Bala Hissar (Ruins)

Nari Gow Kosh

Jad-e Azadi

Sarakh-e Imam Sahib

Jad-e Madru Sarajuddin

Chowk-e Kunduz

Sarakh-e Spinzar

Sarakh-e Khanabad

Jad-e Nashir

Jad-e Mahareif

Mosque

Jad-e Dosti Afghan Aiman

Sarakh-e Kabul

To Taloqan (70km); Ai Khanoum via Taloqan (145km); Faizabad (260km)

To Bandar-e Kabul (700m); Airport (12km); Baghlan (25km); Pul-e Khumri (105km); Kabul (340km)

hotel, this is it. Set in large grounds, the rooms are equally spacious, all with a fridge and a bathroom with water heater. Another popular option for wedding parties.

Lapis Lazuli (☎ 079 9209 503; Jad-e Kulali; s/d incl breakfast & dinner US$45/70; ✖) A joint Afghan-German guesthouse, this is deservedly popular with international workers. Rooms are tidy if sometimes small, and bathrooms are shared. Advance booking is recommended, although a second guesthouse (Lapis Lazuli 2) is being opened to accommodate further guests. The food is a big draw though – the restaurant (open 12pm to 2pm and 6pm to 10pm; mains from US$6) has good meat and pasta dishes, but head here for the 'all you can eat' Monday barbecue from 7pm to fill your plate with German sausage, chicken and meat, and great bowls of delicious salads. There's even draught German lager.

7 Days Guesthouse (☎ 079 9362 992; www.7days -international.com; Jad-e Kulali; s/d US$50/100; ✖) Next door to Lapis Lazuli, this is an unpretentious place also aimed at expats. Rooms are large, and have attached bathrooms with plenty of hot water. The management is extremely helpful, and can organise simple meals for guests, taken in a garden lit up with fairy lights. A small swimming pool was being dug when we visited.

Chaikhanas (Sarakh-e Spinzar; dishes from 50Afg) For the usual kebabs, *pulao* and *shorwa*, there are plenty of chaikhanas clustered west of the main square. Decent fare but no great surprises.

Juice and ice cream (Sarakh-e Iman Sahib; refreshments from 20Afg) Immediately north of the main square, there are several juice stands and shops selling hand-churned ice cream. The usual caveats about where the ice comes from aside, they're a great way to cool down on a hot Kunduz day.

There are plenty of fruit and vegetable sellers near Chowk-e Kunduz.

Getting There & Away

Ariana Afghan Airlines (Sarakh-e Khanabad) normally fly on Sunday and Tuesday to Kabul but the schedule is a very moveable feast. The airport is 12km south of Kunduz, 200Afg by taxi.

Minibuses and shared taxis to Kabul (400Afg, 10 hours), Pul-e Khumri (80Afg, 90 minutes) and Mazar-e Sharif (350Afg, five hours) depart from Bandar-e Kabul

terminal on the road south out of Kunduz. Transport south from Kunduz often stops at the picturesque sugar-producing town of Baghlan. The chaikhanas opposite the pleasantly leafy town square are a relaxing place to break the journey.

Shared taxis to Shir Khan Bandar (80Afg, one hour) for the Tajikistan border leave from opposite the Bala Hissar. For more on crossing this border, see p216.

East of the main square, there are minibuses to Taloqan (50Afg, one hour) and Faizabad (500Afg, 10 hours). Taloqan is another pleasant tree-lined town, with little to do but drink tea and visit the bazaar. One-time capital of the Northern Alliance, it has seen sizeable Iranian funding – note the street signs named for ayatollahs. The sealed road finishes soon after Taloqan, after which it's an extremely bumpy (though very beautiful) ride into Badakhshan.

AI KHANOUM ﺍﻯ ﺧﺎﻧﻢ

In 1961, King Zahir Shah was hunting in the area where the Kokcha River meets the Amu Darya when his party discovered some intriguing archaeological remains. He could never have anticipated that his accident would reveal the site of the easternmost ancient Greek city in the world.

Ai Khanoum ('Moon Lady' in Uzbek) is presumed to be Alexandria-Oxiana, founded by Alexander the Great during his campaigns in the 4th century BC. It's strategic location on a hill overlooking the confluence of the rivers is so immediately apparent it convinces you that Alexander must indeed have stood here.

The site stretches around 2km along the banks of the Amu Darya. Excavation in the 1960s and '70s revealed a temple complex, palace with administrative quarter, theatre, gymnasium and necropolis. Several coin hoards and many statues were also recovered, including an inscription from the Oracles of Delphi haughtily exhorting readers the correct way to live their lives (still in the Kabul Museum – see p88).

Having lain hidden for centuries, the years since discovery have not been kind. Frankly, the site is a mess. Myriad robber holes dot the landscape like giant rabbit holes, reminders that when the war came so did the looters. Anyone but the keenest archaeological mind will need a lot of

A HISTORY TOLD THROUGH COINS

Hellenistic Bactria left few written records. The historians of the day followed Greece and its big players, not the distant high tide marks of empire. Luckily the new city-states left much of their history in the coins they struck. Early 19th century Great Gamers like Charles Masson were the first to note bilingual Greek/Indian coinage, prompting academics to throw new light on the Hellenistic east.

Covering the three centuries following the departure of Alexander the Great, the coin hoards regularly dug up in north Afghanistan have revealed Hellenistic Bactria as a constantly tumbling succession of kings. Some rulers pop up to disappear almost instantly, while a lucky few had long reigns, evidenced by the ageing portraits shown on their coins. The portraits show the fusion of Greek clothing styles and haircuts with Eastern innovations, such as elephant-head helmets. One hoard found near Kunduz in the 1940s contained the largest Greek coins ever minted, the 84g double decadrachms, featuring Zeus and the Persian god Mithras.

Later coins struck show a civilisation on its last legs. The Greek language is debased, and Indian iconography increasingly common. The continuing use of the ancient gods hides the fact that the Graeco-Bactrians had converted to Buddhism, a last grasp at renewing their vigour, but one that couldn't protect them from the encroaching nomadic warriors from the north.

imagination to see the site as an ancient ity. Almost no visible historic remains can e seen. The site hasn't been completely rashed, however, and French archaeologists have received permission to carry out more delicate variety of excavation, particularly in the area around the acropolis nd citadel that sit atop the hill.

Despite this, the Ai Khanoum is still vorth visiting for the scenery. A shingle each sits at the confluence that would nake a fine place for a picnic. On the Afhan side the land sweeps away into wide lains dotted with trees, while the Tajik order is marked by high ochre cliffs and ne strong broad flow of the Amu Darya. There's certainly a romance to the area.

An hour's drive from Ai Khanoum, heading north from Dasht-e Qala is the town f **Khwaja Bahauddin**, the final headquarters f Ahmad Shah Massoud, pinned back by ne Taliban in 2001. It was here on 9 September 2001 that he was murdered by two al-Qaeda operatives posing as journalists. ocals will point out with a heavy heart the uilding where he died. While here, also ook out for the traffic island with the Corinthian columns looted from Ai Khanoum; nere are more in a nearby chaikhana.

letting There & Away

Hiring a car is the simplest way to get to Ai Khanoum. The route via Taloqan is the asiest. From Kunduz the route is spectaclar over some crazy dunes, but it's easy to get lost so it's essential that the driver know where he's going. We were quoted around US$80 for a return trip from Kunduz, around 3½ hours each way. The route passes through the small town of Khwaja Gar and crosses the Kokcha River at Pul-e Kokcha (look for the spectacularly crashed plane near the bridge, the site of the old Taliban/Northern Alliance front line). The road turns west at Dasht-e Qala, following the river a further 5km to Ai Khanoum – the hill at the confluence is on the outskirts of the village of the same name.

Public transport is a challenge. From Taloqan, minibuses run by erratic schedules to Dasht-e Qala, but you'll need to arrange the last leg from there, probably hiring a vehicle outright. Roads are poor throughout this route.

BADAKHSHAN بدخشان

The northeastern province of Badakhshan has always sat slightly apart from the rest of Afghanistan. As the plains become scrunched up into a knot of mountains, and the Hindu Kush collides with the Pamir range, the distance from Kabul seems to be measured in centuries as much as miles.

Badakhshan's history as well as its geography reveals this independent streak. A far outpost of the Achaemenid empire, by the medieval period it was recognised as a sovereign state, its wealth deriving from the trade routes through the mountains between China, Kashmir and Bukhara. Timur tried and failed to subdue it, while his successors sent embassies instead. In the 19th century Badakhshan was finally subsumed into the Afghan state but even Abdur Rahman Khan baulked at having to rule it properly. The Wakhan Corridor, that panhandle of land sticking into China, was only forced on him when the British and Russians decided they needed a buffer between their empires. A century later, Badakhshan was the only part of Afghanistan to resist capture by the Taliban.

It is the scenery that attracts visitors today. The provincial capital of Faizabad provides a gateway to some of the country's most sublime landscapes, from the Kuchi pastures of Lake Shewa to the Pamirs themselves, home of the last nomadic Kyrgyz on earth, in mountains so high that Marco Polo claimed that even birds couldn't fly there. Of equal inspiration to the truly intrepid are the mines of Sar-e Sang, source of most of the world's lapis lazuli. Badakhshan also serves as an entry point into Tajikistan and, potentially, northern Pakistan.

Visitors should be aware that Badakhshan is second only to Helmand for opium production. Controlled by Northern Alliance, opium is the backbone of the local economy. Ironically, security is generally fairly good in the province, but you should be extremely circumspect with cameras and questions if travelling in an area with poppy cultivation. When there have been security problems in Badakhshan, these have tended to coincide with eradication programmes, when being a foreigner in certain areas isn't necessarily a popular thing to be.

FAIZABAD   فیض آباد

Astride the fast-flowing Kokcha River, Faizabad is a largely Tajik town, home to the rump Afghan government during the Taliban era. It's an amiable place with a traditional bazaar, and is good to catch your breath for a few days if travelling to or from the Wakhan Corridor or the Tajikistan border.

The town has been the capital of Badakhshan since the 17th century. Its name ('Blessed Abode') is taken from the cloak of the Prophet Mohammed that was brought here by the ruling mir of the time. The cloak is now kept in a mosque in Kandahar (p193).

The bazaar in the old town follows the street pattern set out during this time, a winding mass of roughly pitted streets between the main square and the river. The bazaar is of great interest to travellers, and knitted socks make good souvenirs. On the street west of the main square there are several lapis lazuli dealers. The blue stone is brought here from Sar-e Sang (p166), although the best goes to Kabul. A kilo of medium quality lapis will set you back around US$100 here. Some jewellery is also made locally, but is generally of inferior quality next to what's available in the capital.

Faizabad has a pleasant climate, its heat moderated by breezes off the river. Given that it's an entry point to the mountains, it's a surprise that it sits at just 1200m – lower than Kabul. The town is particularly pretty in spring and early summer, when the fields and slopes sing with greenery. TV Hill, overlooking the old town, is worth climbing for great views. Nauroz is an interesting time to be here, as the holiday is usually followed by 10 days of *buzkashi* held on the field at the edge of Shahr-e Nau.

Orientation

Faizabad is divided by the Kokcha River, which is crossed by two bridges. The main road in and out of town is on the west bank, passing through the new city (Shahr-e Nau, where most NGO offices are based). The Old Town is on the east bank, centred on a main square (the tall telephone tower is a handy landmark). The main bazaar street runs southeast from here, leading to the southern bridge. Minibuses (15Afg) run throughout the day between the Old Town and Shahr-Nau, via the northern bridge. From the south Faizabad is overlooked by Jilgar Mountain, a corruption of '40 concubines', legendarily ascribed to Genghis Khan when he campaigned here. Faizabad airport is 3.5km west of town, along the main road.

Information

Aria Internet (west of main square, Old Town; per hr 100Afg)

Great Game Travel (☎ 079 9062 033; faizabad@greatgame.travel; Old Town) Branch of Kabul-based travel company; can organise permits, translators and vehicle hire.

Police (Main Sq, Old Town)

Western Union (main bazaar, Old Town) Several money changers also along this street.

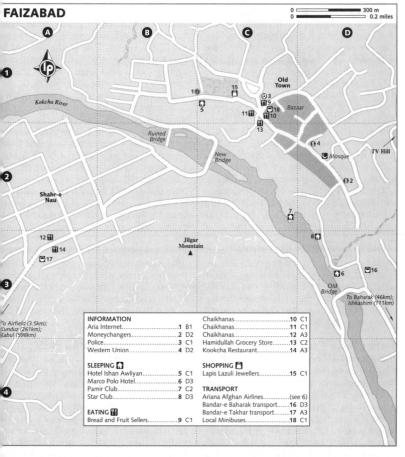

FAIZABAD

INFORMATION
Aria Internet...1 B1
Moneychangers...................................2 D2
Police..3 C1
Western Union.....................................4 D2

SLEEPING
Hotel Ishan Awliyan.............................5 C1
Marco Polo Hotel.................................6 D3
Pamir Club...7 C2
Star Club..8 D3

EATING
Bread and Fruit Sellers.........................9 C1

Chaikhanas...10 C1
Chaikhanas...11 C1
Chaikhanas...12 A3
Hamidullah Grocery Store..................13 C2
Kookcha Restaurant...........................14 A3

SHOPPING
Lapis Lazuli Jewellers.........................15 C1

TRANSPORT
Ariana Afghan Airlines...................(see 6)
Bandar-e Baharak transport...............16 D3
Bandar-e Takhar transport.................17 A3
Local Minibuses.................................18 C1

Sleeping & Eating

Accommodation options in Faizabad are pretty restricted, and though the quality isn't great, several are on the river, allowing the rushing water to soothe you to sleep. Hotels can generally offer meals if requested in advance, otherwise eating out isn't Faizabad's most exciting pastime.

Pamir Club (☎ 079 9443 117; Kokcha River, Old Town; r US$40) If there's a hotel with a better location in Afghanistan, we'd like to know about it. On a promontory surrounded on three sides by the rushing Kokcha River, this government hotel has a hard spot to beat. Rooms are large and reasonably decent with balconies looking over the water, and have shared bathrooms (don't hope too hard

for hot water). Management can rustle up a meal, but are generally resentful of having guests stay at all.

Marco Polo Hotel (☎ 079 9279 018; near southern bridge, Old Town; r US$20) Also known as Number One Guesthouse, this is a basic hotel with hard beds. The shared bathrooms are pretty basic, with squat toilets, but there's a pleasant garden that overlooks the river.

Hotel Ishan Awliyan (West of main square, Old Town; r 300Afg) One step up from a chaikhana, this 1st-floor hotel has a handful of private rooms with two beds and a beaten-up sofa apiece – a little dingy but perfectly serviceable. Meals are in the main restaurant, and a new toilet block was being built when we visited.

Star Club (Kokcha River, Old Town; r around US$20) Reportedly offering similar accommodation to the Marco Polo Hotel, the Star Club was temporarily closed at the time of research. It's right on the river, slightly upstream from the Pamir Club.

Chaikhanas (Main Sq, Old Town; meals from 50Afg) A host of chaikhanas are clustered along the southern edge of the main square – offering exactly what you'd expect from such places.

Kookcha Restaurant (Shahr-e Nau; meals from 60Afg) Here's something blessedly different: chicken and chips. Almost finger-lickin', but after a diet of meat and rice definitely worth the trek to Shahr-e Nau. 'China soup' with noodles is also on offer. Look for the green restaurant front. There are several more standard chaikhanas along the same stretch of the main road.

Self-caterers should head for the main bazaar street running off the main square. Hamidullah grocery store here has a good selection on imported goods, if you're craving chocolate. On the main square, under what looks like a large bus shelter, there are plenty of fresh bread and fruit sellers.

Getting There & Away

Ariana Afghan Airlines (☎ 079 9175 338; in Marco Polo Hotel) fly to Kabul (2500Afg, one hour) three times a week. Go to the office the day before travel to get your name on the manifest, then again on the morning of departure to confirm they're still flying and to get your ticket. Kam Air is reportedly setting up flights to Kabul.

Minibuses and shared taxis for all points outside of Badakhshan depart from the Bandar-e Takhar station in Shahr-e Nau. The main destinations are Taloqan (500Afg, nine hours), Kunduz (550Afg, 10 hours), Pul-e Khumri (600Afg, 12 hours) and Kabul (800Afg, 1½ days, overnighting in Pul-e Khumri).

To get further into Badakhshan, go to Bandar-e Baharak in the old town. HiAces leave for Baharak (150Afg, two hours), Ishkashim (600Afg, eight hours) and Jurm (250Afg, four hours) from here. Travel beyond Ishkashim requires a permit – for more information see p168.

Vehicle hire in Faizabad and throughout Badakhshan is expensive – around US$200 per day.

LAKE SHEWA جهيل شيوه

Three hours (80km) from Faizabad, har against the Tajikistan border, is the beau tiful Lake Shewa. One of the sources of the Amu Darya, the wide pastures tha surround it are the main summer grazin grounds of the northeastern Kuchis.

Every May, Kuchi families arrive in thei hundreds around the lake with their flocks It's a time for weddings and *buzkashi*, an there could hardly be a better landscape fo such pursuits – high peaks and wide gree meadows. The lake itself is a dazzling blu and large enough, we were told, that 'yo can't shoot a Kalashnikov across it'. A com plete trek around would take two days.

Your own vehicle is required to get t Lake Shewa, and you'll need a local guid to introduce you to the Kuchi so that yo can set up camp (and to restrain their fierc dogs if necessary). The lake is accessibl until October, although the nomads ten to leave for their winter grounds by Sep tember. Even if you don't make it here, i you're travelling at this time you're likel to pass their caravans on the road all th way to Kunduz.

SOUTH TO THE ANJOMAN PASS

This route is for the most adventurou travelling from Faizabad along the Kokch River to the Anjoman Pass, leading to th Panjshir Valley. Its main attraction is Sar-Sang, the oldest worked mines in the worl and the source of Afghanistan's – and th ancient world's – lapis lazuli. Like the res of Badakhshan, travel is only really an op tion from late spring to early autumn.

From Faizabad, it's easy to get to th junction town of Baharak (150Afg, tw hours) by public minibus. The road split here, with the southern fork heading fo the town of Jurm (250Afg, four hours). It a poor road but a busy one: most farmer here grow poppies, and aside from culti vation, it's believed that the raw paste i refined into opium in local labs. It's essen tial to get trustworthy security informatio in Faizabad before travelling this road; w were advised that travelling in public trans port decreases the chances of being mis taken for officials involved in eradication.

Sar-e Sang is around another three hour from Jurm. It's a one-street town along valley, with around 20 tunnels current eing worked for lapis. There's a chaikhana, ut it's worth remembering this is a rough-nd-ready mining place. The nearest mines re a stiff two to three hour walk from Sar-e ang. The shafts are 250m deep in places. The lapis is sent either to Kabul, or by orse over the passes to Pakistan. In ancient imes, the seams were mined by lighting res in the tunnels, and then packing the ot rock with snow to crack it. More recent echniques involve using military muni-ions, although the uncontrolled explosions lamage the highest quality lapis.

The track continues for 30km to the fer-ile valley of Iskazer, the last major settle-nent in Badakhshan. Iskazer can be reached rom Faizabad in around 10 hours by 4WD n summer. From here it's a further six ours to the Anjoman Pass (4430m). The istas from here are sublime, to the Panj-hir, Nuristan, and even as far as Pakistan. The road descends into the Panjshir Val-ey (p110), where the sometimes paranoid Panjshiri security officials will be extremely urprised to see you.

SHKASHIM اشکاشم

The small town of Ishkashim sits on the Panj River near the entrance to the Wa-khan Corridor, as well as on the border rossing into Tajikistan. It's a place to ake stock before heading deeper into the nountains.

There are several basic guesthouses in shkashim, which seem to regularly change name – you need to ask for them by owner. All charge around US$20 per person per night. A new guesthouse run by Edi and Boz Muhammad is reportedly good, as is Wafai's Guesthouse. Ayanbeg's Guesthouse has had mixed reviews from international workers passing through.

Minibuses leave daily for Faizabad (600Afg, eight hours), via Baharak (400Afg, six hours). Note that the road between Ish-kashim and Baharak passes through large areas of poppy cultivation, so you're ad-vised to stay in your vehicle and not go exploring. Between Baharak and Faizabad there's no poppy. For information on head-ing into the Wakhan Corridor, see below. A bridge crosses the river into Tajikistan. The border is open Monday to Thursday – see p216 for more details.

WAKHAN & THE AFGHAN PAMIR
واخان و پامیر افغانستان

Afghanistan's Wakhan District is a narrow strip of land that juts eastwards 350km be-tween Tajikistan and Pakistan to touch the Chinese border. Wakhan District has two distinct parts – the Wakhan Corridor and the Afghan Pamir.

The deep valley of the **Wakhan Corridor** is formed by the Panj River as it courses be-tween the lofty mountains of Tajikistan to the north and the snowcapped Hindu Kush Range with 38 summits higher than 7000m to the south. Wakhan is the homeland of 12,000 Wakhi people who live in year-round villages along the Panj River's south bank and its upper tributary, the Wakhan River, where they cultivate wheat, barley, peas, potatoes and a few apricot trees.

LAPIS LAZULI

It's thought that the mines of Sar-e Sang have been worked for over 7000 years, the most important source of lapis lazuli in the world. The gemstone's deep royal blue colour comes from the mineral lazerite, often flecked with gold pyrite and veins of white calcite. Its Persian name, *lajward,* is the origin of the word azure, while the painters of Renaissance Europe knew it as ultramarine, grinding it up to make their most expensive pigments.

Lapis was an important luxury good in the ancient world, and trade networks reached from Badakhshan to Sumer (Iraq) and Egypt, where it was prized for its beads and amulets. The lapis lazuli in Tutankhamen's death mask was mined at Sar-e Sang. Wars were even fought to protect the trade routes.

In the 20th century, the Afghan government exerted a monopoly over the trade, but this collapsed soon after the Soviet invasion. Far from the reach of Kabul, the mujaheddin took over the mines, and traded the rock for guns in the bazaars of Chitral and Peshawar in Pakistan. These powerful interests still control the mines today, with precious little of the profits reaching the Afghan people who would benefit most from this highly lucrative and ancient trade.

The Hindu Kush, Karakoram and Pamir ranges converge in the **Afghan Pamir**, known in Persian as the Bam-e Dunya ('roof of the world'). *Pamir*, U-shaped, high-elevation valleys with lush seasonal meadows and vivid blue lakes, are renowned as summer grazing grounds, but lie snow-covered for more than six months of the year. The Afghan Pamir includes two such grasslands – the Big Pamir and the Little Pamir. Only occasional clusters of shrubs or willow, birch and other small trees break the vast landscape.

A vital branch of the Silk Road flowed through Wakhan. Petroglyphs depicting warriors, hunting scenes, caravans and Buddhist history, along with the occasional *rabot* (travellers' shelter), bear silent witness to the tracks of tradition, and the rich heritage that once traversed remote Wakhan. Trekking is by far the most popular way to experience the natural beauty and cultural diversity of Wakhan, and the only way to visit the roadless Afghan Pamir.

Practicalities

PERMISSION

Permission is required for travel anywhere in Wakhan District. A separate trekking permit is not required.

The process for getting permission changes with some regularity, so cover all your bases. Firstly, in Kabul contact the ATO (p86), who can liaise with government ministries and issue a letter for you to present at government offices in Faizabad and Ishkashim. Second, in Faizabad contact **Engineer Mohammad Deen** (☎ 079 9418 060) at the government's tourist information centre who issues a letter for authorities in Ishkashim. Third, in Ishkashim go to the Border Security Force and the police. The Border Security Force's commander, currently Mir Abdul Wahid Khan, issues another letter of permission to visit Wakhan (and the Afghan Pamir if you want to visit the Big Pamir and/or Little Pamir). He may or may not issue a letter without other letters from Kabul and/or Faizabad. The police in Ishkashim can radio permission to police posts up-valley, although this system is prone to technical breakdowns.

You may be asked to show the letter(s) at various places, but most certainly at the checkpost in Qila-e Panja and in Sarhad-e Broghil. If you don't have permission, you'll be sent back to Ishkashim.

WHEN TO GO

May to September is the optimal trekking season. Snowmelt in July and early August however, swells rivers whose high water can block the sole road. By mid-August, it becomes easier to drive through the rivers. Infamously fierce winds known as *bad-e Wakhan* blow year round, fuelling dust storms. It can snow any month of the year in the Afghan Pamir and by mid-September passes can close.

GUIDES & PORTERS

Wakhan has no fully qualified guides, although handfuls of young men are receiving training in basic mountaineering skills, trek operations, cooking, and English. The daily wage for someone with some training starts at 500Afg.

Hiring a local person with their pack animal (donkey, horse, yak or camel) to transport your gear, help with river crossings, and show the way is the best approach. Villages have a rotational system to equitably assign work. The daily rate in the Afghan Pamir has been fixed at 800Afg, and Noshaq Base Camp at 1000Afg, although it may be possible to negotiate. For some treks, it can be more cost effective to buy an animal (eg a donkey costs between US$150 and US$200), manage it yourself, and sell it afterwards.

Distances in the Afghan Pamir are vast, so you'll likely want to hop a ride during part of your trek. Yaks transport gear and are useful for crossing rivers. Horses are also good mounts on trails, but not on snow. Donkeys are sturdy, but cannot cross deep or swift rivers, and often struggle on passes. In winter when rivers are frozen solid, it's possible to move on the ice in traditional caravans of Bactrian camels.

In Kyrgyz areas, it's common to travel on horseback and you'll likely be asked to hire a Kyrgyz while traversing these areas. Consider retaining a Wakhi person, however, as Kyrgyz people sometimes don't want to travel as far from their homesteads as you may want to go. It's usual for Kyrgyz to ride horses rather than walk, but it's not generally expected for you to pay additional charges for horses they ride. It's also acceptable to pay a proportion of the daily wage for part-days worked.

SLEEPING & EATING

Although village leaders traditionally extend hospitality to guests, travellers should not rely on such generosity in an impoverished society. Minimise your impact by bringing a sleeping bag and tent, and as much food as possible. The local diet of bread and tea, with occasional rice, dairy and meat, is unlikely to be sufficient for most foreign trekkers. Villages have little or no excess food to sell, so plan to cache some food for after your trek.

Most Kyrgyz camps will have a *mehman chana* (guesthouse) or guest yurt, primarily used by local traders. They too welcome anyone to stay and may provide blankets, but these communal sleeping areas aren't appropriate for women and frequently have vermin.

Hot springs with bath houses at Shelk, Sargez and Sarhad-e Broghil, and a few hot springs in the Afghan Pamir (in Alisu and near Chaqmaqtin) provide the only hot water for bathing.

Tourism infrastructure in Wakhan is developing quickly. Newly built guesthouses (with dorms and private rooms) and camping grounds are in Qazideh, Khandud, Goz Khun, Qila-e Panja and Sarhad-e Broghil. Initially priced for NGO employees rather than tourists, competition is now bringing prices down to about 500Afg per night. Be prepared for tough negotiations. A fee of 100Afg per tent is appropriate for pitching your tent in village camping grounds. Elsewhere there is no camping fee.

WHAT TO BRING

Self-reliance is essential, so bring all the cooking and camping gear you need. Limited food (eg rice, flour, lentils, potatoes, onions, tea, sugar, cooking oil, spices, etc) and supplies (eg stove, pressure cooker, cooking pots, utensils, toilet paper, matches, etc) are available in Faizabad, Baharak and, minimally so, in Ishkashim and Khandud. Kerosene, used for aviation fuel, is available only in Kabul and Faizabad. Propane gas in 5kg cylinders is available in Faizabad and Ishkashim. Sheep and goats are readily purchased from herders.

Getting There & Away

Allow two days to drive the 200km-long road between Ishkashim and Sarhad-e

Brog-hil, stopping overnight in Khandud or Qila-e Panja. Special hires cost US$100 per day. Drivers may try to charge for extra days by driving too slowly or because of vehicle breakdowns.

Hire an experienced driver with a 4WD who has previously been to Wakhan and knows how to drive through rivers. Don't hire a Toyota Town-Ace if you're going beyond Khandud. High water, particularly in Ish Murg, may force an overnight in Khandud and can block the road anywhere beyond Khandud. Be prepared to leave the vehicle and travel onwards by foot or horseback at any time.

Lower Wakhan

More than 5000m of vertical relief commands the southern horizon of Lower Wakhan, the villages between Ishkashim and Qila-e Panja, where the valley is only 2km across at its widest point. Snowcapped peaks soar majestically above villages and glaciers descend precipitously to feed the Panj River in this land of immense scale. Afghan urial and ibex thrive in numerous steep and arid side valleys.

QAZIDEH

Qazideh is 20km and less than one hour's drive from Ishkashim. Qazideh Campsite, in the shaded garden of Pir Shah Langar, offers a pleasant, spacious and secure compound to pitch tents. A nearby building provides a safe place for expeditions to store gear. Close by is Madam Bar's house, a several-hundred-year-old home that is a living museum of traditional Wakhi culture.

NOSHAQ BASE CAMP

The base camp of Noshaq (7492m), Afghanistan's highest summit and the second highest peak in the Hindu Kush, is one of Wakhan's best and most easily accessible treks. Trekking to base camp (4450m) is the only way to see Noshaq, which is hidden from view up a narrow side valley. From the trailhead at Qazideh (2800m), the moderate five-day, round-trip trek unveils superb close-up views of four 7000m peaks.

KHANDUD

Khandud, 82km from Ishkashim, is Wakhan District's headquarters, with a police post and government offices. The bazaar is the last place to buy food and basic supplies. The semi-ruined, domed tomb of Fateh Ali Shah is an evocative village landmark called **Ras Malack**. Khandood Campsite, a three-minute walk from the road, is a grassy compound in the village.

QILA-E PANJA

Qila-e Panja, 28km from Khandud, is a large village and home to Pir Shah Ismail, the spiritual leader of Ismailis in Wakhan. Nearby the border police checkpost is the **former hunting lodge** of Afghanistan's last king Zahir Shah. Qila-e Panja (Fort of Panja) was the capital of the former kingdom of Wakhan, and ruins of two forts are near the river. Qila-e Panja, as an historically significant site, also has the sacred shrine of Panja Shah, which is maintained by descendants of the last Mir of Wakhan.

Qila-e-Panjah Camp Site is really a plantation with room to pitch tents between rows of trees. The fenced compound provides a much needed wind break, although water is several minutes' walk away.

Upper Wakhan

The Wakhi villages in Upper Wakhan between Qila-e Panja and Sarhad-e Broghil lie along the narrow Wakhan River, which opens to a dramatic 3km-wide river basin at Sarhad-e Broghil. Wetlands along the river are nesting grounds for geese, ducks and ibises, as well as stopovers for migratory waterfowl and raptors, and marshy flats provide year-round habitat for wading birds.

Wakhi, who depend on livestock to supplement their agriculture, take their herds to seasonal pastures as high as 4500m, where they greet guests with a warm smile, cup of tea and bowl of yogurt.

QILA-E PANJA TO SARHAD-E BROGHIL

The easy walk 90km along the road from Qila-e Panja to Sarhad-e Broghil offers an opportunity to visit friendly villages while acclimatising for longer treks. The main road stays on the Wakhan River's north-side east of Sast, but you can vary the route by crossing the bridge to the river's south bank between Sargez and Baba Tungi, and recrossing to the main road on the bridge between Kret and Rorung.

Less expensive than driving, walking is the only way to go when the road is flooded or blocked by landslides. It takes fou days, camping overnight in Shelk or Sargez Kret and Neshtkhawar or other nearby villages, with good views of snowcappe Baba Tungi (6513m) along the way. You don't have to always walk on the road itsel as some very pleasant trails connect vil lages in a straighter line. You may conside buying a donkey.

BROGHIL PASS

The broad, grassy Broghil Pass (3882m) on the Afghanistan-Pakistan border, is the lowest pass across the Hindu Kush range It is an easy day trip from Nirs on foot o horseback. A half-day side trip on foot to an ancient Tibetan fort high above Korku reveals breathtaking valley views. (Warning crossing the Broghil Pass into Pakistan is not permitted.)

SARHAD-E BROGHIL

Sarhad-e Broghil (3290m), 90km from Qila-e Panja, marks the road's end and the trailhead for treks to the Little Pamir. Qach Beg Guest House has an expansive, grassy area for camping in front of the building Arbob Toshi Boy's Guesthouse is in a tiny walled compound at the village's eastern end. Cold springs throughout the village provide drinking water.

Big Pamir

The 60km long Big Pamir nestles between the Southern Alichur Range to the north and the Wakhan Range to the south. The Big Pamir or Great Pamir is called Pas Pamir in Wakhi, and Pamir-e Kalan o Pamir-e Buzurg in Persian.

GOZ KHUN

Goz Khun (2900m), 11km west of Sas bridge, is the primary trailhead for treks to the Big Pamir. Two guesthouses with the same name, Goz Khan Guesthouse, also have areas for tents.

ZORKOL

Zorkol, the Persian name for the lake tha 19th-century British explorers called Lake Victoria, is the Afghan Pamir's largest lake at 20km by 5km. Two routes via the Big Pamir lead to the lake, which lies on the border between Afghanistan and Tajikistan each taking eight days.

KYRGYZ OF THE AFGHAN PAMIR *John Mock & Kimberley O'Neil*

Central Asia's Altai mountains along Mongolia's western border are the traditional home of the Kyrgyz, a Turkic pastoral nomadic group. Each summer, small bands of Kyrgyz would migrate from lower valleys in Central Asia to the Afghan Pamir, but following the 1917 Soviet revolution, several thousand Kyrgyz settled permanently in the Afghan Pamir. Their once wide-ranging migration became a series of short, seasonal movements between 4000m and 4500m within the Afghan Pamir's closed frontiers. Kyrgyz nomads live in felt yurts, which they move seasonally according to available grasslands, sunlight and shelter from wind. Kyrgyz tend herds of sheep, goats, yaks and camels, and trade with Wakhi neighbours or travelling merchants for all their needs not supplied by livestock. Following the Soviet-backed 1978 coup in Afghanistan, some 1300 Kyrgyz, led by Haji Rahman Qul, left the Afghan Pamir for Pakistan and in 1982 resettled in eastern Turkey. Today, only about 1500 remaining Kyrgyz preserve this vanishing lifestyle.

The demanding 150km-long high route, which starts from Sargez, crosses three challenging passes between 4400m and 4800m, goes through the Wakhi summer settlements of Istimoch, Shikargah, Alisu, and Jermasirt, and offers wildlife watching in the Big Pamir Wildlife Reserve.

A more moderate route along the Pamir River, which starts from Goz Khun, has pleasant scenery, more gradual acclimatisation, and avoids crossing high passes. Several side valleys link this river route to the high route offering many variations.

SPREG SHIR UWEEN & KOTAL-E SHAUR

This 65km-long route between Upper Wakhan and Zorkol is a demanding five-day trek, but offers some of the most impressive high mountain scenery anywhere in Wakhan. It crosses two passes and visits Wakhi summer settlements before reaching Kyrgyz territory near Zorkol. The flower-carpeted Spreg Shir Uween (4723m) just north of Sarhad-e Broghil has outstanding views south to the Hindu Raj Range and leads north to an alpine basin dotted with turquoise lakes.

Crossing Kotal-e Shaur (4890m) involves a short, nontechnical walk on snow and glacier after spending a night in a glacial cirque. This route links up with other routes to and from the Little Pamir and Big Pamir. A yak is helpful for two of the river crossings. Prior acclimatisation is essential.

Little Pamir

The Little Pamir, at 100km long and 10km wide, is actually larger in area than the Big Pamir, yet the more rugged Big Pamir has a higher elevation and so earns its

name. The Little Pamir or Small Pamir is called Wuch Pamir in Wakhi, and Pamir-e Khurd or Pamir-e Kochak in Persian. Its most remote valleys, no longer used for grazing, are pristine alpine grasslands. Tombs called *gumbaz* with distinctive conical mud cupolas mark Kyrgyz graves. Wildlife watchers will find the area home to Marco Polo sheep, snow leopards and brown bears.

KASHCH GOZ

Two routes to the Little Pamir and the nearest Kyrgyz camp of Kashch Goz start from Sarhad-e Broghil, the high route and the river route. The high route is longer and harder, crossing two passes, but is far more scenic. Both routes first cross grassy Daliz Pass (4267m) and descend east to Borak. Kashch Goz is a colourful cluster of yurts whose families welcome visitors.

From Borak, the high route ascends the Shpodkis Valley to the north going through Wakhi summer settlements, including Sang Nevishta with its numerous petroglyphs, to cross snow-covered Uween-e-Sar (4887m). It then turns south and east to cross the flower-carpeted Aqbelis Pass (4595m) with its large lake, and offers views of Chaqmaqtin Lake as you descend to Kashch Goz. The demanding 90km-long route takes five days.

The moderate 65km-long trek along the Wakhan River route takes four days, following the river's north side east from Borak to Kashch Goz. The route goes past several Wakhi winter settlements near the vast plain of Langar, but is typically not used by local people in summer when it can be blocked by high water.

CHAQMAQTIN LAKE

Chaqmaqtin, the Afghan Pamir's second largest lake at 9km by 2km, is the source of the Murghab or Aksu River. From Kashch Goz, allow two days' round trip to visit the lake, the Kyrgyz tombs at **Bozai Gumbaz** (named for a Kyrgyz chief called Bozai who was killed in a battle with men from Hunza around 1840), and additional Kyrgyz camps. A three-day journey beyond Chaqmaqtin leads to the Tegermansu Valley at the Little Pamir's easternmost tip.

WAKHJIR VALLEY

The Wakhjir Valley is the primary source of the Amu Darya or Oxus River, and was the Silk Road's caravan route to Kashgar. Evidence of Kyrgyz winter camps and tombs in the lower valley yield to a remote wilderness lush with wildflowers in the upper valley. Allow three days to reach the base of the Wakhjir Pass, 60km from Kashch Goz.

Cross-Border Routes

A cross-border trek from the Little Pamir to Pakistan's Northern Areas offers world-class adventure. In addition to visas for Afghanistan and Pakistan, special permission is required from both governments sinc there are no established border crossing or immigration checkposts. In Afghanistar contact the ATO (p210). In Pakistan, con tact the **Ministry of Tourism** (☎ 51-9213642; fax 51 9215912; secretary@tourism.gov.pk; Green Tower Trust, 11 fl, Blue Area, Islamabad). Note that all routes int Tajikistan and China are strictly off limits.

An historic trading route from the Lit tle Pamir's Bai Qara Valley to Pakistan' Chapursan Valley crosses the snow-covere **Irshad Uween** (4979m) amidst spectacula multicoloured rock formations. Tradin continues today between the Little Pamir' Kyrgyz and Pakistan's Wakhi at the shrin of Baba Ghundi in Chapursan. This de manding 150km-long route takes eigh days starting from Sarhad-e Broghil an has challenging river crossings, which ca be impassable in midsummer.

Crossing the glaciated **Dilisang Pass** (5290m is a demanding 12-day, 225km-long rout for trekkers with basic mountaineerin experience. From the pass, the Karakoran Range unfolds with distant views of Qaru Koh (7164m). This once-used trade rout starts from Sarhad-e Broghil and goes t Misgar, via the Wakhjir Valley.

LIFE ALONG THE SILK ROAD

Afghanistan's history, culture and politics have always been dominated by its great trading cities of Kabul, Herat, Kandahar and Balkh. In recent years, the urban population has exploded due to the upheavals of war and refugee flight – Kabul's population alone has quadrupled. Overcrowding, broken infrastructure, unemployment, pollution and corruption are all endemic problems, but Afghans continue their struggle to survive supported by the twin ties of family and tradition.

Taking to the Streets

In Afghanistan, while women often dominate private life, the public domain very much belongs to men, who do almost all of the working, selling and even most of the grocery shopping.

If you take a moment to stop, Afghan life unfolds in front of you on the street. Old men push handcarts piled high with scrap metal, women in burqas glide by pulling children, fruit sellers shout out prices while butchers swat flies from their meat. Around all this runs a never-ending flow of traffic, yellow taxis, 4WDs with blacked-out windows overtaking donkey carts, and in the middle a traffic cop waving his arms ineffectually, trying to marshal the chaos. Strip away the cars and the mobile phones, and you'd suspect that little has changed in several centuries.

'While women often dominate private life, the public domain very much belongs to men'

❶ Burqa shop, Herat
A shopkeeper demonstrates that not all burqas are identical – subtle differences in embroidery on the cap and front panel help identify the wearer to her friends and family.

❷ Covered bazaar, Herat
Kabul, Kandahar and Herat all once had great covered bazaars reflecting their status as trading cities. Of these, only Herat's medieval bazaars survive, such as in this brick-vaulted one near Chahar Su in the Old City.

❸ Street food seller
You will find street food everywhere in Afghanistan. Here a pan of kofteh kebab is cooked and served with bread, onions and tomato to be eaten on the go: a quick, tasty and filling meal.

❹ Carpet seller, Herat
A merchant in Herat sits astride piles of Afghanistan's most celebrated export – its carpets. Favoured designs come from the Turkmen and Uzbek in the north and the Baluchis of the southern deserts.

❺ Carpets of Ahmad Shah Massoud
Machine-made carpets display the image of the late Ahmad Shah Massoud, the most nationally celebrated mujaheddin leader, who fought against the Soviets and the Talban.

Enduring Cities

Afghan cities have been the crossroads of the country: important trading centres that stood as islands amid an often unruly countryside. Herat and Balkh grew rich trading with Persia and Central Asia, Kandahar was the gateway to India, while Kabul was one of the great bazaar towns of Asia. Recent Afghan history has dealt them a series of hard blows, with bombs and bullets corroding their landscapes, and unavoidable neglect taking a further toll.

The postwar period has seen a boom in construction, but rapidly growing populations and land-grabs means that expectations for rebuilding have proved hard to meet, with access to adequate shelter, electricity and clean water still lacking for much of the urban population.

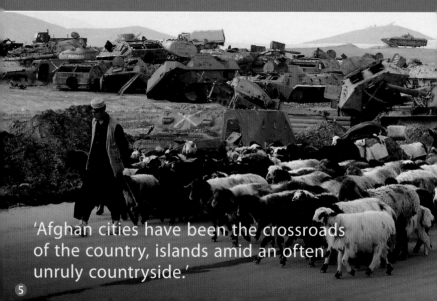

'Afghan cities have been the crossroads of the country, islands amid an often unruly countryside.'

❶ Millie Bus Terminal, Kabul

After almost 30 years of war, Afghanistan's infrastructure has been challenged to the point of destruction. The wrecked Millie Bus Terminal in Kabul is an all-too-visible reminder of the long road ahead in Afghanistan's reconstruction.

❷ View over Herat's Old City

Herat's medieval core is revealed in this rooftop view across the old grain stores to the Friday Mosque. This traditional urban fabric is now under constant threat from unplanned development, with old mud-brick buildings being torn down in favour of glass and concrete.

❸ Teppe Maranjan

The hill of Teppe Maranjan, overlooking eastern Kabul, is one of the oldest continually inhabited parts of the capital. Now the site of a royal mausoleum, its commanding heights also make it the perfect site for the city's annual kite festival, held during Nauroz.

❹ Babur's Gardens

Babur's Gardens are one of the few remaining connections to Kabul's medieval past. Laid out by the first Mughal emperor, they were largely destroyed in the civil war. A conservation project is currently returning the gardens to their former glory – a green spot in a polluted city.

❺ Shepherd & tanks

The slow rhythms of Afghan rural life penetrate even into the cities, with livestock markets a common sight on the edge of the capital. Here, a Kuchi shepherd brings his flocks past a park of ruined Soviet armoured vehicles along the Jalalabad Rd on the outskirts of Kabul.

The Cultural Landscape

Herat, with its old city and many medieval buildings, is the architectural highlight of Afghanistan, and can easily hold its own against the more acclaimed Silk Road cities of Esfahan and Samarkand in neighbouring Iran and Uzbekistan. Yet even today unplanned development threatens to erase much of this proud heritage.

Other Afghan cities have fared even less well. Lashkar Gah and Balkh, once dubbed 'the Mother of Cities', never really recovered from Genghis Khan; while Kapisa, centre of the once-mighty Buddhist Kushan empire, has disappeared almost completely under the tarmac of Bagram airbase.

Valiant efforts at rebuilding the cultural landscape by bodies like the Kabul Museum point the way to a possible resurgence of Afghanistan's artistic heritage.

'Valiant efforts at rebuilding the cultural landscape point the way to a possible resurgence of Afghanistan's artistic heritage'

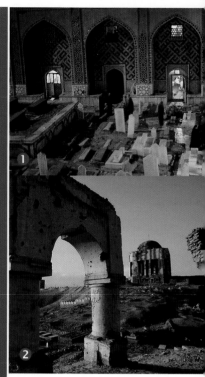

❶ Gazar Gah cemetery, Herat
Gazar Gah in Herat is one of Afghanistan's holiest sites, and its most important intact Timurid monument. Its interior is packed with the graves of those seeking grace by being buried near the tomb of the saint Ansari; the revered amir Dost Mohammed is buried here, too.

❷ Nadir Shah Mausoleum, Kabul
The 1930s Mausoleum of Nadir Shah in Kabul was just one of many historical buildings caught in the crossfire of Afghanistan's civil war. Its wrecked shell provides a perfect example of the challenges facing the country's architectural heritage.

❸ Friday Mosque, Herat

Laid out by the Ghorid Dynasty over 900 years ago, the minarets of Herat's Friday Mosque still dominate the city's skyline today. Its design and decoration keep it ranked as one of the true jewels of Islamic architecture.

❹ Nuristani carvings in Kabul Museum

Pagan carvings from Nuristan can be viewed at the Kabul Museum, which had around 70% of its collection looted during the civil war. Perceived as idols, these carvings were chopped up by the Taliban; their restoration (along with many other artefacts) has provided hope for the future of Afghanistan's cultural heritage.

❺ Mosaic, Herat's Friday Mosque

The mosaics that cover Herat's Friday Mosque give a new face to an old building. Produced by the mosque's tile workshop over the last 70 years, the mosaics are a continually evolving mix of traditional and modern Islamic designs.

❻ Herat Citadel

Herat's monumental citadel is believed to stand on the foundations of a fort built by Alexander the Great. Genghis Khan and Timur took it in turns to reduce the building to dust – the current citadel dates from the 15th century rule of Shah Rukh.

'Shah-e Doh Shamshira Mosque must be one of the most unusual in Islam. Built in the 1920s during Amanullah's drive for modernisation, it looks like it would be more at home in Versailles or Vienna'

Jalalabad & Eastern Afghanistan
جلال آباد و شرق افغانستان

Think of the great clichés of the Afghan character and you'll be transported to Afghanistan's rugged east. Tales of honour, hospitality and revenge abound here, as hardy fighters defend the lonely mountain passes that lead to the Indian subcontinent. For Afghan, read Pashtun: the dominant ethnic group in the east whose tribal links spill across the border deep into Pakistan.

Jalalabad is the region's most important city. Founded by the Mughals as a winter retreat, it sits in an area with links back to when Afghanistan was a Buddhist country and a place of monasteries, pilgrims and prayer wheels. Sweltering in summer, you can quench your thirst with a mango juice before heading for the cooler climes of the Kabul Plateau, via the jaw-dropping Tangi Gharu Gorge.

A stone's throw from Jalalabad is the Khyber Pass, the age-old gateway to the Indian subcontinent. Getting your passport stamped here as you slip between Afghanistan and Pakistan is to experience one of Asia's most evocative border crossings. If you've been in Afghanistan a while, you might find the sudden Pakistani insistence on providing you with an armed guard for your onward journey a little bemusing.

Sadly much of the east remains out of bounds to travellers. The failures of post-conflict reconstruction have allowed an Islamist insurgency to smoulder among the peaks and valleys that dominate this part of the country. The beautiful woods and slopes of Nuristan – long a travellers' grail – remain as distant a goal as ever and the current climate means that carefully checking security issues remains paramount before any trip to the region.

HIGHLIGHTS

- Enjoy the orange blossom of the many gardens in **Jalalabad** (p182)
- Cross the iconic **Khyber Pass** (p185), the gateway to Peshawar in Pakistan
- Take in the shade of the Mughal gardens at **Nimla** (p184)

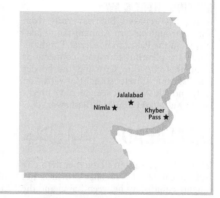

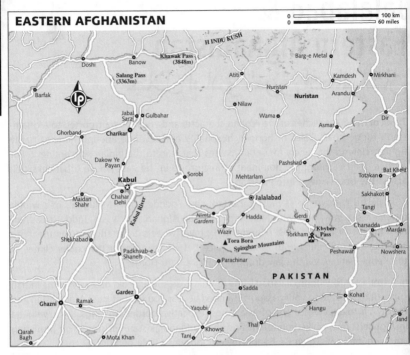

EASTERN AFGHANISTAN

CLIMATE

The plains of the east are hot and dry in the summer, although Jalalabad catches a lot of humidity which can make it a sticky place from mid-June to early September, with temperatures pushing over 30°C. Winters are cool and fall below freezing in the mountains, with snow on the high peaks, including the wooded slopes of Nuristan.

GETTING THERE & AWAY

A recently repaved highway runs from Kabul through eastern Afghanistan to Jalalabad and the Pakistan border at Torkham. There are plentiful transport connections along this corridor. Crossing the border into Pakistan is pretty straightforward – an early enough start can see you have breakfast in Kabul and dinner in Peshawar.

JALALABAD جلال آباد

Jalalabad, Afghanistan's largest eastern city and the capital of Nangahar province, lies roughly equidistant between Kabul and the

Pakistan border at Torkham. It sits in the lee of the Safed Koh Mountains in a fertile plain watered by the Kabul river. Compared to the capital it's something of a green oasis, warm in winter but hot and sticky in summer.

The winter climate meant that Jalalabad was a popular retreat for Afghan rulers since it was founded by the Mughal emperor Akbar in 1570. The region's historical importance predates Islam however. Between the 2nd and 7th centuries AD, the Gandharan culture of the Kushans flourished in the Jalalabad valley and it was a place of pilgrimage rivalling Bamiyan. Nearby, Hadda was a hugely important complex of monasteries and caves used as monk's retreats can be seen on the far side of the river when leaving Jalalabad for Kabul. Islam arrived when Mahmoud of Ghazni tore through to India in the 11th century, and much of the area's subsequent history was tied precisely to controlling the route to the subcontinent through the Khyber Pass.

Jalalabad was a British garrison during the First Anglo-Afghan War and received the one survivor of the disastrous retreat from Kabul in 1842 (see boxed text, p32). Just over 150 years later, the mujaheddin launched an equally disastrous attack on Jalalabad, their first attempt to capture a major city from the government after the Soviet withdrawal. Over 10,000 people died. From 1992 Jalalabad was ruled by a council of mujaheddin called the Nangahar Shura, but the predominantly Pashtun population meant that the city surrendered to the Taliban in 1996 without a fight.

Several of the *shura* leaders returned to power at the close of 2001 and have been heavily implicated in the opium trade for which Nangahar is renowned. Despite this, a provincial ban in 2005 met with popular support and a 96% drop in cultivation. A failure to follow up with alternative livelihood programmes meant that the poppies were back in bloom the following year.

Many people zip through Jalalabad when passing between Kabul and Peshawar. If you've come from Pakistan the city seems like a continuation of the large Pashtun towns of North West Frontier Province, down to the street food and the make of autorickshaws. The heat and humidity can make Jalalabad exhausting in summer and malaria is a serious risk. It's also essential to take note of the political forecast, as the city sits in the heart of the Pashtun areas.

ORIENTATION

Jalalabad runs east–west along the south bank of the Kabul river, and is roughly laid out in a grid. The main junction to orientate yourself by is Chowk-e Mukharabat. The main road leads west from here past the Spinghar Hotel towards Kabul. The main commercial area runs south of the junction to Chowk-e Bazari and Chowk-e Talashi, from where the main road heads east to the airport and the Pakistan border. AIMS (www.aims.org.af) produces an excellent downloadable map of Jalalabad.

INFORMATION

Moneychangers, internet cafés and PCOs can all be found clustered between Chowk-e Mukharabat and Chowk-e Talashi.

ANSO East (☎ 070 606601)

Jalalabad Public Hospital (Sarakh-e Kabul) Next to Spinghar Hotel, with plenty of pharmacies in the immediate area.

Kabul Bank (near Chowk-e Talashi)

Police (☎ 079 9048 154)

SIGHTS

A rule follows that wherever an Afghan ruler settles, he lays out a ceremonial garden. As a favoured winter residence, Jalalabad has several, in varying degrees of maintenance. Akbar's original gardens have long been lost to urban development. The remainder lie between Chowk-e Mukharabat and the Spinghar Hotel.

The **Seraj-ul Emorat Gardens** (Bagh-e Seraj ul-Emorat) are named for the palace of King Habibullah ('Building of Light'), built in the confines of the garden in 1910. The palace was reduced to a shell during the 1929 tribal uprising but the gardens remain a pleasant place for a walk. There are plenty of orange trees for which Jalalabad was once famed and the park still hosts the Mushaira Festival in mid-April, celebrating the blossoming of the orange trees with poetry, storytelling, music and picnics.

Habibullah loved Jalalabad and, ever the moderniser, built the country's first golf course here. When he was assassinated here in 1919, the course was turned into the grounds for his **mausoleum**. Built in the same weird neoclassical style of the time, it also houses the tombs of King Amanullah and his wife Queen Soraya, *doyenne* of Afghan feminism. The gardens are opposite Seraj-ul Emorat.

Between Seraj-ul Emorat and the Kabul river is the peaceful **Kawkab Garden** (Bagh-e Kawkab), planted with roses. A new garden, **Bagh-e Abdul Haq**, is also being laid out here to commemorate the mujaheddin leader Abdul Haq who was killed by the Taliban in 2001. It sits by the Pul-Behsud bridge which leads north to Kunar province. Sunset views of the river here are lovely.

RISK ASSESSMENT

Eastern Afghanistan remains unstable. Security is generally good along the Kabul–Jalalabad–Torkham highway, although extreme caution should be taken around the traditionally problematic Sarobi area and the approaches into Kabul. Take appropriate security precautions in and around Jalalabad city.

We advise against travel off the main highway, due to the large numbers or armed anti-government groups in the region.

SLEEPING & EATING

Spinghar Hotel (☎ 070 604700; Sarakh-e Kabul; r with/ without bathroom US$40/20) This large state-run hotel is set in large gardens in the centre of town. Everyone has stayed here at one point, from Soviet officers to the Taliban's Arab cohorts. Most rooms are en suite and are decent-sized if unexciting. There's a basic restaurant and the shady trees are good for escaping Jalalabad's summer heat.

Nawa Guesthouse (near Chowk-e Mukharabat; r 200Afg; ✷) A basic guesthouse with six tidy rooms and a helpful manager. It's centrally located, near the main moneychangers' area. Food is available, as is hot water (on request).

There are a host of cheap hotels in Jalalabad around Chowk-e Mukharabat, Chowk-e Talashi and the main road east but they are currently extremely reluctant to take foreign guests, citing security concerns. Dotted in between them you'll also find lots of cheap restaurants and chaikhanas. Among the *pulao* and green tea, look for *chapli kabab*, a Pashtun speciality of ground lamb made into a burger and shallow-fried with a sprinkling of spices. In summer, fresh mango and sugar-cane juice make fantastic thirst-quenchers.

GETTING THERE & AROUND

Jalalabad airport is 4km east of the city limits on the road to Torkham. There are no commercial flights, but Pactec has a service to Kabul. The airport is just past the army base, home to the British garrison of 1841. General Elphinstone, leader of the doomed retreat from Kabul is buried here, although his grave has been long-lost.

Minibuses to Kabul (200Afg, three hours) and the border at Torkham (200Afg, 2½ hours) leave regularly throughout the day. Shared taxis are faster but more expensive. Note that transport to Kabul terminates at Begrami Motor Park on the outskirts of the city. The road to Kabul is particularly attractive, following the Kabul River past Sarobi Dam and up the stupendous Tangi Gharu Gorge to the Kabul Plateau. The road has recently been rehabilitated and is excellent quality.

Rickshaws are popular for getting around Jalalabad, but not all roads are paved so they can be a very bumpy experience. Most fares will be under 50Afg.

AROUND JALALABAD

Always check the local security situation before travelling off the Torkham–Jalalabad–Kabul highway.

Hadda

The loss of Hadda remains one of the most grievous disasters to have befallen Afghanistan's cultural heritage since the Soviet invasion. For 500 years to the 7th century AD Hadda was a major Buddhist pilgrimage site with a city that was supported by a host of monasteries. The Buddha himself visited the area to rid it of a vengeful dragon demon and several important relics were kept in the monasteries that sprang up as a result, including his staff, robe, one of his teeth and even part of his skull (which according to a 5th-century Chinese pilgrim was entirely covered with gold leaf and precious stones). Pilgrims venerating such holy items were taxed heavily.

Over 1000 stupas were recorded by 20th century archaeologists in an area covering 15 square kilometres. The most notable was the Teppe Shotor complex, which contained a wealth of carved plaster frescoes and statuary that showed the richness of Kushan culture, freely mixing classical Greek and Indian styles to produce uniquely beautiful Afghan art. Some of the oldest-known Buddhist manuscripts were also found at Hadda. It was the pearl of Afghan archaeological sites.

War destroyed Hadda. The nearby caves once used by monks were favoured as refuges by the mujaheddin and the area was comprehensively bombed by the Soviets. What remained was looted, including most of the excavated artefacts held at the Kabul Museum. Under the Taliban, Hadda was given over to the Arab-Afghans for *jihadi* training purposes and locals were banned from visiting. Today, Afghanistan's celebrated Buddhist site is little more than dust.

Nimla Gardens

These **gardens** (Nimla Bagh) 40km from Jalalabad were laid out in 1610 by the Mughal emperor Jehangir. They follow the quartered *Chahar Bagh*–style of classical Mughal gardens, with beds of plants and trees given order by the addition of terraces, straight paths and channels of water punctuated by fountains. The design echoes the more elebrated Shalimar Bagh in Srinagar, Kashmir, also laid out at this time by Jehangir or his wife Nur Jahan. At Nimla, Nur Jahan is said to have supervised much of the actual planting. As in Srinagar, cypress and hinar trees play an important role in the garden's design.

Until recently much neglected, the gardens have been rehabilitated by the UN's Food and Agriculture Organisation (FAO), although the water channels remain dry. FAO has been working here and elsewhere on extensive nursery and reforestation programmes to repopulate Afghanistan's denuded orchards.

Nimla is southwest of Jalalabad off the Kabul road. The route passes through the village of Sultanpur, where there is a temple dedicated to Guru Nanak, founder of Sikhism. In mid-April, Afghan Sikhs and Hindus visit the temple for its Waisak festival. The village of Gandamak is 11km from Nimla, where the British army made its last desperate (and doomed) stand in January of 1842.

Tora Bora

The Tora Bora cave complex in the Spingar Mountains are a bone-rattling three-hour drive from Jalalabad near the Pakistan border. They became notorious at the end of 2001 as the place where Osama Bin Laden made his last stand in the teeth of an American assault before slipping into hiding. Tora Bora held a series of underground tunnels and bunkers used by the mujahedin during the anti-Soviet Jihad. The area was heavily bombed by the Americans, who were reluctant to put boots on the ground. Their reliance on Afghan warlord proxies ultimately allowed Bin Laden and many Al-Qaeda fighters to slip away in a haze of dust and hefty bribes, proving again the ancient adage that 'you can't buy an Afghan, you can only rent one'.

While we were researching this book, the authorities in Nangahar were making loud noises about developing Tora Bora as a tourist site, even drawing up plans to build several hotels overlooking the caves (which have largely been pounded to dust anyway, although the mountain scenery is spectacular). But as the area remains insecure and visitors require a large complement of armed guards, you probably shouldn't rush to reserve a room just yet.

Torkham

Like many border towns in this part of the world, Torkham is a scruffy place, seeming to consist of little more than auto shops, teahouses, moneychangers and taxi touts. Only the brand new customs building displays any sense of permanence. As an introduction to Afghanistan it's mildly anarchic, although the Pakistani side is a small improvement. There's little reason to hang around other than to get your passport stamped.

As Afghanistan's busiest border post, there's plenty of transport – minibuses to Jalalabad (200Afg, 2½ hours) and Kabul (300Afg, six hours), as well as shared taxis (400Afg and 600Afg respectively). For more details of onward transport through the Khyber Pass to Peshawar in Pakistan, see p215.

THE KHYBER PASS

The road from Torkham to the Pakistani city of Peshawar traverses one of the most famous and strategically important mountain passes in the world. The Khyber Pass stretches for 50km through the Hindu Kush, linking Afghanistan to the Indian subcontinent. Babur drove his army through on his way to set up the Mughal empire and throughout history, Afghans have marauded over the pass to plunder the riches of India.

Not surprisingly, the British weren't too keen on letting the Afghans having the key to this particular back door and made sure that Peshawar and the Khyber Pass stayed on their side of the border, reinforcing it with a network of forts.

Despite this, they never truly conquered the pass itself and had to buy off the local Pashtun tribes to stop them raiding British convoys. Even today, the Pakistani government only controls the main highway – step off the tarmac and you're in tribal land. The local Afridi Pashtuns have built a second road through the pass, away from the highway, to allow them to continue their traditional smuggling unimpeded, carrying everything from opium to DVD players.

NURISTAN نورستان

The fateful telegram 'Can you travel Nuri-stan June?' that kicks off Eric Newby's travel classic *A Short Walk in the Hindu Kush* continues to inspire travellers with dreams of high peaks and wooded mountain slopes, and villagers claiming descent from the troops of Alexander the Great. Sat hard against the Pakistan border, Nuristan was a crucible for the anti-Soviet resistance and sadly remains an important centre for anti-government elements, making it an extremely dangerous region. In a peaceful Afghanistan Nuristan could be heaven for trekkers, but for the foreseeable future all travel is to be avoided.

HISTORY

When Alexander the Great passed through Nuristan en route to India in 327 BC, he was amazed to find a city called Nyas, founded by Dionysus, the Greek god of wine, or so the occupants claimed. This they proved with their groves of ivy and grapes, and copious jars of wine. Alexander celebrated with a party that granted them independence, as well as leading to the mother of all hangovers.

The region remained aloof for most of Afghanistan's history and resisted all attempts

to subdue it. Islam failed to make a dent and the old pantheon of gods continued to hold sway. The steep passes and valleys aided Nuristan's isolation. Now known as Kafiris-tan ('Land of the Unbelievers'), even Timur gave up his campaign here in the 14th century. It wasn't until 1896, when Abdur Rahman Khan launched a bloody invasion, that the region was brought to heel, completing the map of modern Afghanistan. Islam was brought at the tip of a sword and Kafiristan was renamed Nuristan ('Land of Light').

Inaccessibility kept Nuristan isolated throughout most of the 20th century, with barely a road to its name. In 1978 the region was one of the first to rebel against the Afghan communist government, resulting in its heavy bombing. During the Jihad, Nuristan's proximity to the passes to Chitral in Pakistan made it a major arms conduit for the mujaheddin – traffic heavily taxed by the locals, who declared a quasi-independent state, heavily influenced by the Arab-Afghans. Local warlords grew rich on clear-cutting local forests.

Nuristan and neighbouring Kunar province have remained awkwardly independent and an important base for followers of Gulbuddin Hekmatyar and elements of Al Qaeda. The writ for the government is very short here, with little reconstruction work possible and regular US army firefights.

GULBUDDIN HEKMATYAR

Of all the mujaheddin leaders to emerge in the 1980s, Gulbuddin Hekmatyar is undoubtedly the nastiest piece of work. Ironically, this ruthless Ghilzai Pashtun fundamentalist used to be the darling of the CIA in their fight against the Soviets.

Hekmatyar (Afghans call him Gulbuddin) was a firebrand student at Kabul University in the 1970s, where he gained a reputation for throwing acid in the faces of female students; he later fled to Pakistan after his murder of a Maoist student leader. After the Soviet invasion, the ISI (Pakistan's Inter-Services Intelligence agency) found him the perfect pliable stooge. Although Hekmatyar lacked any grassroots support, the ISI bankrolled his Hezb-e Islami party to further their own Afghan agenda and encouraged the USA to do the same. Hekmatyar received hundreds of millions of dollars in aid and plenty of Stinger missiles – many of which he sold immediately to Iran. Instead of fighting the Russians, he spent his time attacking other mujaheddin groups and assassinating moderate Afghan exiles, thus pursuing his own ambition for power.

In 1992 Hekmatyar failed to capture Kabul for his Pakistani handlers and took to raining rockets down on it instead, leaving tens of thousands of civilians dead in the rubble. In a move of depressing Afghan irony, he even briefly served as prime minister while ordering the bombardment.

Pakistan eventually dropped Hekmatyar in favour of the Taliban, who exiled him to Iran in the late 1990s. He returned in the aftermath of their removal, vowing to fight the American 'Crusaders'. At the time of writing he was still at large, with his renamed Hezb-e Islami Gulbuddin party exploring links with Al-Qaeda and the Taliban.

CULTURE

Nuristan remains ethnically and culturally distinct from the rest of Afghanistan. Nuristanis speak their own language and are frequently blonde or red-haired, with blue or green eyes. Their own stories ascribe this to their ancient Greek roots. Modern theories are more sceptical, but recent plans for DNA testing have sadly foundered.

Wood carving holds an important place in Nuristani culture. Houses frequently have elaborately carved posts and shutters, and chairs are an unusual feature in a country where most people sit on carpets. Echoes of their pagan roots can also be found in a penchant for raised wooden coffins. Islam graves were also once marked with carved effigies of gods and ancestors. An important collection remains in the Kabul Museum (p88). The tradition of winemaking also appears to have disappeared due to Quranic strictures.

The drawing of the border in the 1890s split Kafiristan in two. Against the odds, three valleys in Pakistan have clung to their traditional religion and culture, their inhabitants known as the Kalasha.

TRAVEL IN NURISTAN

Nuristan's main town is Kamdesh, linked by a fair road through Asadabad in Kunar to Jalalabad. A second road leads into Nuristan via Mehtarlam and Daulatshah. There are few other roads – mountain tracks are the order of the day. Three main rivers drain Nuristan: the Pech, Alingar and Kunar. Important passes include the Chamar Pass (4570m) leading towards the Panjshir Valley and Mir Samir, the mountain that was the target of *A Short Walk in the Hindu Kush*. Others such as the Ustai lead into Pakistan.

The presence of insurgent groups such as Hezb-e Islami Gulbuddin, and frequent fighting with the US army (who have a base in Kamdesh), make Nuristan an extremely dangerous destination, to be given a very wide berth. No international NGOs currently operate in the area.

Kandahar & Southern Afghanistan

كندهار و جنوب افغانستان

The occasional black turban of a Talib, the white turban of the returning Haj pilgrim, the dirty boys in ragged *shalwar kameez* playing in the street, the fleeting pair of burqas billowing in the wind, the pick-up trucks brimming with rugged fighters, the henna-haired old man with his bird cages, the Pashtuns. Southern Afghanistan and Kandahar, its gateway city, is the crown of Pashtunwali and the Pashtun way of life a culture that is questionably stronger than the religion many mistake it for.

Mullah Omar commanded the Taliban from here, he welcomed Osama Bin Laden here and the first ever democratically elected President of Afghanistan came from here. Politically and historically the south is the most significant region in Afghanistan.

Kandahar city at dusk from a roof top is Asia at its most beguiling – kites swinging in the air, pigeons tinkling back to perch, few buildings higher than two stories, mud roofs, and the desert mountains beyond – this could lull you into believing this was a peaceful, middling city, the hub of a wheel whose spokes lead to Oruzgan in the north, Helmand and Nimroz beyond to the west, Pakistan to the south and a climb to Kabul through Zabul and Ghazni in the east. But its charms remain locked securely behind high-walled compounds and few know the region for more than the draconian regime of the Taliban.

The tragedy of the south is that is has so much to offer in terms of the warm Pashtun culture of welcoming strangers and feeding them the finest fare of the household, world-class fruit and vegetables, and eerie landscapes where you can see a river bed, desert mountains and the curve of the earth in a single vista, but the extreme politics and violence that have and continue to consume the area mean that very few get to see it.

HIGHLIGHTS

- Sunrise over Kandahar and beyond from the **Forty Steps** (p193)
- Climb to the top of **Baba Wali Shrine** (p193) in Kandahar and look out over Arghandab Valley, followed by fresh juices and ice cream
- Explore the **Towers of Victory** (p196) and other remnants of the empire in Ghazni

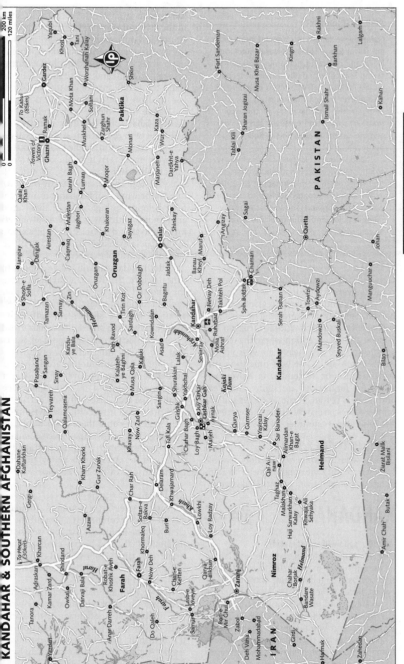

KANDAHAR &
SOUTHERN AFGHANISTAN

RISK ASSESSMENT

Currently we do not recommend independent travel to the south; however numerous NGOs and contractors continue work in the region implementing onerous security mitigating measures. They remain only targets of opportunity and their greatest risk is of being in the 'wrong place at the wrong time'. All road travel outside Kandahar city and the Kandahar–Spin Boldak Route is also not recommended.

Those who are planning to travel to the south for work reasons and whose organisation does not have a permanent footprint in the area are strongly advised to partner with another organisation to host you, or arrange a guide and vehicle for the duration of your visit.

CLIMATE
Generally Southern Afghanistan is the roasting oven of the country with its expansive deserts and dry cities reaching to and beyond 50°C every summer. The northern reaches of the south including Oruzgan and Ghazni are the exception where the climate is much cooler with heavy snows from December to March. The best time to visit is April to June or September to November, when the large skies are sunny and clear and there is colour in the few trees but the temperatures are neither of the extremes felt in winter or summer.

GETTING THERE & AWAY
Due to security concerns the only feasible way of accessing the south is by air to Kandahar or by road from Quetta, Pakistan.

KANDAHAR   کندهار

☎ 030 / pop 1 million (estimated)

The mention of Afghanistan's second-largest city conjures up a collage of terrorist training camps, rugged terrain, warlords, narcotics, fierce tribes and the War on Terror. Its strategic and political importance is understood by the Pashtun proverb: 'Control Kandahar and you'll control Afghanistan'. This was a lesson that Alexander the Great, Genghis Khan and even the Russians failed to learn. Unfortunately since the fall of

the Taliban in 2001, the security situation in the city and surrounding areas has deteriorated significantly to the point where there was an average of one suicide bombing a week in 2006. Although the current players, Afghan and international, understand the significance of controlling Kandahar this Holy Grail continues to elude them.

Despite the violence surrounding them the Kandaharis continue their daily lives, albeit lived with restrictions and a level of fear. Women continue to be the most affected – few women are seen in public on the streets of Kandahar and if ever you do see one the majority will be wearing the nylon burqa. Life for the women of Kandahar is invariably lived behind the high walls of their family compounds with few girls being given permission to attend school still, despite reports in the media extolling the liberation of girls since the arrival of democracy.

Older Kandaharis will tell you about the times before the Russian invasion, when they hosted hippies taking the overland trail in the guesthouses that lined the streets around Chowk-e Shaheedan. Although it may be some time before Kandahar is ready for independent travellers again, it is clear that the NGO, international organisation and contractor communities are desperately needed to improve the lives of Kandaharis. Although millions of aid dollars have been spent in the area, insecurity and corruption have prevented it reaching many people.

In years to come there is no doubt that travellers will enjoy views over Kandahar from the Forty Steps, Pashtun hospitality and picnics in the Arghandab Valley and visits to the Mosque of the Sacred Cloak.

HISTORY
Alexander the Great founded Kandahar city in the 4th century BC, around the ancient city of Mundigak, which was settled in about 3000 BC. The city changed hands numerous times following its founding being fought over by the Arabs, Persians, Indians and Mongols.

In 1743 Ahmad Shah Durrani, a Pashtun and the founder of Afghanistan, took control of Kandahar and made it the capital until the 1780s. The city was occupied by the British in the 19th century during the Anglo-Afghan Wars, and once again by the Soviets throughout the 1980s.

Following the Russian withdrawal war-
rds jostled for control of the city in the en-
uing bloody Civil War. The Taliban seized
andahar in 1994 without a single shot
red, self-proclaimed saviours from the ram-
ant banditry and rape that was gripping
ie country. Although Kabul remained the
apital, the Taliban leader, Mullah Omar,
uled the country from Kandahar.

Shortly after the start of the War on Ter-
or, the regime officially fell in a final clash
ith US Special Forces at the Kandahar
irfield in December 2001. Over 10,000
nternational Security Assistance Force
SAF) troops remain at the airfield and
cross the south, having suffered significant
osses while fighting the insurgency. The
arlords and the drug trade also erode their
fforts. Whichever way you look at it, Kan-
ahar's chequered past is likely to continue
ell into the future.

RIENTATION

andahar city sits on a desert plain sur-
ounded by rocky outcrops. The city's laid
ut in two parts: the once walled Old City, a
byrinth of lanes between mud houses and
azaars; and the New City (Shah-e-Nau),
hich is along three parallel, Pakistani-style
oulevards leading to the west of the Old City.
everal *chowks* (crossroads or town squares)
ake navigating about relatively easy.

To the north of Kandahar is the massive
id Gah mosque, adjacent to Kandahar Uni-
ersity and the Arghandab Valley (15km),
nown for its delicious grapes and pome-
ranates. The road to Kabul heads out of the
ty to the northeast, while Kandahar Airport

(35km) and the Pakistan border (136km) are
to the southeast. South of the city trails off to
the sandy deserts of Registan.

INFORMATION
Emergency
Ambulance (☎ 070 308739)
ANSO South (☎ 070 405697)
Fire Brigade (☎ 070 302008; Eid Gah
Darwarza)
Police (☎ 070 304018; Chowk-e Shaheedan)

Internet Access
New internet cafés are opening all the time.
Most charge 50Afg hour.
Kandahar Internet Café (Chowk-e Kiptan Madad)
Samad Internet Café (Chowk-e Shaheedan)
Wardad Internet Café (Kariz Bazaar)

Medical Services
Al Hadi Farad Private Hospital (☎ 070
301705; Shaheedan Chowk) Has a 24-hour emergency
department and two well-stocked pharmacies at the
entrance.
Mirwais Hospital (☎ 070308739; Shafakhana Sarak,
Shah-e Nau; ☯ 8am-5pm) No 24-hour emergency
department but it does have a well-stocked pharmacy and
is supported by international NGOs.

Money
Afghanistan International Bank (Herat Sarak) Has an
ATM that dispenses US dollars.
Azizi Bank (Chowk-e Shaheedan)
Da Afghanistan Bank (Chowk-e Shaheedan)
Kabul Bank (Chowk-e Shaheedan)
Moneychangers (Chowk-e Shaheedan & Chowk-e Charso)
The best rates for afghanis, US dollars and Pakistani
rupees.

**KANDAHAR &
SOUTHERN AFGHANISTAN**

PISTOL, BATON, POLICE BADGE & BURQA *Nick Walker*

'I am the only woman in Kandahar with a pistol. I also keep a Kalashnikov at home,' Captain Malalai Kakar, the only policewoman in the city, tells me over a cup of chai. While barking orders in
Pashto into her mobile phone, Malalai stands tall in her khaki uniform and utility belt with holster,
cuffs and baton, just like her male counterparts – however she does don the burqa when she is
on the beat outside the HQ. The mother of six fled to Pakistan as a refugee during the Taliban
regime after she learned of her imminent arrest for the 'crime' of being a former policewoman.
Now back in Kandahar she is not only a role model for women in a patriarchal, tribal society but
also an invaluable asset to the Afghan National Police (ANP). She is involved in all women's issues
coming to the attention of police and is on the front line during ANP raids of insurgent hideouts.
As a woman in a high profile position in the ANP, not only does she accept the risks her brother
officers also shoulder, but is she is acutely aware of the fate that has befallen numerous other high
profile women in their very public assassinations. But she will not be deterred, telling me 'I am a
strong woman and want to serve my country…I'm careful, but not afraid.'

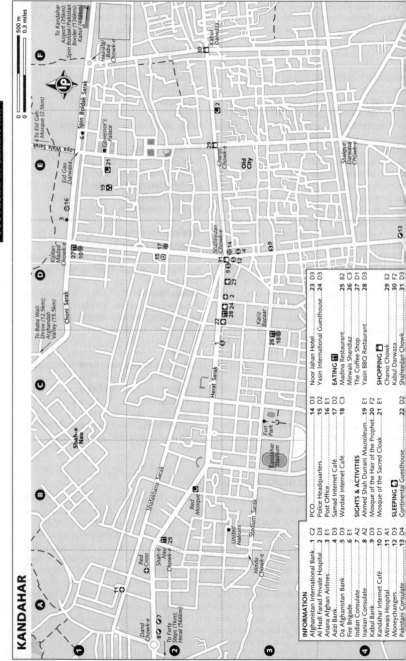

KANDAHAR

INFORMATION
Afghanistan International Bank....1 C2
Al Hadi Farad Private Hospital....2 D3
Ariana Afghan Airlines..............3 E1
Azizi Bank..............................4 D3
Da Afghanistan Bank.................5 D3
Fire Brigade............................6 E1
Indian Consulate.......................7 A2
Iranian Consulate......................8 A2
Kabul Bank.............................9 D3
Kandahar Internet Café.............10 D1
Mirwais Hospital......................11 A1
Moneychangers.......................12 D3
Pakistani Consulate...................13 D4

PCO......................................14 D3
Police Headquarters..................15 D2
Post Office.............................16 E1
Samad Internet Café..................17 D2
Wardad Internet Café................18 C3

SIGHTS & ACTIVITIES
Ahmed Shah Durrani Mausoleum....19 E1
Mosque of the Hair of the Prophet..20 F2
Mosque of the Sacred Cloak.........21 E1

SLEEPING
Continental Guesthouse..............22 D2

Noor Jahan Hotel......................23 D3
Yasin International Guesthouse.....24 D3

EATING
Madina Restaurant.....................25 B2
Mirwais Shandiaz.......................26 C3
The Coffee Shop.......................27 D1
Yasin BBQ Restaurant.................28 D3

SHOPPING
Charso Chowk..........................29 E2
Kabul Darwaza.........................30 F2
Shaheedan Chowk......................31 D3

Post & Telephone

Public Call Offices (PCOs) are scattered throughout the city.

Post Office (Chowk-e Kiptan Madad) Located within the Government Communications Centre (Mukhabarat).

DANGERS & ANNOYANCES

Security remains a primary concern of all internationals in Kandahar city and before you travel, be sure to read the Safety in Afghanistan chapter (p68), particularly the sections on moving around (p73) and emergencies (p74).

Kandahar and its Pashtuns are the most Islamically strict in Afghanistan, if not the world; here, adherence to cultural and Islamic customs is paramount. Visitors need to respect local traditions, both men and women dressing conservatively at the very least.

SIGHTS

Eid Gah Mosque

One of the largest mosques in Afghanistan, Kandahar's **Eid Gah Mosque** (🕓 closed to non-Muslims during Friday & Eid prayers) stands 25m adjacent to the dilapidated Kandahar University. The mosque and the surrounding grounds can accommodate thousands of worshippers, with its construction having taken years at a cost of millions – all funded by Mullah Omar. Apart from Eid times, local youths use the mosque's grounds as cricket pitches, as many of them learned the game whilst growing up in refugee camps in Pakistan. The mullah will show you around and, as a courtesy, a small donation is customary.

Mosque of the Sacred Cloak

A cloak worn by the Prophet Mohammed is housed in the **Mosque of the Sacred Cloak** (Da Kherqa Sharif Ziarat; 🕓 8am-5pm), by far the city's most valued treasure. The mosque is situated opposite the governor's palace. Ahmed Shah Durrani acquired the cloak along with a hair of the beard of the Prophet from the Amir of Bukhara in 1768. When the Taliban took Kandahar in 1994, Mullah Omar wrapped himself in the cloak in front of thousands of loyal Talibs, giving himself god-like status as Amir Al-Momineen (Commander of the Faithful). As a visitor you will be unable to see the cloak but the building is impressive in itself – ornately decorated with green Helmandi marble,

mirrored tile work and gilded archways. Like the Eid Gah Mosque, a small donation is always appreciated.

Ahmed Shah Durrani Mausoleum

The **mausoleum** (Da Kherqa Sharif Ziarat; 🕓 8am-5pm) of the founder of modern-day Afghanistan, Ahmed Shah Durrani, is at the rear of the Mosque of the Sacred Cloak. The octagonal shaped, richly decorated mausoleum is somewhat overshadowed by the mosque.

Mosque of the Hair of the Prophet

Although a little harder to find than the cloak, make sure you make the trip to **Mosque of the Hair of the Prophet** (Jame Mui Mobarak; 🕓 8am-5pm) near Chowk-e Charso in the Old City to see where this unique Islamic relic lies. The hair from the Prophet's beard is encased by a golden sheath in a casket. Like the cloak you will be unable to see the hair; however the Mosque itself is a peaceful haven from the chaos of the Old City bazaars.

Baba Wali Shrine

Sitting on the banks of the Arghandab River is the **Baba Wali Shrine** (Arghandab District Pass), also known as Baba Sahib by Kandaharis. Gul Agha Sherzai, the twice-former Governor of Kandahar, fierce warlord and former mujahideen commander constructed the shrine at a cost of millions of dollars to honour one of his revered tribesmen. It provides a great view to the verdant Arghandab Valley, which is in stark contrast to the rest of the dusty province. The multi-level shrine, marble and mirror-clad, set into a hillside is a popular picnic place for the Kandaharis, with kebabs, hand-made ice cream and local fruit juices available from cart vendors.

Forty Steps

One kilometre west of Chowk-e Dand nestled in a rocky outcrop above the city are the **Forty Steps** (Chihil Zina), which are visible from most of Shah-e-Nau. The steps will take you to a small enclave in the mountain guarded by two stone lions. The statues were carved by Babur, founder of the Mughal empire of India, who took Kandahar in the 16th century. Inside the enclave there is a Persian inscription paying tribute to the conquests of Babur. It's a great place to take the ubiquitous Afghan thermos and drink a cup of green chai while watching the sunrise, but it won't be serene for long as your presence will probably attract an army of kids from the surrounding village.

SLEEPING

Sleeping options in Kandahar are relatively limited, expensive and low quality due to the lack of travellers that make it to the city, with most Afghans staying with friends or family and most internationals staying in their organisations' private guesthouses. The hotels listed all have armed guards, are centrally located and regularly accommodate visiting NGO workers and journalists.

Noor Jahan Hotel (☎ 070 335427; Herat Sarak, Chowk-e Shaheedin; s/d with bathroom 800/1200Afg) The best budget option in Kandahar. It has a small restaurant for guests only, hot water most of the time and all the Bollywood you can watch on Indian satellite TV. Most of the rooms are pretty dilapidated, but compared with the budget alternatives, they're not bad value. The hotel is surrounded by wedding shops that decorate cars for the big day with streamers and gaudy plastic flowers.

Continental Guesthouse (☎ 070 302613; Herat Sarak, Chowk-e Shaheedan; s/d US$40/60) This guesthouse is very popular with journalists, as there is a computer with internet access in every room, and laundry and breakfast are included. It's comfortable and secure, although some of the rooms are pretty tired for the money and few come with private bathroom.

Yasin International Guesthouse (☎ 070 301042, Herat Sarak, Chowk-e Shaheedan; s/d US$40/60) This guesthouse is attached to the Yasin BBQ Restaurant and has six rooms with bathrooms. They have plans for expansion in the near future. Like the Continental, it is comfortable and secure but somewhat overpriced.

EATING & DRINKING

The Pakistani and Baloch influence on Kandahari Pashtun culture is most evident in the food. There is little variance between restaurants in the local cuisine; however, the saving grace of the Kandahar fare is the magnificent seasonal fruits and fresh vegetables.

Mirwais Shandaiz Restaurant (☎ 079 9022 338; Kariz Bazaar; meals from 150Afg; ☽ 8am-10pm) Not surprisingly this is the only restaurant in Kandahar to sport a spinning disco light; don't let the waiters in matching grotty

England soccer shirts put you off, as they serve great Afghan food all day. Offerings include kebab, *pulao* (rice dish), mutton *karai* (diced mutton fried with chilli, tomato and spices and served with bread), *mantu* (steamed meat dumplings) and beef *kufta* (meatballs with different sauces served with rice). The food is fresh, portions are generous and the local seasonal juices and milkshakes are delicious. To finish off, try the home-made ice cream followed by a cup of chai and a *sheesha* pipe on the elevated *takht* area.

The Coffee Shop (☎ 070 300169; Chowk-e Kiptar Madad; meals from 200Afg; ☽ 10am-10pm) The Coffee Shop serves up a wide selection of Western café-style food, Pashtun and English literature and pretty good espresso coffee. It has been dubbed 'the Starbucks of Kandahar' in many Western broadsheets and magazines and has just installed four pool tables. It is the first of its kind in the city and a great place to take a break from kebabs and *pulao*. Here you will find groups of hip, male 20-something Pashtuns sipping lattes and speaking about the latest pirated Hollywood DVDs.

Madina Restaurant (☎ 070 302652; Chowk-e Shah-e Nau; meals from 200Afg; ☽ 8am-10pm) The recently opened Madina Restaurant serves the usual mix of Afghan staples and proudly displays its Western options of burgers and club sandwiches at the top of the menu. Their massive juice bar churns out concoctions of the fruit of the season.

Yasin BBQ Restaurant (☎ 070 301042; Herat Sarak, Chowk-e Shaheedan; BBQ dishes from 350Afg; ☽ 8am-10pm) By far the best Pashtun BBQ restaurant in town, the Yasin serves up tasty lamb kebab, beef shaslik and BBQ whole chicken in a twinkling, plus it will do meals on request. Cleanliness doesn't seem to be too much of a priority, with the occasional cigarette butt kicking around on the greasy floors, but diners shouldn't be overly concerned as the fare is fresh and comes straight off the scorching-hot charcoal grill.

SHOPPING

The main shopping areas are located around the three Old City Chowks. **Chowk-e Shaheedan** is good for mobile phone cards, moneychangers, toiletries and food. Several good antique stores can be found in **Kabul Darwaza**, selling all sorts of trash and treasure from the British and Soviet occupations. The tool stores here sell the favoured souvenir of Western journalists in the south – opium poppy cutters and scrapers. In **Chowk-e Charso** rugs can be found at much cheaper prices than in Kabul. Traditional Pashtun turbans and the quintessential Kandahari prayer hat, the *balotchi*, encrusted with a rainbow of plastic gems, can also be found here.

GETTING THERE & AWAY

Although road travel options exist and the condition of the roads has improved greatly in recent years, the Kandahar–Kabul route (bus/taxi 500/2000Afg, six hours) and the Kandahar–Herat route (bus/taxi 1000/4000Afg, 12 hours) aren't recommended due to the prevailing security situation.

Air remains the best option for accessing Kandahar. Several commercial carriers provide regular services into the recently refurbished civilian terminal building, featured on the 500 Afghani note. **Ariana Afghan Airlines** (☎ 070 300847; Spin Boldak Sarak) has just commenced two regular services; a weekly Kabul–Kandahar–Herat service (one-way 1790Afg) and a weekly Kabul–Kandahar–Dubai service (one-way 8600Afg). Although pricey, the Dubai-based **DFS** (☎ 971-42997556; www.dfsmiddleeast.com; one-way US$600) also take passengers on their weekly cargo run from Dubai–Kandahar.

Several options exist for Kabul–Kandahar flight – exclusively for NGOs registered with the humanitarian air carriers. The ICRC operates a free space-available weekly service, UNHAS have a twice weekly service and PACTEC operates a weekly service.

Kandahar can be reached by road from Quetta in Pakistan. You will need to take a bus or taxi to the Pakistani border town of Chaman, then cross into Spin Boldak in Afghanistan and take a taxi to Kandahar (800Afg, two hours). There is no reason to spend any time in the border towns, which in summer resemble something out of a *Mad Max* movie: full of dust and dirt, with the locals engaged in trading auto parts and smuggling goods. The border generally opens at 8am and can close anytime up until 5pm, or without notice by the security forces on either side. This is the only section of road in the south that is currently being used by NGOs. However, as with all information in this chapter, ensure you have the latest security information before planning a trip.

GETTING AROUND

The Millie buses and minibuses (5Afg) run in a general east–west and north–south direction throughout the day. Taxis will take you anywhere in the city for 50Afg; auto rickshaws cost 25Afg. Movement on foot or by bicycle is not recommended.

THE SOUTH

Due to the security situation outside of Kandahar there are few foreigners here who are not wearing military uniform. The Pakistani influences, more so than Central Asian ones, can be seen in the provinces to the east of Kandahar, such as Zabul and Paktika – in the food, clothing, currency and the insurgency. While in the provinces

---

OPRAH WINFREY AND HANDMADE POMEGRANATE SOAP

Bostonian, Harvard educated, former National Public Radio journalist-turned-humanitarian, Sarah Chayes first came to Afghanistan in 2002. Having first arrived in the country as a journalist, this failed to satisfy her desire to contribute to the needs of the people. Returning to Kandahar to create her own small cooperative Sarah looked to the produce of the south to create products for the export market, and founded Arghand.

The initial capital was provided by numerous benefactors, including Oprah Winfrey. The products of Arghand are soaps, oils and skin care products; the Desert Fields soap with palm and coconut oils and steeped *Artemisia persica* leaves claims to be Arghand's best cleanser.

Along with the products marketed by Arghand, is a collection of organically produced chutneys and jams made almost entirely of pomegranates, plums and apricots – nothing is wasted. Sadly these are yet to be ready for export but can be found in the bazaars of Kandahar.

To learn more about Arghand, visit www.arghand.org.

to the west, particularly Nimroz and parts of Helmand, Iranian influences are evident. Coming down from the mountain ranges in Oruzgan and Ghazni, the desert plains of the south play host to baking heat, sand storms, flash floods, one of the biggest narcotics operations in the world and an active insurgency.

Even with the splendour of the Ghaznavid empire to be explored, independent travel to these areas is not recommended.

GHAZNI   غزنی

The capital of the like-named province of Ghazni is a two-hour drive southwest from Kabul and is now a commercial centre specialising in transport contractors, truck sales and sheepskin coats. It is a shadow of its former glory as the centre of the Ghaznavid empire in the 11th century and one of the most important cities in the Islamic world at the time. Sultan Mahmoud's control extended over modern-day Afghanistan, Iran, Pakistan and Northwest India. He also took Islam to India and returned with plundered riches to keep the empire running, elephants for his stables and priceless artefacts to display in his court, which was filled with poets, artists and scholars.

However Mahmoud's reign was overwhelmed in the 12th century by the Ghorid dynasty. The attacks led by Alauddin, also known as the 'World Burner', gutted the elaborate city. What remained was later decimated by Genghis Khan and his Mongol hoards in 1221. The ruins were reoccupied until once again the city fell, this time in 1839 to the British Army during the first Anglo-Afghan War and has not changed much since that time.

Amongst the feverish paced modern-day trade in Ghazni there are two monuments to the Ghaznavid empire that sit on the side of the road to Kabul. The most visible are two ornate star-shaped **Towers of Victory** or minarets, built in the 11th century by Mahmoud's successors. Both are shorter than they originally were thanks to an earthquake in 1902, and are capped with gaudy corrugated iron roofs. They are

---

A $60 BILLION BUSINESS

Western drug cops talk of busts in grams and kilograms, whereas their relatively ineffective counterparts in Helmand talk in tons. Afghanistan, in terms of volume and quality, is the world leader in opium production – producing 92% of the world crop, or a staggering 6100 metric tons as reported by the UN in 2006, much of it bound for Europe and Russia as heroin. The estimated value of the 2006 crop is nearly $3.5 billion, equating to a street value in excess of US$60 billion. Helmand contributed 42% of the 2006 crop, Badakhshan in the northeast a long second at 8%. Lashkar Gah sports many 'Poppy Palaces' amongst the mud houses – massive, gaudy houses all built with drug money.

A UN survey unsurprisingly lists 'easy cash' as the reason for growing poppies by over 41% of farmers, although 12% cite the high cost of Afghan weddings. However, Afghanistan has not always haemorrhaged opium, in 2001 the Taliban outlawed its cultivation and overnight it stopped; however, the upper Talib echelons still continued the trade. Since the fall of the regime, the poppy fields and the trade has blossomed. President Karzai declared a Jihad on Poppy, which has had little impact. Many of his government officials and security forces are actively involved in the business, cooperating with the narcolords, warlords and criminal gangs who run the trade. This further undermines the international community's efforts of eradication and finding alternative livelihoods for poppy growers; both are failing dismally. Although the level of eradication increased by 210% between 2005 and 2006, the national crop grew by 59%; in Helmand it increased exponentially by 162%.

At 100Afg a hit on the streets, heroin's cheap price has also seen the increase of Afghanistan's intravenous user population, bringing with it the related criminal and health issues such as HIV and AIDS. Having porous international borders with most of its neighbours, making it easy for the heavily armed opium convoys, the Afghan experience is similar in neighbouring countries. The Afghan opium cultivation habit is going to be a hard one to crack, and it is clear that the ancient Silk Road, with its camel caravans of silks and spice, has indeed been replaced by the opium highway, replete with Toyota Hiluxes packed with opium and heavily armed men.

chly decorated in raised brick and ter-
cotta, with each of the panel recesses
etween the start points displaying ornate
atterns and Kufic inscriptions from the
uran. They are thought to be the inspira-
on for the Minaret of Jam (pp126-8).

Mahmoud's elaborately carved marble
mb sits nearby the minarets in a simple
rick mausoleum.

ASHKAR GAH   لشکر گاه

ashkar Gah, the capital of Helmand Prov-
ce and the site of the ancient city of Bost,
a two-hour drive to the west of Kandahar.
ost was the winter palace of Sultan Mah-
oud and his Ghaznavid empire and its
te was the same as Ghazni.

Centuries later it would become a key
S development project during the Cold
Var in the 1960s, so much so that Lashkar
ah was labelled 'Little America'. US engi-
ers and agriculture specialists worked for
ver a decade and laid out the New City in
ashkar Gah and constructed an extensive
etwork of irrigation canals and the mas-
ve Kajaki hydroelectric dam. As the Red
Army invaded in 1979, the programme was
abandoned.

Ironically the canal system, designed to
irrigate food crops, is now used to cultivate
opium poppies with Helmand now receiving
the infamous accolade of being the largest
opium-producing province in Afghanistan.

Helmand is one of the most volatile
provinces in the country, with the UK ISAF
forces experiencing unprecedented violent
clashes with the insurgency throughout the
province. The opium trade serves to further
destabilise the situation.

Little is left of the splendour of the Ghaznavids; parts of the ruins of the Old City can
be found on the far side of the Lashkar Gah
airfield on the Helmand River – in worse
condition than the Ghazni ruins. The expansive **Bost Arch** (featured on the 100 Afghani
note) gives you a glimpse of the ancient city
of Bost. It once served as the entrance to the
city. However, it doesn't look as grand as
the currency depicts; the arch has been filled
with mud brick to prevent it from collapsing,
pending assistance from the international
community for its restoration.

Directory

CONTENTS

Accommodation	198
Activities	200
Business Hours	200
Climate	200
Customs	201
Dangers & Annoyances	201
Documents	201
Electricity	202
Embassies & Consulates	202
Festivals & Events	203
Food	204
Gay & Lesbian Travellers	205
Holidays	205
Insurance	205
Internet Access	206
Legal Matters	206
Maps	206
Money	206
Photography & Video	207
Post	208
Registration	208
Shopping	208
Telephone	209
Time	209
Toilets	209
Tourist Information	210
Travellers with Disabilities	210
Visas	210
Women Travellers	211

ACCOMMODATION

Most levels of accommodation are available in Afghanistan, from top-end hotels and en suite yurts to complete fleapits, and everything in between. Kabul naturally has the widest choice of available options, while outside the cities you may not be presented with any meaningful choice at all.

In the book we have defined budget as up to 2000Afg (US$40), midrange up to 4000Afg (US$80), and top end as anything over 4000Afg. These prices are for doubles, but in many places you'll just be quoted a flat rate for the room irrespective of occupancy. Rooms come without bathrooms unless noted in the text; breakfast is rarely included.

Even though some budget and midrange hotel rooms listed in the text are described as 'clean', this is a relative term and they're unlikely to be absolutely spotless. It's a good idea to bring a sleeping sheet as the quality of bed linen can sometimes leave a bit to be desired. A *pattu* (the woollen blanket carried by many Afghan men) makes an excellent alternative.

Other useful items to pack are a padlock and a torch or candles. Power cuts are frequent, and in some places there just may not be any electricity at all. Earplugs can also be a good idea, particularly if you end up sleeping at a chaikhana.

Some of the cheaper accommodation places in Afghanistan will not take foreign guests, and while we have attempted to account for this in the text, local conditions can change according to the security environment and the whims of local police. This is something we particularly noted in Kabul, where since our last visit many of the cheap hotels popular with independent travellers had closed their doors to foreigners. At the opposite end of spectrum, many midrange and all top end hotels and guesthouses employ security guards outside their premises.

If travelling in winter, you'll find many places are heated by a *bukhari*, a simple heater run off paraffin, gas or petrol. While undoubtedly warming, these devices can be extremely dangerous. Stories of exploding *bukharis* or people dying of asphyxiation due to carbon monoxide poisoning are a staple of the local press during the colder months. Never sleep in a room with a lit *bukhari*. If you're in Afghanistan long term, investing in a carbon monoxide and smoke detector is recommended.

Finally, Afghan hospitality is famous and people you meet on the road may invite you to your home. Remember that most ordinary Afghans have very limited resources and may just be offering hospitality they may ill be able to afford for the sake of honour. If the offer is genuine (and you're satisfied as to the safety aspects of the situation), consider carefully as to whether you can accept without burdening your potenial host. A gift for your hosts, such as fruit or sweets, is appropriate.

Camping

We advise against rough camping in Afghanistan, where a tent will quickly draw the attention of locals. In October 2006 two German journalists were murdered when they were camping in Baghlan province, increasing the chances that should the police spot a tent they'll move you on and insist you stay at a hotel or chaikhana. An exception is the peaceable Wakhan Corridor, where you're likely to be trekking with local guides. Camping here is sometimes the only option.

Chaikhanas

The simplest form of accommodation available in Afghanistan is the chaikhana (teahouse). In small towns and places off the beaten track (the central route for instance), they're likely to be the only type of accommodation on offer. In addition, when long trips by public transport demand an overnight stop, it's at a chaikhana where the driver will pull up.

At its most basic form, sleeping arrangements in a chaikhana are no more than the large communal room where meals are taken, either on the floor or on a *takht* (raised platforms). Bed and board are as one – if you eat your evening meal at the chaikhana then you've also paid to stay, so a night should weigh in at under 100Afg. You simply grab a corner, unroll your sleeping bag or blanket and you're away. There's no peace or privacy (and as a foreigner, you're instantly a figure of interest), and no security for your belongings either. Bathroom facilities tend towards the extremely basic, often just a drum of water fixed with a tap. Outside the towns and cities, enquiries as to where the toilet is may find you directed to either a pit latrine or just being waved towards the street outside.

Female travellers won't be allowed to sleep in a communal room with men, but most chaikhanas have at least one or two private rooms, for which you'll pay a small supplement. They're a much better bet for privacy and security, but don't always have a lock. These rooms often come with some bedding, which you may or may not want to examine too closely.

A torch or candles are essential in a chaikhana. In the remote areas a car battery is commonly used to power the lights and blaring TV, as it's cheaper to run than a generator.

Guesthouses

Private guesthouses were very much a feature of the accommodation scene in the immediate aftermath of the collapse of the Taliban regime, when there was a huge influx of foreigners and a shortage of hotel capacity. Although less popular now than they once were, they can still make a good choice, and are a preferred option for those staying in the country for longer time periods. Prices are normally negotiable for extended stays.

Guesthouses in Afghanistan are essentially private houses that have been converted into B&Bs, and typically have just a handful of rooms and one bathroom shared by all guests. They are often contained in a small compound behind a high wall that offers privacy and security; the best will have a nicely tended garden. Rates normally include breakfast, with other meals offered for extra. Amenities vary widely, but usually include satellite TV and, increasingly, internet access. A private generator should provide a reliable electricity supply. The guesthouse will be run by a *chowkidar* (caretaker), who usually lives on-site. If you're staying long term, you'll find a good *chowkidar* to be worth his weight in gold.

Hammams

If you're staying in cheap accommodation, the local hammam (bathhouse) may be the best way of getting clean. They're busy sociable places, and in the country often the only source of hot water. Prices are usually around 15Afg or 25Afg if there's a private room, and about 100Afg to be washed and massaged by the staff (tips are always appreciated). Bring toiletries and flip-flops (thongs) and keep your underwear on – Afghans of both sexes will be surprised to discover you don't shave your intimate areas.

Locals will generally be happy to direct travellers to the nearest hammam. In the cities there are separate hammams for men and women; in the country access for women is often restricted to a particular time every week. Herat has the best and most traditional hammams; Kabul has relatively few old hammams left.

Hotels

Hotels come in a variety of stripes in Afghanistan. By the standard of neighbouring countries like Pakistan and Iran rooms tend to be overpriced, especially in the midrange, where 2500Afg may just get you a slightly dreary room with attached bathroom, hopefully with hot water. At the top and bottom ends of the price range, prices more accurately reflect what you get for the money. In Kabul, the choice and quality of hotels has improved significantly in the last few years.

At the higher price range, you should expect air-conditioning, and a constant electricity supply to power it. Satellite TV and internet is also usually on offer, and maybe even a few extras like a gym or pool in some places. As rates decrease, so does the quality – air-con becomes a fan, private bathrooms become shared, and broken fixtures less likely to be replaced. At the bottom end, you'll end up with a thin mattress looking at grubby walls, but thankful that the smelly (squat) toilets are at the far end of the corridor. Hot water isn't likely to be an option at this budget, so ask about the local hammam, which will have it by the bucket-load.

Most hotels have a restaurant, and even the cheapest places should be able to rustle up a simple breakfast of tea, bread and eggs or jam.

ACTIVITIES

The mountains of Afghanistan could rival Nepal for trekking opportunities, but for the most part, potential is all there is. There's no infrastructure, and anyone setting out will be genuinely breaking new ground – you'll be unsupported in very remote areas.

The one area where the seeds of a trekking industry are taking root is in Badakhshan, where the Aga Khan Development Network has been assisting with setting up guesthouses and formalising guide and animal hire rates. Several mountaineering teams have also tackled Mt Noshaq, Afghanistan's highest peak (7492m). The Panjshir Valley also offers great hiking potential, but you should seek permission from the local commander. A few expats in Kabul have also taken their own canoes to kayak on the Panjshir River, which has good white-water.

Mir Samir, the unattained target for Eric Newby's *A Short Walk in the Hindu Kush*, remains unreachable for the foreseeable future due to its location in high-risk Nuristan (ironically Nuristan itself was heavily trekked in the 1980s by journalists crossing from Pakistan with the mujaheddin).

BUSINESS HOURS

Government offices and banks are open from 9am to 4pm. The official weekend is Friday, although many offices and business close early on Thursday lunchtime or afternoon. Official business is better conducted in the mornings, before the two-hour lunch break at midday. Private businesses and shops tend to keep longer hours, opening earlier and closing far later, especially where there's money to be made.

Chaikhanas keep the longest hours, usually opening around dawn and closing late into the night, meaning there's almost always somewhere to get food.

During Ramazan, opening hours are shortened by most government offices and businesses. Restaurants (aside from those directly serving the international community) are closed from dawn to dusk, and many take the opportunity to close for the entire month.

CLIMATE

Afghanistan has a four distinct seasons. There's fine weather in spring (March to May) and the country blooms, but rain and melting snow can make many roads difficult to traverse. Summers (June to August) can be blisteringly hot everywhere except

---

DUST!

The comparative rarity of paved roads can make Afghanistan feel like the dustiest country in the world; even Kabul is regularly engulfed in swirling dust storms. Chest infections are common complaints among visitors. Both Afghan men and women use their scarves to keep out the dust on bumpy roads – you should do the same.

the mountains – Herat, Mazar-e Sharif, Jalalabad and Kandahar all swelter, but Kabul, Bamiyan and Faizabad enjoy pleasant, cool nights. Sandstorms at this time can affect air travel. Autumn (September to November) is one of the best times to visit with pleasant dry weather, and plenty of delicious Afghan fruit. From the end of November, winter sets in, and snow is common across much of the country. Travel

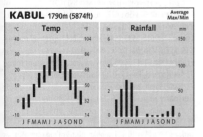

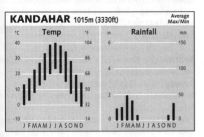

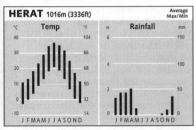

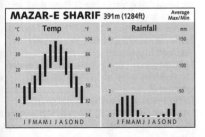

in the mountains is particularly tricky at this time, with some remote regions cut off from transport links completely.

CUSTOMS

Customs procedures and restrictions aren't very transparent. Checks on arrival (by air or land) tend to be lax, with officials only really interested in guns and drugs. Other restricted items that could potentially land you in trouble are alcoholic drinks and large quantities of (non-Islamic) religious material. Foreign currency over US$20,000 must be declared on arrival (see p212).

On leaving, an easy-to-miss sign at Kabul Airport's passport control announces that carpets and 'handicrafts' must be declared to customs, although no one seems to want to check your bags. Duty must be paid if you're exporting more than 30 sq metres of carpets. Carrying items considered antiquities is liable to bring either a fine or confiscation. Export permits can be requested at the **Ministry of Information & Culture** (☎ 020 2101301; Pul-e Bagh-e Omomi) in Kabul.

If you are importing goods for business, information about customs can be found on the website of the **Ministry of Finance** (www.mof.gov.af).

DANGERS & ANNOYANCES

Afghanistan presents unique potential risks to the traveller, with the danger of an insurgency in the south, plus warlordism and terrorist violence in some other parts of the country. It's essential to keep abreast of the current political and security assessments both before travelling and while in-country. For a more detailed discussion of these issues see the chapter Safety in Afghanistan, p68, and the risk assessment boxes at the front of the regional chapters.

DOCUMENTS

We recommend that you carry at least one photocopy of your passport (front and visa pages), travel insurance policy and airline tickets on your person. It's also a good idea to leave copies with someone you can contact at home (or make scanned copies and keep them in a webmail account). Passport photocopies can also be useful for casual inspection at checkpoints.

Permits aren't needed for travel within Afghanistan, with the exception of entering the Wakhan Corridor. For more details on the paperwork needed here, see p168.

Student and youth cards are of no use, although as with any photographic ID they can be useful as a decoy if someone wants to keep your passport.

ELECTRICITY

Mains electricity, when available, is 220V, 50Hz AC. Plug sockets take round two-pronged plugs. Availability is the key issue – a constant and stable electricity supply is a huge problem in Afghanistan. Kabul currently receives between two to six hours of mains electricity a day, and the roar and drone of generators provides a constant aural backdrop. Herat and Mazar-e Sharif, both of which import electricity from neighbouring countries have more reliable electricity supplies, but power cuts are still common. Travelling along the highway between Kabul and Mazar-e Sharif it's possible to see the great rows of destroyed power lines, along with the newly built pylons intended to finally provide a reliable electricity supply to the capital by around 2008 – seven years after the fall of the Taliban.

If you're using any electric equipment, particularly computers, it's vital to have a surge protector and uninterruptible power supply (UPS) plugged in between your equipment and electricity socket. Both are widely available in larger towns and cities across the country.

EMBASSIES & CONSULATES

We strongly advise that travellers register with their embassy on arrival in Kabul, but you should be aware of what your embassy can and can't do for you. Your embassy general won't help much in an emergency if the trouble you're in is remotely your fault. Embassies won't be sympathetic if you end up in jail after committing a crime locally, even if such actions are legal in your own country. Embassy attitudes may also be compounded if your government is currently advising against travel to Afghanistan. In genuine emergencies you might get some assistance (such as a new passport) but you'll be expected to have your own insurance.

For details of all Afghan embassies abroad, go to the website of the **Ministry of Foreign Affairs** (www.mfa.gov.af).

Afghan Embassies & Consulates

Afghanistan has diplomatic representation in the following countries, among others. Where there is more than one listing per country, the embassy is listed first, followed by the consulates in alphabetical order:

Australia (☎ 02-6282 7311; www.afghanembassy.net; PO Box 155, Deakin West, ACT 2600) Hosts nonresident envoy to New Zealand.

Belgium (☎ 02-761 3166; ambassade.afghanistan@skynet .be; 281 Rue Francoise Gay, Brussels B-1150)

Canada (☎ 613-563 4223/65; www.afghanemb-canada .net; 246 Queen St, Ottawa K1P 5E4)

China (☎ 010-6532 1582; afgemb.beijing@gmail.com; 8 Dong Zhi Men Wai Da Jie, Beijing)

France (☎ 01-45 25 05 29; www.ambafghane-paris.com; 32 Ave Raphael, Paris 75016) Hosts nonresident envoys to Portugal, Spain, and Switzerland.

Germany Berlin (☎ 030-224 87229; afghanische-bots chaft@t-online.de; Wilhelmstrasse 65 D, 10117); Bonn (0228-256797; Liebfrauenweg 1A, 53125)

India (☎ 011- 410 331; afghanspirit@yahoo.com; Plat No 5, Block 50F, Chanakyapuri, Delhi 110021)

Iran Tehran (☎ 021-873 7050; afghanembassytehran@ hotmail.com; 4th St, Dr Beheshti Ave); Mashad (☎ 0511-854 4829; afghanistan_ge_con_mashad@samanir .net; Sevom Isfand Sq, off Doshahid St, Emam Khomeini Ave); Zahedan (☎ 0541-243 7113; g_c_afgh_i_zahedan@ yahoo.com; Kheyaban-e Daneshga, Koi Estandari)

Italy (☎ 06-8621 6111; afghanembassy.rome@flashnet .it; Via Nomentana 120, Rome 00161) Hosts nonresident envoy to Greece.

Japan (☎ 03-5465 1219; www.afghanembassyjp.com; 3-37-8-B Nishihara, Shibuya-ku, Tokyo 151-0066)

Kazakhstan (☎ 327-255 2792; Khan Tengri 59, Almaty)

Kyrgystan (☎ 312-426372; afghanemb_bishkek@ yahoo.com; cnr Ayni & Toktonalieva, Bishkek)

Netherlands (☎ 20-6721311; afconsulholland@yahoo .com; Wellemsparkweg 114, Amsterdam)

Norway (☎ 22 83 84 10; www.afghanemb.com; 17 Kronprinsens Gt, 0244, Oslo) Hosts nonresident envoys to Denmark and Sweden.

Pakistan Islamabad (☎ 051-282 4505/6; nstarzi1@yahoo .com; House 8, Street 90, G-6/3); Karachi (☎ 021-582 1264; agc_karachi@yahoo.com; 33/2 9th St, Khayaban-e Shamsi, Phase V, Defence 75500); Peshawar (☎ 091-285962; The Mall, Saddar Bazaar); Quetta (☎ 081-843364; 45 Prince Rd)

Russia (☎ 095-9287581; safarat_moscow@yahoo.com; Sverchkov Per 3/2, Moscow)

Tajikistan Dushanbe (☎ 372-216394; afghanemintj@yahoo .com; Pushkin 34); Khorog (☎ 35220-2492; Kheyaban Kermshayef 17)

Turkey Ankara (☎ 312-4381121; 88 Cinnah Caddesi, Cankaya); Istanbul (☎ 212-361 5500; info@afghanconsula teistanbul.com; Pamuk Palas 13/7, Taksim)

Turkmenistan (☎ 12-480757; Garashsyzlyk köçesi, Berzengi, Ashgabat)

UK (☎ 020-7589 8891/2; www.afghanembassy.co.uk; 31 Prince's Gate, London SW7 1QU)

United Arab Emirates Abu Dhabi (☎ 2-665 5560; PO Box 5687); Dubai (☎ 4-398 8229; PO Box 113233)

USA Los Angeles (☎ 310-473 6583; afghanconsulate@hotmail.com; 11040 Santa Monica Blvd, CA 90025); New York (☎ 212-972 2276; info@afghanconsulateny.org; 11th fl, 360 Lexington Ave, NY 10017); Washington DC (☎ 202-416 1620; www.embassyofafghanistan.org; 2341 Wyoming Ave NW, 20036)

Uzbekistan (☎ 71-134 8432; Murtazayev 6/84, Tashkent)

Embassies & Consulates in Afghanistan

All of the following embassies and consulates are in Kabul unless otherwise noted. New Zealand and Ireland do not maintain diplomatic representation in Afghanistan. For information on visas for onward travel to neighbouring countries see p211.

Australia (☎ 020 2104474; in Kabul Serena Hotel, Jade-e Froshgah)

Belgium (Map p85; ☎ 070 200135; House 40, Lane 3, Street 15, Wazir Akbar Khan)

Canada (Map p85; ☎ 079 9742 822; House 256, Street 15, Wazir Akbar Khan)

China (☎ 020 2102548/9; Shah Mahmoud Wat, Shahr-e Nau)

France (Map p85; ☎ 070 284032; near Charahi Zambak & Charahi Ariana, Shahr-e Nau)

Germany (Map p85; ☎ 020 2101512; Charahi Zambak, Shahr-e Nau)

India Herat (☎ 040 224432; Sarakh-e Qulurdo); Kabul (Map p85; ☎ 020 2200133; Interior Ministry Rd, Shahr-e Nau); Mazar-e Sharif (☎ 070 309982; Dand Chowk, District 6); Mazar-e Sharif (☎ 070 500372, Darwaza-ye Balkh)

Iran Herat (☎ 040 220015; Jad-e Walayat); Kabul (Map p85; ☎ 020 2101393/4; Charahi Sherpur, Shahr-e Nau); Mazar-e Sharif (Kheyaban-e Nasir Khusrau)

Italy (Map p85; ☎ 020 2103144; Charahi Ariana, Shahr-e Nau)

Japan (Map p85; ☎ 020 290172; Street 15, Wazir Akbar Khan)

Kazakhstan (☎ 070 277450; House 1, Street 10, Wazir Akbar Khan)

Netherlands (Map p85; ☎ 070 286640/1; Ghiyassudin Wat, Shahr-e Nau)

Norway (☎ 020 2300900/0899; Lane 4, Street 15, Wazir Akbar Khan)

Pakistan Jalalabad (Charahi Marastoon); Kabul (Map p85; ☎ 020 2300911/3; Street 10, Wazir Akbar Khan); Kandahar (☎ 070 302520; Noorzo Shah Bridge, District 2)

Russia (☎ 020 2300500; Darulman Wat, Karte Se)

Sweden (Map p85; ☎ 020 2301416; House 70, Lane 1, Street 15, Wazir Akbar Khan)

Switzerland (Map p85; ☎ 020 2301565; House 486, Lane 3, Street 13, Wazir Akbar Khan)

Tajikistan (Map p85; ☎ 020 2101080; Street 10, Wazir Akbar Khan)

Turkey Kabul (Map p85; ☎ 020 2101581/79; Shah Mahmoud Wat); Mazar-e Sharif (☎ 070 500501; Baba Yadgar Kamarband)

Turkmenistan Herat (☎ 040 223534; Jad-e Walayat); Kabul (Map p85; ☎ 020 2301504; Lane 3, Street 13, Wazir Akbar Khan); Mazar-e Sharif (☎ 050 5023; Darwaza-ye Tashkurgan)

UK (Map p85; ☎ 070 102000; Street 15, Wazir Akbar Khan)

USA (Map p85; ☎ 020 2300436; Charahi Massoud)

Uzbekistan Kabul (Map p85; ☎ 020 2300124; House 14, Street 13, Wazir Akbar Khan); Mazar-e Sharif (☎ 050 3042; Darwaza-ye Tashkurgan)

FESTIVALS & EVENTS

Afghanistan's new year (Nauroz; p204) is a major cause for celebration, but there are several important holy days for travellers to be aware of.

Islamic Holy Days

The Muslim calendar is lunar, and shorter than the Western solar calendar, meaning that the calendar begins around 11 days earlier in each solar year. Dates run from sunset to the next sunset. The Hejira year is dated from the time of the Prophet Mohammed's flight from Mecca to Medina in AD 622.

Each month begins with the sighting of the new moon. Religious officials have the authority to declare the sighting, so while future holy days can be estimated, the precise dates are in doubt until a few days before the start of that month. Ask an anxious Afghan what date the Ramazan fast is going to end and you'll understand the frustrations. For this reason, the dates given here are only approximate. Offices and businesses all shut on these days, except for the first day of Ramazan.

Of the Muslim holy days, the most important is Eid-e Qurban. The Feast of Sacrifice (called Eid ul-Adha elsewhere in the Muslim world) commemorates the Prophet Ibrahim's readiness to obey Allah even to the point of sacrificing his son. In the run up to Eid-e Qurban, markets throng with goats and sheep; those who can afford it slaughter one, sharing the meat with relatives and the less privileged. The holiday takes place at

ISLAMIC HOLIDAYS

Hejira year	Prophet's Birthday	Ramazan begins	Eid al-Fitr	Eid-e Qurban	Ashura
1428	31 Mar 2007	13 Sep 2007	13 Oct 2007	20 Dec 2007	29 Jan 2007
1429	20 Mar 2008	2 Sep 2008	2 Oct 2008	9 Dec 2008	19 Jan 2008
1430	9 Mar 2009	23 Aug 2009	21 Sep 2009	29 Nov 2009	8 Jan 2009

Actual dates may occur a day later, but not earlier, depending on western hemisphere moon sightings.

the end of the Haj season, roughly 70 days after the end of Ramazan. It lasts for three days, during which Afghanistan effectively shuts down.

Ashura is an important Shiite festival. It marks the death of Hussain at Karbala in Iraq in 680, the event that provoked the schism between Sunni and Shiite Islam. Men pound their chests and chant the name of Hussain and his companions. Some practise self-flagellation, bloodying their backs with blade-tipped chains. The mourning period for Hussain continues for 40 days.

For more on Ramazan, the month of fasting, see right.

Nauroz

Nauroz, or New Year, is the most widely celebrated holiday in Afghanistan apart from Eid-e Qurban. The holiday is an adaptation of pre-Islamic renewal celebrations held on the spring equinox. The date is now fixed on 21 March. It probably has Zoroastrian roots, and was being celebrated in the country before Alexander the Great. Given these ancient roots, it's no surprise that the Taliban tried to ban it.

Nauroz is a time for picnics and visiting relations. Wheat seedlings are often grown and small fires are lit to be leapt over to symbolise renewal after the winter. Tables are traditionally laid with seven items beginning with the Dari letter 's': sabzeh (wheat, for rebirth), samanak (a sweet pudding, for affluence), sir (garlic, for health), sib (apples, for beauty), sumaq (berries, representing sunrise), serkeh (vinegar, for patience) and sekkeh (coins, for prosperity). Haft-mewah, a dish of seven fruits is also specially prepared. Rain on Nauroz augurs a good harvest. The sabzeh is thrown away into running water 13 days after Nauroz, by which time it has symbolically collected all the family's bad luck for the year.

Across the north, the holiday is often marked with buzkashi matches (see p57). Afghanistan's biggest public Nauroz celebrations are held in Mazar-e Sharif, attended by tens of thousands of people (p152).

FOOD

Eating is relatively inexpensive in Afghanistan, but if you spend much time out of Kabul and on the road you're liable to become bored with the limited variety of food on offer. Pulao (rice dish) and kebabs are mostly the order of the day, sometimes enlivened with soup or a small qorma (stewed vegetables).

The chaikhana is the backbone of the Afghan eating experience. Diners normally sit on the floor or on takhts (raised platforms) in front of a large roll of oil cloth that acts as a table substitute. Many chaikhanas will have a separate 'family room' for women and children to eat in, often just a sheet partition. Prices include tea and often a space to sleep for the night (see the Accommodation section, p199).

In larger towns you'll find a little more variety, including approximations of Western fast-food outlets. Street stalls are often a better bet, serving up cheap plates of boloni (stuffed vegetable pancakes), samosas, mantu (steamed meat dumplings) and the like. In season, there is always plenty of fruit on offer, from juicy melons from the north to plump Kandahari pomegranates.

Kabul has a wide variety of international restaurants aimed at the expat community. Expensive by Afghan standards, they offer a break from meat and rice. Alcohol availability has recently been severely clamped down on due to popular disapproval.

Ramazan

Ramazan (Ramadan elsewhere in the Muslim world) is the auspicious holy month of sunrise-to-sunset fasting, marking the period when the Prophet Mohammed received his revelations. No eating, drinking or smoking is permitted during daylight hours, although children, the pregnant, sick or elderly are exempt.

Non-Muslims are not expected to fast, but in practice you end up adapting to some degree. Local restaurants close during daylight, and many shut for the entire month. You'll do a lot of eating and drinking in private. Eating in public should be strenuously avoided – it's incredibly rude to indulge in front of those who are abstaining, and it's possible you might attract negative attention for being culturally disrespectful.

This said, the celebratory aspects of Ramazan can almost compensate for the hardships of the day just passed. *Iftar*, the breaking of the fast, is a time of great activity, when people come together to eat, drink and pray. As in the rest of the Muslim world, dates are traditionally the first thing to be eaten, but *boloni* are also popular. Traffic can be terrible in the approach to sunset, with everyone clamouring to get home – hungry taxi drivers don't appreciate being flagged down at this time.

The end of Ramazan is marked by the festival of Eid ul-Fitr, which can last up to three days, and Afghans usually spend it visiting family and friends. For approximate dates of Ramazan, see opposite.

GAY & LESBIAN TRAVELLERS

Homosexuality is illegal in Afghanistan, and penalties are theoretically harsh, including jail terms – the Taliban used to debate whether the appropriate punishment should be being pushed off a cliff or crushed under a toppled wall. Afghan men often hold hands in public, but this is an accepted expression of nonsexual friendship. Like heterosexual foreign couples in Afghanistan, gay and lesbian travellers should respect local sensibilities and refrain from all public displays of affection.

For all this, there is a tradition in some strands of Afghan (and particularly Pashtun) society where men seek sex with younger males, so-called *bacha baaz* (boy players). Something of an open secret, this behaviour is not recognised as formally homosexual in any way and is widely tolerated.

HOLIDAYS

On the days listed below (and on the Islamic holidays noted on opposite), businesses and government offices are closed.

21 March Nauroz; new year (see opposite)

28 April Victory Day; celebrating the mujaheddin victory over communist rule in 1992.

1 May National Labour Day

4 May Remembrance Day for Martyrs and the Disabled

19 August Independence Day; celebrating victory in the Third Anglo-Afghan War in 1919.

9 September Ahmad Shah Massoud Day; commemorating the assassination of the Northern Alliance leader in 2001.

INSURANCE

To say Afghanistan can be an unpredictable place is something of an understatement, so travel insurance is essential. However, many insurance companies regard Afghanistan as a conflict zone. Coupled with advice from government travel advisories, this means that not all brokers will issue insurance for a trip to Afghanistan. Discuss this with your broker and check the small print for exclusions on the policy before signing up. Note that insurers may make a distinction between 'active' and 'passive' war zones, where premiums reflect the level of risk. Cover for land mine injuries are often specifically excluded by some companies. A minimum of US$1 million medical cover and a 'medivac' clause covering the costs of being flown to another country for treatment is essential.

Specialist policies are available with some brokers aimed specifically for those working in conflict zones, although they're not always cheap. **AKE Group** (☎ in the UK 020 7816 5454, in the USA 678-560 2336; www.akegroup.com), a dedicated security and risk management company has been recommended. In the UK, also try **Medicare** (☎ 020 7816 2033; www.medicare.co.uk) or **J&M Insurance** (☎ 01992 566939; www.jmi.co.uk). In the USA, try **New York International Group** (☎ 212-268 8520; www.nyig.com) or **Safe Passage International** (☎ 303-988 9666; www.spibrokers.com).

In Afghanistan, medical services insist on payment on the spot, so collect all the paperwork you can when being treated for a claim later. Some policies ask you to call them (they'll usually call you back) so that an assessment of your problem can be made.

INTERNET ACCESS

The internet has caught on in a big way in Afghanistan. All major towns have cyber-cafés or 'internet clubs', with prices varying between 50Afg to 80Afg. Connections are usually good, and offer facilities like Skype and burning CDs of digital photos.

LEGAL MATTERS

Although corruption is rife in the Afghan National Police, it's unlikely that you'll actually be arrested unless there are supportable charges against you. Always keep your embassy's contact details on your person and try to contact them without delay if you are arrested. Remember that all visitors are subject to the laws of Afghanistan. If the 'problem' is an imaginary one, the ability to be extremely patient and drink large quantities of tea may eventually see the issue disappear.

MAPS

Some maps of Afghanistan are available in bookshops in Kabul, but they tend to be expensive. *Afghanistan* (produced by Nelles) is a good 1:1.5 million map. For those going further east, the 1:2 million *Afghanistan & Pakistan* map by GeoCenter is also recommended. Both maps have good mountain coverage, but can be vague with detail in some areas – village names are often hazy.

AIMS (www.aims.org.af) has excellent reference and topographical maps of the country, serving the Afghan government and assistance community. Maps include street plans and highly detailed provincial and district maps. They can be downloaded as PDF files, or ordered as poster-sized maps from the AIMS office in Kabul (p84). On all maps, beware variants in spelling: Tarin Kowt on one map may be Tirin Kot on another, or even Teren Kotte.

MONEY

Afghanistan's currency is the afghani (Afg). Paper notes come in denominations of one, two, five, 10, 20, 50, 100, 500 and 1000. One, two and five afghani coins are slowly replacing the grubbiest small notes. When the afghani was relaunched in 2002 to encourage economic stability, there were around 10,000Afg to the US dollar; since then the currency has consistently floated at around 45Afg to 50Afg to the dollar.

Afghanistan's war-shattered banking system has been slowly rebuilding itself, but the distinction between the formal and black economy remains vague in many places. Despite government attempts at regulation, the country effectively operates a two-currency system – US dollars are an accepted form of payment for many goods and services (including hotels). Throughout the guide we have followed local practices, listing the currency payment is usually requested in. For smaller sums, including public transport and local restaurants, payment in afghanis is usually demanded. In some places, payment may even be accepted in currencies from neighbouring countries – Pakistani rupees in Jalalabad and Kandahar for instance.

ATMs

Automatic teller machines (ATMs) have slowly been introduced in Kabul, operated either by Afghanistan International Bank (AIB) or Standard Chartered. These accept MasterCard and Visa, but not always all cards (technically the machines are also wired for Cirrus and Maestro, but we didn't have much luck on this front). Check with your bank before departing that your card can access international banking networks. The ATMs give either afghanis or dollars according to the machine, and tend to have set working hours. While very useful, they shouldn't be relied on as your sole source of cash if possible. At the time of research, the only ATM outside Kabul was at Bagram Airbase.

Cash

We prefer not to recommend that travellers carry large amounts of cash with them, but in Afghanistan this is largely unavoidable. This is a country where cash – or rather the US dollar – is king. There are a few precautions to minimise the risk of losing your stash to misadventure.

It's unwise to carry wads of money in your wallet, and you're similarly more prone to being robbed if you carry valuables in a shoulder bag, which can easily be snatched. Keep a small amount of money for the day in a handy but concealed place (eg in an inner pocket), and the bulk of your resources more deeply hidden. A well-concealed money belt is one of the safest ways of carrying your money as well as important documents such as your passport. It's also a good idea to have emergency cash (say US$100 in small bills) stashed away from your main hoard, as a backup.

One alternative to carrying large sums of money with you on the road (and away from Kabul's ATMs) is fast international money transfer by Western Union. These are found in almost every Afghan town, and often in branches of Kabul Bank in the cities – see regional chapters for details. Fees are paid by the person wiring the funds, not by the person collecting.

Changing Money

It's far easier to change money on the street than in a bank, and in our experience some tellers will actually advise you to do just the same. Only Kabul Bank seems to consistently change money, but in a country where much of the economy operates outside the banking system, almost everyone uses moneychangers.

Moneychangers tend to operate on the street, with small stands rather than formal shops. The main moneychanging areas are listed in the text – look out for men holding thick wedges of afghanis and clutches of US$100 bills. Afghan moneychangers are a pretty honest bunch as a whole, but always take your time to count out the bills, and don't hand over your money until you've done so. Insist on smaller denominations if you're handed everything in 1000Afg notes.

If you're not happy to change money standing on the street, doing it from a taxi is an acceptable practice. Alternatively, most hotels and many shops (particularly those dealing with imported goods, or carpet shops) are usually willing to change money. When bringing currency to Afghanistan get new dollar bills; higher denominations are preferred. Euros and sterling can be easily changed in the cities, but other currencies can be problematic. Currencies from neighbouring countries are freely exchangeable, but you get better rates closer to the relevant border – eg Iranian rials in Herat, or Tajik somani in Kunduz.

Credit Cards

Flashing your plastic is currently of limited use in Afghanistan, and then only really in the capital. Only the most upmarket Kabul hotels accept payment by credit card. Most Kabul airline offices and travel agents will take them (plus a few enterprising carpet shops), but as a general rule banks won't give cash advances on credit cards.

Travellers Cheques

Most banks in Afghanistan will look at travellers cheques with some curiosity before pushing them back over the counter for you to take elsewhere. A few lucky (and pushy) people have managed to change travellers cheques at the main branch of Da Afghanistan Bank in Kabul, with punishing commission rates, but this is the exception rather than the norm.

This said, it can sometimes be possible to cash travellers cheques with moneychangers. The moneychangers bazaar in Kabul is the best place to try, but you might also have luck at the congregations of changers in Herat and Mazar-e Sharif. Their stalls might be lo-tech, but mobile phones put them in instant contact with the international currency markets. A little persistence, and a willingness to pay commission might work wonders – we've even heard of moneychangers cashing cheques drawn on travellers' personal bank accounts.

If you do try bringing travellers cheque, always carry the purchase receipts and a note of the serial numbers in a separate place from the cheques.

PHOTOGRAPHY

Afghanistan is a photographer's dream, so bring more film or digital memory sticks than you think you'll need. Lonely Planet's *Travel Photography* has been designed to take on the road, and has valuable tips and techniques on shooting everything from mountains to portraits.

Film & Processing

International-brand colour film and processing are available in all cities and most large towns, but check use-by dates when buying film. Photographic studios increasingly offer digital services, although only in the cities will you find much choice if you need to buy another flash-card.

Restrictions & Etiquette

The Taliban famously banned all photography of living things, a move that becomes

DIRECTORY

PINHOLE PORTRAITS

As digital cameras catch on in Afghanistan, it's a surprise to see street photographers still taking portraits with old-fashioned box pinhole cameras on wooden tripods. Sitting for your shot, the photographer takes the cover off the lens to directly expose the photographic paper inside. This is printed to make a negative, which is then photographed and the process repeated to produce a slightly blurred and ethereal portrait that looks like it was taken in the 19th century, rather than the 21st. Allow at least 30 minutes to get an unusual, but very Afghan, souvenir.

deeply ironic as soon as you realise the Afghans' great love of having their picture taken. Always ask *'aks gerefti?'* ('May I take your photo?') before snapping away. This love of being photographed only extends to male Afghans, however, and open photography of women should be avoided. It is deeply insulting to take pictures of women without permission and doing so can easily lead to an ugly scene, especially if a male relative is nearby. This can even apply if you're shooting a street scene and a woman happens to be in the foreground. Although the 'burqa shot' is one of Afghanistan's more iconic images, resist the temptation. Even if no protest is made, don't underestimate the grave offence you might have unwittingly caused. Women photographers are often permitted more access than men, especially if they've established some rapport.

As in many developing countries, prohibited subjects include military sites, airports and embassies. Avoid these completely, along with photos of international military forces.

POST

International post is generally reliable but can be very slow. It can take anything between two weeks and a month for letters to reach their destinations, irrespective of where they're headed. Either way, if you're only on a short trip you're likely to beat your postcards home. A postcard currently costs 34Afg to send to Europe or Australia, and 40Afg to North America. Stamp-lovers will enjoy the process of sending mail, as the clerk picks out designs of various ages

and then carefully franks them. One card we sent reached its destination with stamps from 1969, 1984 and 2003 on it!

Mail is best sent from the major cities (Kabul by preference), which is faster and more reliable. Although many small towns have post offices, mail is liable to go astray; we're not sure we'd entirely trust the crudely made wooden 'post box' we saw nailed to a tree in Samangan's bazaar.

Sending packages is a daylong process involving a complicated customs declaration paper chase. It's more efficient (if more expensive) to use an international shipping company. DHL, TNT and Federal Express all have offices in Kabul. A 500g package sent from Kabul costs around US$130 to the USA or Europe, taking five days to arrive.

It's just about possible to receive mail by post restante. Have mail addressed to the main post office (eg Shahr-e Nau, Kabul), with your name underlined. Take your passport; there's a nominal fee for collection.

If you're based in Afghanistan longer term, a more reliable way of receiving mail is to set up a PO Box. You need proof of identity (usually accompanied by a letter from your employer vouching for you) and a couple of passport photos. The fee is 530Afg per six months. Mail takes around two to three weeks from Europe or the USA.

REGISTRATION

There's no need for travellers to register with the authorities on arrival in Afghanistan. In towns not used to seeing foreigners, some hotels may ask that you register with the police before allowing you to check in. This is more common at the cheaper end of the accommodation, where local authorities sometimes place restrictions on where foreigners can and can't stay overnight – the police and security services tend to do nightly checks of cheap hotels.

SHOPPING

Afghanistan is full of enough interesting handicrafts and souvenirs to have you worrying about your baggage allowance on the plane. Kabul has the widest choice (and highest prices); Herat and Mazar-e Sharif are also good places to go shopping.

Prices are never fixed, so be prepared to haggle. There's no rule on how much to offer, but it's best to treat the deal-making

---

TOP AFGHAN SOUVENIRS

After the obligatory carpet, here are some of our most iconic souvenirs from Afghanistan:

- A *chapan*, the striped and quilted silk Uzbek robe that Hamid Karzai is never seen without
- A *pakul*, the pancake-flat hat immortalised by Ahmad Shah Massoud
- Lapis lazuli jewellery, from the mines of Badakhshan
- A delicately embroidered *suzani*, an Uzbek hanging or bedspread in silk or wool
- Handmade green and blue Herati glass
- Rustic blue and brown pottery from Istalif
- A cover for bottles in the shape of a miniature *burqa*
- A CD of music by Ahmad Zahir
- Opium cutter and scraper

---

as a game rather than becoming obsessed with driving the price into the ground. Both sides will take it in turns to be disinterested and then outraged at the prices offered before finding common ground.

For more on that most famous of exports, the Afghan carpet, see p53.

TELEPHONE

A limited fixed-line telephone network exists in Kabul, Herat, Kandahar, Mazar-e Sharif and Jalalabad, managed by the state-run Afghan Telecom. However, Afghanistan has quickly taken to mobile phones. Three companies currently compete for custom: **Roshan** (www.roshan.af; prefix 079/075), **AWCC** (www.afghanwireless.com; prefix 070) and **Areeba** (www.areeba.com.af; prefix 077). A fourth network, run by **Etisalat** (www.etisalat.co.ae) was due to launch soon after we went to press. Afghanistan uses the GSM system, although demand frequently overloads the different networks at different times. As a result, it's not uncommon to see Afghan businessmen clutching a handful of phones, one for each network. At the time of writing, Roshan was Afghanistan's most popular network, with the widest coverage.

The networks have international roaming agreements with many foreign networks, but it can work out cheaper to buy a local SIM card on arrival in Afghanistan for about 2000Afg (including several hundred afghanis credit). Take a copy of your passport to the dealer. Calls within Afghanistan cost around 5Afg to 7Afg per minute according to the network, and around 20Afg per minute overseas. Top-up scratchcards for more credit are available everywhere from shops and street sellers.

If you're going to be spending time outside the reach of mobile phone coverage, a satellite phone from **Thuraya** (www.thuraya.com; prefix 088216) can be a good investment, albeit not a cheap one. Handsets cost US$750 in Kabul, and phone calls cost US$1 a minute to any phone worldwide, or US$0.50 to another Thuraya number. To use a Thuraya phone, dial 00 to get the international code, followed by the country code, and then the number.

In the big cities, it's easiest to place a call at a post office or an Afghan Telecom office. You give the number to a clerk who directs you to a booth and places the call. Calls to the US cost around 22Afg per minute, 22Afg to Europe and 25Afg to Australia. Local calls cost around 5Afg per minute. In addition, public call offices (PCOs) are common in the major cities, usually just an office with a desk and phone, or simply someone on the street with a table and chairs and a pile of mobile phones.

TIME

Afghanistan runs on GMT plus 4½ hours. There is no daylight saving. The clocks are an hour ahead of Iran, and 30 minutes behind all its other neighbours.

TOILETS

Public toilets are effectively non-existent in Afghanistan. While midrange hotels and international restaurants will have sit-down toilets, everywhere else you'll find squat toilets giving your thigh muscles a work-out.

CROSSED LINES

Afghanistan's telephone system is in a constant state of flux. While we have taken every care to check all telephone numbers at the time of research, it is highly likely that many numbers will change during the lifetime of this guide.

Only at the top-end of the spectrum will you find toilet paper on offer, otherwise a tap or ewer of water will be provided for ablutions (the left hand is used, which is why Afghans eat with the right).

In the countryside, a pit latrine is often the best that can be hoped for, which often demand nostrils of steel to overcome the smell. Otherwise, requests for the tashnab or joab-e chai (literally 'the answer to tea') will result in you walking to the nearest bush, which can be an issue for female travellers If you're on the road, always remain aware of the risk of landmines before stepping off the path.

TOURIST INFORMATION

The **Afghan Tourist Organisation** (ATO; ☎ 020 2300338; Great Massoud Rd) is struggling to bring back the tourist heyday of the 1970s. ATO also has offices at the airport, in Kabul at the Intercontinental Hotel and on Asmai Wat (near the National Gallery), as well as branches in Bamiyan, Herat and Faizabad. Available services are somewhat limited, as staff don't actually expect to see many tourists, but ATO can organise drivers and translators, and sell you copies of Nancy Dupree's 1970s guidebooks. Government plans to train official guides have yet to come to much. Better quality tourist information can usually come from the new private tour operators in Kabul – see p86. There are no ATO offices outside Afghanistan.

TRAVELLERS WITH DISABILITIES

Travel in Afghanistan presents severe challenges for a physically disabled person. The rigours of road travel, the lack of decent footpaths and wheelchair-accessible buildings all pose serious problems. However, travel is possible for those with an iron will, plenty of stamina and the willingness to adapt to whatever hurdles present themselves. Travelling with an able-bodied companion can help immensely in overcoming these obstacles. At the very least, hiring a vehicle and guide will make moving around a great deal easier.

Despite the many difficulties, physically disabled travellers may actually get a more positive response from locals than in other countries in the region. One legacy of decades of war is the high number of amputees, those impaired by polio and other disabili-

ties. With between 700,000 and one million disabled Afghans, it's thought that up to 15% of the population is affected directly or indirectly by disability. Making contact with local disability groups could potentially prove a strong focus for your trip.

For more information, consider contacting **Mobility International USA** (MIUSA; ☎ 541-343 1284; www.miusa.org; 132 E Broadway, Suite 343, Eugene OR 97401), who offer general travel advice for physically disabled travellers. Its website has links to disability organisations working in Afghanistan, and MIUSA has operated exchange programmes in other parts of Central Asia.

VISAS

All nationalities need visas to visit Afghanistan. Visas are relatively straightforward to obtain, but must be applied for in advance as they are not issued on arrival at Kabul airport or at any land border.

All visa applications require a letter of introduction, stating the purpose and duration of your trip. If you're travelling for work purposes this should be from your employer. The situation for tourist visas depends on the embassy you apply at. If you're travelling independently, a letter written by yourself stating your purpose and itinerary often suffices. Bemused consular officials have been known to request applications be made in person so they can interview applicants as to why they want to holiday in Afghanistan. Otherwise, the Afghan tour operators listed on p217 should be able to provide you with a letter of introduction for a small fee. Call your nearest embassy well in advance of travel to check current requirements.

At the time of writing a one-month single-entry visa in London costs UK£30, UK£55 for a three-month multiple-entry visa, and UK£115 for a six-month multiple-entry visa, all issued in two days. The embassy in Washington charges US$50 for a one-month single-entry visa, US$100 for a three-month multiple-entry visa, and US$180 for a six-month multiple-entry visa. Visas take two weeks to process, with a premium charged for same-day issue.

In neighbouring countries, Peshawar, Tehran, Mashad and Tashkent are good places to apply for an Afghan visa. One month single-entry visas cost US$30 to US$45 and are generally issued on the same day.

Visa Extensions

Visas can be extended in Kabul at the **Interior Central Passport Department** (Map p85; Passport Lane, off Interior Ministry Rd, Shahr-e Nau). Tourists require one passport photo and a letter requesting an extension from the head office of the ATO. The letter costs US$10 for a one-month extension. The process takes about an hour if the queues aren't too long.

If you're working in Afghanistan, you'll need a letter of support from your organisation, or in the case of journalists, a letter from the **Ministry of Information & Culture** (☎ 020 2101301; Pul-e Bagh-e Omomi) in Kabul. Visa extensions cost US$30 for three months, which must be paid into the central branch of Da Afghanistan Bank, with the receipt presented at the passport office along with one passport photo.

Visas for Onward Travel

For contact details of embassies and consulates in Afghanistan, see p203. Be warned that the Iranian and Pakistani embassies attract huge queues of visa applicants.

India Applications can only be made at the embassy in Kabul (open 9am to noon Monday to Thursday). Six-month visa issued in 24 hours for US$65. Bring three passport photos.

Iran Transit visas from Kabul or Herat (both open 8am to 2pm Saturday to Wednesday, 8am to noon Thursday) cost from US$20 to US$60 according to nationality. One-month tourist visas cost from US$60. Both require two photos, and possibly a letter of introduction from your home embassy. Issue time is one day to a fortnight, again according to nationality: Americans and British are given the hardest time.

Pakistan The embassy in Kabul (open 9am to noon Sunday to Thursday) is picky about issuing visas for nonwork purposes. Tourist visas cost about US$60 according to nationality, and take several days, with two photos.

Tajikistan One-month visas cost US$80; a letter of introduction from your embassy is sometimes requested. Be there as soon as the embassy opens (9am to noon Saturday and Sunday) and be persistent to have your application processed. Visas can take up to a fortnight to issue.

Turkmenistan Visas issued in Kabul (open 9am to noon and 2pm to 4pm Monday to Thursday) and Herat (open 9am to noon Saturday to Wednesday). Transit visas costs US$31, one-month tourist visas around US$125. As well as two photos, you need a letter of invitation from a Turkmen travel agency specifying your point of entry. Applications can take up to a fortnight to process.

Uzbekistan Visas issued in Kabul (open 9am to noon Monday to Thursday) only. A one-month visa costs US$100 with two photos and a letter of invitation from an Uzbek travel agency. Visas are issued on the spot.

WOMEN TRAVELLERS

Afghanistan has a conservative culture where attitudes to women are bound up with the protection of honour. Society generally seeks to minimise contact between unrelated men and women. As a result foreign women travelling or working on their own, away from male relatives, are often viewed with a mixture of curiosity and astonishment. Being disregarded is a common reaction, and if you're with a male companion you shouldn't be surprised if an Afghan directs his attention and conversation in that direction.

There is no legal obligation to wear a headscarf, but in practice all foreign women do. Walking around Kabul with a bare head would attract a lot of attention; in the countryside such behaviour would be nothing short of scandalous. As a general rule, the more conservative or rural the area you are in, the more discreetly you should dress. In keeping with local sensibilities, your clothes should hide the shape of your body. Bare arms and tight fitting clothes should be avoided, but whatever you wear you'll still have to get used to being stared at. Trying to wear the burqa is both unnecessary and a cultural no-no for foreign women. The *pirhan tonban* (traditional male clothes; also called *shalwar kameez*) of baggy trousers and long shirt is comfortable and popular with many women working in Afghanistan. Baggy clothes can also provide useful cover should you need to go to the toilet while travelling off the beaten track. Facilities in chaikhanas are usually limited.

Foreign women can interact with Afghan women in a way impossible for men. Afghan men may also make special allowances for your status. 'I often joke that there are three genders here: male, female, and foreign woman', commented one female NGO worker we met during research. Afghan men can sometimes be unsure about the correct protocol of dealing with a foreign woman. It's best to wait for them to offer a hand to shake rather than offering your own, and try to avoid excessive eye contact with Afghan men you don't know. If harassed in a public place, several women have advised making a loud scene to shame your harasser. Avoiding walking alone at night is advice we'd equally extend to foreign men. You'll also need to cultivate patience and learn to trust your own instincts.

Transport

CONTENTS

Getting There & Away	**212**
Entering Afghanistan	212
Air	212
Land	215
Tours	217
Getting Around	**218**
Air	218
Bus & Minibus	218
Car	219
Hitching	220

TRANSPORT

GETTING THERE & AWAY

There are few direct flights to Afghanistan from outside the immediate region. The most popular route from Europe or North America is to fly to Dubai, from where there are plenty of connections to Kabul. Coming from the east, the most convenient hubs to catch flights from are Delhi and Islamabad.

Entering by land, Afghanistan maintains open border crossings with all its neighbours except China.

ENTERING AFGHANISTAN

When entering the country by air, formalities are fairly simple, but be prepared for long queues. You'll have to fill in an entry form stating the purpose of your visit and your profession. Baggage reclaim can sometimes be something of a scrum, but at least the carousel normally has electricity these days. Customs checks on arrival are fairly cursory.

Crossing land borders is also usually straightforward, but customs checks on leaving Afghanistan to neighbouring countries, particularly the Central Asian republics and Iran, can often be exceedingly thorough.

There is no currency declaration unless you're carrying cash worth more than 1,000,000Afg (US$20,000), in which case you need a Currency and Negotiable Bearer Instrument Report. In practice, this is only checked on exiting Afghanistan, and can b obtained before leaving at Da Afghanista Bank in Kabul or at the airport.

AIR

Airports & Airlines

Currently only **Kabul International Airport** (KB ☎ 020 2300 016) receives commercial flight into Afghanistan. There is an ATM and cur rency exchange at the airport. At the tim of research, Ariana had announced a direc Kandahar–Dubai service.

There's a restricted choice of airlines fly ing to Kabul. Since the fall of the Taliban plenty of airlines have announced services including Lufthansa, Qatar Airways an Turkish Airlines – only to cancel then abruptly, either due to security concerns or (it's rumoured) pressure from vested Af ghan interests.

INTERNATIONAL AIRLINES IN AFGHANISTAN

Air Arabia (G9; ☎ 079 9700 095; www.airarabia.com; hub Sharjah International Airport) Flights suspended at the time of research.

Ariana Afghan Airlines (FG; ☎ 020 2100 271; www .flyariana.com; hub Kabul International Airport)

Azerbaijan Airlines (J2; ☎ 070 296 914; www.azal.az; hub Heydar Aliyev Airport, Baku)

Indian Airlines (IC; ☎ 079 9308 303; www.indian-air lines.nic.in; hub Indira Gandhi International Airport, Delhi)

Kam Air (RQ; ☎ 020 2301 753; www.flykamair.com; hu Kabul International Airport)

Pakistan International Airlines (PK; ☎ 020 2203 500; www.piac.com.pk; hub Islamabad International Airport)

THINGS CHANGE...

The information in this chapter is particularly vulnerable to change. Check directly with your airline or travel agent to make sure you understand how a fare (and ticket you may buy) works and be aware of the security requirements for international travel. Shop carefully. The details given in this chapter should be regarded as pointers and are not a substitute for your own careful, up-to-date research.

In addition to the international carriers, there are also three carriers serving the international community: the International Committee of the Red Cross (ICRC), Pactec and the UN Humanitarian Air Service (UNHAS). While primarily operating domestic flights, they do offer some international connections to Islamabad (Pactec and UNHAS), Dubai and Dushanbe (UNHAS only). ICRC flights all originate in Peshawar. Flights are only open to accredited NGO workers. For more information see p218.

Tickets

Not many travel agencies (traditional or online) outside Afghanistan will issue tickets for Ariana or Kam Air – see individual regions in this chapter for more information. It's now possible to book online with Ariana, with Kam Air about to follow suit as this book was being researched. Note that when booking return flights, both Ariana and Kam Air frequently issue open returns by default so it's essential to check this when booking, and always reconfirm your tickets in Kabul.

There is very little seasonal variation in pricing for flights to Afghanistan, but demand can be heavy in the run-up to the Nauroz and Eid al-Adha holidays.

Airline Safety

Flying into Kabul has always been a bit of an adventure. In the 1980s and '90s, approaching planes had to steeply corkscrew when approaching the airport as an anti-missile defence, while as recently as 2006, new arrivals were greeted by the sight of the 'Ariana Graveyard', a twisted and shattered junkpile of destroyed airliners. The same year also finally saw the installation of a radar system at the airport.

Poor maintenance has been a worry for Ariana flights, and the UN and many embassies ban their staff from flying with the airline, which has also been barred from EU airspace. Much of the fleet are second-hand planes from Indian Airlines, but these are slowly being replaced. Kam Air uses newer planes and is generally regarded as being better run, but it has Afghanistan's one recent fatal crash to its name: a flight between Herat and Kabul crashed in February 2005 with the loss of 104 lives. Snowy conditions were blamed.

Winter can cause severe problems at the 1800m-high Kabul airport, and flights are frequently cancelled due to snow and poor visibility. Factor in extra travel time if visiting Afghanistan during the winter, as delays can last several days.

TRANSPORT

TRANSPORT

DEPARTURE TAX

There is a 500Afg/US$10 departure tax upon flying out of Afghanistan. Domestic flights have a departure tax of 50Afg/US$1.

Europe

Ariana operates a weekly flight between Frankfurt (Germany) and Kabul, as well as a weekly flight every Monday between Moscow and Kabul, with a stopover in Baku (Azerbaijan). The Frankfurt flight uses new planes to allow Ariana to operate in EU airspace. There are flights between Istanbul (Turkey) and Kabul every Tuesday and Friday, the latter via Ankara (Turkey). Ariana has offices in these countries:

Azerbaijan (☎ 12 93805; 16 Pushkin St, intersection 28th of May, Baku 1010)
Germany (☎ 69 2562 7940; Frankfurt Airport)
Russia (☎ 495-2026269; 8/1 Povarskaia St, 121069 Moscow)
Turkey (☎ 212-664 6930; Yenidoğan Mh. 42, sok 76 Zeytinbumu, Istanbul)

At the time of research, Kam Air had just announced a weekly Istanbul–Kabul service, and **Azerbaijan Airways** (☎ 12 493 4004; booking@azal.az; 66-68 28th of May St, Baku 1010) flies between Baku and Kabul every Wednesday.

In the UK, agents selling Ariana and Kam Air tickets include **Ariana Travel** (☎ 020 8843 0011; arianatravel@hotmail.com; 136 The Broadway, Southall, IB1 1QN) and **Afghan Travel Centre** (☎ 020 7580 7000; 107 Great Portland Street, London).

Middle East

Dubai is the busiest route into Kabul, with Ariana and Kam Air both operating daily flights, as well as a new Ariana Kandahar–Dubai route.

It's important to note that while the vast majority of international flights to Dubai arrive at Terminal 1, flights to Kabul are via the completely separate Terminal 2. There is a free airport bus (15 minutes) linking the two, alternatively a taxi will cost about 25AED. As flying via Dubai involves a change of airline as well as terminal, passengers cannot normally check their bags through all the way to Kabul. This means having to go through UAE immigration on arrival at Dubai before transiting to Terminal 2. Visas are not required for citizens of most developed countries including all EU states, the USA, Canada, Australia, New Zealand, Japan, Korea and Singapore – but check requirements before travel.

The cargo airline **DFS** (☎ 04 299 7556; www .dfsmiddleeast.com) sometimes sells seats on its Dubai–Kandahar flight.

In Dubai, **Eisa Travels** (☎ 04 223 7348; PO Box 11266) represents Ariana. **Kam Air** (☎ 04 223 6060; kamairdubai@hotmail.com; near Emirates Bank, Baniyas Rd) sells tickets direct.

From Iran, **Ariana** (☎ 021 8855 0156; Block 29, Kheyaban Khalid, Tehran) run a weekly service from Tehran, while Kam Air have a weekly flight to Mashhad. **Iran Asseman** (☎ 021 8889 5567; www .iaa.ir; Enqelab Ave, Nejatollahi St, Tehran) have one flight a week from Tehran to Kabul via Mashhad. Ariana also fly to Jeddah, Saudi Arabia.

Asia

From India, both **Ariana** (☎ 11-2687 7808; Ashok Hotel, Chanakyapuri, New Delhi) and Kam Air fly twice weekly from Delhi. Ariana also has an Amritsar–Kabul flight. **Indian Airlines** (☎ 11-2331 0517; Malhotra Bldg, Connaught Pl, New Delhi) fly between the Indian and Afghan capitals twice a week.

From Pakistan, **Ariana** (☎ 051 287 0618; Kashmir Commercial Complex, Fazel-e-Haq Rd, Blue Area, Islamabad) fly once a week from Islamabad. **PIA** (☎ 111-786-786; Quaid-i-Azam Airport, Karachi) operate an identical schedule.

Both Ariana and Kam Air fly once a week to Almaty (Kazakhstan). There's also a weekly flight to Dushanbe (Tajikistan) with **Ariana** (☎ 1413-669 880).

North America

There are no direct flights between North America and Afghanistan. In 2006 **Ariana** (☎ 866-330 3431) started offering online booking packages from the USA and Canada to Kabul, including connecting flights with either Lufthansa or Air France to their direct Frankfurt–Kabul service. In Canada, you can also try the **Ariana GSA** (☎ 905-389-0999; 203-801 Mohawk Rd West, Hamilton, Ontario, L9C 6C2). For Kam Air tickets in the USA or Canada contact **Kam Air** (☎ 888-952-6247; sales@flykamair.ca).

In the USA, other agents who can arrange flights to Afghanistan include **Afghan Tours & Travel** (☎ 703-998 7676, ext 222; ahmedb1961@yahoo .com; 4300 King Street, Suite 139; Alexandria, VA 22302) or **Pamir Travel** (☎ 510-791 5566; hashmat@pamirtravels .com; 37477 Fremont Blvd. Suite C, Fremont, CA 94536).

LAND

Afghanistan's traditional position as the crossroads of Asia can make entering the country by land an evocative trip. Sneaking over the high passes like so many Great Gamers or journalists with the mujaheddin (Islamic fighters) is, however, no longer necessary: border procedures are, for the most part, a formality these days.

Iran

Crossing from Mashhad in Iran to Herat is one of the most straightforward entry points to Afghanistan. Alexander the Great pioneered this overland route, followed nearly 2500 years later by the Hippy Trail. In the 1970s, as some Afghans grew weary of the kaftan-clad hordes, a sign appeared in the consulate in Mashhad: 'Visas will not be given to people with long beards or hair like that of beetle.'

The highway between Herat and the border crossing at Islam Qala (Taybad in Iran) has recently been upgraded, allowing a quick transit. Direct buses run daily from Mashhad to Herat (IR70,000, seven hours), which is slightly cheaper than travelling piecemeal from Mashhad. On the Afghan side of the border, note the huge parks of vehicles imported from Dubai and waiting to clear customs. From Islam Qala it's around 90 minutes' drive to Herat. There are plenty of shared taxis (60Afg) after immigration. There are also direct Herat–Mashhad buses (see p141 for details).

Mashhad is an excellent jumping-off point for Herat. The Great Mosque in the vast Emam Reza Shrine Complex is the most outstanding surviving building commissioned by Gowhar Shad (p138). A dazzling confection of Timurid mosaic tiling, it gives a taste of how Herat's Musalla Complex must once have looked, and should not be missed.

Pakistan

There are two official border crossings open to foreigners between Pakistan and Afghanistan: at Torkham between Peshawar and Jalalabad through the Khyber Pass, and at Spin Boldak (Chaman on the Pakistani side), equidistant between Quetta and Kandahar. In the current political climate, we strongly advise against attempting to cross the latter border independently – see p190 for more information. For trekking into north Pakistan from the Wakhan Corridor, see p172.

Minibuses and shared taxis run daily from Kabul and Jalalabad to Torkham. Border formalities on the Afghan side are relaxed, but more chaotic on entering Pakistan. The road from Torkham to Peshawar passes through the Tribal Areas of North West Frontier Province, an autonomous area belonging to the Pashtun tribes where the Pakistan government's writ is light. It is forbidden for foreigners to travel on this road without an armed guard from the Khyber Rifles – you'll be assigned one after immigration. There's no fee, but the soldier will expect a tip of around Rs200 once you get to Peshawar. Technically foreigners are also forbidden to take public transport on this road, leaving a taxi (Rs1200, two hours) the only option, although we've heard of a few travellers who have snuck onto local buses.

From Peshawar to Torkham, some paperwork is involved. You need a Tribal Area Permit, obtained for free at the **Home Department of Tribal Affairs** (☎ 9210507; off Saddar Rd), to travel to the border. Take your passport plus photocopies of your Afghan and Pakistani visas and the photo page to the Foreign Section staff office on the third floor. The permit specifies the exact date of travel, and should be applied for no more than two days in advance. With luck, the process takes around an hour. Make three or four photocopies of the permit to give to police checkpoints along the route.

Ideally arrange a taxi the day before travel. Before leaving Peshawar you must go to the **Khyber Political Agent** (Stadium Rd) to collect your gunman. Without him you'll be turned back at the first checkpoint. There's plenty to see as you drive through the Khyber. Look out for the army badges on the hills near Jamrud Fort, belonging to British and Pakistani regiments who served here. The massive fortified home of the notorious drug smuggler Ayub Afridi at Landi Kotal (complete with anti-aircraft guns) is also unmissable, and a keen reminder about who really rules this part of the country. There are good views of the Khyber and across to Torkham from Michni checkpoint, but ignore the children who assail you trying to sell afghani banknotes at over-inflated rates.

Onward transport from Torkham is plentiful, and you'll probably get mobbed by touts so keep control of your bags. Travelling straight through, if you leave Peshawar at 8am, you should arrive in Kabul by around 4pm. See p185 for transport options once in Afghanistan.

Afghan and Pakistani authorities make regular pronouncements on establishing a direct Peshawar–Jalalabad bus service, but at the time of research, there had only been a few erratic departures. It's not known whether foreigners will be allowed to take this service if it runs regularly in the future.

Tajikistan

There are three crossing points between Afghanistan and Tajikistan, two of which are in Badakhshan. The busiest and most accessible is at Shir Khan Bandar near Kunduz. The Badakhshan border posts are at Ishkashim and Khorog.

From Shir Khan Bandar there is a daily ferry (US$10) across the Amu Darya to the Tajik town of Panj-e Payon (Nizhniy Panj on old maps). The ferry leaves Panj-e Payon at 10am, and Shir Khan Bandar after lunch. There's no ferry on Sundays. A new bridge has been built across the river here that will make this border crossing quicker, and was due to be inaugurated as we went to press.

There are daily shared taxis between Panj-e Payon to Dushanbe (TJS50, four hours). On the Afghan side, it's one hour by shared taxi to Kunduz (80Afg). With a very early start, it's just about possible to travel overland between Dushanbe and Kabul in one long day.

The borders in Badakhshan are easier crossing into Afghanistan. The Tajik side of the border is the Gorno–Badakhshan Autonomous Oblast (GBAO) for which a special permit is required. This is normally only available in Dushanbe, but anecdotal evidence suggests that persistence can sometimes persuade the Tajik embassy in Kabul to issue the necessary paperwork. Contact Great Game Travel (see opposite) which also has an office in Dushanbe, and can help arrange GBAO permits.

The border crossing at Ishkashim is open Monday to Thursday. There's a bridge across the Panj River here, a couple of kilometres from both towns. There's a daily minibus between Afghan Ishkashim to Faizabad (600Afg, eight hours). On the Tajik side there are a couple of homestays, and onward transport to Khorog (TJS20, three hours).

The largest town in Tajik Badakhshan, Khorog also has a border crossing, as well an Afghan consulate. The border crossing is a bridge over the Panj. While a good road connects Khorog to the rest of Tajikistan, transport connections are extremely scant on the Afghan side. If you don't have your own vehicle, hire is very expensive. A bad road leads west past Lake Shewa to Faizabad, but despite what some maps say, there's no road south along the river to Ishkashim.

Turkmenistan

There are two official border crossings on the Afghan–Turkmen border. Torghundi in Afghanistan to Serkhetabat in Turkmenistan (Kushka or Gushgi on some maps) is the border crossing more commonly used, due to its proximity to Herat. A more obscure alternative is at Imam Nazar, near Andkhoi.

The Turkmen authorities love paperwork. To enter the country overland, you need to have your point of entry marked on your visa. For tourist visas, you generally also have to be met at the border by an official guide.

From Herat, shared taxis run irregularly to Torghundi, and you'll probably end up having to hire one outright (1000Afg, two hours). The road is poorly maintained and may be problematic in winter. Make sure the driver takes you to the actual border, which is 4km past the town. There's a customs fee of 550Afg. The Turkmen border is a 1.5km walk past the Afghan post, and the waiting customs officials will probably take your luggage apart. There's an entry tax of US$10 (with US$1 bank fee). You must also declare all foreign currency and register with the police on arrival – keep the receipt as it's checked when leaving the country.

There's no accommodation at Serkhetabat, so the best option is to head to Mary. As the border is regarded as sensitive by the Turkmen authorities, a special permit from the capital is required to stop overnight in the area. There are road and rail links to Mary (the railway actually extends a few kilometres into Afghanistan for freight trains).

The border post in the flat steppe at Imam Nazar is far more remote, and not even marked on all maps. The exact demarcation of the border has become disputed in recent years due to the shifting Amu Darya and Murghab rivers, with Turkmenistan now claiming areas that have always been Afghan. As a result, cross-border traffic has dwindled to a trickle, but is still possible for the adventurous.

There is no public transport linking Andkhoi to Imam Nazar or on to Kerki once you're in Turkmenistan, and as there's barely a road a 4WD is recommended. Anticipate paying around 1000Afg for the two-hour trip. Wet conditions can make this route very tough in spring and into summer. The Turkmen border post is a 2.5km walk past Afghan immigration. Once in, take whatever transport is available to Kerki, another two hours on a rough and rolling track.

Uzbekistan
The Friendship Bridge across the Amu Darya links Hairatan in Afghanistan to Termiz in Uzbekistan. Its name became something of a bad joke when it turned into the main invasion route into Afghanistan for the Red Army in 1979. Although technically an open border, Uzbekistan's police-state paranoia can make crossing here something of an unknown quantity at times.

The border was officially opened to tourist traffic in 2005, but the message doesn't seem to have reached all the Uzbek officials at the bridge. While we've had several reports of independent crossing here without problems, a few have reported that only people on accredited business were being allowed to enter or leave Uzbekistan here. For humanitarian workers, this involves a letter being sent to the Termiz UN office, where your details are accredited and passed on to the border officials who put your name on a list of those approved to cross the border on that particular date.

If the border continues to be subject to the whims of the bureaucrats, we suggest contacting the Uzbek embassy in Kabul before heading to the border, and asking for written permission to cross to Termiz. If you're in Uzbekistan, talk to a reliable Tashkent travel agency or contact the **Office of Visas & Registration** (OVIR; ☎ 132 6570) in Tashkent directly.

Assuming the border is open, the easiest way to get to Hairatan is from Mazar-e

Sharif by private taxi (500Afg, 30 minutes). Shared taxis are scarce. The Amu Darya is wide here and it takes around 10 minutes to walk across the bridge. The Uzbek border guards are pretty surly. The bridge is 10km from the centre of Termiz, and there are a few *marshrutka* (minibuses) that make the run into town (S200, 20 minutes).

Termiz has several interesting Buddhist and Islamic sites that make lingering a day worthwhile, but note that its location on a sensitive border means you need to register with OVIR on arrival if staying overnight.

TOURS
The changeable nature of Afghanistan means that travelling with a reliable tour operator can sometimes be a better option than going independently. Always ask about the company's security procedures before booking.

Afghanistan
Afghan Logistics & Tours (Pvt) Ltd (☎ 070 277408/ 079 9391 462; www.afghanlogisticstours.com; House 106, Street 1, Charahi Ansari, Shahr-e Nau, Kabul) Experienced operator with individual and group tours across the country. Also offer translators and vehicle hire.
Great Game Travel (☎ 079 9489 120/077 9489 120; www.greatgametravel.com; Street 3/1 House 3, Proje Wazirabad, Proje Taimani, Kabul) High-quality secure jeep tours and mountain trekking mainly in northern Afghanistan. Also has offices in Faizabad and Dushanbe.

UK
Hinterland (☎ 01883 743584; www.hinterlandtravel.com) Rugged overland trips crossing Afghanistan from Iran to Pakistan.
Live! Travel (☎ 020 8894 6104; www.live-travel.com; 120 Hounslow Rd, Twickenham, TW2 7HB) Tailor-made cultural trips.
Wild Frontiers (☎ 020 7736 3968; www.wildfrontiers .co.uk; Unit 6, Townmead Business Centre, William Morris Way, London SW6 2SZ) Group tours to north Afghanistan, including Badakhshan.

USA
Distant Horizons (☎ 800 333 1240; www.distant -horizons.com; 350 Elm Avenue Long Beach, CA 90802) Cultural tours of Afghanistan, often in conjunction with Tajikistan or Pakistan.
Reality Tours (☎ 415 255 7296; www.globalexchange .org; 2017 Mission Street #303, San Francisco, CA 94110) Alternative travel, centred on visiting community groups and NGOs working in Afghanistan.

TRANSPORT

TRANSPORT

GETTING AROUND

AIR

The two Afghan airlines, **Ariana** (☎ 020 2100 271; www.flyariana.com) and **Kam Air** (☎ 020 2301 753; www.flykamair.com) both operate domestic schedules, linking Kabul with daily flights to Herat and Mazar-e Sharif, and Kandahar several times a week. There's also a weekly Ariana Kandahar–Herat flight. For other destinations, the schedule is an extremely moveable feast. In theory, Ariana also operates a twice-weekly flight to Faizabad, and weekly flights to Kunduz, Maimana and Shiberghan. In practice, these services can be cancelled for months at a time. Contact Ariana in Kabul, as the provincial offices are usually shut except on days immediately preceding a rare flight. Neither airlines' websites are much help for domestic flights.

Kam Air operates a reliable twice-weekly flight between Herat and Mazar-e Sharif. It has toyed with a Kabul–Faizabad service but has only operated a few flights and has yet to open an office in the town. Kandahar and Maimana flights are also apparently planned.

Demand is high for flights, so book as far in advance as you can. Ariana's Kabul office can be chaotic but is surprisingly efficient. Kam Air run a slightly tighter ship. Elsewhere, things are more disorganised so you might need to be persistent to get your name on the list. You'll need your passport when you book your ticket.

Always recheck the time of departure the day before you fly. Schedule changes are both common and unexplained. If you're in the provinces you'll probably depart late anyway, as you wait for the plane to arrive from Kabul.

Humanitarian Airlines in Afghanistan

Three airlines serve the humanitarian community within Afghanistan, with flights only open to those working for accredited NGOs and nonprofit organisations. Most of the flights are operated with small Beechcraft planes, and for certain routes stricter than normal baggage limits may be applied due to flying conditions.

ICRC Air Operations (International Committee of the Red Cross; ☎ 070 285948; kabul.kab@icrc.org; Charahi Haji Yaqub) Scheduled flights to Jalalabad, Mazar-e Sharif,

Herat, Kunduz, Faizabad and Kandahar. Flights originate in Peshawar and are via Kabul. No flights on Fridays.
Pactec (☎ 070 282679/079 9300 837; bookingkbl@pactec.net; Street 15, Right Lane 1, House 12, Wazir Akbar Khan, Kabul) Scheduled flights to Bamiyan, Chaghcheran, Faizabad, Farah, Herat, Kandahar, Kunduz, Lashkar Gah, Maimana, Qala-e Nau, Taloqan and Yawkawlang. Can also arrange charter flights.
United Nations Humanitarian Air Service (UNHAS; ☎ 070 284070/282559; kabul.unhas@wfp.org; WFP Compound, btwn Charahi Zambak & Charahi Ariana, Shahr-e Nau, Kabul) Scheduled flights to Bamiyan, Faizabad, Herat, Jalalabad, Kandahar, Kunduz, Maimana and Mazar-e Sharif.

BUS & MINIBUS

Getting around by bus and minibus isn't always terrifically comfortable, but it's undeniably cheap and services run to most places you'll want to get to. The road distances chart (opposite) shows approximate road distances between major towns and cities.

Afghanistan is held together by the minibus. Toyota HiAces are the most favoured, and are seemingly indestructible in the face of terrible road conditions. They're known locally as *falang,* a corruption of 'flying coach'. Also popular are the slightly smaller TownAces. Passengers are squeezed in four to a row, or three in a TownAce. If you're male, don't be surprised if your arrival forces a change in seating arrangements, to stop you sitting next to an Afghan woman. There are no timetables, vehicles just leave when they've collected enough passengers. The smaller TownAces tend to fill up and depart quicker, and are also slightly faster, so there's a slight increase in the fare. A fare that costs 450Afg in a HiAce would be about 100Afg more in a TownAce. Prices also fluctuate according to demand – a trip to Kabul would normally be cheaper than a journey to Faizabad of the same length. Unless you've got particularly huge bags, there shouldn't be a luggage charge.

Transport generally leaves from motor parks on the edges of towns. They're lively places, with touts barking out their destinations, beggars and kids hawking snacks and goods. Most places will have some sort of chaikhana where you can get a cup of tea while waiting for your vehicle to fill. Shared taxis can also be found here.

The comfort factor of your trip depends on the destination as much as the size of the passengers you're squeezed next to. Simple journeys along sealed roads are usually fine but anywhere else can be bumpy and painful, particularly over long distances. It can sometimes be a good idea to buy an extra seat to give yourself some extra room, a tactic we highly recommend if tackling the central route or northwest Afghanistan. Drivers tend to stop every three or four hours for prayers and at chaikhanas for food. On long trips you might end up staying the night at one, so ensure you have a blanket or sleeping bag easily accessible (for more information see p199).

Clunky old German buses also ply Afghanistan's roads. Painfully slow and overcrowded, they're only used by the poorest locals and those unconcerned about time or comfort. On a slightly higher level, there are coaches running along the Ring Rd from Mazar-e Sharif to Kabul and on to Herat. Cheaper than a HiAce, tickets can normally be bought a day in advance from a bus office. As the Kabul-Herat leg passes through Kandahar and the restive south, we strongly advise against foreigners taking this route in the current climate.

CAR

Roads are generally of a poor quality in Kabul. The Ring Rd from Herat to Kandahar, Kabul and up to Mazar-e Sharif is paved, along with link highways from the Pakistan border to Kabul, and from Iran to Herat. Elsewhere, roads are gravel or worse, and road reconstruction continues to be depressingly slow.

Road rules are extremely lax, but most vehicles at least aspire to drive on the right. Wherever tarmac allows drivers to get some speed up, accidents are common. The Kabul–Mazar-e Sharif highway is particularly bad in this respect, where drivers seem to view the road more as a venue for a game of motorised *buzkashi* rather than a conduit for getting from A to B. Watch out for the very Afghan practice of turning old tank tracks into speed bumps.

Beware of driving off-road due to the risk of landmines and unexploded ordnances (UXOs). In areas of instability, high-visibility white NGO vehicles have sometimes been deliberately targeted by criminals and insurgents. Travel at night is not recommended.

TRANSPORT

ROAD DISTANCES (KM)

	Bamiyan	Chaghcheran	Faizabad	Ghanzi	Herat	Jalalabad	Kabul	Kandahar	Kunduz	Lashkar Gah	Maimana	Mazar-e Sharif	Pul-e Khumri	Shiberghan	Torkham
Bamiyan	---														
Chaghcheran	398	---													
Faizabad	692	1090	---												
Ghanzi	382	780	742	---											
Herat	892	492	1329	915	---										
Jalalabad	387	785	747	195	1203	---									
Kabul	237	635	597	145	1053	150	---								
Kandahar	725	1200	1085	350	565	638	488	---							
Kunduz	432	830	260	482	1390	487	337	825	---						
Lashkar Gah	862	1337	1222	487	435	775	625	137	962	---					
Maimana	1352	952	869	877	460	880	773	1025	609	895	---				
Mazar-e Sharif	525	923	567	573	800	578	428	916	307	1053	302	---			
Pul-e Khumri	325	723	110	373	1000	378	228	716	107	853	502	200	---		
Shiberghan	657	1055	699	705	630	710	560	1048	439	1185	170	132	332	---	
Torkham	462	860	822	370	1280	75	225	713	562	850	955	653	455	785	---

If travelling in remote areas or in winter, your vehicle should contain adequate tools and spares, emergency rations and (ideally) communication equipment. For more security tips for the road, see p73.

Hire

It's not possible to hire cars without drivers in Afghanistan. In Kabul there are a number of private companies that hire out reliable vehicles with drivers such as Afghan Logistics & Tours (see p104). Outside Kabul, the best bet is to ask at your hotel or the transport park, and get trustworthy recommendations if possible.

Hiring a 4WD with driver (typically a Toyota Landcruiser or Surf) typically costs around US$150 per day, including fuel.

Taxi

There are two main ways of travelling by car in Afghanistan if you don't have your own vehicle: ordinary taxi or shared taxi.

ORDINARY TAXI

In this case you'd hire an entire taxi for a special route, ideal for reaching off-the-beaten-track places, or where minibus connections are hit-and-miss. A private taxi allows you to stop at will and will hopefully give you some control over the manic tendencies latent in many Afghan drivers – don't be afraid to suggest a preference for the brake over the accelerator pedal. Select your driver with care, and always look over his vehicle. If you're travelling solo, it's often recommended to visibly note the car's registration number and phone it through to a friend with your itinerary.

You'll have to negotiate a price before setting off. Along routes where there are also shared taxis this is simple arithmetic, adding up the total number of individual fares. Make sure everyone is clear which route you'll be taking, how long you want the driver to wait for you at the destination and whether or not fuel is included. You may have to haggle hard, as many drivers will see the opportunity to add 'foreigner inflation' to the price.

SHARED TAXI

Aside from minibuses, shared taxi is the main form of road transport around Afghanistan, and operates on the same principle, whereby a yellow taxi or private car does a regular run between two destinations and charges a set fare for each of the seats in the car. These cars can almost always be found in the same transport depots as minibuses. Fares are more expensive than a minibus, but you reach your destination faster.

Most shared taxis are yellow Toyota Corollas, and typically take two passengers in the front seat and three in the back seat. The front middle seat can be quite uncomfortable on bad roads, leaving you getting friendly with either the driver or the gear stick. Drivers will often sell the front seat to just one passenger at a slight premium. It's always possible to buy an extra seat for comfort or just to get the car to depart faster.

HITCHING

Hitching is never entirely safe in any country in the world, and we certainly don't recommend it in Afghanistan. Travellers who decide to hitch should understand that they are taking a small, but potentially very serious risk. Never try flagging down a lift in areas where security is known to be poor.

In Afghanistan there is little meaningful distinction between hitching and taking a taxis. Anyone with a car will stop if you flag them down. Drivers usually expect some money for picking you up, so it's best to offer a little; it may be refused, but it's more likely not to be. Keep public transport fares in mind so that, should you strike someone trying to extort silly amounts from you, you'll have some idea of how much is fair to offer. Many Afghans will be baffled by the sight of a foreigner without a vehicle and pick you up out of curiosity.

In some parts of Afghanistan, hitching a ride on trucks can sometimes be the only way of getting around – for example on the central route in winter. The big Kamaz trucks normally get through, but can be painfully slow. Most NGOs are banned from picking up passengers on the road.

Health

CONTENTS

Before You Go	**221**
Insurance	221
Recommended Vaccinations	221
Medical Checklist	222
Internet Resources	222
Further Reading	222
In Transit	**222**
Deep Vein Thrombosis (DVT)	222
Jet Lag & Motion Sickness	223
In Afghanistan	**223**
Availability & Cost of Health Care	223
Traveller's Diarrhoea	223
Infectious Diseases	223
Environmental Hazards	225
Women's Health	226

Prevention is the key to staying healthy while travelling in Afghanistan. With luck, the worst complaint you might come down with on your trip is a bad stomach; while serious infectious diseases can and do occur in Afghanistan, these are usually associated with poor living conditions and can be avoided with a few precautions.

BEFORE YOU GO

Health matters often get left to the last minute before travelling. A little planning is advisable, however – some vaccines don't ensure immunity for two weeks, so visit a doctor four to eight weeks before departure.

Travellers can register with the **International Association for Medical Advice to Travellers** (IAMAT; www.iamat.org). Their website can help travellers to find a doctor with recognised training. Those heading off to very remote areas (particularly for work) may find a first-aid course useful.

Bring medications in their original, clearly labelled, containers. A signed and dated letter from your physician describing your medical conditions and medications, including generic names, is also a good idea. If carrying syringes or needles, be sure to have a physician's letter documenting their medical necessity. See your dentist before a long trip; carry a spare pair of contact lenses and glasses (and take your optical prescription with you).

INSURANCE

Adequate health insurance is vital when travelling to Afghanistan. Check in advance that your insurance plan will make payments directly to providers or reimburse you later for overseas health expenditures – doctors in Afghanistan expect payment on the spot. Your policy should ideally also cover emergency air-evacuation home, which may be essential for serious problems. For more on insurance issues regarding Afghanistan as a conflict zone see p205.

RECOMMENDED VACCINATIONS

Specialised travel-medicine clinics are your best source of information; they stock all available vaccines and will be able to give specific recommendations for you and your trip. Ask your doctor for an International Certificate of Vaccination (otherwise known as the yellow booklet), which will list all the vaccinations you've received.

Yellow fever vaccination is mandatory if arriving from a country where the disease is endemic. The World Health Organization also recommends the following vaccinations for travellers to Afghanistan:

Adult Diphtheria & Tetanus Single booster recommended if none in the previous 10 years. Side effects include sore arm and fever.

Hepatitis A Provides almost 100% protection for up to a year; a booster after 12 months provides at least another 20 years' protection. Mild side effects such as headache and sore arm occur in 5% to 10% of people.

Hepatitis B Now considered routine for most travellers. Usually given as three shots over six months, a rapid schedule is also available, as is a combined vaccination with Hepatitis A. Side effects are mild and uncommon, usually headache and sore arm. In 95% of people lifetime protection results.

Measles, Mumps & Rubella Two doses required unless you have had the diseases. Occasionally a rash and flulike illness can develop a week after receiving the vaccine. Many young adults require a booster.

Polio Only one booster is required as an adult for lifetime protection.

Typhoid Recommended unless your trip is for less than a week. The vaccine offers around 70% protection, lasts for two to three years and comes as a single shot. Tablets are also available, but the injection is usually recommended as it has fewer side effects. Sore arm and fever may occur.

These immunisations are recommended for long-term visitors (more than one month) or those at special risk:

Japanese B Encephalitis Three injections, with a booster recommended after two years. Sore arm and headache are the most common side-effects.

Meningitis Single injection. There are two types: the quadrivalent vaccine gives two to three years' protection; the meningitis group C vaccine gives around 10 years' protection. Recommended for long-term visitors aged under 25.

Rabies Three injections in all. A booster after one year provides 10 years' protection Side effects are rare – occasionally headache and sore arm.

MEDICAL CHECKLIST

Following is a list of other items you should consider packing in your medical kit when you are travelling.

- Antibiotics (if travelling off the beaten track)
- Antibacterial hand gel
- Antidiarrhoeal drugs (eg loperamide)
- Paracetamol (eg Tylenol) or aspirin
- Anti-inflammatory drugs (eg ibuprofen)
- Antihistamines (for hay fever and allergic reactions)
- Antibacterial ointment (eg Bactroban) for cuts and abrasions
- Steroid cream or cortisone (allergic rashes)
- Bandages, gauze, gauze rolls
- Adhesive or paper tape
- Scissors, safety pins, tweezers
- Thermometer
- Pocket knife
- DEET-containing insect repellent for the skin
- Permethrin-containing insect spray for clothing, tents, and bed nets
- Sun block
- Oral rehydration salts
- Iodine tablets (for water purification)
- Syringes and sterile needles (if travelling to remote areas)

INTERNET RESOURCES

There is a wealth of travel health advice on the Internet. The **World Health Organization** (www.who.int/ith/) is an excellent resource

> **TRAVEL HEALTH WEBSITES**
>
> The following government travel health websites are useful resources to consult prior to departure:
> **Australia** (www.smartraveller.gov.au)
> **Canada** (www.hc-sc.gc.ca/english/index.html)
> **UK** (www.dh.gov.uk/policyandguidance/health advicefortravellers/)
> **United States** (www.cdc.gov/travel/)

for travel health information, along with **MD Travel Health** (www.mdtravelhealth.com), which provides complete travel health recommendations for every country.

FURTHER READING

Lonely Planet's *Healthy Travel Asia & India* is packed with useful information including pretrip planning, emergency first aid, immunisation and disease information, and what to do if you get sick on the road. Other recommended references include *Travellers' Health* by Dr Richard Dawood (Oxford University Press) and *The Travellers' Good Health Guide* by Ted Lankester (Sheldon Press), an especially useful health guide for long-term expatriates working in the region.

IN TRANSIT

DEEP VEIN THROMBOSIS (DVT)

Deep vein thrombosis occurs when blood clots form in the legs during plane flights, chiefly because of prolonged immobility. The longer the flight, the greater the risk. Though most clots are reabsorbed uneventfully, some may break off and travel through the blood vessels to the lungs, where they may cause life-threatening complications.

The chief symptom of DVT is swelling or pain in the lower leg, usually but not always on just one side. When a blood clot travels to the lungs, it may cause chest pain and difficulty breathing. Travellers with any of these symptoms should immediately seek medical attention.

To prevent the development of DVT on long flights you should walk about the cabin, regularly contract your leg muscles while sitting and drink plenty of fluids. Recent research also indicates that flight socks, which gently compress the leg from the knee down, encourage blood to flow properly in the legs and reduce the risk of DVT by up to 90%.

JET LAG & MOTION SICKNESS

Jet lag is common when crossing more than five time zones; it results in insomnia, fatigue or nausea. To avoid jet lag, set your watch to your destination's time zone when you board your plane, drink plenty of (non-alcoholic) fluids and eat lightly. Upon arrival, seek exposure to natural sunlight and readjust your eating and sleeping schedule as soon as possible.

Antihistamines such as dimenhydrinate (Dramamine) and meclizine (Antivert, Bonine) are usually the first choice for treating motion sickness. Their main side-effect is drowsiness. A herbal alternative is ginger, which works like a charm for some people.

IN AFGHANISTAN

AVAILABILITY & COST OF HEALTH CARE

Health care in Afghanistan is basic at best, and there is a nationwide shortage of doctors. Although there are a handful of good hospitals in Kabul, medical facilities are not generally up to international standards and serious cases are likely to require evacuation. While most towns have pharmacies, it can nevertheless be difficult to find reliable medical care outside the cities. Take care when buying medication, as fake, poorly stored or out-of date drugs are common.

Self-treatment may be appropriate if your problem is minor. If you think you may have a serious disease, especially malaria, do not waste time; travel to the nearest quality facility immediately to receive attention. Recommended hospitals are listed under Information in the major city sections of regional chapters in this book; your embassy may also be a useful contact.

TRAVELLER'S DIARRHOEA

The strains of travel – unfamiliar food, heat, long days and erratic sleeping patterns – can all make your body more susceptible to stomach upsets.

In terms of prevention, eat only fresh fruits or vegetables if they are cooked or if you have washed or peeled them yourself. Water should be treated before drinking. Meals freshly cooked in front of you (like much street food), or served in a busy restaurant are more likely to be safe. It's also very important to pay close attention to personal hygiene while on the road. Afghan meals are eaten with the hand, so always wash before eating (even the smallest restaurant will have water and soap) and after using the toilet. Antibacterial hand gel, which cleans without needing water, is a real travellers' friend.

If you develop diarrhoea, drink plenty of fluids, preferably an oral rehydration solution – readily available in pharmacies. Avoid fatty food and dairy products. A few loose stools don't require treatment but, if you start having more than four or five watery stools a day, you should start taking an antibiotic (usually a quinolone drug) and an antidiarrhoeal agent (such as loperamide). If diarrhoea is bloody, persists for more than 72 hours, is accompanied by fever, shaking chills or severe abdominal pain you should seek medical attention.

Amoebic Dysentery

Amoebic dysentery is actually rare in travellers but is often misdiagnosed. Symptoms are similar to bacterial diarrhoea, ie fever, bloody diarrhoea and generally feeling unwell. You should always seek reliable medical care if you have blood in your diarrhoea. Treatment involves two drugs: Tinidazole or Metroniadzole to kill the parasite in your gut, and a second drug to kill the cysts. If left untreated, complications such as liver or gut abscesses can occur.

Giardiasis

Giardia is a parasite that is relatively common in travellers. Symptoms include nausea, bloating, excess gas, fatigue and intermittent diarrhoea. 'Eggy' burps are often attributed solely to giardia, but work in Nepal has shown that they are not specific to giardia. The parasite will eventually go away if left untreated, but this can take months. The treatment of choice is Tinidazole; Metronidazole is a second option.

INFECTIOUS DISEASES
Diphtheria

Diphtheria is spread through close respiratory contact. It causes a high temperature and severe sore throat. Sometimes a membrane forms across the throat requiring a tracheostomy to prevent suffocation. Vaccination is recommended for those likely to be in close contact with locals in infected areas. The vaccine is given as an injection alone, or with tetanus, and lasts 10 years. Diphtheria outbreaks are not uncommon in Afghanistan, particularly in and around IDP camps.

HIV

HIV is spread via infected blood and blood products and through sexual intercourse with an infected partner. There is a small risk of infection through medical procedures, such as blood transfusion and improperly sterilised medical instruments. At the time of researching this book, Afghanistan had less than 100 officially recorded cases of HIV, but screening was limited to blood donors and the real figure is presumed to be far higher. Increasing drug use and lack of public information may lead to greater infection rates. Be aware that clinics in Kabul treating expats regularly report other sexually transmitted diseases.

Leishmaniasis

Spread through the bite of an infected sand fly, leishmaniasis can cause a slowly growing skin lump or ulcer, leading to disfigurement. It may develop into a serious life-threatening fever usually accompanied with anaemia and weight loss. Sand fly bites (most common between dusk and dawn) should be avoided whenever possible.

Kabul is the largest centre of cutaneous leishmaniasis in the world, although WHO-distributed insecticide-treated bednets are attempting to address the problem, in tandem with its malaria-control programme.

Malaria

There is a significant malaria risk in Afghanistan between May to November in parts of the country below 2000m (including Kabul). Outbreaks most commonly occur after rains or flooding, especially in rural areas. Spread by a parasite transmitted by the bite of an infected mosquito, both *Plasmodium vivax* and *P. falciparum* strains exist in Afghanistan. Remember that malaria can be fatal and the risk of contracting the disease far outweighs the risk of any antimalarial tablet side effects.

The most important symptom of malaria is fever, but general symptoms such as headaches, diarrhoea, cough and chills may also occur. Diagnosis can only be confirmed through a blood sample. Two strategies should be combined to prevent malaria – mosquito avoidance, and prophylactic antimalarial medication.

Travellers are advised to prevent mosquito bites by taking these steps:

- Use a DEET-containing insect repellent on exposed skin. Natural repellents like citronella can be effective, but must be applied more frequently than those containing DEET
- Mosquitoes bite between dusk and dawn: sleep under a permethrin-impregnated mosquito net
- Wear long sleeves and trousers (not a problem with Afghanistan's dress code) in light colours
- Use mosquito coils
- Spray your room with insect repellent

There are a variety of antimalarial medications available. Before travelling, seek medical advice about the right medication and dosage for you. Women should take particular advice if pregnant or taking the contraceptive pill. Note that chloroquine and sulfadoxine-pyrimethamine resistance has been recorded in Afghanistan.

Doxycline A broad-spectrum antibiotic. Potential side-effects include photosensitivity (a tendency to sunburn), indigestion, nausea, and thrush in women. More serious side effects include ulceration of the oesophagus – you can prevent this by taking the tablets with a meal and plenty of water, and never lying down within 30 minutes of taking them. Doxycycline must be taken for four weeks after leaving the risk area.

Larium (Mefloquine) This has received much bad press among travellers, some justified but most not, and the weekly tablet suits many people. Side effects are rare but can include depression, psychosis and fits, so anyone with a history of these conditions should not take it. Larium must be taken for four weeks after leaving the risk area.

Malarone This drug is a combination of Atovaquone and Proguanil. Side effects are uncommon and mild, most commonly nausea and headache. It's the best tablet for short trips to high-risk areas, and must be taken for one week after leaving the risk area.

Poliomyelitis

Generally spread through contaminated food and water. It is one of the vaccines given in childhood and should be boosted every 10 years, either orally (a drop on the tongue), or as an injection. Afghanistan is one of the few countries in the word where polio is still endemic. Polio may be carried asymptomatically, although it can cause a transient fever and, in rare cases, potentially permanent muscle weakness or paralysis.

Rabies

Spread through bites or licks on broken skin from an infected mammal, rabies is fatal and endemic to Afghanistan. Animal handlers should be vaccinated, as should those travelling to remote areas where a reliable source of post-bite vaccine is not available within 24 hours. If an animal bites you, gently wash the wound with soap and water, and apply iodine-based antiseptic. If you are not vaccinated you will need to receive rabies immunoglobulin as soon as possible and seek medical advice. Vaccination does not provide you with immunity, it merely buys you more time to seek appropriate medical help.

Tuberculosis (TB)

Along with Malaria, TB is one of the most serious health issues facing Afghanistan. Medical and aid workers, and long-term travellers who have significant contact with the local population should take precautions against TB. Vaccination is usually given only to children under the age of five, but pre-and post-travel TB testing is strongly recommended for adults at risk. The main symptoms are fever, cough, weight loss, night sweats and tiredness.

Typhoid

This serious bacterial infection is spread via food and water. It gives a high and slowly progressive fever and headache, and may be accompanied by a dry cough and stomach pain. Be aware that vaccination is not 100% effective so you must still be careful what you eat and drink.

ENVIRONMENTAL HAZARDS
Air Pollution

Air pollution is an increasing problem in Afghanistan's cities, particularly in Kabul where a combination of dust and the pollution from vehicle congestion and massed generators gets everyone coughing. If you have severe respiratory problems speak with your doctor before travelling. Air pollution can cause minor respiratory problems such as sinusitis, dry throat and irritated eyes. If troubled, leave the city for a few days and get some fresher air.

Altitude Sickness

Lack of oxygen at high altitudes (over 2500m) affects most people to some extent. The effect may be mild or severe and occurs because less oxygen reaches the muscles and the brain at high altitudes, requiring the heart and lungs to compensate by working harder. Symptoms of Acute Mountain Sickness (AMS) usually (but not always) develop during the first 24 hours at altitude. Mild symptoms include headache, lethargy, dizziness, difficulty sleeping and loss of appetite. AMS may become more severe without warning and can be fatal. Severe symptoms include breathlessness, a dry, irritative cough (which may progress to the production of pink, frothy sputum), severe headache, lack of coordination, confusion, irrational behaviour, vomiting, drowsiness and unconsciousness. There is no hard-and-fast rule as to what is too high: AMS has been fatal at 3000m, although 3500m to 4500m is the usual range. Note that quick ascents and descents – such as traversing the Salang Pass between Kabul and northern Afghanistan in a vehicle – are extremely unlikely to cause AMS.

Treat mild symptoms by resting at the same altitude until recovery, or preferably descend – even 500m can help. Paracetamol or aspirin can be taken for headaches. If symptoms persist or become worse, however, immediate descent is necessary. Drug treatments should never be used to avoid descent or to enable further ascent.

Diamox (acetazolamide) reduces the headache of AMS and helps the body acclimatise to the lack of oxygen. It is only available on prescription and those who are allergic to the sulfonamide antibiotics may also be allergic to Diamox.

The **British Mountaineering Council** (www.thebmc.co.uk) has an excellent series of downloadable fact sheets on altitude sickness.

Sunburn

Even on a cloudy day sunburn can occur rapidly, especially at high altitudes. Always use a strong sunscreen (at least SPF30), and always wear a wide-brimmed hat and sunglasses outdoors. If you become sunburnt stay out of the sun until you have recovered, apply cool compresses and take painkillers for the discomfort. One percent hydrocortisone cream applied twice daily is also helpful.

Insect Bites & Stings

Bedbugs don't carry disease but their bites are very itchy. They live in the cracks of furniture and walls and then migrate to the bed at night to feed on you. You can treat the itch with an antihistamine.

Lice can inhabit various parts of your body but most commonly your head and pubic area. Transmission is via close contact with an infected person. They can be difficult to treat and you may need numerous applications of an antilice shampoo such as permethrin. Pubic lice are usually contracted from sexual contact.

Ticks are contracted after walking in rural areas. They are commonly found behind the ears, on the belly and in the armpits. If you have had a tick bite and experience symptoms such as a rash at the site of the bite or elsewhere, fever or muscle aches, you should see a doctor. Doxycycline prevents tick-borne diseases.

Anyone with a serious bee or wasp allergy should carry an injection of adrenaline (eg an Epipen) for emergency treatment. For others, apply ice to the sting and take painkillers.

WOMEN'S HEALTH

Emotional stress, exhaustion and travelling through different time zones can all contribute to an upset in the menstrual pattern. If using oral contraceptives, remember some antibiotics, diarrhoea and vomiting can stop the pill from working and lead to the risk of pregnancy, so remember to take condoms with you just in case. Sanitary towels are available in the larger cities, but tampons are hard to find outside Kabul.

Heat, humidity and antibiotics can all contribute to thrush. Treatment is with antifungal creams and pessaries such as clotrimazole. A practical alternative is a single tablet of fluconazole (Diflucan). Urinary tract infections can be precipitated by dehydration or long bus journeys without toilet stops; bring suitable antibiotics.

HEALTH

Language

CONTENTS

Dari 227
Pashto 231

Dari and Pashto are the official languages of Afghanistan, but Dari is the one most commonly used as a lingua franca (linking or market language). Like Farsi, Dari and Pashto are written using a modified alphabet of the cursive Arabic script (see p228).

Tajik, Uzbek, Turkmen, Kyrgyz and Wakhi are all spoken by minorities in northern Afghanistan. All these languages (along with Pashto) are covered in Lonely Planet's *Central Asia Phrasebook*.

DARI

Dari is so similar to Farsi (the language of Iran) that even Afghanis will often refer to it as Farsi. The principal difference between the two is that Farsi contains more loan words from Arabic and Turkish.

Dari is an Indo-Iranian language and a member of the Indo-European language family. While it is written in Arabic script, and runs from right to left, it isn't related to Arabic at all. For a more comprehensive guide to the language, pick up a copy of Lonely Planet's *Farsi Phrasebook*.

PRONUNCIATION & TRANSLITERATION

Transliterating Dari from its non-Roman script into the Roman alphabet is a tricky affair. In this language guide the system used was designed to be as simple as possible for spoken communication, even at the expense of absolute accuracy.

In general, the last syllable of a multi-syllable word is stressed.

Vowels

Like Arabic, Dari script has only one letter (*alef*) dedicated solely to cover vowel sounds, and many vowels that would otherwise be represented in written English are

simply left out. It is some consolation that the English vowel sounds **i** (as in 'marine') and **u** (as in 'rule') are represented in the script by the letters *ye* (ی) and *ve* (و) respectively (which are also used to repersent the consonant sounds **y** and **v/w** respectively). Some vowel sounds do have long variants, but pronouncing them short won't overly affect meaning. We transliterate Dari and Pashto using the following five English vowel equivalents.

a	as in 'father'
e	as in 'bed'
i	as in 'marine'
o	as in 'mole'
u	as in 'rule'

Consonants

Dari consonants sounds are shown in the alphabet table on p228. There are many consonants represented in the script with only subtle sound differences; the transliterations in this book reduce these variants to their closest English equivalent. The following are the only really tricky sounds:

gh	a guttural sound like a heavy French 'r' pronounced at the back of the mouth
'	a very weak glottal stop, like the sound made between the words 'uh-oh' or the 'tt' in Cockney 'bottle'

ACCOMMODATION

Do you have any rooms available?	*otagh khali darin?*

I'd like a ... room.	*yak otagh e ... mikhaham*
single	*yak nafara*
shared	*chand nafara*

How much is it for ...?	*baraye ... cheghadr misha?*
one night	*yak shab*
a week	*yak hafta*
two people	*du nafar*

CONVERSATION & ESSENTIALS

The all-purpose Dari greeting is *salam aleykom*, which does duty for 'good morning', 'good afternoon' and 'good evening'.

THE DARI/FARSI ALPHABET

Final	Medial	Initial	Alone	Transliteration	Pronunciation
ا			ا	a	short, as in 'act', long, as in 'father'
ـب	ـبـ	بـ	ب	b	as in 'bet'
ـپ	ـپـ	پـ	پ	p	as in 'pet'
ـت	ـتـ	تـ	ت	t	as in 'ten'
ـث	ـثـ	ثـ	ث	s	as in 'set'
ـج	ـجـ	جـ	ج	j	as in 'jet'
ـچ	ـچـ	چـ	چ	ch	as in 'chat'
ـح	ـحـ	حـ	ح	h	as in 'hot'
ـخ	ـخـ	خـ	خ	kh	as the 'ch' in Scottish *loch*
ـد			د	d	as in 'dot'
ـذ			ذ	z	as in 'zoo'
ـر			ر	r	as in 'run'
ـز			ز	z	as **z** above
ـژ			ژ	zh	as the 's' in 'measure'
ـس	ـسـ	سـ	س	s	as **s** above
ـش	ـشـ	شـ	ش	sh	as in 'shed'
ـص	ـصـ	صـ	ص	s	as **s** above
ـض	ـضـ	ضـ	ض	z	as **z** above
ـط	ـطـ	طـ	ط	t	as **t** above
ـظ	ـظـ	ظـ	ظ	z	as **z** above
ـع	ـعـ	عـ	ع	'	a glottal stop (see p227)
ـغ	ـغـ	غـ	غ	gh	a rough, guttural sound (see p227)
ـف	ـفـ	فـ	ف	f	as in 'fact'
ـق	ـقـ	قـ	ق	gh	as **gh** above
ـک	ـکـ	کـ	ک	k	as in 'kit'
ـگ	ـگـ	گـ	گ	g	as in 'get'
ـل	ـلـ	لـ	ل	l	as in 'let'
ـم	ـمـ	مـ	م	m	as in 'met'
ـن	ـنـ	نـ	ن	n	as in 'net'
ـو			و	v	as in 'very' (in Dari only)
				w	as in 'wary'
				u	as in 'rule'
ـه	ـهـ	هـ	ه	h	as **h** above
ـی	ـیـ	یـ	ی	y	as in 'yacht'
				i	as in 'marine'

Welcome.	*khosh amadin*	**Fine – and you?**	*khubam – shoma chetorin?*
Greetings.	*salam aleykom*	**Yes.**	*bala*
Hello.	*salam*	**No.**	*na*
Good morning.	*sob bekhayr*	**Please.**	*lotfan*
Good day. (noon)	*rux bekhayr*	**Thank you.**	*tashakor*
Good evening.	*shab bekhayr*	**Thank you very much.**	*besyar tashakkor*
Goodbye.	*khoda hafez*	**You're welcome.**	*khahesh mikonam*
How are you?	*haletan chetor hast?*	**Excuse me/I'm sorry.**	*bebakhshid*

LANGUAGE

I like ...	man ... dust daram
I don't like ...	man ... dust nadaram
What's your name?	nametan chist?
My name is ...	namam...hast
Where are you from?	az koja hastin?
I'm from ...	man az ... hastam
It is God's will.	mashallah
mother	madar
father	pedar
sister	khwahar
brother	baradar
daughter	dokhtar
son	bacha
aunt	ameh (maternal)/
	khaleh (paternal)
uncle	kaka (maternal)/
	mama (paternal)
wife	zan
husband	shuy

DIRECTIONS

Where is the ...?	... koja st?
Can you show me (on the map)?	mitanin (dar naghshe) be man neshan bedin?
Is it far from here?	un az inja dur hast?
Go straight ahead.	mostaghim berin
To the left.	taraf e chap
To the right.	taraf e rast
here	inja
there	unja
behind	poshte sar
in front of	pishe ru
far (from)	dur az
near (to)	nazdik be
opposite	moghabele

HEALTH

Where is the ...?	... koja st?
chemist	davakhana
doctor	daktar
hospital	shafakhana
I have ...	... daram
asthma	asma
diabetes	maraze shakar
I'm allergic to ...	be ... hassasiyat daram
antibiotics	antibiyutik
aspirin	asperin
peanuts	mumpali
penicillin	penisilin
I'm sick.	mariz am
antiseptic	zedd e ufuni konanda

EMERGENCIES – DARI

Help!	komak!
Stop!	tavaghof!
Go away!	gom sho!
Call ...!	... khabar konin!
a doctor	yak daktar
an ambulance	yak ambulans
the police	polis

I wish to contact my embassy/consulate.
mikhaham ba sefarat/konsulgari khod am tamas begiram
Where is the toilet?
tashnab koja st?
Shame on you!
khejalat bekash! (said by a woman to a man bothering her)

aspirin	asperin
diarrhoea	es-hal
medicine	dava
sunblock	kerem e zedd e aftab

LANGUAGE DIFFICULTIES

Do you speak English?
shoma ingilisi midanin?
Does anyone here speak English?
inja kasi ingilisi midanad?
I (don't) understand.
(na) mifahman
How do you say ... in Dari?
... ra dar dari chi migin?
Please write it down.
lotfan un ra benevisin

NUMBERS

0	sifir	•
1	yak	١
2	du	٢
3	se	٣
4	chahar	٤
5	panj	۵
6	shash	۶
7	haft	٧
8	hasht	٨
9	noh	٩
10	dah	١•
11	yazdah	١١
12	duwazdah	١٢
13	sizdah	١٣
14	chahardah	١٤
15	panzdah	١۵
16	shanzdah	١۶

LANGUAGE

17	havdah	۱۷
18	hajdah	۱۸
19	nuzdah	۱۹
20	bist	۲۰
21	bist o yak	۲۱
22	bist o du	۲۲
30	si	۳۰
40	chehel	۴۰
50	panjah	۵۰
60	shast	۶۰
70	haftad	۷۰
80	hashtad	۸۰
90	navad	۹۰
100	sad	۱۰۰
167	sad o shast o haft	۱۶۷
200	do sad	۲۰۰
1000	hazar	۱۰۰۰

SHOPPING & SERVICES

Where is the ...?	... koja st?
bank	bank
city centre	markaz e shahr
consulate	konsulgari
embassy	safarat
hotel	hotal
lodging house	mosaferkhana
mosque	masjed
market	bazar
office	daftar
police	polis
post office	posta khana
public toilet	tashnab e umumi
tourist office	edare ye turizem

I'd like to buy ...	mikhaham ... bekharan
How much is it?	Kimatesh chand hast?
I don't like it.	az un khosh am nemiyad
May I look at it?	mitanamun ra seyr konam?
I'm just looking.	faghat seyr mikonam
I think it's too expensive.	fekr mikonam un ziyad geran hast
I'll take it.	un ra mikharam

Do you accept credit cards?
kredit kard ghabul mikonin?
Do you accept travellers cheques?
shoma cheke safari ghabul mikonin?

TIME & DATES

What time is it?	sa'at chand hast?
today	emruz
tomorrow	farda
yesterday	diruz
tonight	emshab
morning, am	sob

afternoon, pm	ba'd az zohr
day	ruz
month	mah
year	sal

Monday	dushanba
Tuesday	se shanba
Wednesday	chahar shanba
Thursday	panj shanba
Friday	jom'a
Saturday	shanba
Sunday	yakshanba

TRANSPORT

What time does the ... leave/arrive?	... che sa'ati harekat mikone/mirese?
bus	sarvis
plane	tayara

What time is the ... bus?	sarvis e ... key miyad?
first	awal
last	akher
next	ba'di

I'd like a	... mikhaham
one-way ticket	tikete yak tarafa
return ticket	tikete du tarafa

I'd like to hire a ...	mikhaham ... keraye konam
car	motar
4WD	forwildrayv

Where is the bus stop?	istgah e sarvis koja st?
Where's a service station?	petrol estayshen e ba'di kojast?
Please fill it up.	lotfan tanki ra por konin
I'd like ... litres.	... litr petrol mikhaham
Is this the road to ...?	in sarak be ... mira?

| diesel | dizal |
| petrol/gasoline | petrol |

SAFE TRAVEL

Is it safe/dangerous?	un mason hast?
Are there landmines?	mayn hast?
aid-worker	komakgar
bomb	bam
gun	tofang
landmine	mayn
refugee	panahanda
rocket	rakat
security (forces)	amniyat
soldier	asgar
war/fighting	jang

LANGUAGE

PASHTO

Pashto is the speech of the Pashtuns across southern and eastern Afghanistan, and Pakistan's North-West Frontier Province and Baluchistan. Though there are some regional differences in pronunciation between the Swati and Afghan dialects (eg the northerners call themselves Pakhtun, the southerners Pashtun), this is still the lingua franca from the Indus to Kabul. For a more detailed coverage of Pashto, get a copy of Lonely Planet's *Central Asia Phrasebook*.

PRONUNCIATION

The Pashto language is written in an Arabic script. Most Pashto sounds are also found in the English language, while a few additional ones must be learned. Intonation is important and this can be learned quickly by listening to Pashtuns speak.

Pronunciation of Pashto vowels and consonants is more or less the same as it is for Dari (see p227).

ACCOMMODATION

hotel/inn	otel/sarai
guesthouse	mehman khana
youth hostel	da zawanano hastel
Do you have any rooms available?	kota sheta?
How much is it per night?	te yawy shepy tso paisy di?
I'd like a ...	ze ghuarum yawa ...
single room	singel kota
twin room	dua ghebargy koty
double bed	dua bestery

CONVERSATION & ESSENTIALS

Greetings.	assalam u alaikum (lit: peace be upon you)
And upon you peace.	wa alaikum u ssalam
Goodbye.	de kuday pe aman
Good night.	shpa dey pe khair
Thank you.	sta na shukria
Excuse/Pardon me.	bakhena ghuarum
Yes.	hoo
No.	na
Sorry.	wobakha
How are you?	ta tsanga yei?
I'm fine, and you?.	ze khe yem aw ta?
What's your name?	sta noom tse day?

What country do you come from?	ta la kuom hiwad na raghelay yi?
I come from ...	za la ... na raghelay yem
Do you speak English?	ta pe angrezai pohegy?
Do you understand?	poh shwey?
I (don't) understand.	ze (ne) pohigam
I don't speak Pashto.	ze pe pashto ne pohigam

DIRECTIONS

Can you tell me where ... is?	cherta dai ...?
Do you have a local map?	da die alaki naksha darsara sheta?
Go straight ahead.	negh lar sha
Turn right/left.	khai/chap taraf ta wagarza
Is it far?	da lirey dai?
Can I walk there?	pe pakho telalai shem?
left/right	chap/khai
far away	deyr lirey
near (to ...)	(... ta) negdey
north/south	shimal/janub
east/west	shark/gharb

HEALTH

I have ...	ze ...
asthma	sa landai
diabetes	diabetes/(da shakar maraz)
diarrhoea	diarrhoea/eshal
I'm sick.	ze naroogh yem
I am allergic to antibiotics.	ze de antibiotiks sara hasasiat larem
antiseptic	antiseptic
aspirin	aspirin
clinic	klinik
doctor	dokter
hospital	roghtoon/haspatal
painkillers	aram rawronke golai
pharmacy	dawakhana
sanitary napkins	zanana dusmalona

NUMBERS

See p228 for the script used with numbers.

0	sefer
1	yau
2	dua
3	drei
4	tsalare
5	penza
6	shpag
7	owa
8	ata
9	naha
10	las
11	yauolas
20	shal
21	yau wisht
30	dirsh
39	naha dirsh
40	tsalwekht
50	panzos
60	shpeta
70	awia
80	atia
90	nawi
100	sal
101	yau sal yau
200	dua sawa
1000	zer
1001	yau zer yau

SHOPPING & SERVICES

Where's the nearest ...?	kum ... negdy dai?
bazaar	bazar
grocery store	khuraka feroshi
market	market
pharmacy	dawa khana

Where can I buy a ...?	... cherta akhestelay shem?
How much does this cost?	da pe tso dai?
It's very expensive.	da deir gran dai
Can you reduce the price?	baia kamawalay shey?
credit card	credit card
money exchange	paisy badlawal
travellers cheque	safari chek

TIME & DATE

When?	kala?
What time is it?	tso bajy dhi?
morning	sahar
afternoon	da gharmy na wrosta
evening	makham
today	nan wraz
tonight	nan shpa
tomorrow	saba

Monday	pir/doshanba
Tuesday	naha/mangle
Wednesday	sharow/budh
Thursday	ziarat/jumarat
Friday	juma
Saturday	hafta/shanba
Sunday	atwar/yakshanba

TRANSPORT

I'd like to go to ...	ze ghuaram che ... ta lar shem
What time does the next bus leave?	bal ba pe tso bajo bus rarasigi?
Where is the bus terminal?	cherta dai bus ada?
I want to get off at ...	ze ghuaram pe ... ke kooz shem
How much?	karaya tso da?

return ticket	wapasi tiket
ticket office	tiketono dafter
car	motor
fill up	dakawal
map	naksha
motorbike	motor saikel
petrol	petrol

SAFE TRAVEL

Is it safe/dangerous?	khatar day?
Are there landmines?	dalta nazhde kum mayn shta? (mayn as in English 'mine')
aid-worker	mrastanduy
bomb	bam
gun	topak
refugee	kadwal/mahajir
rocket	raket
soldier	askar
war/fighting	jang

Glossary

ab – water
ACBAR – Agency Coordinating Body for Afghan Relief
Afghani – currency of Afghanistan
Aimaq – Dari-speaking nomads of central and western Afghanistan
Allah – God
amir – chieftan or nobleman
amu – river
ANA – Afghan National Army
ANP – Afghan National Police
ANSO – Afghan NGO Security Office
asalaam aleikum – Muslim greeting, literally 'peace be with you'; the usual response is *wa aleikum salaam* (and peace be with you too).
Ashura – Muslim holiday particularly celebrated by Shiites, marking the death of Hussein at Karbala in AD 680.
atan – national dance of Afghanistan
ATO – Afghan Tourist Organisation
azan – Muslim call to prayer

Bactria – ancient name for northern Afghanistan, centred on Balkh
badgir – traditional tower built on roofs in semidesert regions, to funnel in breezes
bagh – garden
baksheesh – donation, tip or bribe
bala hissar – 'high fortress', citadel and traditional seat of royal power
bandar – port
beg – landlord, gentleman
bukhari – room heater
burqa – enveloping veil worn by many Afghan women
buzkashi – traditional pololike game of northern Afghanistan, played with a headless goat carcass

caravanserai – basic accommodation for travelling traders
chaderi – see *burqa*
chai – tea; can be either green (*chai sabz*) or black (*chai siah*)
chaikhana – teahouse
chapan – long-sleeved silk coat worn in northern Afghanistan
charahi – crossroads or roundabout
charas – marijuana
chowk – crossroads or town square
chowkidar – caretaker, night watchman
commandan – leader of local militia

daff – flat-framed drum, often played to accompany Sufi rituals
daftar – office
Dari – national language of Afghanistan, also referred to as Farsi
darya – river
dasht – desert
Deobandism – Indian anticolonialist school of Muslim teaching, a large influence on Taliban ideology
dotar – long-necked lute
Durand Line – border between Afghanistan and Pakistan, imposed in1893 by Sir Mortimer Durand

falang – large minibus (from the term 'flying coach')
Farsiwan – Dari-speaking Shiites from northwest Afghanistan
feringhee – foreigner, see also *khareji*

gilim – woven carpet
ghazal – sung verses of poetry
Ghaznavid – Turkic-Afghan empire ruled from Ghazni, 10th to12th centuries AD
Ghorid – 12th century Afghan empire, founded by Alauddin 'the World Burner'
gombad – dome or domed monument
Graeco-Bactrian – Hellenistic kingdoms and culture in north Afghanistan following conquest by Alexander the Great
Great Game – geopolitical 'Cold War' of territorial expansion between imperial Russia and Britain in 19th century Central Asia

Hadith – collected acts and sayings of the Prophet Mohammed
haj – the pilgrimage to Mecca, to be made by devout Muslims at least once during their lifetime
haji – honorific title denoting someone who has performed the haj
hammam – bathhouse
Hazara – Shiite ethnic group of Mongol descent from central Afghanistan
hazrat – honorific title meaning 'holy'
Hejira – the flight of the Prophet Mohammed and his followers from Mecca to Medina in AD 622 (taken as the start of the Islamic calendar)
Hezb-e Islami – Party of Islam; largely Pashtun fundamentalist party, founded by Islamist Gulbuddin Hekmatyar
Hezb-e Wahdat – Party of Islamic Unity; Hazara-dominated Shiite political party
hijab – Muslim woman's veil or headscarf (literally 'modest dress')

IDP – Internally Displaced Person
IED – Improvised Explosive Device
iftar – breaking of the *Ramazan* fast at sunset
imam – Muslim religious leader
insha'Allah – 'If God wills it', universal Muslim saying
ISAF – International Security Assistance Force, led by NATO
Ismaili – a branch of Shiite Islam
iwan – open-ended barrel-vaulted hall used in mosque architecture

jad – road, street
jamaat khana – Ismaili community hall, their closest equivalent to a mosque
Jamiat-e Islami – Society of Islam Party; moderate Tajik political party and leading player in the Northern Alliance, with the late Ahmad Shah Massoud as its figurehead
jang – war
jihad – holy struggle or holy war
Jihad, the – popular name given to the Afghan anti-Soviet war
jirga – council of community elders and leaders
Jumbesh-e Melli – National Islamic Movement; almost exclusively Uzbek political party, dominated by General Abdul Rashid Dostum

kafir – Islamic term for a nonbeliever
Kalimeh – Muslim declaration of faith ('There is no God but Allah and Mohammed is His prophet'; shahadah in Arabic)
karakol – breed of Afghan sheep; also the pelt from newborn lambs used in Afghan hats
karez – subterranean irrigation canal
khan – Muslim title, typically referring to landed elite
khanka – opium (Pashto); also called *tareyak* (Dari)
khareji – foreigner
khel – Pashtun clan
Khoda – God (Dari)
koh – mountain
kolah – turban cap
Koran – see *Quran*
kot (kotal) – mountain pass
kowk – partridge kept for bird fighting
Kuchi – nomad, usually Pashtun
Kushan – Buddhist empire that ruled Afghanistan from 1st century AD
Kyrgyz – Nomadic tribe of the Wakhan Corridor

landay – Pashtun folk poetry, composed in couplets
lakh – 100,000
loya jirga – grand tribal council
lungi – turban

madrassa – Islamic college
malang – wandering holy man, usually a *Sufi*

malik – Pashtun tribal chief
masjid – mosque
maulana – Islamic cleric
mazar – tomb
mehman – guest
mehmankhana – guesthouse, hotel
melmastia – hospitality, a key pillar of *Pashtunwali*
Meshrano Jirga – House of the Elders; the upper house of the Afghan parliament, acting in a primarily advisory role
mir – honorific title given to some Afghan leaders
muezzin – one who calls Muslims to prayer, traditionally from the minaret of a mosque
Mughal – Muslim India empire founded in Afghanistan in 16th century
mujaheddin – Muslim fighter engaged in *jihad*
mullah – Islamic cleric
Muslim – adherent of the Islamic faith

namaz – Muslim prayer
nan – bread
nang – honour, a key pillar of Pahstunwali
Nauroz – Afghan new year with pre-Islamic roots, celebrated on the spring equinox (March 21)
NGO – Non-Governmental Organisation
Northern Alliance – coalition of anti-Taliban Afghan forces, dominated by Panjshiri Tajiks; also called the *United Front*

Oxus – historic name of Amu Darya River

pakul – flat pancake-shaped hat
Pashto – second language of Afghanistan, spoken by *Pashtuns*
Pashtun – dominant ethnic group of Afghanistan, divided into two main branches, the Durrani and Ghilzai
Pashtunistan – Pashtun tribal region spanning the Afghan–Pakistan border
Pashtunwali – Pashtun tribal code
pattu – the woollen blanket carried by many Afghan men
PCO – Public Call Office; for making telephone calls
PDPA – People's Democratic Part of Afghanistan; former ruling communist party, divided into opposing *Khalq* and *Parcham* factions
pir – holy man; given to the head of a Sufi order
pirhan tonban – traditional male clothes, of knee-length shirt and baggy trousers
PRT – Provincial Reconstruction Team
pulao – Afghan meal of rice with meat or vegetables

qala – fort
qawwali – Islamic devotional singing
qazi – Judge overseeing Islamic law
Qizilbash – Turkic Shiite ethnic group living in Kabul
Quran – the holy book of Islam; also spelt *Koran*

Ramazan – Islamic holy month of sunrise-to-sunset fasting; referred to as Ramadan outside Afghanistan
rebab – short-necked lute; the Afghan national instrument

Safavid – Persian dynasty ruling west and southern Afghanistan in 16th to 18th centuries
samovar – tea/hot water urn found in *chaikhanas*
sayyid – descendent of the Prophet Mohammed
sefarat – embassy or consulate
shah – king
shahid – martyr
shahr – town or city
shalwar kameez – see *pirhan tonban*
sharia – Islamic law, derived primarily from the Quran and Hadith
Shiite – minority Muslim sect
shura – Muslim consultative council
Sufi – follower of Islamic mysticism
Sufism – Islamic mysticism
Sunni – Muslim sect; dominant worldwide and in Afghanistan
suzani – traditional Uzbek embroidery of wool or silk on cotton cloth

Tajik – second-largest ethnic group in Afghanistan
takht – throne; also raised platform for seating in a chaikhana
talib – religious student
Taliban – Pashtun Islamist political movement that ruled Afghanistan from the mid-1990s to 2001
tangi – gorge
tareyak – see *khanka*
tariqah – Sufi order or brotherhood
tashnab – toilet

teppe – hill
Thuraya – brand of satellite phone
Timurid – Central Asian empire of the 14th to15th centuries, ruling Afghanistan from Samarkand and Herat
tofan – gun
Tribal Areas – primarily Pashtun autonomous areas of North West Frontier Province and Baluchistan in Pakistan that border Afghanistan
Turkmen – minority ethnic group concentrated in the northwest of Afghanistan

Ulema – collection of Muslim scholars and clergy; traditional arbiters of sharia
UNAMA – UN Assistance Mission to Afghanistan; umbrella body for all UN agencies in Afghanistan
UNHAS – UN Humanitarian Air Service
United Front – see *Northern Alliance*
UXO – Unexploded Ordnance
Uzbek – minority ethnic group concentrated in the northwest of Afghanistan

Wahabbi – conservative and literalist Muslim orthodoxy from Saudi Arabia
Wakhi – ethnic group living in the Wakhan Corridor
wat – street
watan – country, homeland
White Huns – nomadic group that settled in Afghanistan around AD 400 and carved the Bamiyan Buddha statues
Wolesi Jirga – House of the People; the lower house of the Afghan parliament and primary law-makers

zakat – charitable donation; the third pillar of Islam
ziarat – shrine
zikr – *Sufi* devotional ritual, often involving music and recitation of the names of Allah

Contributing Authors

Lina Abirafeh 'Women in Afghanistan' boxed text, The Culture; Photographer

Lina Abirafeh is a gender and development practitioner with 11 years of development experience. She recently completed work in Sierra Leone and is relocating to Papua New Guinea to focus on gender-based violence and HIV/AIDS. Abirafeh spent four years in Afghanistan running programmes for women with various UN agencies and international NGOs. In addition, she spent four years at the World Bank in Washington, DC. She is nearing completion of a PhD under the auspices of the London School of Economics Institute of Development Studies, researching the effects of gender-focused international aid in post-conflict contexts.

Tamim Ansary 'Exile & Return' boxed text, The Culture

Tamim Ansary wrote *West of Kabul, East of New York* and co-authored *The Other Side of the Sky* with Afghan land-mine victim Farah Ahmadi. The son of an Afghan father and an American mother, he was born and raised in Afghanistan and moved to the United States when he was 16. His work has appeared in the *San Francisco Chronicle*, *Salon*, *Alternet*, TomPaine.com, *Zyzzyva* and *Edutopia*, as well as on Encarta.com, where he writes a monthly column. He directs the San Francisco Writers Workshop as well as a workshop for young Afghan American writers in the San Francisco Bay Area.

Christina Lamb 'Reporting from Afghanistan' boxed text, Working in Afghanistan

Christina Lamb started reporting on Afghanistan in 1987 when she was just 21 and the country was under Russian occupation. Her daring reports on travelling in and out of the country with the mujaheddin earned her the Young Journalist of the Year in the British Press Awards. Since then she has reported everywhere from Iraq to Zimbabwe. She returned to Afghanistan shortly after the September 11 attacks and has travelled back and forth ever since. She was named Foreign Correspondent of the Year in the British Press Awards and What the Papers Say Awards in both 2002 and 2006. She is currently roving Foreign Affairs correspondent for the *Sunday Times* and the author of several books including *The Sewing Circles of Herat* and *Tea with Pinochet*.

John Mock & Kimberley O'Neil Wakhan & the Afghan Corridor and 'Kyrgyz of the Afghan Pamir' boxed text, Mazar-e Sharif & Northeastern Afghanistan

John Mock and Kimberley O'Neil, a hardcore trekking couple, have logged more than 10,000km, 60 passes, and 50 glacier traverses through the Karakoram, Hindu Kush, and Himalaya. Since 2004 their focus has been on Wakhan and the Afghan Pamir, reconnoitring new trekking routes and re-establishing old routes. Their recent trips include a journey to the source of the Oxus River and two cross-border treks into Pakistan's Northern Areas. They are also working in Wakhan as consultants on tourism development, and on community conservation for a wildlife conservation project.

LONELY PLANET AUTHORS

Why is our travel information the best in the world? It's simple: our authors are independent, dedicated travellers. They don't research using just the internet or phone, and they don't take freebies in exchange for positive coverage. They travel widely, to all the popular spots and off the beaten track. They personally visit thousands of hotels, restaurants, cafés, bars, galleries, palaces, museums and more – and they take pride in getting all the details right, and telling it how it is. Think you can do it? Find out how at lonelyplanet.com.

Ash Sweeting   Photographer

In early 2004 Ash Sweeting came to Afghanistan for a month, and he's still there. His photography career started off covering adventure travel, climbing and mountaineering, with much of his early work in the Australian deserts and New Zealand. Since arriving in Afghanistan he has moved onto to covering all the many aspects of Afghanistan today: the conflict, drugs, history, people and the complex political situation there. He has, however, still managed to take some time out in between to do the odd climbing story in Afghanistan, Thailand and China.

Nick Walker   Kandahar & Southern Afghanistan, Safety in Afghanistan

Originally a scientist from Auckland, Nick Walker has spent the last decade travelling, studying, living and volunteering in Central Asia, the subcontinent, the Middle East and Southeast Asia. He was also one of the few travellers who ventured into Afghanistan when the Taliban were in power.

Tony Wheeler   Afghanistan in the Hippy Era...and 35 Years Later' boxed text, History

Tony's travels across Asia in 1972 took him through Afghanistan and led to him writing *Across Asia on the Cheap,* the very first Lonely Planet guidebook. When he flew into Kabul from Dubai in 2006 it was his first return visit. His recent Afghan travels appear in *Bad Lands,* a book aptly subtitled 'A Tourist on the Axis of Evil'. Regrettably, the Buddhas of Bamiyan, which Tony missed on his first visit to Afghanistan, had been destroyed by the Taliban.

Behind the Scenes

THIS BOOK

This first edition of *Afghanistan* was coordinated by Paul Clammer. It was commissioned in Lonely Planet's Melbourne office, and produced by the following:

Commissioning Editor Lucy Monie
Coordinating Editors Holly Alexander, Brooke Lyons
Coordinating Cartographer Joshua Geoghegan
Coordinating Layout Designer Indra Kilfoyle
Managing Editors Imogen Bannister, Geoff Howard, Katie Lynch
Managing Cartographers Amanda Sierp, Shahara Ahmed
Assisting Editors Gennifer Ciavarra, Chris Girdler, Carly Hall, Kate McLeod, Rosie Nicholson
Assisting Cartographers Anita Banh, Darwun Chau, Monique Elsley, Joanne Luke, Erin McManus

Cover Designer Rebecca Dandens
Project Manager Glenn van der Knijff
Language Content Coordinator Quentin Frayne
Thanks to David Carroll, Sin Choo, Sally Darmody, Janine Eberle, James Ellis, Bruce Evans, Emma Gilmour, Graham Imeson, Margot Kilgour, Yvonne Kirk, Bradley Mayhew, Wayne Murphy, Iain Shearer, Simon Tillema, Celia Wood

THANKS
PAUL CLAMMER

This book is for Wais Faizi of the Mustafa Hotel in Kabul, who died during the write-up. A good friend to travellers and journalists, and much missed.

In Afghanistan, my thanks above all go to Muqim Jamshady for his help and friendship. *Yek roz didi dost, digar roz didi baradar.* Huge thanks to Stephen

---

LONELY PLANET: TRAVEL WIDELY, TREAD LIGHTLY, GIVE SUSTAINABLY

The Lonely Planet Story

The story begins with a classic travel adventure: Tony and Maureen Wheeler's 1972 journey across Europe and Asia to Australia. There was no useful information about the overland trail then, so Tony and Maureen published the first Lonely Planet guidebook to meet a growing need.

From a kitchen table, Lonely Planet has grown to become the largest independent travel publisher in the world, with offices in Melbourne (Australia), Oakland (USA) and London (UK). Today Lonely Planet guidebooks cover the globe. There is an ever-growing list of books and information in a variety of media. Some things haven't changed. The main aim is still to make it possible for adventurous individuals to get out there – to explore and better understand the world.

The Lonely Planet Foundation

The Lonely Planet Foundation proudly supports nimble nonprofit institutions working for change in the world. Each year the foundation donates 5% of Lonely Planet company profits to projects selected by staff and authors. Our partners range from Kabissa, which provides small nonprofits across Africa with access to technology, to the Foundation for Developing Cambodian Orphans, which supports girls at risk of falling victim to sex traffickers.

Our nonprofit partners are linked by a grass-roots approach to the areas of health, education or sustainable tourism. Many projects we support – such as one with BaAka (Pygmy) children in the forested areas of Central African Republic – choose to focus on women and children as one of the most effective ways to support the whole community.

Sometimes Foundation assistance is as simple as assisting in the conservation and recording of an archaeological site such as the Minaret of Jam in Afghanistan. The Lonely Planet Foundation is training Afghan archaeologists in the field, recording illegal looting of the site and providing educational material for children and adults in Dari and Pashto. The incredible Minaret of Jam monument now draws intrepid tourists and Afghans alike to the area and encourages the local community to preserve its heritage.

Just as travel is often about learning to see with new eyes, so many of the groups we work with aim to change the way people see themselves and the future for their children and communities.

Shucart for sharing some good times and very bad roads. Thanks also to Andre Mann, Vanni Cappelli, Dominic Medley, Omar Massoudi at the Kabul Museum, Jason Kerr, Mr Shafiqullah, Alex Strick Van Linschoten, Rory Stewart, Mobin and Wahid Jamshady, Jonathan Bean, Ted Chang, Iraj Rais and all the drivers at Afghan Logistics & Tours.

At Lonely Planet, thanks to Lucy Monie for her invaluable support, the brilliant Holly Alexander, Marg Toohey and not least to Janine Eberle who helped get the book off the ground but didn't stick around long enough to see it through. My particular thanks to my coauthor Nick Walker, and contributors John Mock, Kim O'Neil, Christina Lamb, Tamim Ansary, Lina Abirafeh and Tony Wheeler.

Finally, thanks and love to my parents and to Jo, for their continued indulgence of my Afghan obsessions.

OUR READERS

Many thanks to the travellers who wrote to us with helpful hints, useful advice and interesting anecdotes:

Peter Higgins, Jason Mason

ACKNOWLEDGMENTS

Many thanks to the following for the use of their content:

Globe on title page © Mountain High Maps 1993 Digital Wisdom, Inc.

Internal photographs: all photographs by Ash Sweeting except p173, p174 (#5), p175 (#3) and p177 (#3) by Lina Abirafeh, unless otherwise indicated.

SEND US YOUR FEEDBACK

We love to hear from travellers – your comments keep us on our toes and help make our books better. Our well-travelled team reads every word on what you loved or loathed about this book. Although we cannot reply individually to postal submissions, we always guarantee that your feedback goes straight to the appropriate authors, in time for the next edition. Each person who sends us information is thanked in the next edition – and the most useful submissions are rewarded with a free book.

To send us your updates – and find out about Lonely Planet events, newsletters and travel news – visit our award-winning website: **www.lonelyplanet.com/contact**.

Note: we may edit, reproduce and incorporate your comments in Lonely Planet products such as guidebooks, websites and digital products, so let us know if you don't want your comments reproduced or your name acknowledged. For a copy of our privacy policy visit www.lonelyplanet.com/privacy.

All images are the copyright of the photographers unless otherwise indicated. Many of the images in this guide are available for licensing from Lonely Planet Images: www.lonelyplanetimages.com.

The boundaries of India and Pakistan on maps throughout this guide have not been authenticated and may not be correct.

Index

A

Abdur Rahman Khan 93
Ab-i-Estada 66
accommodation 198-200, *see also
    individual locations*
activities 200
    golf 109, **12**
    kayaking 110
    trekking 24, 168-9
Afghan Pamir 24, 167-72
Ai Khanoum 162-3
air travel
    to/from Afghanistan 212-14
    within Afghanistan 218
Ajar Valley 66
Alexander the Great 25, 111, 137, 186
Al-Qaeda 38-9, 110, 163, 185
Andkhoi 144-5
animals 64-5
Anjoman Pass 166-7
Ansari, Khoja Abdullah 138-9
architecture 18, 55-6
    Balkh 156, 157
    Herat 137-8
    Kabul 94
    Minaret of Jam 127, **7**
    Samangan 158-9
area codes, *see inside front cover*
Arghandab 193, **12**
art galleries, *see* galleries
arts 49-57, *see also individual arts*
ATMs 206

B

Baba Wali Shrine 193
Babur, Zahiruddin 28-9, 88
Babur's Gardens 87-8, **174**
Bactrian Gold 89
Badakhshan 163-72
Badghis province 142
Bagram 109-10
Bala Hissar 90, 157
Bala Murghab 143
Balkh 155-8, **156**
Balkhi, Rabi'a 157
Baluchi 46-7
Bamiyan 114-22, **115**, **6**
Band-e Amir 66, 122-4, **122**, **7**, **11**
Barf-e Awal 95
bathrooms 209-10
Bibi Mahru Hill 95
Big Pamir 66, 170-1

Bin Laden, Osama 36, 38-9, 67,
    185, 188
birds 65, 90, 170
books 18-19, 41
border crossings 215-17
Bost Arch 197
Broghil Pass 170
Buddha Niches 117-19, **6**
Buddhism 26-7, 114-15, 118, 158, 184
Buddhist sites
    Bagram 109-10
    Balkh 156
    Bamiyan 117-19, **6**
    Hadda 184
    Samangan 158-9
    Surkh Kotal 160
    Takht-e Rostam 158-9
    Termiz 217
burqas 16, 38, 46, 211, **174**
business hours 200
bus travel 218-19
buzkashi 57, **12**

C

camping 199
cannabis 155
car travel 219-20
carpets 53-4, **174**, **175**
cash 206-7
caves
    Jalalabad 182
    Takht-e Rostam 159
    Tora Bora 185
cemeteries
    Kabul 89, 90
    Gazar Gah 138-9, **178**
Chaghcheran 126
chaikhanas 199
Chaqmaqtin Lake 172
Chist-e Sharif 128
Christianity 49
cinema 56-7
citadels
    Bamiyan 119
    Herat 137, **179**
    Kabul 90
climate 17, 200-1
clothing, *see* dress codes
Cold War 35
consulates 202-3
costs 18, *see also inside front cover*
credit cards 207

crime 72
culture 41-58
customs regulations 60, 201

D

dangers, *see* safety
Darya Ajdahar 120
Dasht-e Laili 144
Durrani, Ahmed Shah 29, 45, 81,
    190, 193
deep vein thrombosis 222-3
deforestation 67
diarrhoea 223
Dilisang Pass 172
diphtheria 223-4
disabilities, travellers with 210
Dostum, General Abdul Rashid 145
dress codes 16, 42, 46, *see also* burqas
drinks 61
driving 73
drugs 15, 73, 155, 196

E

economy 15, 43-7
Eid Gah Mosque 193
electricity 202
embassies 202-3
emergencies 74-5, *see also inside
    front cover*
environmental issues 66-7
exchange rates, *see inside front cover*

F

Faizabad 164-6, **165**, **10**
festivals & events
    Barf-e Awal 95
    Islamic holy days 203-4
    Nauroz 17, 95, 204
flights
    to/from Afghanistan 212-14
    within Afghanistan 218
food 59-63, 204-5
football 57
Forty Steps 193-4
Friday Mosque 136-7, **179**

G

galleries 91-2, 103
gardens, *see* parks & gardens
gay travellers 205
Gazar Gah 138-9, **178**
Geneva Accords 36

geography 64
Ghazni 196-7
golf 109, 12
Goz Khun 170
Great Game, the 30, 125

H
Hadda 184
hammam 199-200
Hazaras 45
Hazrat Ali, Shrine of 157, 7
health 221-6
Hekmatyar, Gulbuddin 186
Herat 132-42, **133**, 5, 174, 175,
   177, 179
   accommodation 140
   attractions 135-40
   drinking 140-1
   food 140-1
   shopping 141
   travel to/from 141-2
   travel within 142
hiking 167-72, 200
Hinduism 49
history 25-40
hitching 220
HIV 224
holidays 17, 205
hot springs 128-9, 169
hunting 67

I
immigration 212
insect bites & stings 226
insurance
   health 221
   travel 205
insurgency 71
internet access 206
internet resources 19
Irshad Uween 172
Ishkashim 167
Islam 47-9
Islamic holy days 203-4
Istalif 107-8
itineraries 20-4

J
Jalalabad 182-4, 8
Jam, Minaret of 127, 7
Jami, Mawlana Abdur Rahman 139
Jebal Saraj 112
Judaism 49

K
Ka Faroshi Bird Market 90, 6
Kabul 79-105, **80**, **85**, **93**, 9, 10,
   176, 179
   accommodation 95-8
   attractions 87-95
   drinking 101-2
   entertainment 102
   events 95
   festivals 95
   food 98-101
   itineraries 20
   shopping 102-3
   travel to/from 103-4
   travel within 104-5
Kabul Museum 88-9, 179
Kakrak Valley 119
Kamdesh 187
Kandahar 190-5, **192**, 12
Karzaid, Hamid 38
Kashch Goz 171
kayaking 110, 200
Khan, Genghis 28
Khandud 169-70
Khoja Abu Nasr Parsa, Shrine of
   156-7, 6
Khwaja Bahauddin 163
Khyber Pass 185
kidnapping 72-3
kite flying 58, 93, 95, 117
Kol-e Hashmat Khan 66
Kotal-e Shaur 171
Kuchi 46
Kunduz 160-2, **161**

L
Lake Shewa 166
Lal-o-Sar Jangal 125-6
landays 52
landmines 67
languages
   Dari 227-30
   Pashto 231-2
Lashkar Gah 197
legal matters 206
leishmaniasis 224
lesbian travellers 205
Little Pamir 171-2
Lower Wakhan 169-70

M
Mahmoud the Great
   27
mail services 208
Maimana 143-4
malaria 224
maps 206

markets
   Herat 141
   Kabul 90, 93, 101, 6
   Samangan 158
Massoud, Ahmad Shah 38, 39, 111
mausoleums
   Herat 138
   Jalalabad 183
   Kabul 92-3, 94, 178
   Kandahar 193
Mazar-e Sharif 148-55
medical services 223
metric conversions, *see inside front
   cover*
Minaret of Jam 126-8, 7
mines 71-2
Mir Samir 187, 11
Mohammed, Prophet 47-9, 193
monasteries 158-9
money 18, 206-7, *see also inside
   front cover*
mosques 21, 55-6
   Balkh 157
   Friday Mosque 136-7, 177, 179
   Herat 136-7, 177, 179
   Kabul 88, 94-5
   Kandahar 193
mujaheddin 35-6
Musalla Complex 137-8
museums 88-9, 92, 93-4, 179
music 54-5

N
Nangahar province 182, 9
National Archive 92
National Gallery 91-2
national parks, sanctuaries &
   wildlife reserves 66
   Ab-i-Estada 66
   Ajar Valley 66
   Band-e Amir National Park 66,
      122-4, **122**, 7, 11
   Big Pamir 66, 170-1
   Kol-e Hashmat Khan 66
   Registan Desert Reserve 66
Nauroz 95, 204
newspapers 58
Nimla Gardens 184-5
No Gombad Mosque 157
Noshaq 169
Nuristan 186-7

O
Obey 128-9
OMAR Land Mine Museum 93-4
opium 15, 43, 73, 164, 183, 196, 197, 8

INDEX

P
Paghman 108
Pamir 24, 167-72
Panjshir Valley 110-12, **8**, **10**
parks & gardens
    Babur's Gardens 87-8, **177**
    Herat 140
    Jalalabad 183
    Kabul 87-8
    Nimla Gardens 184-5
Pashtuns 44-5
pashtunwali 44
phone codes, see inside front cover
photography 207-8
planning 16-19, see also itineraries
plants 66
poaching 67
poetry 49-53
poliomyelitis 224-5
politics 15, 30, 41-2, 43, 45, 50-1, 57-8, 82, 149
pollution 67
population 44-7
postal services 208
Prophet Mohammed 47-9, 193
Pul-e Khumri 159-60
Pul-e Malan 140

Q
Qala-e Nau 142-3
Qargha Lake 108-9
Qazideh 169
Qila-e Panja 170

R
rabies 225
radio 57-8
Rahman, Abdur 31-2
Ramazan 204-5
Registan Desert Reserve 66
registration 208
religion 47-9, see also individual religions
religious festivals 203-4
Rostam 159
Rukh, Shah 28

S
safety 16-19, 68-75, 201
    accommodation 97
    air travel 213
    Badghis province 142
    Bamiyan 114
    Eastern Afghanistan 183
    Herat 132, 135

Kabul 81, 87
Kandahar 193
Mazar-e Sharif 149, 152
Northwestern Afghanistan 132
Paghman 108
Panjshir Valley 110, 111
Southern Afghanistan 190
Salang Pass 112, **9**
Samangan (Aibak) 158
sanctuaries, see national parks, sanctuaries & wildlife reserves
Sarhad-e Broghil 170
security, see safety
Shad, Gowhar 138
Shah, Nadir 92
Shah, Timur 28, 94
Shahr-e Doh Shamshira Mosque 94-95, **180**
Shahr-e Gholghola 119
Shahr-e Zohak 119-20
Shahzada Abdullah 139
Shibar Pass 121
Shiberghan 145-6
shopping 208-9
Shrine of Hazrat Ali 152, **7**
Shrine of Khoja Abu Nasr Parsa 156-7, **6**
Sikhism 49
Silk Road, the 26, 27
Soviet Union 30, 36, 37, 43, 81
sports 57
Spreg Shir Uween 171
Sultani Museum 92
Surkh Kotal 160

T
Tajiks 45
Takht-e Rostam 159
Takht-e Safar 140
Taliban 15, 16, 37-9, 40, 45, 50, 68, 77, 145
    alcohol 61
    Bamiyan 114, 116, 119
    books 18, 41
    cinema 56-7
    economy 43
    Hadda 184
    Herat 132, 134-5
    Kabul 82, 88, 89, 91
    Kandahar 190, 191
    Mazar-e Sharif 151
    music 55
    religion 48-9
    sport 57, 58
Tashkurgan 158
taxi travel 220

telephone services 209, see also inside front cover
time 209
toilets 209-10
tombs
    Balkh 157
    Chaqmaqtin Lake 172
    Chist-e Sharif 128
    Herat 138, 139
    Kabul 87, 92-3
    Mazar-e Sharif 152
    Panjshir Valley 111
Tora Bora 185
Torkham 185
tourist information 210
tours 17, 217
travellers cheques 207
travel to/from Afghanistan 212
travel within Afghanistan 218-20
trekking 24, 168-9, 200
tuberculosis 225
Turkmen 46-7
TV 58
typhoid 225

U
Upper Wakhan 170
UXOs 71-2
Uzbeks 45-6

V
vacations 17, 205
vaccinations 221-2
vegetarian travellers 61
visas 210-11

W
Wakhan 24, 167-72
Wakhjir Valley 172
War on Terror, the 15, 40, 110, 190, 191
weather 200-1
wildlife reserves, see national parks, sanctuaries & wildlife reserves
women in Afghanistan 42, 46, 50-1, 52, 191
women travellers 211
women's health 226
working in Afghanistan 76-8

Y
Yawkawlang 125

Z
Zahir, Ahmad 54
Zarnegar Khana 139
Ziarats 49
zoos 91
Zorkol 170-1

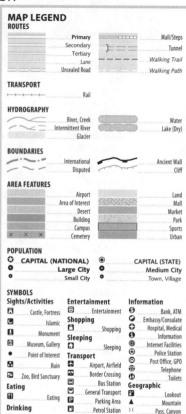

MAP LEGEND

ROUTES

- Primary
- Secondary
- Tertiary
- Lane
- Unsealed Road
- Mall/Steps
- Tunnel
- Walking Trail
- Walking Path

TRANSPORT

- Rail

HYDROGRAPHY

- River, Creek
- Intermittent River
- Glacier
- Water
- Lake (Dry)

BOUNDARIES

- International
- Disputed
- Ancient Wall
- Cliff

AREA FEATURES

- Airport
- Area of Interest
- Desert
- Building
- Campus
- Cemetery
- Land
- Mall
- Market
- Park
- Sports
- Urban

POPULATION

- ◎ **CAPITAL (NATIONAL)**
- ● **Large City**
- ○ Small City
- ◉ **CAPITAL (STATE)**
- ● **Medium City**
- ○ Town, Village

SYMBOLS

Sights/Activities
- Castle, Fortress
- Islamic
- Monument
- Museum, Gallery
- Point of Interest
- Ruin
- Zoo, Bird Sanctuary

Eating
- Eating

Drinking
- Drinking

Entertainment
- Entertainment

Shopping
- Shopping

Sleeping
- Sleeping

Transport
- Airport, Airfield
- Border Crossing
- Bus Station
- General Transport
- Parking Area
- Petrol Station
- Taxi Rank

Information
- Bank, ATM
- Embassy/Consulate
- Hospital, Medical
- Information
- Internet Facilities
- Police Station
- Post Office, GPO
- Telephone
- Toilets

Geographic
- Lookout
- Mountain
- Pass, Canyon
- River Flow

LONELY PLANET OFFICES

Australia
Head Office
Locked Bag 1, Footscray, Victoria 3011
☎ 03 8379 8000, fax 03 8379 8111
talk2us@lonelyplanet.com.au

USA
150 Linden St, Oakland, CA 94607
☎ 510 893 8555, toll free 800 275 8555
fax 510 893 8572
info@lonelyplanet.com

UK
72–82 Rosebery Ave,
Clerkenwell, London EC1R 4RW
☎ 020 7841 9000, fax 020 7841 9001
go@lonelyplanet.co.uk

Published by Lonely Planet Publications Pty Ltd
ABN 36 005 607 983

© Lonely Planet Publications Pty Ltd 2007

© photographers as indicated 2007

Cover photograph: the owner of a burqa shop in downtown Kabul spends time with his son; Paula Bronstein/Getty Images. Many of the images in this guide are available for licensing from Lonely Planet Images: www.lonelyplanetimages.com.

Printed through The Bookmaker International Ltd
Printed in China